FROM
SHIELD
TO
STORM

Also by James F. Dunnigan and Austin Bay

A Quick and Dirty Guide to War

Also by James F. Dunnigan

How to Stop War (with William Martel)

How to Make War

The Complete Wargames Handbook

Dirty Little Secrets (with Albert A. Nofi)

Shooting Blanks (with Albert A. Nofi)

Also by Austin Bay

The Coyote Cried Twice

FROM
SHIELD
TO
STORM

High-Tech Weapons, Military Strategy,
and Coalition Warfare in the Persian Gulf

James F. Dunnigan
and
Austin Bay

WILLIAM MORROW AND COMPANY, INC.
New York

Library of Congress Cataloging-in-Publication Data
Dunnigan, James F.
From shield to storm: high-tech weapons, military strategy, and coalition warfare in the Persian Gulf / James F. Dunnigan and Austin Bay.
p.   cm.
Includes bibliographical references and index.
ISBN 0-688-11034-7
1. Persian Gulf War, 1991.   I. Bay, Austin. II. Title.
DS79.72.D86   1991
956.704'3—dc20   91-24588   CIP

Printed in the United States of America

First Edition

1 2 3 4 5 6 7 8 9 10

BOOK DESIGN BY RHEA BRAUNSTEIN

To the troops,
who did all the work

Foreword

———

Among the many side effects of a war are an avalanche of books explaining, or trying to explain, what happened and what it all means. In the case of the Persian Gulf War, this is the first of "those books," written while memories and impressions are still fresh and published ten short months after the fighting stopped. Six months after the chaos more or less ends is just about the time many people begin to wonder about exactly what *did* happen.

We, the authors, have written many books on modern warfare, both of us have military experience, and we both remain active in studying military affairs. Thus equipped, we have attempted to present an in-depth study of what ignited the war and how the war was fought. We also analyze what the war means and what it *may* mean.

You can bet on it: There will be more books just like this one, *many* more books. We may write some of them. Wars, like all intense human historical endeavors, are windows on both the past and future. Historians pick and cull through the events and evidence again and again, examining, testing, and questioning. Futurists gaze into the conflict's bloody crystal.

The Persian Gulf War will be no exception. Time will fill in missing details as well as define the conflict's particular significance. Perhaps history will ultimately see the war as just one of three crucial events witnessed during the tumultuous years of 1989 through 1991— the thousand days which concluded the

Cold War with a series of rapid political changes and global power rearrangements. (The others? The fall of Eastern European Communism after the Berlin Wall cracked and the division and restructuring of the USSR.) But history, historians, and readers have got to start somewhere. This is the place.

—JAMES F. DUNNIGAN
New York
August 1, 1991
—AUSTIN BAY
Austin, Texas
August 1, 1991

Acknowledgments

—

Many people made this book possible. Here's a rough list of heartfelt "thank-yous":

Kathleen Ford Bay, Dave Tschanz, Joyce Gusner, Corbulo Keith Schlesinger, Charles Kamps, Major Jeff Phillips, Ray Macedonia, Susan Leon, Virginia Kiggins, Name Withheld by Request, Ben Fitzgerald, the partners at Hays and Anson, the newspaper clipper in Baghdad, David Langworthy, Frank Michel, Paul Henze, Mark Simonitch (for the maps), Mark Herman, Name Withheld by Request, Al Nofi, Michael D'Alessandro, Frank Bay, sundry discreet friends in the Eastern Province, Nicole Van den Heuvel, Jodi Van den Heuvel, Linda Zorich, Colonel Rick Kiernan, CPT Bill Buckner, Lisa Cabaj, Major Mike Kelly, Ben Jones, Bill Rosenmund, Name Withheld by Request, the staff of the Army and Navy Club, the work crew in MRD, and Major Roy Peterson

Contents

Maps and Diagrams

List of Charts

———

For the Benefit of Readers: Weapons Ranges

Throughout this book, the reader will encounter weapons and weapons' range data. For those of you who are particularly range-minded, here is a brief list of some significant weapons and their ranges:

- M16A2 assault rifle: 300 meters (maximum effective range)
- M1A1 tank thermal (night) sight—1,500 meters (to identify), 6,000 meters (to know if something warm is out there).
- 25-mm automatic "chain gun" (mounted on M2 and M3 Bradley Infantry Fighting Vehicle): 1,600 meters
- TOW Antitank Guided Missile (ATGM): 3,750 meters
- M1A1 120-mm tank gun: 4,000 meters (or more)
- Hellfire antitank missiles: 8,000 meters
- Sidewinder air-to-air missile: 18 km
- Maverick air-to-ground missile: 24 km
- MLRS rocket: 40 km (maximum; 30 km expected)
- 16-inch gun on U.S. battleship: 40 km
- Sparrow air-to-air missile: 50 km
- GBU (laser-guided bomb): 4–80 km (depends on height and speed of aircraft)
- Phoenix air-to-air missile: 200 km (maximum)
- AWACS radar: 200–600 km (depending on size and height of target aircraft)

PART I

Storm Signals

The Persian Gulf crises of 1990 have ancient roots. The region's tensions, antagonisms, and disputes span the several thousand years of recorded history. Archeologists, sifting through the carbon burn of a destroyed city, know the area's troubles pre-date literacy. From the perspective of the post-Renaissance West and the industrialized world, however, Kuwait and the other Bedouin lands of Mesopotamia and Arabia were easy to ignore, at least until the twentieth century's discovery of oil—lots of oil. Oil turns a hotbed of conflict into one of the world's genuine flash points. The ancient and the modern combined to create the Persian Gulf War, the latest of hundreds of wars fought in the area. It won't be the last.

CHAPTER 1

Roots of Conflict

August 2, 1990. Iraq, under the Baath regime of Saddam Hussein, invades the nation of Kuwait. Within twenty-four hours, Kuwait City falls to a combined tank, mechanized infantry, and airmobile infantry assault. Kuwaiti resistance is scattered and haphazard, although fits of resistance continue for several days until the remnants of the Kuwaiti armed forces retreat into Saudi Arabia. "We didn't think the Iraqis would attack, not even until ten minutes before they came," a Kuwaiti Army officer will lament to Western journalists a long ten days later.

Against the casual military forces of a Gulf Arab emirate, the Iraqi war machine looks like a juggernaut. Kuwait's A-4 Skyhawk aircraft squadron and a handful of other aircraft flee and fly south to Saudi and Bahraini bases. Disrupted and confused Kuwaiti Army units either surrender or wisely retreat across the border into neighboring—and suddenly vulnerable—Saudi Arabia.

The door to control of the Arabian Peninsula's vast oil fields had been kicked open with an invader's boot. Kuwait City in hand, an Iraqi Republican Guard armored division begins to clank down the coast road through the Kuwaiti town of Mina Sa'ud toward the Saudi border.

The world's first post–Cold War military crisis is under way, a crisis cut sharp with dangerous economic, military, and political angles. Turmoil among dollars and dinars tosses world financial markets. Westerners focus on the immediate five-dollar-a-barrel leap in oil prices. Petroleum prices spiral higher—and the thinning Amero-Euro-Tokyo wallet takes a painful economic thump.

Move from dollars to mass destruction, and this dagger dangles: Iraq's possession of technologically advanced weapons. Discover a regional power ideologically opposed to the West and a demonstrated menace to its neighbors now possessing long-range missiles, chemical weapons, and several thousand main battle tanks. Add the hard fact that Iraq is desperately seeking nuclear technology. How does the rest of the world react, in particular the planet's remaining Superpower, the United States?

These troubles nest in a global corner of deep political troubles. In the Middle East, a land of current borders, former borders, and long memories, two distinct visions of Iraq's attack quickly emerge. The first is the so-called conservative and moderate Arab viewpoint: One Arab nation had invaded another Arab nation. Naked aggression. A blatant power grab by a thug regime. Saddam must be stopped. Is this viewpoint the basis for unified "Arab political action" to force the Iraqis to leave?

Not with the potential power of the contra view. There is a second version, the so-called disenfranchised "Arab Street" vision: Kuwaitis are rich and arrogant. Palestinians and Yemenis have next to nothing. Saddam Hussein represents active Arab power. The Kuwaitis sold out to the West a long time ago, and fat sheikhs are Western pawns. The West created and supports Israel. Saddam's Iraq confronts Israel. Iraqis do not placate like Egyptians or hide like Saudis. Saddam says half of Israel will be burning when he finishes dealing with the Zionists.

Blitzkrieg or blunder? Or will history show Iraq's invasion of Kuwait to have been a sad mix of both, another tragic outcome of a string of strategic political miscalculations?

The truth pains and astonishes: Western powers, industrializing South American nations, China, but especially the Soviet Union, sold and supplied the Iraqi war machine with its more lethal weapons systems. Russia traded 3,000 tanks and 500 aircraft for political clout and foreign exchange. China sold missiles, bombs, bullets, and artillery. South Africa, while still in its most virulent apartheid stage, sold Iraq some of the world's most advanced tube artillery pieces (the G-5 155-mm howitzer). German chemical and electronics companies provided equipment and expertise to Iraq's chemical-weapons programs. Brazil sold armored cars and rocket launchers. Chile pushed ammunition and bombs. France sold advanced aircraft and nuclear reactors. From the United States and Great Britain leaked high-tech equipment capable of supporting a nuclear-weapons research program. The entire world made a buck, deutsche mark, and dinar in the Iraqi weapons bazaar.

With the exception of Iraq's worst enemies, Israel and Iran, almost every other nation (including Iraq's quiet enemy, Syria) treated Saddam Hussein's regime with a gentle diplomacy. Already the U.S. press has slapped the State Department for taking a placating diplomatic tone toward Iraq in the weeks immediately prior to the invasion. The tone up to that moment *was* soft, considering the United States was dealing with Saddam Hussein, one of the world's most aggressive and yet curiously isolated gangsters. Even though the American ambassador's last message to Saddam was strongly put, Saddam was more fixated on the previous five years of soothing words.

Clearly, a major layer of blame for the disaster falls on Kuwait. Kuwait sat on its bankroll and ignored all of the war signals. Iraq had rattled sabers before—a week after Kuwait proclaimed independence from Britain on June 19, 1961, Iraq claimed Kuwait and threatened invasion. The Iraqi Army, in fact, had rolled to the border several times since then, both as would-be invader and as protector. One could say Kuwait had cried wolf before, but the Iraqi wolf was not an imaginary beast. Kuwait foolishly misread the meaning of 130,000 troops on its border. Few Kuwaiti troops were on duty.

But there is also blame for Saudi Arabia, the Gulf Cooperation Council, and other Arab moderate regimes. The Saudi game had been to pay off any threat with cash, and attempt to keep a hard political distance from its economic (and ultimately military) partners in the West. One might blame the Arab world in general, a world caught in the continual bind of advancing economic integration undermined by historical fragmentation, the bind of chafing feudalism in a world of high technology and increasingly democratic aspirations.

And surely there's blame to pass around the international table—but the center of miscalculation and mistake is *Iraq* and its dictator, Saddam Hussein.

In the short months between Iraq's invasion and the Allied counterattack, a common description of Saddam was to call him

a new Hitler. An analogy to Italian Fascist Mussolini might have
been more accurate. Like the Italian Fascist dictator, Saddam
had romantic dreams of power and military aspirations fed by a
Baathist ideology based as much on notions of an imperial past
as on ethnic connections. Saddam spoke of his intention to "lead
the Arab world," and of a "greater Iraq" dominating the whole
of the Arabian Peninsula and Mesopotamia. The aspiration was
but a step from reestablishing the caliphate of Baghdad. Saddam's Baghdad would be his equivalent of Mussolini's New
Rome. In fact, the origins of the Baath party have roots in Italian Fascism, making the analogy even more pertinent.

When he invaded Kuwait, Saddam gambled that the Saudis
and the rest of the world would tremble, then ignore the tiny
emirate just as the world essentially ignored Mussolini's invasion
of Ethiopia in the 1930s. (In fact, some Saudis were willing to
do just that—worry and pray that Saddam would go no further.)
Unfortunately, Saddam missed a critical bit of information:
Ethiopia wasn't in the oil business. Saddam raised a dagger—an
economic, political, and military dagger—to the world's petroleum artery.

Indeed, one of the key historical questions following this
crisis will be this: Could the Iraqi leadership have been so
blind as to expect little more than United Nations grousing
and regional lamentations, but no military response, to its
invasion of Kuwait?

The looming answer seems to be a quiet Yes—the Iraqi leadership operated in a bag of self-inflicted sightlessness. Surviving
eight years of terrible war with Iran led Saddam to *suspect* he
could contend with any military response from the rest of the
world. But he felt that in all likelihood there would be no military confrontation after he took Kuwait. Saddam reasoned (if
one calls this reasoning) that fragile Arab relations with the
West (read United States), weak Gulf Arab armies, the existence of Israel, and his own armies' power would reduce resistance to political howls. There was also the question of the
United States itself, the Superpower that survived the Cold War.
Yes, the United States had military might, but with the legacy
of Vietnam, with its frustrating experience in Lebanon, with its
dependence on oil . . . was the moment ripe?

As early as February 1990, Saddam seemed to think so.

The Speech: February 24, 1990

He was live and on television, at the podium of the Royal Cultural Center in Amman, Jordan. He was addressing the Arab Cooperation Council, the ACC, and paying obeisance to his version of "pan-Arab issues." With King Hussein of Jordan as host and President Hosni Mubarak of Egypt in attendance, he mentioned the beckoning "lights of Jerusalem," held by the "Zionists" who had taken power and Arab land with the aid of Western imperialists, the imperialists who had drawn the false borders dividing Arabs from one another. The "loss of Palestine," however, was not due to Israeli success but to the "Arabs' abandonment of the Arab cause."

Shifting gears, the intense speaker began to sketch his vision of recent political history. After World War II, France and Britain had "declined." Two Superpowers arose, the United States and the USSR. The West helped create the "Zionist entity." The East bloc had supported the "Arabs' basic rights" against the West. The USSR balanced the United States as "global policy continued on the basis of the existence of two poles that were balanced in terms of force."

He paused. "And suddenly the situation," Saddam Hussein observed, "changed in a dramatic way." His black, rabbity eyes ran across the cool political faces in the audience.

In the text of the speech, the changed "situation" Saddam overtly referred to was the end of the Cold War, perceived in his terms as the result of an internal Soviet decision to confront its domestic problems instead of the United States.

Yet in the historical lens it isn't too farfetched to conclude that Saddam, in a curious rhetorical turn, was hinting at other dramatic changes, changes in the international political situation he, the president of Iraq, was already preparing to initiate. In fact, this very speech in Amman was part of that groundwork, a hazily framed plan based on blurry Iraqi political assessments of what looked like a definite goal: Arab unification under Saddam's dictatorship.

There were specific steps in that plan, however, achievable in what Saddam saw as a regional context ripe for exploitation, given what he called American political and military "fatigue."

Saddam's seminal Amman speech continued, with a rambling

suggestion that ultimately American power would fade, but "throughout the next five years, until new forces of balance are formed" the United States would be relatively politically unrestricted. This meant Israel could, with impunity, "embark on new stupidities" against Arabs and Palestinians.

Yes, in vague contradiction, the United States, as Saddam's source of evil in the world, was both powerful and weak, potent after its Cold War victory but immobilized by Vietnam. The marine withdrawal from Beirut after the 1983 terror bombing of the marine barracks loomed large in Saddam's perception. This powerful United States didn't have any staying power, Saddam concluded, if confronted *correctly*. (Curiouser and curiouser: He seemed to ignore the U.S. staying power in the Cold War.) Correct confrontation with the United States, Saddam's speech suggested, meant attacking the scar of Vietnam and threatening massive American casualties. "Fatigue" and domestic self-recrimination would stall U.S. military power.

Saddam's Amman speech is one of the few windows the world had on his political and strategic assessments prior to the date of the invasion of Kuwait on August 2, 1990. The speech, like much of what Saddam had to say in the past and what he had to say during the crisis, was a mix of shrewdness, standard-issue Baath political rhetoric, and utter blindness. The speech contains instances of calculated disinformation—obvious in retrospect, since basic Iraqi planning for an invasion of Kuwait was well along. In Saddam's speech, Kuwait is referred to as a "sisterly state." Hypocritical statements regarding the need to quell inter-Arab conflict are part and parcel of the display. Pan-Arabism is trumpeted at every rhetorical turn, and the appeal to Arab pride, wounded at the success of the West, is given ample coverage. The thorn of Israel is always twisted one notch deeper. The actual or looming domination of an aggressive United States, but a United States lacking will, receives constant amplification.

Yet in the retrospect of a year, one crucial line will stand out larger than the rest. "The big," Saddam said, glancing out at his audience, "does not become big nor does the great earn such a description unless he is in the arena of comparison or fighting with someone else on a different level." (Translation: If a minor-leaguer wants to move up, he has to take on the majors.)

In the speech, Saddam directly refers to American domination of Arab countries in order to maintain its supply of Arab oil. But the statement had a greater echo as a momentary reflection of Saddam's own ego. He, the already self-proclaimed new Nebuchadnezzar, the second Saladin, the center of the Iraqi Baath police state, was no longer satisfied with Iraq. Dramatic change would take place. The end of the Cold War had produced a moment where all of the terrible regional problems swirling through the Middle East offered an opportunity to create an Arab world power, with Saddam as its dictator.

The trouble was that in order to establish this Arab world power, the Arab nations of Kuwait and Saudi Arabia would have to be destroyed by the Arab nation of Iraq.

Whose Map, Whose History?

Political borders are, indeed, sometimes things. History, one line of thought goes, is only written by the winners. There are philosophical debates on these propositions that will forever rage in academic settings and the coffeehouses. In point of fact, however, since the 1930s such political and historical relativism had been fodder for various fascist enterprises, Saddam's territorial demands on Kuwait being in line with Hitler's absorption of Austria, Czechoslovakia, and parts of Poland into the Nazi German state. Both Saddam and Hitler could point to British and French political maneuvering that redrew borders that proved to be problems for the dictators.

Saddam was an admirer of Hitler and had studied Nazi methods and accomplishments. Saddam believed that what Hitler set out to do could have been done, at least if he had not invaded Russia. Kuwait, however, looked like Czechoslovakia's Sudetenland.

The act makes the fact. That Iraq invaded Kuwait indicates that Saddam thought he could get away with the assault and actually win. This was an aspect of his grandiose dreams, his megalomania, and his self-imposed isolation in a circle of yesmen. (Indeed, Saddam has only visited the West once, a trip to France.) He had no real grasp of the United States' power. Hitler also had contempt for the United States and doubted its ability to bring power to bear in Europe.

Still, one does not have to be a Hitler to invade a neighbor.

Land claims are often used by all types of governments as excuses to take a nation into war. Irredentist claims abound throughout the world. "Irredenta" comes from the Italian for "unredeemed," and such claims are made on the basis of ethnicity ("Members of our tribe live on the other side of the political divide") or historical claim ("In the glorious past, our nation rightfully ruled the land we no longer rule"). In the early part of this century, Italian "irredentists" saw parts of Italy as being separated from the new Italian state. Their land claims became tightly linked to the growth of Italian Fascism and the rise to power of Benito Mussolini. The Balkans are an unrelieved hodgepodge of mutual claim and counterclaim on land. Serbia claims parts of Croatia, Croatia claims parts of Serbia. Bulgaria, with dreams of a Greater Bulgarian state, eyes Macedonia, Grecian Thrace, Turkish Thrace, and slices of Romania.

The Iraqi invasion used an irredentist claim as historical cover. Iraq's land claims in and around Kuwait are legion. When the Turks controlled the Gulf coastal region, from 1550 to 1918, Kuwait was, in theory, administered by the local governor in Basra Province. Iraq had pressed that claim—no matter that at the time the Iraqi town of Mosul was solidly Turk or that at other times in the past Basra had solid Persian connections (and is still a Shiite area). There is also the matter of the Rumalia oil field, which straddles the Iraq and Kuwait border. The Kuwaitis had been pumping oil—excessively, the Iraqis claimed—from their small sliver of the field: In other words, the Kuwaitis were robbing Iraq. The next rhetorical step was to make the point that all of the Gulf Arabs were conspiring to keep oil prices low and were therefore "stealing" from Iraq. Forget the fact that the Gulf Arabs had given Iraq billions of dollars in aid during the 1980–88 Iran-Iraq War. Likewise, Saddam's regime had its eyes on owning the Khawr Abd-Allah, a brine channel situated between the Iraqi coast and Kuwait's Bubiyan Island that circumvents the Shatt-al-Arab (the mouth of the Euphrates and Tigris rivers). Since 1988, Baghdad had devoted time and money to turning the town of Umm Qasr into an improved seaport that Iran could not shut by closing the Shatt-al-Arab. Kuwait, the Iraqis ominously proposed, might deny Iraq access to Umm Qasr just as the Iranians had shut down

Basra, and thus must give Iraq Bubiyan or at the least allow a long-term lease.

As to the validity of these claims, Iraq ignored several other facts. The Al-Sabah dynasty had been ruling Kuwait for two-and-a-half centuries, whether under Turkish suzerainty or British hegemony. Kuwait existed as a clearly autonomous entity, made so by its geographic position as a port cut off from the Arabian hinterland by desert and separated from the Tigris and Euphrates Delta by a sand sea and religious differences. Populated by Arab pearl divers and fishermen, the Kuwait area saw in the early eighteenth century an influx of nomadic Bedouin Arabs from the Arabian Peninsula (the 'Anizah tribe). The Turks were aware of this movement, but only dimly so, for backwaters in the Persian Gulf were of little concern to Constantinople as long as the Bedouin remained peaceful. Living in a city made it easier for the Turks to control a local population.

When the local population in Kuwait selected as their emir (prince) a sheikh in the Sabah family, the Turkish imperial government had no quarrel as long as the al-Sabahs recognized supreme Turkish power. The area already fell under control of the Turkish "millet" (province) of Basra, a loose political administrative unit centered on the port of Basra and containing large Shiite Muslim populations. The millet of Basra was an imperial convenience for the Turks, for the people of Kuwait were Sunnis with more in common with the other tiny Arab emirates dotting the Persian Gulf littoral and stronger ties to the unruly Bedouin tribes of Arabia than the settled peoples of Mesopotamia.

As Turkish power diminished, Kuwait eased out of even the administrative control of Basra. Great Britain officially made Kuwait a protectorate in 1899 (protecting it against Turkey), though the Royal Navy had effectively been controlling Kuwait, as it had a dozen other ports in the region, since the mid-nineteenth century. (The British had also wanted to block Russian efforts to establish a coaling station in the port, and had suspected as well that the Germans wanted to extend the Berlin to Baghdad railroad to Kuwait.) In 1913, Turkey, loser of two Balkan wars and a fight with Italy over Libya, relinquished all claims to the Arab ports and emirates from Kuwait to Oman. Constantinople, however, did not give up its claim to Basra. The Ottomans also claimed Bubiyan Island.

Actually, the British, instead of inventing Kuwait as Saddam claimed, victimized the emirate by cutting it in half. At one time, Kuwaiti control extended well into what is now northeastern Saudi Arabia, almost 150 miles further south. When the British set up the Hashemite Iraqi monarchy in 1921, they also came to the aid of their ally King 'Abd 'al-Aziz ibn Sa'ūd and attached the southern half of Kuwait to the Saudis' Nejd (central Arabia) possessions. Thus Kuwait, without the British and with a little luck, could have been Saudi Arabia, or something close to it. Some of the land between Kuwait and Saudi Arabia remained in dispute and was administered until the 1960s as a Kuwaiti-Saudi Neutral zone, similar to the old Iraqi-Saudi Neutral Zone that straddled the Iraq and Saudi border west of Kuwait.

All of this, however, was of little consequence to Saddam. The overriding facts, from Saddam's point of view, were that Kuwait was Arab, had oil, and could be taken. The existence of definite international rules and precedents for settling claims on shared oil pools and Kuwaiti willingness to abide by them made no difference either. As for Bubiyan, Kuwait wouldn't lease the island, but obviously Kuwaitis did not have the inclination or the ability to deny use of the channel—or much of anything else—to Iraq.

IMPERIALISM IN THE MIDDLE EAST

Europeans did not invent empires and imperialism. The Middle East has been a land of grand empires, rising, expanding, absorbing, and fading throughout historical time. Before oil, water and control of water resources defined wealth and the wherewithal to found and maintain empires.

From prehistoric times, the two major sources in the otherwise-parched Middle East were the Nile and the Tigris-Euphrates river valleys. From the Nile sprang a string of Egyptian empires that waned only when conquered by the "Western" invader Alexander the Great and his Greek spearmen (2,300 years ago). Alexander also took over the Tigris-Euphrates area, but independent empires in that region had already fallen to the Persians, an "Eastern" power that still exists in this day and age as modern Iran.

After the Greeks declined, the Romans arrived (2,000 years ago). Direct "Roman" influence faded in the fourth century, but lingered in the guise of the "Eastern" (Byzantine) Empire. Then, in the 700s, the Arabs erupted from Arabia and created, for a few centuries, the Islamic Arab Empire. This fragile empire fell to sundry Asiatic marauders and conquerors (Baghdad being sacked by Mongols in A.D. 1258) until the Turks grabbed everything in sight during the 1500s. The Turks gripped the Middle East until one more group of Westerners (Britain and France) arrived in 1918 and "freed" the Arabs from the "Ottoman yoke."

The Westerners brought in modern technology, discovered oil, and paid hundreds of billions of dollars for it. These last points are often lost on many in the area who continue to complain of the depredations of "Western imperialism."

BREAKING THE RULES, WRITING NEW RULES

The attack on Kuwait directly challenged the "inviolability" of political frontiers. Almost all of the "lines in the sand" demarcating the boundaries between states in the region have been drawn in the twentieth century, with most of the artwork supplied by Britain and France. The border between Iran and "Arab lands" was drawn by Turkey and Iran in 1914, with Russian and British backing. Likewise, Saddam's attack destroyed any remaining substance to the "rule" prohibiting inter-Arab warfare. Much less a rule than an aspiration, the bias against Arabs taking arms against other Arabs had a dampening effect on warfare.

Arabs have fought other Arabs: Oman and South Yemen waged a quiet "camel war" for a decade in the Dhofar Province. South Yemen and North Yemen, in the twenty years prior to their rapprochement, fought a continual series of border wars. Algeria and Morocco have been essentially at war for fifteen years in the Western Sahara. Algeria was sponsoring the Polisario guerrilla movement while Morocco tried to absorb the old Spanish province. Libya has fought Muslim tribesmen in Chad; Egypt and Libya fought a brief border war. Libya has also squared off against Tunisia. Syria and Jordan have had several near clashes, and Iraq and Syria have faced off across their mutual border a half-dozen times since 1970. And Christian and Muslim Arabs have of course bloodied themselves in continual warfare in Lebanon.

Yet to a great extent, these conflicts have been restrained. Saddam's invasion of Kuwait and slaughter of Arab civilians snapped, perhaps forever, any notion of inter-Arab moderation. The extent of the damage could be measured by the torrent of Arab-supported UN resolutions.

The UN by the Numbers: 666 Was No Armageddon

When the war started, it crossed several theologic minds that the United Nations was fast approaching UN Security Council Resolution 666. With the real possibility that the world faced a nuclear-armed Saddam, who had already threatened to destroy Israel, readers of the Book of Revelations began to think prophecies were a mite too close. . . .

The UN resolutions were the political framework for the united action against Iraq.

Here is a list of the relevant Security Council resolutions (SCR) with date, summary, and vote count:

SCR Number	Date Passed	Description
660	August 2, 1990	Condemned invasion; demanded withdrawal 14–0–1, Yemen abstaining
661	August 6, 1990	Imposed embargo on Iraq; 13–0–2, Cuba and Yemen abstaining
662	August 9, 1990	Declared Iraq's annexation of Kuwait null and void; adopted unanimously
664	August 18, 1990	Demanded immediate release of foreigners held hostage; unanimous

665	August 25, 1990	Called on UN members to enforce sanctions and verify cargoes (i.e., made naval inspections legal); 13–2, Cuba and Yemen against
666	Sept. 13, 1990	Reaffirmed Iraq was responsible for foreign nationals held hostage; established guidelines for mercy shipments to Iraq; 13–2, Cuba and Yemen against
667	Sept. 16, 1990	Condemned Iraqi actions against diplomats. Demanded immediate release of hostages; unanimous
669	Sept. 24, 1990	Emphasized only special UN sanctions committee could authorize mercy shipments to Iraq; unanimous
670	Sept. 25, 1990	Expanded embargo to include air traffic and called for detention of Iraqi ships; 14–1, Cuba against
674	Oct. 29, 1990	Demanded Iraq stop mistreating Kuwaitis, foreign nationals. Reminded Iraq it was liable for damages; 13–0–2, Cuba and Yemen abstaining
677	Nov. 28, 1990	Condemned Iraq's attempt to absorb Kuwait demographically and the destruction of Kuwait's civil records
678	Nov. 29, 1990	Authorized UN members to use "all means necessary" to enforce previous resolutions if Iraq does not leave Kuwait by Jan. 15, 1991; 12–2–1, Cuba and Yemen against, China abstaining

686   March 2, 1991   Demanded Iraq stop hostile ac-
                                    tion, return all POWs and de-
                                    tainees, rescind annexation,
                                    accept liability, return Kuwaiti
                                    property, and disclose location
                                    of mines; 11–1–3, Cuba against,
                                    Yemen, China, and India ab-
                                    staining

CHAPTER 2

The Iraqi Dilemmas

The Iran-Iraq War left Saddam Hussein and the Baath Revolutionary Command Council with well-equipped and experienced (although battle-weary) armed forces. With over 700 Iraqi frontline fighter-bomber aircraft and an army that could swell to over sixty-five division equivalents (when the reserves were fully activated), only Israel and Turkey rivaled Iraq's regional military power.

From a strategic perspective, Saddam saw Russia declining, thus the growing "preponderance" of Israeli power as linked to the increasing U.S. power to intervene in the Gulf. If Iraq stagnated, if an "Arab power" did not fill the vacuum created by Soviet political and military retreat, then a great opportunity would be lost.

Yet in 1990, both Israel's and Turkey's regional "freedom of action," Saddam believed, were limited by domestic and international politics. In Israel's case, the Palestinian issue, the physical imposition of Jordan, the continuing "intifada," and Israel's general regional isolation impeded potential Israeli action against Iraq to air strikes (such as the 1981 attack on the Osiraq nuclear reactor) and Mossad-sponsored covert operations.

Turkey had a string of domestic and developmental crises to contend with. Its NATO alliance, in Baghdad's view, was a double-edged scimitar. Yes, the alliance brought "the West" in the guise of Western military forces to Iraq's northern border. But in Arab eyes the alliance further stigmatized the historically distrusted Turks, whose "meddling" in "Arab affairs" was already political dynamite in Ankara. Nonetheless, opposition Turkish political parties and Turgut Ozal's Turkish government made it clear that they both wished to avoid further regional political strain between Arabs and Turks (not to mention Kurds). Granted, the Turks still pressed the Southeast Anatolian Dam Project (SADP), the damming of the Euphrates River. Iraq and Syria had both protested vehemently the filling of the giant Atatürk Dam reservoir in early 1990. The Turks had proceeded to fill the reservoir anyway, but had spent a lot of time assuring the Iraqi and Syrian governments that the Arabs had no cause to fear Turk intentions. Saddam also felt he had some economic leverage over oil-poor Turkey. The Turks had been receiving $200–$500 million a year in oil-pipeline fees, while the transport and supply trade from Europe to Iraq was worth several billion dollars to Turkey. Finally, Turkey's southeastern air defenses, indeed its entire defense system in that area, was primitive. Saddam had already shown in 1988 and 1989 that he would gas Kurds. The Turks could put up no defenses against Iraqi surface-to-surface missiles. Turk and Kurd populations in the whole of eastern Turkey could be held "at risk" to the chemically tipped Scuds and Scud-derivative missiles Saddam claimed to possess.

In truth, if viewed in regional terms, the Iraqi Army emerging from the Iran-Iraq War was an especially powerful force. Iran had large infantry forces with no offensive bite. Syria was still bogged down in Lebanon and *always* had to leave forces facing Israel, while in Beirut, Syrian intervention had become something of a Syrian Vietnam.

Kuwait, on the other hand, had four weak brigades and a small air force. Saudi Arabia possessed an outstanding air force, but its ground forces were divided into two commands (Saudi Army and Saudi National Guard), and several units were ill trained. Pakistani mercenary ground forces, used to reinforce the Saudi Army, were being withdrawn at the request of the government of Pakistan from their Saudi Arabian base near Hafir al Batin, while Jordan, whose forces faced Israel and Syria, had essentially become an economic limb of the Iraqi economy. The Egyptian Army was formidable but well away from the immediate battlefield.

In tactical terms, the Iraqi Army appeared to have a huge edge over all regional forces with the exception of the Israelis, and Saddam encouraged that perception. The Saladin (10th) Armored Division gained the reputation (rightly or wrongly) as the best "non-Israeli" division in the Middle East. It was regarded by some military analysts as being at least as good as any Turkish mechanized or armored unit of equivalent size. The Saladin Division also had the cream of Iraqi Regular Army personnel, with well-trained tankers and a strong cadre of company-grade officers and battalion commanders. But even second-line reserve infantry divisions had troops with combat experience, and to be more explicit, *successful* combat experience. The Iraqi Army knew what it was to win.

The quantity and quality of Iraqi Army weapons had been upgraded during the Iran-Iraq War. New South African–made G-5 howitzers (with a 39–41 kilometer range when using "base bleed" extended-range ammunition) were deployed with Republican Guards and Regular Army units. Brazilian Astros multiple-rocket launchers were also in the weapons inventory. Ammunition for artillery, tanks, and individual arms was plentiful, and much of the ammunition stockage was new.

But ammunition, like all military equipment and supplies, ages. This logistical dilemma was small potatoes—but it illustrates in the microcosm Saddam's rock and hard place: He had the weapons and capabilities *now*. If not used, the equipment and troop expertise would begin to rust and rot.

The human equation was an important factor, if one that was difficult to gauge. At the end of the Iran-Iraq War in 1988 Iraqi Army morale was sky-high, which is as important a fact politically as it is militarily. And yet, certainly, the Iraqis were tired of war. Even the controlled press in Baghdad reflected both the public jubilation and relief at the end of that conflict.

Unlike the Iranians, however, the Iraqis were not beaten and exhausted. Of course, they had not gained control of the Shatt-al-Arab or incorporated Iranian Khuzistan (called Arabistan in Baghdad) into the Iraqi state. Yet in the long slugfest, a new Iraqi Army had been born, a strong, tough fighting force. The Republican Guard Forces Corps now formed an elite body of troops. While functioning as a political counterweight to the Iraqi regular forces, by the end of the Iran-Iraq War the Guards were regarded as a potent ground-battle group with offensive punch.

Yet military establishments, like all organizations, tend to lapse in efficiency and corrode over time. Equipment could be upgraded and ammunition stockpiles increased; perhaps nuclear weapons and a usable chemical-weapons capability could be added to the Iraqi weapons inventory. But the human element—the battle "edge" of Iraqi personnel—would year by year begin to dull. And by early 1989, Saddam could see that the Iraqi Army had reached a peak in operational capability.

Not so with the Iraqi economy—yet another dilemma for Saddam. In the aftermath of the Iran-Iraq War, the Iraqi economy, in its best description, was "highly stressed." Those troops with the fighting edge were returning to civilian life. In general the Iraqi economy had atrophied; every stitch and dinar had gone into the war effort or into the "propaganda effort." Roads had been improved where they would aid troop supply and tactical operations. Bridges had been improved, again to help the war effort.

Likewise there had been no slack in monumental architectural efforts that enhanced Saddam's prestige. These monuments to military successes and to Saddam were built throughout Iraq. One of the more extreme is a memorial arch in Baghdad, the so-called "Victory Swords," which comprises two huge fifteen-meter forearms holding crossed swords. The forearms were cast in Britain, supposedly from plaster-cast models made of Saddam's own forearms. Helmets taken from dead Iranians and welded into a waterfall of iron tumble from nets hung near the arms. The Victory Arch, however, is only one of many similar ego projects on which Saddam squandered millions of dollars.

And the bills for the battle were coming in, slamming at the Iraqi economy and the Baghdad regime like a postwar tidal wave of debt. Iraq owed Kuwait $17 billion (by Kuwaiti figures), $25 billion to other Gulf Arab states (including Saudi Arabia), and another $35–$45 billion to non-Arab countries. Iraq had earned $130 billion in oil income in the 1979–early 1990 time period. That had all been spent on the war or on immediate projects. Ninety billion dollars in loans had been floated, and less than $5 billion had been paid back. Iraq, the military victor, faced a credit squeeze.

The bills for the war hounded Saddam. The Iraqi dictator always believed others (groups, individuals, nations) were conspiring against him, and he acted against opponents to his regime swiftly and violently. The continuing Kurdish rebellion confirmed the Kurd conspiracy. The looming demands by Gulf Arab states (the nations Iraq had protected, he argued, ignoring the fact that Iraq had invaded Iran) were clear evidence of an economic conspiracy. And certainly America was involved in this plot. The United States, as a particular problem, was putting a technology squeeze on Iraq (despite the continual U.S. sale of dual-use technologies; that is, those that could be used for legitimate industrial purposes *and* chemical- and nuclear-weapons development). Indeed, Iraq was the strongest Arab country. The West was trying to weaken it, in cahoots with arrogant local allies like Kuwait and Saudi Arabia. For instance, Kuwait, Saddam argued publicly, was overproducing oil because it was forced to by Washington, in an indirect effort to weaken Iraq.

Propaganda? Of course. But illustrative of the Iraqi economic straits—lies with just enough outline of truth. Threatening Kuwait might force that government to cut production and help raise the price of oil. The Rumalia oil field (located in northern Kuwait and southern Iraq and jointly operated by both nations) became a physical example of the conspiracy.

The Kuwaitis admitted they had been pumping more than their allotment from the field. From the Kuwaiti perspective, it was a down payment on the Iraqi debt, which Iraq was not honoring. Saddam called it theft—theft by an "ungrateful" regime.

But why threaten Kuwait? *Taking* Kuwait would be a clever bank robbery. It would both erase a creditor and add to Iraq's reserves another 15 percent of the world's oil wealth. From that position, Saddam could dominate the oil business in the rest of the peninsula and set the world price for oil. Baathist expansionism had always cast eyes at wealthy Kuwait. At the least, gaining Bubiyan Island would give Iraq complete control of the Kawhr Abd-Allah, the channel leading to the Iraqi port of Umm Qasr.

But in the eyes of an expansionist, Kuwait may have been seen as a way station to an even bigger prize, Saudi Arabia. Its own vast reserves and domination of the oil-rich Arab states on the peninsula notwithstanding, the Arabian Peninsula yielded something that could have as much power as the oil: Mecca. Saddam saw Mecca as an ultimate objective to be controlled by this new and oil-enriched Greater Iraqi Arab state. Mecca

Strategic Map:
The Middle East and Kuwait Theater of
Operations (KTO)

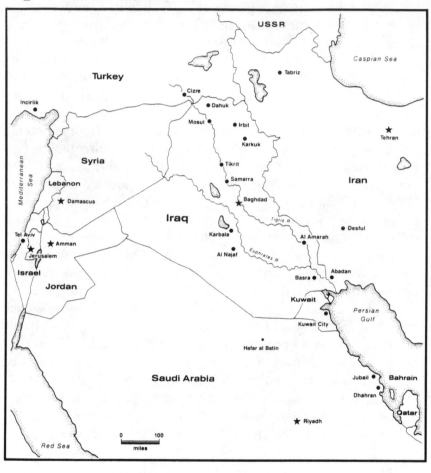

would give him, the great leader, an ideological lever over the world's 400 million Muslims.

From Saddam's perspective, Mecca was in fact an answer to his personal dilemma—the springboard to world power. With it, the political vacuum resulting from Soviet retreat left no balance to the United States. While the secular Baathists were presently limited in their ability to politicize the Muslim faithful, control of Mecca would provide Saddam with an ideological lever worldwide in scope. He would have, at the least, propaganda input running from Indonesia and Malaysia to Pakistan, into the Soviet Turkish republics, and across the Middle East and northern Africa.

Then came the last dilemma—would the United States stand in his way? True, America was increasing in power. Yet it was a wounded great power—fatigued was what Saddam had called it in Amman, and still haunted by the specter of Vietnam. America could not withstand casualties, he concluded. Would the Vietnam wound still be there in five years? Would the bloody thread of Vietnam, the thread that could unravel the entire tapestry of U.S. foreign policy, be there to pull by the time Iraq had nuclear weapons? Would Israel ever allow Iraq to build a nuclear weapon? The 1981 Osiraq attack was a lesson and a bitter one to Saddam. Wait too long to act and the West and Israel will take away the ability to act.

Iraq had a ready and able military force. Iraq had economic troubles. Kuwait could be painted as provocative. The long-range correlation of forces, from Saddam's perspective, had swung strongly to the West and Israel, but the Vietnam-illness of the United States was still sapping the body politic. Dilemmas and dilemmas . . .

The invasion of Kuwait would be his resolution.

CHAPTER 3

The Coalition Prepares for War

Military and political preparations by the United States and its allies for war in the Middle East stemming from an attack on Kuwait or Saudi Arabia by either Iraq or Iran (or even the Soviet Union) began long before August 2, 1990. Here is a brief look at the major coalition members' military, political, and, in some cases, financial preparations for armed conflict.

Kuwait

The four-brigade Kuwait Army of July 1990 was little more than a constabulary force. Most of the troops weren't even Kuwaiti citizens. The Kuwait Air Force, consisting of two squadrons, one of French Mirage F-1s and one of A-4 Skyhawk attack aircraft, was a capable force but one that would be readily overpowered by the Iraqis. Kuwait had on order a squadron of F/A-18 Hornets, but these would not be available until sometime in late 1991.

The multimission Hornets, however, would not have made enough of a difference. One new squadron wouldn't deter Saddam's Iraq. What would have made a difference for Kuwait was a political and military establishment ready to believe its own intelligence reports. Put simply, the Kuwaiti government and military did not think Iraq would attack. Over the past thirty years, Iraq had three times gone through the same drill of massing on the border. Each time Iraq had backed off.

If alerted and in position, the Kuwaiti military claimed that its 24,000 troops could have held out for four days against the invading Iraqi forces, time enough to get aid from Saudi Arabia. Such a holding action would have been on the far edge of the possible, if the Kuwaitis had invested in layered defensive fortifications, scatterable mines, and long-range multiple-rocket launchers. If the Kuwaitis also had preplanned arrangements to get assistance from the very capable Saudi Air Force, the Iraqis might have been stalled in the desert border area and might have thought twice before bulling their way through to Kuwait City.

The Kuwaitis, however, did not build fortifications. Fortifications might have been interpreted in Iraq as a "provocation." The Kuwaiti forces didn't have sufficient scatterable mines or MLRS (rocket launchers). Most important, unlike the three previous times the Iraqis had massed on the border, the Kuwaitis thought they could talk their way out of the problem without the embarrassment of calling on an outside power to face down the Iraqis. Big mistake, made bigger by a lack of readiness on the part of the Kuwaiti military.

Ill prepared as the Kuwaiti military was, the Kuwaiti government *had* prepared for "long periods of stress" by salting away billions of dollars around the world. Of course, Kuwaiti investments weren't solely for a rainy day. With a cash surplus of petrodollars, Kuwait had the capital wherewithal to pick and choose its investments. And by July 1990, the Kuwaiti investment portfolio (which included "Q8" gas stations in Europe and the Santa Fe Pipeline corporation) had an estimated worth of $150–$200 billion. After the Iraqi invasion, that financial stockpile proved its worth. The emir of Kuwait hired first-rate public-relations talent (Hill and Knowlton) to press Kuwait's case to the world media. The Committee for a Free Kuwait became a well-financed advocacy group, using well-placed and highly educated Kuwaitis living around the world as its spokespersons. And Kuwaiti students studying in American colleges also became a valuable and effective manpower pool. Ironically, Kuwait's four brigades weren't ready for war, but its portfolio managers were.

Saudi Arabia

Saudi Arabia has essentially had two armies: the Regular Army and the Saudi National Guard. In peacetime their missions are to watch the Saudi borders, watch one another, protect the extended Saudi royal family, and ensure peace and stability during the "hajj" to Mecca when anywhere from 2 million to 4 million Muslim pilgrims flood the western half of the kingdom (the Hejaz).

The Saudi National Guard is primarily manned by Bedouin tribesmen. National Guard units conduct border patrol, take on paramilitary missions, and, in a pinch, defend the Saudi royal family. The Guard is considered to be a reliable light-infantry force. During the war when two of its battalions were chosen to counterattack the Iraqis who had invaded and taken the abandoned Saudi town of Khafji on January 31, the guardsmen acquitted themselves well.

Saudi Army combat units, on the other hand, had a mix of highly trained and motivated soldiers, poorly trained soldiers, and some mercenaries. After the 1973 Arab-Israeli October War, the Saudi government began a program of reequipping the army. In the early 1980s, it stepped up the pace, largely due to the fundamentalist Shiite threat from Ayatollah Khomeini's revolutionary Iran. As part of their arms buildup, the Saudis bougth U.S. M60A3 tanks and French surface-to-air missiles (SAMs) such as the Crotale.

At the time they began to improve their equipment, the Saudis also started to upgrade army basic training and improve their officer cadres throughout the force. This is a key point: In Saudi Arabia, it is fine to be in an elite unit (an armored cavalry reconnaissance squadron or an air-force unit) but it is not socially attractive to be in the mechanized infantry or tanks. Thus the ground forces were a weak point.

Lacking troops and a motivated populace, the Saudis supplemented their ground forces by hiring a mechanized infantry division from Pakistan. The Pakistani soldiers were Muslim and highly trained. A forward brigade group operated out of the big Saudi base area around Hafir al Batin. However, in late 1988, in part due to political problems in Pakistan but also the increasing hostility between Pakistan and India over Kashmir, the Pakistani government decided to withdraw some of its division. By the summer of 1990, all but a few advisers and parts of one armored task force had been withdrawn.

It is no secret that the Iraqis thought the Pakistanis to be good soldiers—professional military scuttlebutt gets around. Did the withdrawal of the Pakistani units encourage Saddam? This is one question that may eventually be answered as the Iraqi battle plan leaks out of postwar Baghdad. The Pakistanis did send a brigade back to Saudi Arabia in the fall of 1990, but the brigade did not participate in offensive operations.

Saudi Arabia prides itself on its air force. The Saudis own a half-dozen AWACS aircraft, manned by Saudi personnel mainly, and by U.S. Air Force personnel as needed. The Saudis purchased the AWACS to give them early warning of Iranian air attacks on Saudi ports and oil fields, but their eye was also always turned toward Iraq.

Traditionally, the high-tech Saudi Air Force has perhaps been the key to the defense of the nation. The Saudis operate four squadrons of U.S.-supplied F-15s (plus two squadrons of Tornado interceptors and sundry other aircraft), and the Saudi Air Force pilots are well trained. During the war, the first "twin kill" (two planes downed by the same pilot) was accomplished by a Saudi F-15 pilot. Most Saudi Air Force maintenance is, however, provided by civilian contractors. Several American defense consulting firms have been involved in advising the Saudis on logistics and maintenance.

At one time, the Saudi government touted the big air base at Tebuk as being its main forward base as it is the base closest to Israel. In point of fact, however, since the late 1970s Saudi defensive preparations centered on protecting the critical eastern province. Between 1975 and 1990, layers of surface-to-air missile defenses began to ring Dhahran and Riyadh. One source even asserts that there are *seven* SAM and antiaircraft artillery belts protecting the Dhahran area, which is the economic and political center of eastern Saudi Arabia and the headquarters of the Arabian-American Oil Company (ARAMCO).

Gulf Cooperation Council (GCC)

The Gulf Cooperation Council (formal name: the Cooperation Council of the Arab States of the Gulf) consists of Saudi Arabia, Kuwait, Bahrain, the United Arab Emirates (UAE), Qatar, and Oman. Organzied in May 1981, the GCC began as less of a defensive "pact" than as a political statement announcing that the member nations were already linked by common interests of trade, culture, language, and custom. The formation of the GCC was also intended to show "foreign powers" (Iran) that the small Persian Gulf states were willing to defend themselves. The security side of the GCC developed into a defensive planning council.

Prior to the formation of the GCC, Qatar and the UAE discussed with the Saudis mutual defense arrangements. Qatar, with an army largely equipped with French equipment, had a poorly regarded ground force. The UAE troops were looked upon as little more than constabulary troops. Then, in the mid-1980s, both small nations increased defense cooperation with France and the United Kingdom. The war would show that the Qatari armored troops were well trained and confident (if slack on discipline): A Qatari tank company led the counterattack on Khafji and its tank platoons outmaneuvered and outgunned the Iraqi attackers.

GCC nations originally intended to cooperate in sharing intelligence data, combating terrorism, and buying military equipment and weapons. Prior to the invasion of Kuwait, the GCC was doing a mediocre job on all three counts. Membership in the GCC did not exclude other defensive agreements (though one of the stated aims of the GCC was to keep all "all foreign forces" from the Gulf region). Oman in particular maintained close ties to both the United States and Britain. Interestingly, GCC military forces held several joint defensive exercises in the mid-1980s. The code name for those operations? *Desert Shield.*

Egypt

After President Anwar Sadat tossed Soviet military advisers out of his country in the mid-1970s and began the Camp David peace process that would lead to the Egyptian-Israeli peace agreements, Egypt began to edge ever closer to the United States. At first the flow was primarily one of American economic subsidies, but then the trickle of weapons became a torrent. The Egyptians acquired F-4 Phantoms and M-60A3 tanks. U.S. M-113 armored personnel carriers (APCs) replaced Soviet BTRs and BMPs as the primary Egyptian mechanized infantry troop carrier. Defensively, the Egyptians also began to move away from the static Soviet tactics to more flexible U.S. ground tactics.

Egypt also began a series of mutual defense exercises with the United States, the "Bright Star" desert training series that brought U.S. Army, Marine, Air Force, and Navy units into Egypt. The Bright Star exercises greatly benefited the U.S. central command (CENTCOM), but the Egyptian Army and Air Force also gained useful modern combined arms training experience. A sixth major "Bright Star" exercise took place as late as early 1990. There, the 1st Brigade of the U.S. 24th Mechanized Infantry Division and several brigades of the Egyptian Army maneuvered with and against one another in Egypt's rugged Wadi al-Natrun training area. A battalion from the U.S. 82nd Airborne Division flew out of Fort Bragg, North Carolina, and thirteen hours later parachuted into the Egyptian desert.

Egypt and Saudi Arabia had been at terrible odds during the Nasser era. The Egyptians had invaded Yemen in the early 1960s in an attempt to establish a pro-Egyptian, secular "pan-Arab" government at Saudi Arabia's back door, and used mustard gas on the Yemeni loyalists (that is, tribal-oriented traditionalists). The Yemeni traditionalists, with extensive Saudi support, fought a hard and bitter guerrilla war, and Yemen became the graveyard of Egyptian paratroopers. Finally, in 1970, the war petered out, and Egypt withdrew. Yemen remained separated into socialist-oriented city slickers and tribal nomads until reunification in 1990. After the August invasion of Kuwait, the city boys running Yemen said nice things about Saddam while the tribal chiefs sent messages of support to the Saudi king.

The Sadat government moved to mend fences with the Saudis, but the repairs came apart when Egypt made peace with Israel. Still, after the assassination of Anwar Sadat in 1981, the Saudis and Egyptians achieved a private, then public rapproachement. By 1988, perceiving an increasingly radical Iraq, close Saudi and Egyptian political cooperation had become fact (and encouraged by the United States). In 1990 the Saudis were considering building a causeway across the Strait of Tiran, connecting the Sinai Peninsula with Saudi Arabia. The bridge would allow Egyptian armored units to move rapidly from Egypt to Saudi Arabia in case of an "emergency." The bridge, however, was opposed by ecological activists because it threatened sensitive coral reefs.

France

The French FAR (Rapid Action Force) was built after 1960, with African and Middle Eastern contingencies in mind. The French 6th Light Armored Division provided the FAR's armored striking power. Elite Foreign Legion airborne infantry battalions, a Foreign Legion light-armored battalion, infantry, and Special Forces units from the 11th Airborne Division, and selected French "marine" units (light infantry, formerly colonial-based troops) flesh out the FAR.

France has remained politically and militarily active throughout the Middle East, most significantly in the area of arms sales. French arms may be found in the inventories of all of the coalition armies, with the exception of the United States, and its arms ($10 billion worth) also added to Iraqi might.

The French protectorate of Djibouti is an important regional logistics, naval, and intelligence base on the Red Sea. Likewise, over the years, French advisers had shown up throughout the Persian Gulf, in particular in Qatar and the UAE.

United Kingdom

Britain and the United States have a long legacy of military cooperation. The UK also has many friends—and enemies—from its old imperial days. As late as 1968, Britain maintained a base in Aden. Since 1956 and the Suez Crisis, however, the UK had been in the process of withdrawing from "east of Suez." Still, Britain never totally withdrew. British Army officers and noncoms remained "seconded" (or "temporarily transferred") to the Omani Army, where these troops acted as advisers throughout the "camel war" fought between Oman and South Yemen during the 1970s.

British Tornado fighter-bombers, both in their IDS (interdiction, or ground attack) and ADV (air defense variant) versions were sold to Saudi Arabia, and this brought Royal Air Force technical advisers into the Saudi kingdom.

And the Royal Navy never left its old Persian Gulf haunts. The "Armilla patrol," a small Royal Navy task force, remained permanently assigned to the region. Usually, the task force consisted of two frigates and a support ship while British military bases on the island of Cyprus provided useful intelligence listening posts and logistics and refueling points for operations in the Middle East.

United States

The U.S. Central Command (CENTCOM) has its direct origins in the Rapid Deployment Force (RDF). The RDF was the military offspring of the Carter Doctrine, formulated by President Jimmy

Carter and his national-security adviser, Zbigniew Brzezinski. The Carter Doctrine stated that for the foreseeable future, the Middle East (the Arabian Peninsula) was of vital military, political, and economic interest to the United States, the intention being to stop the Soviet Union from attacking south (either into Iran to seize the Strait of Hormuz and cut the jugular vein of oil-tanker traffic sailing to Japan, the Western Allies) and after Khomeini took power in Iran, to counter Iranian expansion.

Yet American plans for military action in the Gulf predated the RDF. Even in the early 1960s, contingency plans existed for U.S. Marine and airborne forces to land in the Middle East and wait for an "armor sea package" (tank division) to arrive.

The truth was, however, when the Carter Doctrine was formulated, U.S. sealift and airlift capabilities for the long haul to the Middle East were decidedly limited. The infantryman's joke went like this: What is the RDF? You and me and our M-16s and two tickets on Pan Am.

CENTCOM thus evolved as a headquarters dedicated to resolving both the force planning and logistics problems. Headquartered at MacDill Air Force Base (near Tampa, Florida), CENTCOM began organizing and training specific U.S. Army units for Middle Eastern deployment. Army Ranger units and the 82nd Airborne Division received more and more desert training. The Bright Star exercises proved to be of unusual benefit, especially for solving helicopter maintenance and operational problems. The 24th Infantry Division (Mechanized) was reorganized and reequipped as a desert unit. Its M1A1 tanks were painted in desert camouflage. Likewise, marine units were organized for use in the Middle East. The marines' acquisition of the mobile Light Attack Vehicle (LAV) was made with the Middle Eastern mission definitely in mind.

CENTCOM also developed a rapid air-force redeployment plan, both for fighter-bomber aircraft and for the transport planes of the Military Airlift Command (MAC). Several squadrons were pinpointed for early deployment in the event of a crisis in the Middle East. In particular, the USAF marked a "wing" (approximately sixty to seventy aircraft) of F-15 air-superiority fighters for quick deployment to the Middle East.

Ever since the fall of the shah of Iran, the navy had kept at least one aircraft-carrier battle group in the Indian Ocean. Like the Royal Navy, the U.S. Navy also kept a small task force

(Middle East Task Force or METF) deployed in the Persian Gulf, based in Bahrain. The METF usually consisted of two destroyers or frigates, a supply ship, and one command ship, most often the *USS LaSalle,* a floating command and intelligence ship, glittering with advanced electronics.

One of the keys to American strategic planning is the strength of its base on the island of Diego Garcia. Lying in the middle of the Indian Ocean some 2,500 miles from the Strait of Hormuz, Diego Garcia is the "springboard" for U.S. Middle East operations. The air base is a regular stopping point for B-52s, and during the war B-52s shuttled from the United States across Iraq to it. CENTCOM also kept large prepositioned supplies on Diego Garcia and aboard ships sitting in the island's harbor. The fleet of merchant ships carried everything from tanks and ammunition to food and water.

Another key element in U.S. preparation was the 1986 Goldwater-Nichols Act, which made the chairman of the Joint Chiefs of Staff the key military adviser to the president and vested military decision-making authority in "unified" joint field commands like CENTCOM. In a unified command, the general or admiral in charge commands all armed forces, be they naval, ground, or air units. This quashes much interservice rivalry and duplication of effort. It also makes for direct responsibility and, if the president allows it, less politicking and more military concentration.

In addition, the United States attempted to maintain extensive diplomatic contact with all of the nations in the region, with the singular exception of Iran. While American diplomatic "leverage" in the region was always limited, it was also always apparent. No other nation had the economic, political, and military prestige to act as a conduit between even the most bitter enemies, such as Syria and Israel. But then, no other nation on the globe has as many international interests as the United States.

Turkey

Since the rise of the Turkish Republic, Turkey has emphasized its European connections and European aspirations. Indeed, in the eyes of many Turks, Turkey *was* Europe, and in fact NATO remains a major Turkish commitment. Not insignificantly, the Turkish-Iraqi border is a NATO border, which also added an interesting dimension to the crisis.

Turkey has long complained to its NATO allies that Turks are treated as Europeans when the rest of Europe needs a Turk Army; Turks, however, become semi-Asian "others" when they start mentioning their desire to join the European Economic Community (EEC). Turkey bridles that its 55 million people are denied membership in the EEC by 9 million Greeks. But the Iraqi invasion of Kuwait directly affected the European economy, and the Turks made no secret that they did not want a nuclear-armed gangster regime on their border.

Turkey built an army designed to defend the Turkish Straits against a Soviet and Bulgarian attack and defend eastern Turkey against Soviet attack from Armenia SSR. The Turkish Army is still primarily an infantry force, ill equipped to face chemical and nuclear weapons but otherwise a well-trained and well-led *defensive* combat force. The Turks also deployed significant mountain infantry forces and a paramilitary constabulary. (These forces have usually been found in southeastern Turkey fighting Kurdish insurgents.) The Turks were not prepared to fight Iraq on their own, but when the United States and Saudi Arabia proved to Ankara that they meant to stick it out, the Turks saw a political opportunity to serve as "the European Army of the North."

When Iraq attacked Kuwait, Turkey's southeastern army consisted of around 80,000 troops. The Turks rapidly reinforced, bringing the troop count in the area to between 120,000 and 150,000 men—enough to threaten a second front. Were the Turks prepared to fight? Iraq left nearly 80,000 troops in the north to face that possibility. Although these troops would have slowed the Turks down, the Iraqis kept their northern areas heavily garrisoned, mainly to keep an eye on the Kurds.

GOLDWATER-NICHOLS:
WHAT A DIFFERENCE A NEW CHAIN
OF COMMAND MAKES

Before 1986 there was never a genuinely unified command in the American military. Up until 1947, there was a supreme commander for the army and another for the navy. In 1947, as part of the fallout from World War II, the Department of Defense was established with a Joint Chiefs of Staff. The newly created air force (split off from the army) joined the army and navy (along with the Marine Corps, actually a part of the navy but in 1947 larger than the pre–WWII army). A fifth member of the Joint Chiefs was the chairman. This was an unwieldy organization because the chairman of the Joint Chiefs of Staff was not the commander of the armed forces (the president was "commander in chief") and did not have any significant authority over the other "chiefs of staff" (as the commanders of the services were called). The result was the now infamous interservice rivalries.

Interestingly, the effects of this setup on battlefield operations was not keenly felt during the Korean War (1950–53), largely because most of the officers had recent World War II experience and knew how to cooperate. But by the time of the Vietnam War (1964–75), U.S. officers had had sufficient time to develop some really bad habits. In Vietnam, interservice cooperation had to be arranged back at the Pentagon, often after bruising and lengthy debates among the "chiefs" of the respective services. It was no way to fight a war, and the problem was recognized during and after the Vietnam War.

It took over ten years to implement a solution at the Joint Chiefs level (the 1986 Goldwater-Nichols Act reorganizing the chain of command) and it wasn't until the Persian Gulf War that it became clear that a solution was in the works at the troop level. General Norman Schwarzkopf was an army man, but he was the officer in charge of *all* U.S. troops in the region, and the buck stopped at his desk for all three services. Any calls back to the Pentagon by a disgruntled navy, air-force, or marine officer went unanswered. The prosecution of the campaign speaks for itself. The air force was allowed to do the logical thing and pound the Iraqis from the air. This left the largest American mechanized army since World War II impatiently sitting out there in the desert, watching. Despite having been a paratrooper, General Schwarzkopf did not allow a parachute drop, fearing that it would be too risky for whatever advantage it might gain. The same reasoning prevented the marine amphibious force from seizing a more activist role for itself. Thus, an army general allowed the air force to walk away with the show. But that was the prudent solution; it was what a commander in chief should have done. The classic chain of command, with the general in the field having full authority to use all his forces as he saw fit, was finally implemented in a post–World War II U.S. force. It worked.

GEORGE BUSH'S SECRET

The world was amazed at the quick diplomatic response to the crisis engineered by the Bush administration. Between August 2 and August 5, 1990, President Bush forged what would have been regarded on August 1 as an "impossible political coalition." Certainly the "coalition" of conservative Arab monarchies, creaky Arab authoritarian states, an Arab dictatorship (Syria), Western European nations, an authoritarian democracy (Turkey), and the United States looked like a fragile mosaic cemented by little more than spit and a prayer. To break it apart, it seemed, Saddam would only have to whisper, "Israel," and watch the incredible structure topple.

Likewise, the United Nations had served as little more than a reason for elitist diplomats to live in New York City. During the height of the Cold War, the UN Security Council was a gaggle of rhetoric punctuated by an occasional veto delivered by one of the Security Council's permanent members, usually the Soviet Union, but often, in defense of Israel, by the United States.

Yet during the crisis and the conflict, the "Allied coalition" (as it came to be called) proved to be resilient. The United Nations provided the legal sanctions for economic and military action against Iraq, something its ill-fated and ineffectual predecessor, the League of Nations, had failed to do in the 1930s when Fascist Italy, militarist Japan, and Nazi Germany began to devour their neighbors.

Admittedly, deep mutual economic, political, and military interests bolted the coalition. The end of the Cold War and *perestroika* policies that increased Russian cooperation with Western Europe and the United States laid the groundwork for dialogue and decision in the UN Security Council. The People's Republic of China's interest in maintaining positive ties with America and Western Europe earned Chinese abstentions rather than vetoes when it came to voting in the Security Council.

But behind all of this lay rapid and effective personal leadership by the American president. In some respects, George Bush's résumé suggests he had spent his professional life training for such a crisis. Conspiracy theorists will make much of this point, but only because conspiracy theories sell books and enliven the chatter of otherwise dull TV talk shows. Bush had served as United States ambassador to the UN, envoy to China, and had been director of the Central Intelligence Agency. As a result of these experiences, Bush had a keener awareness than most politicians of what to tell and what to keep private when it came to international diplomacy. He was definitely more aware than most other American politicians, and past presidents, of the inner workings of other governments and how they act and interact (or fail to do so) with the U.S. government. Bush also has a knack for "the personal touch" in politics. Bush is well known for the personal cards he mails to friends and supporters. He uses the same personal touch in international diplomacy. During the hectic first days following the invasion, his personal knowledge of King Hussein, President Mubarak, Prime Minister Ozal (of Turkey), King Fahd of Saudi Arabia, and all of the other key players (including Gorbachev) was an ineluctable but relevant diplomatic tool. The only key player completely outside the circle was Saddam Hussein.

Bush also has the ability to allow talented people to function as a team. By plan, accident, and circumstance, the U.S. "command group" in the crisis (the key decision makers and executives) proved to be a capable crew. Secretary of State James Baker and National Security Adviser Brent Scowcroft were there by plan. Secretary of Defense Richard Cheney ended up in the administration because the Senate Armed Services Committee rejected Bush's first choice, Senator John Tower. Chairman of the Joint Chiefs of Staff General Colin Powell and CENTCOM commander General Norman Schwarzkopf were there on military merit. Under President Bush's direction, they would untangle one of the trickiest diplomatic thickets since World War II. Not even German reunification (October 1990) and separatist troubles in the USSR (December 1990) would untrack them.

The Bush team's military plans tended to evolve as the crisis progressed. According to General Colin Powell, the decision to go for a decisive offensive edge wasn't a single, sudden determination. "There wasn't a single decision, but a gradual increase in forces based on the expanding presence of Iraqi troops," General Powell replied to a query by the authors.

COALITION POLITICS ON THE BATTLEFIELD

Getting what became the three dozen national contingents comprising Allied coalition forces to the Gulf battlefield was one minor miracle. Effectively integrating them on the battlefield was a major achievement. Consider some of the difficulties that had to be dealt with.

1. Differences in Training and Preparedness. This was the underlying factor that influenced all other problems. Fortunately, American forces were sufficiently plentiful to take care of all the fighting (if the need arose), although that was not the intention of the coalition. All those who sent forces to the Gulf *expected* their troops to be involved. Those nations that did not want their troops to fight other Arabs, as in the case of the Pakistanis, were not a problem; these units were simply put to work providing security within Saudi Arabia. On the other hand, those contingents that were supposed to fight presented most of the problems.

The British, French, and Italians were up to U.S. standards and had the further advantage of regularly training with U.S. forces in NATO exercises. The Egyptian forces also trained annually with American forces flown over to Eygpt each year, although as we have seen, only a small number of units were involved. The Egyptians could not afford the expense of a lot of large-scale exercises. However, the months they had to wait before the Gulf battle began were put to good use in conducting large-scale training exercises (which the Saudis paid for, especially by absorbing the enormous fuel costs). The Syrians were somewhat less well prepared than were the Egyptians, but they also trained in the desert for several months during the fall of 1990, and had some experience under fire in Lebanon.

Most other national contingents were less well trained than the American and European forces. As we know, the Saudis had received some training assistance from American advisers, but used a lot of French equipment and also maintained two separate armies. And because the smaller National Guard existed primarily to protect the king and his extended family in case the Regular Army got any funny ideas, for political reasons, the Sa'ūds therefore (as in the House of Sa'ūd, the ruling family) did not encourage professionalism in the ground forces. The Saudis accepted more training assistance from the United States after August 2, and got their forces in much better shape by the time the ground war started. (The Saudi Air Force, conversely, attracts a lot of very capable personnel, and they are allowed to fly more than most Western pilots.)

The Kuwaitis insisted on rebuilding their shattered ground forces, and did this with American assistance. As most of the Kuwaiti recruits had no military experience at all, and Kuwaiti forces were to play a leading role in the liberation of their homeland, much effort was put into getting the Kuwaiti units into passable shape. Meanwhile, other Gulf nations contributed forces that varied widely in their readiness, and received training assistance where necessary. The smaller Muslim contingents were mostly too small to take on a significant part of the offensive or, as in the case of the Pakistanis, not willing to attack other Muslims. Most of these contingents were put into various support tasks where they would be unlikely to have any problems.

2. Differences in Equipment. There was a wide disparity in types and condition of equipment among the ground forces. Most of the equipment was American or Russian (especially those of the Syrians and Kuwaitis). The French and the British had their own as well, and many of the smaller contingents were equipped by a hodgepodge of gear from suppliers as diverse as Germany and China. Thus, each national contingent had to take care of its own gear. Because of differences in manufacturing quality (the Russian stuff was a bit shoddy) and different attitudes toward maintenance (the Western forces were fanatical about maintenance, while most other contingents took a less zealous attitude), equipment readiness was uneven. For this reason (among others), the U.S. ground forces were given the assignments requiring the most effort from their equipment. Saudi and Kuwaiti air forces used civilian (largely Western) technicians to maintain their equipment. Thus, a major problem that had to be addressed was the differences in communications equipment and procedures. The Western (NATO) forces already had experience in dealing with these problems. But new procedures had to be developed on the spot to communicate effectively with the Muslim contingents.

3. *Diplomatic Problems.* The willingness to fight was not the same for all contingents. The Kuwaitis were the most keen on getting into combat, but were the least prepared to deal with it. The Saudis were also eager to liberate Kuwait, and as the Saudis were in somewhat better shape, the Kuwaiti units served under Saudi command and alongside Saudi units. The other small Arab contingents from the Gulf area were also keen on taking care of the Iraqis, so they also served with the Saudis. The Egyptians were eager to do their part, while the Syrians kept changing their minds about fighting their way into Kuwait or just defending Saudi Arabia. The Syrians were kept close to the Egyptians, to go into Kuwait alongside them, behind them, or to stay in Saudi Arabia. When the ground war started, the Syrians finally decided to go into Kuwait behind the Egyptians. The Pakistanis were opposed to fighting fellow Muslims, but they did want to defend Saudi Arabia. So the Pakistani contingent was put to work guarding the holy cities of Mecca and Medina. (The Pakistanis were good troops, so this guard duty freed up some Saudi units.) Most of the other small contingents were given similar guard duty or support functions through Saudi Arabia. In the end, all the Allies were content that they had done their part. This was no small diplomatic accomplishment.

4. *Similarities Between Some Allied and Iraqi Weapons.* Many Allied nations used equipment identical to what Iraq was using (e.g., French Mirage fighters) or very similar (e.g., wheeled armored vehicles with 20- or 25-mm auto cannons). American marines and British infantry both suffered friendly-fire casualties because their wheeled combat vehicles looked similar (especially

from the air) to the wheeled Russian-built vehicles used by Iraq. For this reason, the Allied Mirages were not used much until February, after most of the Iraqi Mirages had been destroyed or had fled to Iran. The problems of Allied armored vehicles being mistaken for Iraqi ones was never completely solved. In one case, it was thought that these weapon similarities would be an advantage. The most effective (on paper, anyway) Iraqi missiles were of French manufacture. However, the French adamantly refused to share technical knowledge of these weapons with their allies, and the issue was dropped before it became a diplomatic problem.

5. Deployment of Non-U.S. Contingents. The lineup of troops for the liberation of Kuwait was heavily influenced by diplomatic considerations. Obviously, the Kuwaitis and Saudis wanted to go straight for Kuwait City. So Kuwaiti and Saudi (and some other Gulf-area troops) were placed on the coast road. Next to them, inland, were the two U.S. Marine divisions who would do most of the work clearing out the Iraqi divisions and making the Saudi/Kuwaiti push up the coast road possible.

Next to the marines were the Egyptians, who were willing to go into Kuwait to fight Iraqis but not into Iraq itself. Actually, some Egyptian units did cross into Iraq. The Egyptian soldiers were less reluctant about entering Iraq than their political leaders.

The Syrians were placed behind the Egyptians because, almost up to the last moment, the Syrians were unsure if they wanted to fight Iraqis to liberate Kuwait or simply continue to "defend Saudi Arabia." The Syrians eventually advanced behind the Egyptians.

The British 1st Armored Division was originally to assist the marines in piercing the Iraqi fortified line. But the British resisted such a mundane task (for an armored division, even though they were quite good at breaching fortifications). So the Brits were shifted to the west and assigned to form the right flank of the U.S.-led mechanized advance into Iraq's open flank.

The French were also a problem. They were equipped with light armored vehicles and did not want to get bogged down in slogging through fortified lines, or get mixed up in a firefight with heavier Iraqi tanks. So the French were given the task of covering the wide-open western flank of the U.S. mechanized advance. This the French did admirably.

Many other Muslim contingents were either unwilling or ill prepared to go up against Iraqi units. So these units were assigned to security functions. The 300 Afghan partisans who arrived (to repay Saudi support for their struggle) were also assigned security duties. It all worked out, a diplomatic as well as a military triumph.

CHAPTER 4

Why Fight?
War and Peace on the Home Front

The United States and several of its European allies came to the support of Saudi Arabia and Kuwait for a variety of economic, political, diplomatic, and military reasons. Not everyone on the American home front agreed with these reasons. For many, Kuwait looked like "another Vietnam."

Counting Oil Barrels and Petrodollars: The Economic Imperatives

Economic concerns were fundamental to the formation of the Allied coalition. The industrialized nations of the world, particularly the Western alliance (the United States, NATO, and Japan), cannot thrive without Persian Gulf oil. Each year, the Gulf region exports 3.5 billion barrels of oil, more than one third of the world's annual production yield. Iraq and Kuwait normally export over a billion barrels a year each, Saudi Arabia ships over 1.3 billion barrels. On the receiving end, the United States imports 2.4 billion barrels (45 percent of its oil needs), with 27 percent (650 million barrels) coming from the Gulf. Japan imports 1.2 billion barrels a year, virtually 99 percent of its oil consumption, with over half of that coming from the Gulf, (and the remaining 1 percent coming from its own domestic production). American allies in Europe import over 2 billion barrels a year (over 90 percent of oil needs), with over 500 million barrels coming from the Gulf (a quarter of the total).

Math says that the major industrial powers draw around 2 billion barrels of oil a year from the Gulf.

After seizing Kuwait, Iraq controlled a billion barrels of production a year. If Baghdad took Saudi Arabia's oil (or trashed those oil fields), another 1.3 billion barrels a year would have been lost. The smaller Gulf states add another 600 million barrels a year. Loss, or prolonged interruption, of this oil would shut down the industrialized economies, causing an economic depression until adjustments were made.

But strangling the oil spigot results in more dire consequences than mere economic disruption and recession in the wealthy, industrialized countries. The Third World nations, which depend on the industrial nations for trade and aid (particularly food), suffer even more bitterly when oil prices increase. Sadly, recession and depression among the rich places millions of the Third World's poor in danger of starvation. It's an aspect of the "integrated global economy" that is often ignored. Oil-price increases and rapid fluctuations severely injure the economies of industrializing Third World nations, which is precisely what happened after the OPEC oil embargo of 1973. These nations cannot afford conservation technologies, and their foreign exchanges reserves (used to buy oil) are slender.

More to the point, in the summer of 1990, according to several estimates (econometric and "oil patch" windage), oil cost about 150 percent what it should if only market conditions set the price. The Saudis, to a degree, were limiting their own production. With the price of oil nearly doubling again because of Iraq's invasion, citizens of industrialized nations suffered. For inhabitants of Third World nations, calamity loomed.

Many people in the West, and especially the media, neglected to consider the "interconnecting" effects of price disruption and price blackmail in the world's global economy. In the United States, many "opinion leaders" looked only to the possible increases in gasoline costs.

But stable petroleum costs and reliable supply are major factors in overall world economic performance. When the industrialized economies falter, unemployment increases. With rising unemployment come tangible social ills such as increased death rates, social disorder, and generally lower living standards. The

Third World nations, which live on the edge of catastrophe in the best of times, see even greater suffering as aid from the developed nations disappears. Going to war over Persian Gulf oil was ultimately more than a matter of keeping the price of fuel down and keeping the Cadillac and Corvette crowd happy; it became a matter of life and death for millions of people who don't even know what a Cadillac looks like.

There was another "economic" aspect to Iraq's aggression, albeit an indirect one and one with a much more specific enemy in mind. Saddam Hussein had made no secret of his desire to unite all Arab nations under his leadership, at the point of a gun if necessary. This program of conquest included the extermination of Israel and relentless war on any Arab neighbors who chose to resist his dream of Arab Renaissance. But Saddam could only accomplish this goal if he had the means to finance it. Three billion barrels of oil a year provide a lot of economic grease. The fact that the UN quickly closed ranks against Iraq shows how clearly a wide variety of nations saw the danger of Iraq getting a stranglehold on world oil production. If Iraq were allowed to seize all the Gulf oil (except Iran's, they already tried that and failed), it would control a third of the world's oil production and dominate 55 to 60 percent of its proven oil reserves.

Such wealth would make Iraq a regional economic superpower. (With an oil price of over thirty dollars a barrel, the GNP of "Greater Iraq" would be about $250 billion a year). Even with the larger population in the conquered territories, the total population of "Greater Iraq" would still be under 30 million and per capita income nearly twice what it was before a successful war. This GNP would be greater than that of Turkey, Iran, and Egypt combined.

Because oil therefore plays such an essential role in the world's economy, the distant industrial nations could not look upon Iraq's invasion of Kuwait as just another deplorable but ignorable Third World dispute.

War Fever, Peace Fever, Resolution Temperatures: The Political Imperatives

Going to war is a political act. President George Bush could not have considered military assistance to Saudi Arabia unless he thought doing so had sufficient domestic political support.

Historically, military action tends to unify a nation politically. This has been the case in the United States, at least most of the time. Yet Vietnam was not the first war that had ugly domestic political repercussions. Korea was unpopular, there was much resistance to America's entry into World War I and World War II, and the 1898 Spanish-American War also had some Vietnamlike undertones domestically. The Civil War had its draft resisters; Henry David Thoreau objected to the Mexican War. And if one wants to be very technical, American Tories in 1776 certainly thought the Revolutionary War was a politically objectionable conflict.

The U.S. failure in Vietnam deeply divided Americans on the issue of military action, a division between so-called "war hawks" and "peace doves." The 1980s had provided three American successes (Libya, Grenada, Panama) and one failure (Lebanon) in the use of military power, but no consensus had emerged. Then Saddam invaded Kuwait. Saddam Hussein loomed large in the public's view as one of the planet's big-time bad guys. From a purely television-*image* point of view, Saddam offered the hawks a perfect target. If the doves wouldn't confront this guy, whom would they take on?

Yet America faced three political risks to military action in the Gulf. Risk One: Military action might fail. Military failure, however, was unlikely, as most students of military history (and students of the Iraqi Army's recent performance against Iran) could have pointed out.

The second risk was more tangible: a large, terrible toll of American casualties. Again, past experience held out the probability of a low U.S. casualty count if the Iraqis were bombed and isolated in the desert before the ground troops were sent in. But the possibility, and political risk, remained.

There was a third political "consideration" that was in some respects less immediately significant than the other two risks, but a risk that could grow out of hand if military action in the Gulf failed. The third risk dealt with two questions: Why are we fighting? and Is it worth it? Usually, every American political decision brings forth a stream of protest from the loyal opposition. The prospect of war turns the stream into a torrent. During the U.S. military buildup in the Gulf, a lot of such rhetorical firepower was unleashed. Indeed, they remain difficult questions to answer, particularly when the rhetoric gets thick enough and loud enough to obscure central issues.

More than enough time elapsed between the Iraqi invasion of Kuwait and the U.S. congressional debate on the Persian Gulf War Resolution for a lot of touchy issues to be raised. Admittedly, many of the "issues" border on diatribe and suffer from demonstrably skewed and half-baked notions of the world, but then virtually all legitimate political controversies in a free society must carry a certain burden of posturing. Nonetheless, a quick rundown of some of the issues raised by those on what we might very crudely call the "prowar" and "antiwar" sides of the issue provides an insight into the entire political process.

Consider these "antiwar" contentions:

Contention One: Is the Principal Reason for Going to War Because the United States Oppposes Aggression?

The "antiwar" argument was that the United States is highly *selective* in its opposition to aggression. In effect, the doves said the United States accepted aggression if the "aggression" was in our interests. Military aggression is "bad," the argument continued, only if it is against our interests. Seen in this light, the U.S. invasions of Grenada and Panama were held up as examples of this selective opposition to aggression.

The "proconfrontation" crowd, conversely, pointed out that the people of Panama and Grenada cheered the incoming U.S. invaders and called them liberators (as did, ultimately, the people of Kuwait, and even many of those Iraqis who came under Allied control).

But the antiwar crowd raised other examples of America's alleged selective opposition to aggression. Turkey invaded northern Cyprus in 1974, established a Turkish state separate from Greek-populated Cyprus, killed over 1,000 people, and drove out 200,000 people. According to the dove argument, this example poses the following question: If the United States goes to war with Iraq, then the United States should have gone to war with Turkey to get the Turks out of Cyprus. Typically, the "Cyprus argument" ignores glaring factual differences between Kuwait and Cyprus, in particular the fact that the Greeks on Cyprus (through the terror organization EOKA-B) were engaging in an armed movement to make Cyprus a part of Greece ("*enosis*"), in violation of an agreement that would have kept the island independent while protecting the sizable Turkish minority.

The Israeli invasion of Lebanon in 1982 is also often held up as another example of selective U.S. opposition to aggression. This invasion killed over 10,000 people and established a pro-Israeli Christian Lebanese (with some Shiite support) buffer zone in southern Lebanon policed by the army of South Lebanon. The United States vetoed a series of UN Security Council resolutions that condemned Israel's action and called for an immediate end to the war. Israel was, in the dove argument, allowed to do what it wanted to do. In other words, the United States condemns Iraq but looks the other way when Israeli tanks roll. Isn't this the height of imperialist (and Republican) hypocrisy?

Again, the antiwar argument ignored the fact that Israelis were being attacked and killed on a daily basis by terrorists crossing the Israeli-Lebanese border. More ominously, Russia and several other nations were helping the Palestinians to build a three-division army in southern Lebanon, complete with artillery, tanks, communications equipment, and antiaircraft missiles. By 1983 this army was expected to be operational. It may not have been able to attack Israel with any success, but it would certainly have been a source of further anarchy in Lebanon. Seen in this way, Israel attacked a growing military threat. Was Kuwait a military threat to Iraq?

The antiwar criticism of American policy on aggression asserted a U.S. double standard. The criticism ignored the limited resources, both financial and diplomatic, that prevent any nation from stepping in and resolving all the world's real or imagined cases of international aggression. Iraq invading Kuwait was a clear-cut example of international aggression, while most other cases of aggression (including Syria's depredations in Lebanon) are internal conflicts spilling over a border or are international only by a very dubious standard.

Other oft-mentioned examples of the "double standard" were Indonesia's annexation of the former Portuguese colony of East Timor (1975) and the former Dutch colony of Irian Barat (1963). Both of these annexations were resisted by the locals, and the death toll over the years, from both combat and deprivation, has been hundreds of thousands. Both East Timor and

Irian Barat were, and still are, beset with dozens of fractious groups of rebels. Both are poor, out-of-the-way, and have nothing to do with U.S. national interests (real or perceived). Did the United States object to Indonesia's aggression? Yes. Did it defend East Timor? No. The U.S. economy wasn't threatened by the attack. Is the United States hypocritical? In this case perhaps, but from a larger lens this question begged a countering observation: The same people who made this claim were conspicuous by their lack of agitation for any American action to aid these two areas.

The Iraqi invasion of Iran in 1980 has been offered as yet another example of the U.S. double standard, even though Iraq attacked during a time when Iran was waging a global terror campaign against American citizens. America did maintain a more neutral stance than the other major powers, who generally sold arms to Iran and Iraq indiscriminately. United States appeals for peace between Iran and Iraq eventually played a role in securing a cease-fire. In any event, Iraqi requests for a cease-fire and return to prewar boundaries (after Iran had successfully repulsed the invasion) were ignored. Iran spent most of the war trying to invade Iraq. The U.S. dilemma, had it wanted to intervene, would have been which side to attack first.

The theme of an Amercian double standard on aggression is played loud, long, and without much attention to detail. Many members of the antiwar movement take a cynical attitude about media attention and are prone to come up with outrageous statements to support their positions if it will get them more media exposure. If a war is unpopular, and Vietnam was just one of many unpopular wars in this century, people will look for additional reasons to oppose it.

Unfortunately, many of the fringe elements of the antiwar crowd are not interested in what's right or wrong in American foreign policy, or America in general. In their eyes, there is nothing right, and this pervasive negativism appeals to a variable, but generally small, segment of the population. It does play well in the media, though, and the media attention is what keeps a lot of the anti-this and anti-that rhetoric going.

Connection Two: It's Not Our War.

This is a well-heeled, apple-pie American isolationist rap. The flip side is that one can only avoid those wars that one can afford to avoid. With most of the world's exportable oil threatened by an armed megalomaniac, the hawks argued, it wasn't prudent to sit this one out.

Contention three: No Blood for Oil.

A more specific "It's not our war" theme. Based on the premise that the United States government takes its orders from U.S. oil companies (or U.S. oil consumers, take your pick).

Contention Four: We're Being Hired by the Saudis and Kuwaitis to Defend Them.

A few cynics in Saudi Arabia got caught mentioning this one ("We will have our American slaves do the fighting"). Every foreign war is subject to this contention, and it's in the same league with "Marriage is legal prostitution."

Contention Five: We Have More Serious Problems at Home.

Absolutely—the United States does have serious domestic troubles. Yet this argument assumes that all else must come to a grinding halt until our principal domestic problems are taken care of. The trouble is, not everyone agrees on what most serious domestic problems are. That's why we have government budgets with thousands of different programs, and a democracy to keep the jostling from turning into civil war. In one sense, this argument is a mask for U.S. isolationism, always a strong factor in American politics. Isolationism runs deep in both the far right and far left of the U.S. political spectrum. It also exerts a fundamental pull on most of the center: Wouldn't our world be great if we could ignore the rest of it? Isolationism carries a lot more weight than a lot of the slogans.

Contention Six: There Goes the Peace Dividend.

Ouch. The end of the Cold War was supposed to permit massive disarmament and subsequent savings. This was a hollow argument but one that got lots of airplay. Most (if not all) of the additional costs of the war are being paid for by noncombatant (and Gulf state) contributions. A lot of the equipment and munitions used were slated for destruction according to the disarmament treaties signed with the Russians (previous to the Kuwait War).

Contention Seven: It's a plot by the military to avoid budget cuts.

It's unlikely that Saddam Hussein allowed his country to be turned into an Allied live-fire range as a gesture of professional courtesy to Western defense establishments. This plot, however, will work well in a number of yet-to-be written adventure novels.

Contention Eight: It's Part of the United States' Grand Plan to Dominate the Planet.

This one was invented by someone who avoided taking any economics courses in college. The United States already dominates the planet.

Contention Nine: Saddam Is a Big-time Baddie, but So What?

Only a few sightings on this one. A variation on the theme, "If we don't fight all the thugs, we shouldn't go after any of them."

Contention Ten: We're Fighting to Protect Israel.

Sort of. The coalition organized to protect all of Iraq's neighbors (or anyone within range of Iraqi missiles).

Contention Eleven: Call This One Not So Much a Question as "Sympathy for the Underdog and the Kuwait Catch-22"

A number of antiwar activists saw Iraq as the underdog and the Kuwaitis as a bunch of rich pigs who finally got what they deserved. (This didn't play well beyond the "smash the state" left-wing protest crowd.) In the end, however, the various rhetorical objections to liberating Kuwait were swamped by what most Americans perceived as the most decent, well-considered, and correct action.

Diplomatic Reasons for U.S. Involvement

There were ample diplomatic reasons for taking military action against Iraq's aggression. Diplomacy, like any other human relationship, puts a premium on trust and reliability, ultimately, alas, it is backed up by the threat of force. If force is not brought to bear when words fail, then future aggressors will be less dissuaded by nonviolent entreaties.

The United States took a big hit in its diplomatic capabilities when it abandoned Vietnam. Vietnam was a civil war, and America was seen as overreaching when it attempted to take sides. The United States overreached, but became marked as a paper tiger when it essentially abandoned the South Vietnamese. As a result, Americans have had difficulty coming to grips with how they are perceived by most of the rest of the world.

Indeed, America was (and still is) seen as unstable in many of its diplomatic relationships. Part of this was the result of America's democratic form of government, which is unique in the world and its complexities somewhat tricky to manage. The U.S. system often works at the expense of consistency in many government policies. At the very least, with the constant domestic political debate that is part of the American scene, our foreign policy always appears to be in a state of flux.

Still, through the 1980s U.S. policy was consistent in its opposition to totalitarianism and aggression. America supported the demise of many right-wing dictators that it had previously supported and, when the Communist dictators went like lemmings over the abyss in 1989, the United States experienced an unusually high demand for economic, diplomatic, and military leadership. It was a new age, if not a New World Order, and Iraq's invasion of Kuwait signaled a major test of America's ability to handle the load.

The diplomatic opportunities the Kuwait situation presented were immense. If a coalition could be formed to deal with the crisis, even if the United States did most of the fighting, the diplomatic message would be substantial. A UN-sponsored response to Iraqi aggression would tell any other would-be aggressors for the foreseeable future that they could not reasonably expect to get away with it.

On a more mundane level, the United States had built up its diplomatic relationships with several Persian Gulf states since the early 1940s. One of the many casualties of President Franklin Roosevelt's death in office in 1945 was the abandonment of his "tilt" toward the Arab position on the establishment of a Jewish state in Palestine after World War II. Truman, and subsequent American presidents, have taken a lot of heat from Arab leaders for pro-Israeli positions. Nonetheless, American diplomacy has managed the formidable task of maintaining good relations with both Arab states (particularly in the Gulf) *and* Israel. But Kuwait and Saudi Arabia's call for protection from Iraqi aggression in August 1990 put America in a difficult position. Were U.S. proclamations that it would resist aggression worth anything? Replacing a dictatorship in Grenada and getting chased out of Beirut in 1983, bombing Libyan terrorist bases in 1986 and deposing another dictator in Panama in 1989, produced a mixed record. Iraq had a million men under arms and over 5,000 tanks. In early August, the world watched, and wondered.

Military Reasons for U.S. Involvement

In truth, military "reasons" are diplomatic and political reasons in uniform. Among allies, especially among *threatened* allies, the military test is the ultimate test of political reliability. The question may be stated bluntly: Will you show up when you say you will?

One cannot prove what did not happen. But the argument that aggression breeds aggresssion is far older than Mussolini and Hitler. In the "post–Cold War world" the stability of the East-West bloc confrontation had been destroyed. On this planet, there are literally thousands of "irredentist" land claims, (border claims of one nation, or would-be nation, upon the territory or parts of the territory of a neighbor). In the post–Cold War world, there is only one Superpower. Like it or not, Superpower action or inaction when aggression occurs does set a tone for behavior.

Thus the first military reason for American involvement—a strategic argument—revolved around the conclusion that fighting *now* may prevent other wars.

The second reason had to do with the size and flexibility of U.S. forces. Virtually no other nation on earth could have led and conducted the Persian Gulf War's military operations except the United States. Russia could have destroyed Iraq conventionally, but would have had to project its forces overland, through Turkey or Iran. The Russians, lacking sufficient and flexible strategic sea and airlift assets, would not have been able to move heavy mechanized forces to Saudi Arabia by sea and sustain them. By applying overwhelming military force against the Iraqis, it was felt, the ultimate toll of American and Allied lives needed to defang Iraq and liberate Kuwait would be much lower. This proved to be a correct assessment, although it was a calculated risk, as such a lopsided victory against such a large army was without historical precedent. And even with over 20,000 Iraqi dead, the toll for Iraq could have been much higher had the war been fought as a World War I–style slugfest by evenly matched opponents.

Could Kuwait Have Been Liberated Without Fighting?

The supreme diplomatic achievement of the United States in getting the United Nations to condemn Iraq (which it should have done in any event) and then to authorize a blockade (a much rarer event) was capped off by the authorization to use force if Iraq did not leave Kuwait by January 15, 1991 (five months after it invaded). Though appalled at the looting and killings in Kuwait, no one was eager to displace the Iraqi Army by military means. The embargo was, in Iraq's case, easily enforced, and would eventually have considerable impact.

Iraq was a Third World country that had become accustomed to First World amenities. Iraq also imported most of its food and needed spare parts and technical assistance to keep its public utilities (electricity and water supplies) operating. But even optimistic observers accepted that it would take at least a year for the embargo to put Iraq on the ropes. Meanwhile, the United States and other Allies were pouring troops into Saudi Arabia. All that UN-sponsored military force sitting in the desert was expensive, both in terms of cash and political currency. The question that is still asked is, could Iraq have been forced out just with the embargo? The question will be posed for a long time to come, so we might as well deal with it here.

Iraq is a police state. Secret police, terror, and tight control of essential institutions enable the ruling Baath party to withstand a lot of shock and keep going. The aftermath of the Kuwait War has demonstrated this fact. How could the embargo have forced Iraq to leave Kuwait? Naturally, the Iraqi government would have had to decide that Kuwait was not worth the suffering its citizens were undergoing. But the Baath party has never taken the sufferings of Iraqi citizens into account. Moreover, Iraq loudly proclaimed its seizure of Kuwait as a blow for Arab dignity and pride. Entire populations have endured much for that line, and in Iraq you are not given much choice. If true to form, the Baath party would have kept its members and functionaries fed, and let the world see the sufferings of those it would not feed. How long would an embargo last in the light of all those pictures of dying Shiite and Kurdish children?

Quick Study 1:
The Iraqi Army, or, Why Counting Rifles Doesn't Work

Since 1980, Iraq has been "an army with a country attached" rather than a nation with an army. The numbers tell part of the story. Throughout the 1980s, over 5 percent of the population (over 20 percent of the adult males) have been in uniform. An equal number have been enrolled in the armed civilian militia or other paramilitary organizations. But not all the people in the Iraqi Army were soldiers in the Western sense of the word. Hundreds of thousands are essentially civilians (without military training) performing military-support duties that in other nations would be done by uniformed personnel. These include supply, transportation, medical, signal, and so on.

In the Russian style, civilians are conscripted and sent to their units with no initial training. The unit then provides the conscripts with a varying degree of training, which is often fitful and uneven. There were exceptions to this pattern during the Iran-Iraq War when Iraq utilized a more centralized and formal training regimen. During the military mobilization after the Kuwait invasion, however, training was still not a high priority with the Iraqi high command. Most existing and

newly called-up troops (both former soldiers and new conscripts) went right off to a border area and began preparing
field fortifications. Many of these new recruits were not even
given complete uniforms. This is a "muddle through" approach to military affairs that has always been characteristic
of the Iraqi armed forces.

The backbone of the ground forces are its 120,000 officers,
most of whom are Baath party members. This does not mean
that all officers are dedicated, or even loyal, members of the
Baath party. This does mean that the ruling Baath party cares
enough about the loyalty of the army to "encourage" all officers
to join and then to use the existing security agencies and party
leaders to monitor loyalty and performance. (Among the many
duties of Baath party members is the requirement that they keep
an eye on other Baath party members.) Often, officers merely
go through the motions of "loyalty spying," but still the loyalty
reports are checked, double-checked, and cross-checked. That
an occasional officer is halfhearted and sloppy in performing his
Baath party duties and is caught tends to keep the others nervous. If some army officers are not exactly loyal, they certainly
have good reason to be wary. Only about half the officers are
on active duty all the time, the rest are "reserve" officers and
are only called to duty for an emergency (like war with Iran or
invading Kuwait).

As a result of the political priorities, many Iraqi officers are
not very dedicated to the profession of arms. During the Iran-
Iraq War, it was noted that surrenders by Iraqi brigades and
battalions were much more likely to occur if a lot of reserve
officers were involved. This situation repeated itself in Kuwait,
where many reserve officers were present and only the Republican Guard divisions, officered largely by career army officers,
managed to keep their units reasonably together. Yet incompe-
tence and lack of determination bred by politicization also in-
fects elements of the regular officer corps. Many Regular Army
officers abandoned their units in Kuwait as soon as the punish-
ing aerial bombardment began to take its toll.

If Iraqi troops are ill served, they are also often mistreated,
especially if they do not belong to the Baath ruling elite. From
the earliest years, Iraqi attitudes toward its troops were more
Turkish than British: i.e., the troops received harsh discipline,
and unquestioned obedience was required. This creates condi-

tions where ill-led troops are prone to choose surrender rather than resistance.

Nevertheless, the Iraqi Army was a formidable force. Most Westerners only saw the Iraqi Army as masses of dispirited prisoners. But before they were bombed and bludgeoned by superior Allied forces, the Iraqi armed forces were pretty impressive. This section will detail just how impressive the Iraqi armed forces were. Billions of dollars' worth of Russian and Western weapons and equipment as well as a large cadre of experienced NCOs and officers had made it one of the more competent fighting forces in the region. Much was known about the Iraqi armed forces, if only because of all the attention they got during the 1980–88 Iran-Iraq War and the authors' official, and unofficial, studies of the Middle Eastern armed forces since the 1960s. What follows is a detailed look at the Iraqi Army. Despite their collapse in the face of even more formidable Western air and ground firepower, the Iraqi armed forces will remain a strong regional influence for some time to come.

Organization and Equipment of the Iraqi Army

First, a short primer on the components of army units. If you were a soldier, you would belong to a squad or section of five to fifteen troops. Three or more of these would form a platoon. Three or more platoons form a company, and three or more companies form a battalion (or squadron). Three or more battalions form a brigade (or regiment), and three or more brigades form a division. Three or more divisions form a corps, and three or more corps form an army. That's it. And so ends the naming of the parts.

By February 1991, Iraqi ground forces consisted of about sixty divisions and thirty separate brigades (see the Orders of Battle section; Iraq never gave out exact numbers). If at full strength, these combat units would have contained over 800,000 troops. Most units were never at full strength, even with the call-up of reservists. And while over a million Iraqi soldiers were put on duty, many of those were used for support and other noncombat functions.

The Iraqi Army in mid-1990 had eight corps (numbered 1–7) plus the Republican Guards Corps. Each corps had about eight divisions, plus a Special Forces brigade and additional artillery, supply, maintenance, and other support units. It is important to understand that these are not corps in the Western sense, but are (as with the Egyptian and Syrian armies) a formation similar to what the Russians call an "army" (between a U.S. Field Army and Corps in size, number of support units, and use in combat). The Iraqi corps structure was flexible, and several additional corps were formed during the course of the war by simply taking divisions from existing corps and attaching them to new corps headquarters.

The Republican Guard Force Corps (RGFC) had eight divisions. Most of the RGFC was used to invade Kuwait. The Regular Army's elite Saladin Armored Division was also involved. In the past, Saddam Hussein had been wary about letting all of the Republican Guards stray too far from Baghdad, though the entire corps was eventually dug-in north of Kuwait.

The rest of the Iraqi Army was largely an infantry force, but the army did have some tank and mechanized infantry divisions. The army had five armored divisions, including one mobilized in the weeks after August 2. One of these armored divisions, the "Saladin" Division, was considered to be the combat equal of any Republican Guard Force division. Each armored division had 250–300 tanks. There were three mechanized divisions. Each of these had about 200 tanks. Rounding out the armored forces were six armored brigades, each with 100–120 tanks. Brigades were sometimes be added to armored divisions to beef them up.

To ensure loyalty, there were eighteen Special Forces brigades, including six mobilized after August 2. These units often have sufficient trucks to move all personnel. Each corps had two or three Special Forces brigades, often referred to as a "division" although these units are commonly used as separate brigades.

Most of the army's manpower was in fifty-one infantry divisions, twenty-four of which were mobilized after August 1990, some of which had only two brigades. About ten reserve divisions, some of them People's Army militia, were raised after November 1990. About twenty of these divisions had a battalion of forty tanks each.

For amphibious operations, there were three marine brigades—usually organized into a division. These were reinforced units.

There was one air-assault commando infantry brigade, apparently kept in reserve throughout the war.

Largely for internal security (like watching the Kurds), there were twenty-two infantry brigades, including two mobilized after August 2.

The Iraqi Army infantry divisions and brigades lacked sufficient trucks to move themselves. They required trucks, aircraft, trains, or watercraft for transportation; otherwise they marched on foot at the rate of ten to twenty miles a day.

Palestinian Militia.   There was a "division" of "Palestinian Militia" raised in Kuwait in late September 1990 for service with the Iraqi Army. These were local Palestinians, and apparently they were never able to muster more than a few thousand men. This unit was somewhere between an armed mob and a rabble in effectiveness. These armed men were used mainly against local Kuwaitis.

By February 1991, there were forty-three divisions in Kuwait or adjacent portions of Iraq (the Kuwait Theater of Operations or KTO). The remainder of the Iraqi Army was deployed along the Iranian, Turkish, and Syrian frontiers. Most of the Iraqi Army (especially the infantry divisions and brigades), were relatively low-grade infantry who depend as much on their shovels as their weapons for their effectiveness.

The Iraqi Special Forces (SF).   Every Iraqi division included a Special Forces unit, a brigade in the best mobile divisions, and battalion in most, and a company in low-quality infantry units. Corps also included an SF brigade, although the Guards Corps reportedly had three brigades that were grouped into its 8th Division. The Iraqi Special Forces are not the same as U.S. Special Forces "Green Beret" commando units. The Iraqi SF are always motorized and often mechanized (via armored personnel carriers) and have the best weapons and vehicles. They served a dual purpose. First, they were the most dependable troops in the unit they were a part of, and as such they were used to lead assaults or to cover retreats. The SF also functioned as politically reliable military-police units to ensure the loyalty and reliability of less trustworthy army units. Together with the secret-police informers found in every army unit, the Special Forces kept the army troops stable in situations the army troops would rather not be in. The presence of Special Forces units and secret-police spies ensured that, before January 17, 1991, only troops authorized leave to visit home did so. After the bombing began, the Special Forces staffed the "death squads" mentioned in the press, which sought to prevent Iraqi troops deserting to the Allies.

Ground-Combat Division Types

There are four division types: Tank, Mechanized Infantry, Infantry, and Special Forces (sort of motorized infantry with some tanks). Iraq uses a Russian-type unit organization with 11,000–13,000 men per full-strength division. Each division is composed of two to four combat brigades. In the Russian Army, these brigades are called regiments, so don't let that confuse you. Otherwise, a Russian regiment and an Iraqi brigade are not organized all that differently. In both cases, the regiment/brigade is composed of three to four battalions and some smaller units. Half the division's manpower is organized into other support and maintenance units.

Tank divisions have two tank brigades (each with three tank battalions and one mechanized infantry battalion) and one mechanized infantry (three mechanized infantry battalions and one tank battalion) brigade.

Infantry divisions simply have three infantry brigades plus one tank battalion of forty-four tanks. Using the Russian model, each division had ten to fourteen ground combat battalions (infantry and tank) plus artillery, reconnaissance, and so on. One major difference from Russian practice is the presence of many infantry divisions (the Russians eliminated the last of their nonmotorized "leg" infantry divisions in the 1950s). An Iraqi infantry division generally had nine infantry battalions and one or more tank battalions as well as some divisional support units.

The organization and, especially, equipment of Iraqi divisions deployed during the Persian Gulf War varied enormously. The Republican Guard divisions not only had the best equipment, but usually had all the equipment they were supposed to have.

Many of the Iraqi Army Reserve infantry divisions raised after August 1990 had only two brigades and only one or two battalions of artillery. These divisions had little of the signal, medical, engineer, or other specialized equipment they were supposed to have. The officers were recently recalled reservists, and many of the troops had never been in the army before. The Republican Guard troops had plenty of time to learn how to use their equipment and even spent a fair amount of time maintaining it.

While the two to four infantry and tank brigades formed the core of a division's combat strength, about half the division's manpower was in a collection of additional support units. These units were:

- One reconnaissance battalion with 30–50 armored vehicles, (infantry divisions use trucks) and 400–500 men. This unit scouts ahead when the division is on the move, or provides outer security and patrols when the division is in fixed positions. Division commanders usually try to get some of their best and most reliable troops into their recon battalion. The recon unit is also sometimes used as a reserve, as it can also function as a rear guard during a retreat. Some division commanders have also been known to use it as their personal bodyguard.
- Three to five artillery battalions. Each with eighteen guns or rocket launchers, and about 250 troops. Most divisions have towed 152-mm or 122-mm howitzers. The forty-three divisions in the KTO (Kuwaiti Theater of Operations, Kuwait and southern Iraq) had an average of seventy-two guns each. But up to 20 percent of those guns would be "nondivisional." That is, they would be under the control of corps or theater headquarters. So while some of the Republican Guard divisions might have over 100 guns (six battalions, most of them self-propelled guns), some of the lower-grade infantry divisions would only have two or three battalions. Infantry divisions would also tend to have the less capable 122-mm howitzers and less well trained gun crews. Artillery received an intensive pounding from Allied air power, and little of it was in operating condition by the middle of February.
- One antitank battalion. Usually armed with twelve to twenty-four antitank guided missile (ATGM) launchers, although some still have ancient Russian 100-mm towed

antitank guns. Units consist of about 150 men. The Iraqis bought thousands of French Milan ATGMs and as many of the more recent Russian models. The infantry division generally got stuck with the older, and less effective, ATGMs. One of the reasons for Allied ground units hitting Iraqi units quickly and unexpectedly was to prevent these antitank missiles from being used. While the M1A1 tanks were largely invulnerable, the lighter Allied armored vehicles were not.

• One or two antiaircraft battalions of about 100–300 men each. Equipment consisted mostly of 23-mm and 57-mm artillery, one to three dozen guns per battalion, and usually towed. The mechanized units have all or some of their antiaircraft guns self-propelled.
• One or two engineer battalions. One for construction and maintaining electrical and mechanical equipment, the other for combat. Each battalion had 300–400 men.
• One signal battalion of 240–260 men, and 50–60 vehicles. Split between troops for laying and maintaining telephone lines and those operating and maintaining long-range radio communications.
• One chemical-defense battalion of 140–60 men, 50–60 trucks. Some vehicles carried equipment for detecting the presence of chemicals, others have gear for decontaminating vehicles and troops. There was actually relatively little equipment for these units, and the Iraqis were much less prepared to deal with chemical warfare than the Allies.
• One transportation battalion consisting of 100–200 heavy trucks for moving supplies, carrying one, sometimes two, men per truck plus a few dozen in battalion headquarters.
• Medical battalion. Consisted of 20–30 trucks, and 100–150 men (including one or more doctors), which was not nearly enough to take care of all the casualties from a major battle. As a support unit, it's barely enough to deal with normal sickness, disease, and accidents.
• Maintenance battalion. Included 200–300 men and 50–100 trucks, and consisted of mechanics, tools, and spare parts for repairing and maintaining much of the divisions' equipment. Good mechanics were always in short supply, and Iraqi equipment tended to be poorly maintained.
• Traffic control. Had 50–100 troops and a dozen or so ve-

hicles. This was basically traffic police, charged with keeping the divisions' vehicles moving in the right direction. This was crucial in the desert, where regular supply convoys could, and did, get lost.

- Supply depot, consisting of 100–200 men and 30–40 trucks to maintain stored supplies and give them out to units that needed them. These units were favorite targets of the bombing.
- Division headquarters. Consisting of 100–150 men, and 30–40 trucks, this unit often split into two or more headquarters so that if one was destroyed, the other could still control the division. Allied bombing often tracked down and destroyed all elements of the division headquarters, because the Iraqis had to use radios to issue orders and radio transmitters could be easily located.

Brigade Organization

The brigade was the principal combat organization for both Iraqis and Allies.

Tank brigades had three tank battalions (each 44 tanks, 200 men) and a mechanized battalion (50 APCs, 700 men); mechanized brigades had the reverse. At least some Guards brigades had two tank and two mech battalions.

Infantry brigades had only three rifle battalions of about 600 men each. Motorized infantry battalions had a dozen or more trucks, just enough to move all the troops and their equipment on wheels.

Many brigades had Special Forces companies. Mechanized and armored brigades had a bridge company, and often a recon company. All brigades had a supply company and a chemical decontamination platoon. In addition, brigades had company-size units for recon, engineers (mobile bridge, because much of Iraq is rivers and streams) and some other support troops as needed (signal, medical, maintenance, etc.).

Nearly all brigades had an artillery component, although this was usually a battery of six mortars (82 mm in infantry units, 120 mm in mechanized units). Guards brigades had a complete artillery battalion (sometimes two, plus the mortar battery).

Battalion Organization

Battalions are the basic building block of all armies. A battalion is the smallest unit that can support itself with different weapons and its own supply system in the field.

Iraqi battalions had three combat companies. Rifle battalions had about 600 men; tank battalions had 44 tanks. (Republican Guards tank battalions had sixty tanks, divided into four companies.) Companies had three platoons, about thirty riflemen or four tanks each. Infantry companies also had a heavy-weapons platoon with machine guns, and antitank and antiaircraft weapons. Republican Guards companies had 81-mm or 82-mm mortars; army rifle companies usually had no mortars (some had smaller 60-mm mortars).

Artillery battalions had eighteen guns, except heavy artillery and large-caliber rocket battalions, which usually had twelve weapons. Keep in mind that nearly all Iraqi artillery is towed, usually by trucks.

Independent Brigade Operations

Unlike their mentors the Russians, the Iraqis are prone to use brigades independently. In part they do this because it allows them to use key mobile units more flexibly, and the Iraqis never had mastered the concept of keeping a division-sized unit going with all its support elements.

Iraqi support units are not that effective, and divisions tend to put down roots where they are stationed. For example, the troops take shelter in local buildings (because the Iraqi Army doesn't have a lot of tents for field operations) and give their trucks a rest (there were not enough of these, and they were not well maintained). Basically, the Iraqi Army does not travel well, so the Iraqis move it as infrequently as possible, and when they do move, move as little of it as possible.

The Long-Range Rocket Troops: Missile Units

Iraqi missile units comprised four Laith (Russian Frog-7 type unguided rockets) regiments (five to six launchers each, 40-km range, several hundred missiles) and five Scud brigades (ten to eleven launchers each, firing Russian Scuds or Iraqi-

modified Russian Scud missiles, up to 900-km range). At the
start of the war, Iraq was believed to have over 300 Al Abbas
or Al Hussein missiles available for these launchers. In addition there were several dozen fixed launchers, most of which
were bombed during the first days of the air war. The Iraqis
also proved adept at quickly turning flatbed tractor-trailer
trucks into Scud launchers.

Iraq promised to "scourage its enemies with rockets," and it
did just that, launching over eighty Scud-type missiles at Israel
and Saudi Arabia. The Scud attacks had far more political than
military impact. The Iraqi Al Hussein variant of the Scud was
apparently used. The Al Hussein accuracy was, at best, capable
of putting 50 percent of the warheads within 1,000 meters of the
target. The missile warheads weighed only half a ton (far less
than what a fighter-bomber can carry on one sortie). The Al
Abbas had longer range, but was available in smaller quantities.

The four missiles that were available to the Iraqis are:

IRAQI MISSILES

	Weight (Tons)	Warhead (Pounds)	Length (Feet)	Range (Km/Miles)	CEP (Meters)
Scud	6.3	2,000	37	300/187	1,000
Al Hussein	7	1,100	39	650/406	2,000
Al Abbas	8	770	44	900/562	3,000
Laith*	2	500	30	60/37	2,000

*Laith was Russian Frog-7 variant.

The weight of the rocket (in tons) gives an indication of what
damage the rocket could do; as only half the weight was fuel,
the rest would land somewhere and do damage even if the warhead did not explode. About two thirds of the warhead weight
was explosives. The range shows the trade-off between reaching
distant targets and smaller warheads and decreased accuracy.

The CEP is the Circular Area Probable, or, in plain English,
the distance from the target within which 50 percent of missiles
fired will land. The theoretical distance of the CEP is a bit better
than the actual one. The Iraqis tend to be sloppy, and their actual CEP is probably much worse than the figures shown. Not

that it makes a lot of difference, as the missiles were largely fired at area targets (cities), so just getting the missile in the general area of the target will do the job.

Iraq's Army Arsenal

The principal weapons of the Iraqi ground forces were:

- 5,500 tanks, comprising 1,600 T-55 (forty-year-old design), 500 Type 59 (Chinese clone of T-55), 900 Type 62 (updated Type 59), 1,500 T-62 (thirty-year-old design), 1,000 T-72 (twenty-year-old design)
- 1,000 Infantry Fighting Vehicles (BMP-1 and variants, similar to U.S. Bradley)
- 1,100 reconnaissance vehicles (wheeled armored vehicles)
- 6,000 APCs (Armored Personnel Carriers, older wheeled armored vehicles)
- 2,800 towed artillery (includes 300 long range. 30–40 km)
- 500 self-propelled guns (Russian 122-mm and 152-mm models)
- 200 multiple-rocket launchers (Russian and Brazilian)

Where the Tanks Were

Iraqi tank battalions had forty-four tanks each (at full strength), while Republican Guard battalions often had sixty tanks. With a total tank strength of 5,000, this gives a total (with reserve, spare, and under repair tanks) of as many as 110 tank battalions. Prior to their destruction by the coalition forces, there were eleven armored and mechanized divisions, with about sixty-six tank battalions, in the ground forces. Six armored brigades contained another twenty tank battalions. The remaining twenty-four battalions were distributed in ones and twos (usually ones) among the infantry divisions.

Where the Guns Were

Iraq had over 4,000 major artillery pieces. In the inventory are over a dozen different models, and nearly as many calibers (122 mm, 130 mm, 152 mm, 155 mm, 203 mm, etc., as well as several different types of artillery rockets). Each division had 40–100 of these, thus absorbing over 3,000 guns. A division rarely had more than one battalion of rocket launchers. The remaining guns and rocket launchers were in nondivisional units controlled by corps or army headquarters and used to support major operations. There were also over a dozen counterbattery radars. These were used to spot incoming enemy fire and calculate where the shells were coming from so that Iraqi artillery could accurately fire back. The Allies shut down these radars before they could do any damage. The large number of different calibers complicated ammunition supply significantly.

Manpower Strength

Total prewar personnel strength was generally estimated as about 1 million men (including 50,000 in the air force and 5,000 in the navy). A third of these are regulars (to one degree or another); the remainder are draftees and recalled reservists. The reservists, numbering about 250,000, are those who fought in the Iran-Iraq War and were discharged between 1988 and 1990. About 300,000 are conscripts undergoing their mandatory service. Nearly 100,000 more men were simply grabbed wherever they could be found. With about seventy division-size units, this comes out to about 14,000 men per division. Headquarters and nondivisional units (artillery, engineer, signal, supply, transportation, etc.) reduce the actual strength of each division to 8,000–12,000. The lower figure is for some of the newly raised divisions, the higher figure for the Republican Guard units. While the million-man figure may have been achieved for a few months in late 1990, it appears that desertions began to cut into this number by late 1990. By mid-January 1991, Iraq probably had fewer than 700,000 troops under any kind of central control. Two months later, during the March rebellions, the number probably fell to less than 300,000 troops. Still enough to beat the Kurdish partisans and Shiite rebels.

Mobility

Most of Iraq's divisions are not motorized. As a Third World nation, Iraq was always short of trucks. During its war with Iran, most of the troops were merely occupying trench lines and had no need for mobility. Thus, aside from about twenty mechanized and motorized units, and trucks assigned to the support units of each division, all the remaining trucks available to the Iraqi Army formed a pool of nearly 20,000 vehicles that could be used to motorize a dozen or more infantry divisions or provide additional resupply capacity for units out in the desert. Some of these motorized divisions had enough APCs (Armored Personnel Carriers) for one battalion. Some had a tank battalion. Iraq had several thousand tank-transporter trucks. These are capable of lifting three armored or mechanized divisions at one time, speeding up long-range moves (but also providing excellent targets for U.S. Air Force A-10s). These were needed because most of Iraq's tanks are older (and less reliable) Russian models. Iraq does not have a lot of tank mechanics, so it's been more efficient (and easier) to maintain the wheeled tank transporters (large, flatbed tractor-trailer trucks that can also carry other loads). Moreover, tanks tear up roads, and keeping them off the roads saves on road-repair expense.

Military Background of the Iraqi Army

The Iraqi Army that invaded Kuwait was not an unknown entity. The Iraqi Army's experience and that of its increasingly numerous opponents across the border in Saudi Arabia were well known. Here are a few points to consider, especially in light of the 1980–88 war fought with Iran:

1. The victors of the trench warfare of 1914–18 were soundly defeated by the more mobile German "blitzkrieg" of 1939–41. Iraq fought its eight-year war with Iran in fixed positions—that is, through trench warfare. The Iraqis thought this would work for them in Kuwait. The thousands of Iraqi tanks in the Iran war were used only for short advances and most of the time were simply dug-in as part of fixed defenses. The one Iraqi experience with mobile warfare, the initial advance into Iran in 1980, was a disaster (although not as bad as press reports since 1980 would have it).

2. Mobile warfare is much more difficult to master than static defense. Iraqi troops are masters of the shovel and defending prepared positions. On the road, it's a different story. Iraqi troops are not trained for mobile warfare

and are not comfortable or confident doing it. The invasion of Kuwait was basically a dash across the border and into Kuwait City. Even though they were outnumbered six to one, the Kuwaiti troops kept the Iraqis tied up for several days, and then managed to retreat into Saudi Arabia with many of their troops and much of their equipment.

3. Iraq never demonstrated an ability to competently and consistently use technologically sophisticated equipment. This became a particularly crucial shortcoming when the tempo of operations increased, as it did during the ground war in Kuwait.

4. Most of the UN forces in Saudi Arabia (particularly the Americans, French, and British) have trained for years at mobile warfare. Their equipment and tactics are built around a war of movement.

5. The UN forces had a significant "information" advantage. Air superiority and several satellites could provide, in many cases, instant information on where Iraqi forces were and what they were doing. The Iraqis, however, knew little of where the UN units were and what they were doing.

6. Iraq fought a successful logistical war with Iran. Right behind the border, Iraq had a well-developed road network and nearby bases that allowed it to move supplies and troops easily and quickly. Iraqi forces in Kuwait were supplied by a few roads from the north. They were surrounded by desert and were dependent on a desalination plant for drinking water. Any water they had stockpiled could be destroyed by air attacks. The truck convoys from the north were attacked by aircraft (and the roads constantly monitored by satellite and aircraft). During its war with Iraq, Iran had serious logistics problems getting all its supplies over a mountain range from distant bases. This time it was Iraq that was at the end of a very slender and vulnerable supply line.

7. Iraqi troops proved inept in the attack. Their few successful offensives against demoralized Iranian troops in the late 1980s were carefully planned and heavily supported operations. Even then, the Iraqis were not always successful. Moreover, many of the Iraqi officers who

planned and executed these attacks were later purged by
Saddam lest they become too popular. Unless the UN
forces abandoned their thousands of armored vehicles
and attacked dug-in Iraqi infantry as the Iranians did,
Iraqi success on the battlefield was unlikely.

8. Iraq had air superiority for most of its war with Iran.
This was not the case in 1991. As Israel had demonstrated many times, air superiority in the desert is a decided disadvantage if you don't have it. UN air units
operated night and day and often in foul weather. This
meant that any movement of Iraqi units made them vulnerable to delay, disruption, and, ultimately, destruction. This was equally true of the vital supply columns
carrying water, fuel, food, and ammunition. If you cannot maneuver in the desert, you soon die.

9. Iraq did have some experience in mobile warfare, in
1980. There was even one major tank battle, the Battle
of Susangerd. In January 1981, the Iranian 16th Armored Division and the 55th Paratroop Brigade counterattacked an Iraqi armored division near Susangerd, Iran.
The purpose of this attack was to open the road to Ah-
waz and relieve the Iraqi siege of the key Iranian port
town Abadan. There was a lot of political pressure on
the Iranian Army to lift the siege of Abadan. This was
coupled with incompetent military leadership, and the
result was the Iranian 16th Armored Division and the
55th Paratroop Brigade attacked down a single road
without adequate infantry support (most of the local Iranian infantry were controlled by the Revolutionary
Guard, who were hostile to the Regular Army). On both
sides of the road was nothing but mud and water, and it
was in the middle of the rainy season. The 300 Chieftains
and M-60s of the Iranian 16th delivered themselves
piecemeal into the 300 T-62 tanks of the Iraqi Armored
Division. Two thirds of the Iranian tanks got shot to
pieces in an ambush near the village of Achmed Abad
before the Iranians gave up. Both sides demonstrated
lack of skill in the battle. Most tanks had to get close to
score hits, sometimes as close as 200 meters (this in relatively open and featureless terrain). In similar terrain
during the 1991 battles, U.S. tanks routinely scored hits

from as far away as 3,000 meters. The poor performance of both Iraqi and Iranian gunners was due to poorly maintained (and used) fire-control systems. The Iranians lost over 200 tanks. Some were destroyed by Iraqi tanks, others broke down, and many were simply abandoned by inexperienced crews after they bogged them down in the mud. The Iraqis lost about 100 T-62s in the engagement but recovered all of them and were able to repair most after the battle.

The Experience Factor by the Numbers

Iraq had about 1.5 million men (18–30 years old) available through the 1980s for military service in 1990. Each year, about 150,000 men reach age eighteen and become available for military service. There would be more, but large segments of the population are either of suspect loyalty, disabled, or are needed for more urgent work. Only about half the population is literate, which places more restrictions on which men can be used for which job. During the 1980–88 Iran-Iraq War, Iraq mobilized nearly 2 million men, including several hundred thousand under age eighteen and over thirty. Over 150,000 of these troops were killed (or died of other causes), and nearly 250,000 were disabled to the point where they could no longer serve (a larger number were wounded or became ill but returned to service). Over 70,000 troops were captured, and many more deserted. This was a world-class military effort, with nearly half the adult male population directly involved. Most of the combat was defensive, fending off waves of Iranian infantry or enduring lengthy artillery barrages. The battlefront with Iran was 1,100 kilometers long, and over half the troops spent the war manning inactive areas along it. Of those stationed on the active areas (mostly in the south, near Basra), over half would become casualties, and many of the rest would absorb more terror than experience.

The effect of the war on Iraqis was similar to the European experience in World War I. Few veterans came out of the trenches with any enthusiasm for another war. Wisely, Iraq placed many of its best-trained, experienced, and nonshell-shocked troops into the Republican Guard Corps. These 100,000 troops were the best it had, but to build up this elite, most of the remaining army units were left with a larger proportion of less capable troops and equipment. Not surprisingly, a disproportionate number of troops (and even more officers) come from the province of Tikrit (north of Baghdad), which is the home area of Iraqi leader Saddam Hussein. Tikrit has been shown much favor politically and economically in the twenty years Saddam has been in power, and the Tikritis are expected to repay those favors with exceptional loyalty. However, this meant that many key positions in the Republican Guard force were filled with officers noted more for loyalty than military skill.

Quick Study 2:
Iraq Is Divided into Three Parts

Iraq is at once one of the oldest and newest nations on earth. The modern nation of Iraq dates back only to 1932. Yet Iraq is also the land of Babylon and of Abraham, the patriarch of Jews and Muslims.

Around 2100 B.C., Abraham left his hometown of Ur (in southern Iraq, not far from Babylon and Baghdad), wandered into what is now Israel, and became the first Hebrew. The Jews ended up in exile in Egypt, but by 1200 B.C. or thereabouts they were back in Palestine and in charge.

Back in what is now Iraq, things got more complicated. The following list of events in the history of the territory we now know of as Iraq is intended to offer some perspective. Note that the items after 1918 are covered again elsewhere, but we keep them here also for easier reference.

- 7000 B.C.—First farming in the area. Includes some of the earliest known farming communities in the world.
- 5000 B.C.—Irrigation from Tigris and Euphrates rivers used to extend farming into adjacent desert.
- 3000 B.C.—First cities built in the area; first evidence of written language (commercial records on clay tablets).

- 1720–1530 B.C.—Babylonian Empire under Hammurabi. One of the most prominent ancient empires.
- 1350–615 B.C.—Assyrian tribes from up north conquer area and establish empire, although for long periods there is chaos and no one is in control.
- 625–539 B.C.—New Babylonian Empire (Assyrians are still around, but no longer running things).
- 539–331 B.C.—Persians move in from the east (Iran) and take over.
- 331–150 B.C.—Alexander the Great and his Greek Army conquer area, and Greeks become the new ruling class. Alexander noted that the Kurds gave him some trouble when his army passed through what is now northern Iraq.
- 150 B.C.—A.D. 660—Various Persian (Iranian) empires rule the area, often using it as a battleground for wars with Romans and Byzantines to the west. Sometimes chaos rules.
- 661–1258—Conquest by Muslim Arabs from the south (Arabia). Area converted to Islam and most of the population in the Tigris-Euphrates river valleys adopts Arabic language. Area still used as a battleground during the frequent civil wars between various Muslim rulers attempting to restore the unified Arab Empire (which didn't survive more than a few centuries after the birth of Islam). At times Byzantine (Greek) Empire controls area.
- 1258–1355—Mongols enter the area, trash much of what the Muslims have built up, and rule with an iron fist.
- 1355–1405—Timur (Tamerlane), leading an Oriental nomad army enters and outdoes the Mongols in the destruction department. After Timur, disorder reigns.
- 1500–1534—Persians make a comeback and rule the area briefly.
- 1534–1918—The Turks, yet another group of Oriental nomads, conquer the area (after finishing off the Byzantine Empire in what is now Turkey). The Persians remain across the Shatt-al-Arab, and sporadic wars occur. Throughout all this, no one bothers with Arabia, because there's nothing there but Bedouin nomads minding their flocks.
- 1897—Kuwait becomes a British protectorate (voluntarily). This enabled the Kuwaitis to guarantee that the

Turkish governor of Basra Province to the north would not try again to seize Kuwait (whose primary assets are an excellent harbor, trade with the interior tribes, and oyster beds producing many pearls).

- 1917—British take Baghdad and Iraq from Turks. The northern part of Iraq is initially under French control, but the British get it back in 1920.
- 1918—Britain and the Sharif Hussein of Mecca (Hashemite king, descendent of prophet Muhammad) join forces, and Iraq is formed as a country. (Lawrence of Arabia supported the Hashemites.)
- 1919—Saudi Arabian religious fanatics march on Kuwait. British repel Saudis, who blockade country for twenty years.
- 1920—League of Nations makes Iraq a territory under British administration. Soon the Iraqis rebel against British. The rebellion is put down, and a Hashemite prince is installed as ruler (and soon to become the king). These developments take place during the 1920s, in stages. Part of the deal was that there was to be a vote in northern Iraq (where the Kurds live) to determine what the people in that area wanted to do. Iraq has never held that vote.
- 1932—League of Nations mandate ends, Iraq gains independence.
- 1934–36—Iraqi Army puts down series of tribal (Shiite) uprisings in central Iraq. This establishes the army as a major power in the government.
- 1936–41—Six successful coups (and several that aren't) are backed by or led by the army. The army asserts its newfound authority by making and unmaking new governments at will. The king is left alone.
- 1942—Britain invades and defeats Iraqi attempt to ally with Nazi Germany. The army went too far when it took over and tried to gain Nazi support to keep the British out. Britain had a treaty that allowed the British back into Iraq if Britain saw a need to do so.
- 1948—Rebellion causes change of government. Popular uprisings over economic issues. Army puts them down, but new political leaders installed.
- 1952—Iraq renews ancient claim to Kuwait which is re-

jected by Britain. British warn that they will resist, with armed force, any Iraqi actions.

- 1952–53—Popular rebellion for democratic rights. Army puts these down, but more clandestine political parties form.
- 1958—Army takes over, executes king and his family. This was largely a revolt of the conservative middle class that wanted law and order and modernization. Communists and other radicals persecuted. The wealthy landlord class was broken by a series of land reforms that benefited the poor, and often landless, farmers.
- 1961—After sixty years, Kuwait becomes completely independent of Britain (which had controlled Kuwaiti foreign affairs for over 60 years). However, an Iraqi attempt to march into Kuwait that year is stopped by the presence of a few thousand British troops.
- 1963—Baath party coup. The Baath party (a middle-class group of radicals) formed a coalition with the landlords and upper class in general to overwhelm the middle-class army officers. The Baath party also preaches Arab nationalism and unity.
- 1963—Late in the year the military again take over. The Baath use of terror and its attempt to oust its allies from power are fatal moves. The army allies with Arab nationalists and socialists. As a result, the middle-class base of the Baath power is attacked with a program of nationalization.
- 1963—Iraq and Kuwait sign agreement that Kuwait is free and sovereign.
- 1968—Increasing economic problems, and diligent political organizing, gives the Baath party another chance to seize power. This time they succeeded, and are determined not to lose it again. A combination of terror against real, imagined, or potential opponents plus heavy use of patronage to maintain loyalty of party members proves successful.
- 1969—Kuwait and Saudi Arabia agree on a boundary in the disputed area from 1919.
- 1973—Iraq joins war against Israel. Iraqi forces impress neither the Allies nor the Arabs.
- 1975—Iraq threatens to invade Kuwait, but backs off

after Saudi Arabia sends 15,000 troops to aid Kuwait.
- 1976—Iraq and Syria quarrel over Syria's intervention in Lebanon. Iraq provides support to factions that will oppose Syria, which helps keep the civil war going.
- 1977—The United Nations declares that Iraq is systematically destroying its Kurdish minority and asks Iraq to stop, please. Baath also hammers Shiite separatists during this period.
- 1979—Saddam Hussein, since 1968 the vice president of Iraq and the chief architect of the Baath party security services, takes over from his sickly cousin. One of the few times a major change in leadership occurs without the incumbent being killed. Saddam proceeds to conduct a purge, killing, jailing, and otherwise rearranging thousands of Baath party members.
- 1980—Iraq and Iran begin open war after skirmishing for nearly a year. Iraq had early success.
- 1981—Israel bombs Iraqi Osiraq nuclear reactor.
- 1982—Iraq is pushed back to prewar Iran-Iraq boundary.
- 1984—War expands into Gulf area. Shipping threatened, and Iranian ships and oil facilities attacked.
- 1987—*USS Stark* is hit by missile from Iraqi plane, killing thirty-seven sailors. Iraq apologizes for mistake. Iraqi pilot involved is apparently shot.
- 1988—Iran and Iraq begin cease-fire after many Iranian troops lose will to fight and Iraqi forces win a few victories.
- 1990—Iraq invades Kuwait in dispute over oil field and shipping access to Gulf.
- 1991—UN forces attack Iraq seventeen hours after UN deadline for Iraqi withdrawal from Kuwait expires. Five weeks later, the ground forces go in, and five days after that, the Iraqi forces are defeated and smashed.

A Larger Lebanon

Keeping the Iraqi population happy has never been an easy task, largely because the population is not homogeneous. Iraq is similar to Lebanon in the diversity of its ethnic makeup. No one wants ten or twenty years of civil war in Iraq, but that's what could eventually occur (if not this decade, then eventually).

In some ways, Iraq is the least "Arab" of all Arab nations, with only a quarter of its population being true "Arabs"—that is, Sunni Arabs. Half of the population (mostly in the Basra area and lower reaches of the Tigris and Euphrates rivers) were Shiite Muslim Arabs, who are considered somewhat heretical by the mainline Sunni Arabs. The Basra Arabs have also yearned for independence. But this was not practical, as many Shiite Arabs already lived (and were persecuted) across the border in Persia, and the Persians (now Iranians) were always keen to grab the rest of the Shiite Arabs in Basra (and further south along the Persian Gulf coast and further west in Syria and Lebanon.) So the Shiite Arabs in Basra generally put up with the Sunni Arabs in Baghdad as the lesser of two evils. The Baghdad Sunnis, mindful of the many Shiite holy places in the Basra area, and the larger number of Shiites, were generally careful in their dealings with the Shiite Arabs.

Kurds living in Mosul Province (northern Iraq) make up another fifth of the population. The Kurds were almost always in revolt against Arabs (and Persians and Turks) in their centuries-long quest for an independent Kurdish state. This "Kurdistan" would incorporate those portions of Iran and Turkey occupied by the rest of the 10 million (or more) Kurds in the area. The area would also include the oil fields in the current Kirkuk Province (near Mosul). Kirkuk is also claimed by Turkey.

The remainder of the population comprises several other minorities, including a sizable number of Christians (some Arab, some not). Most of the minority groups are Shiite, giving Iraq a Shiite majority. This majority is even more striking when you realize that nearly half the Sunni population are Kurds, who care nothing for Sunni or Shiite Arabs.

Iraq the Nation

People have always lived in the Iraq region because of its plentiful water supply and lush agriculture. The merging of the Tigris and Euphrates rivers as they flowed into the Persian Gulf formed a river delta of enormous agricultural potential. Irrigation aided the process, but also caused the land to become saturated with salt every thousand years or so, after which food production would plummet, along with the population. Eventually, fertility would return, along with population growth.

As a consequence, population varied in the Baghdad and Basra areas until earlier this century, with 2 million being the maximum population sustainable with the then-primitive irrigation and farming methods. (Seven hundred years ago, the shape of the rivers changed, largely destroying the ancient fertility cycle. Population did not move over the 2 million mark until this century, with the introduction of better farming methods and the availability of cheap imported food.) During the periods when intensive agriculture was not possible, the land was used for grazing. In these dry periods, more Bedouin would wander up from the Arabian Peninsula, graze their flocks, make war on the locals, and often settle down. This is the basis of the Iraqi dislike for the Bedouin to their south. Note also that "traditional Bedouin grazing areas" extend into southern Iraq, Syria, and Jordan.

The area around Baghdad was always the primary province in the region, usually with less than a million people and populated by Sunni Muslim Arabs for the last 1,200 years. North of the Baghdad Province was the slightly less populous province of Mosul, populated (for over 2,000 years) by Kurds, along with many Arabs, Turks, and sundry other groups.

As we have seen, the Kurds (ethnically similar to the Iranians) in the Northern and Eastern mountains wanted nothing to do with the Arabs on the Baghdad plain (and to a lesser extent, Turks and Persians); and this has not changed over the centuries. South of Baghdad was the buffer zone province of Basra, populated largely by Shiite Muslims (and some Bedouins) and exposed to invasions by the Persians to the east, Turks and other Arabs from the west, and the nomadic Arab Bedouins from the south.

Just south of Basra lay largely empty desert wastes thinly inhabited by Bedouin nomad tribes. The area just to the south of Basra eventually became the emirate of Kuwait, centered around the fortified port city of Kuwait. This area did not become a factor in local politics until the 1700s, when a particularly bad drought in the Arabian Peninsula drove several Bedouin clans to the coast, where they built up the town of Kuwait and have ruled the area ever since. The area around Kuwait City had been settled for thousands of years, primarily because it was one of the few sheltered bays in the Persian Gulf. The Sunnis in Kuwait traded with the Shiites in Basra and others in the Persian Gulf, but largely kept to themselves. When another people conquered Basra, be they Turks or Persians, they usually left the feisty and poverty-stricken Kuwaitis alone. Bedouin were too tough, too mobile, and too poor to bother with. Until the discovery of oil during the early part of this century, there was nothing in the Arabian Peninsula for an outsider to fight over. The Bedouin and a small number of town dwellers were left alone and largely independent.

When World War I broke out in 1914, the Ottoman (Turkish) Empire sided with the Germans. So in 1917, the British moved in and seized the Baghdad and Basra areas. Through the 1800s, Britain had been establishing relationships with the Arab Gulf states. The Kuwaitis, who were no friends of the Turks, had always sided with the British and friendly British diplomatic ties continued to the present day.

Baghdadi Arabs provided many officers for the Turkish Army, largely because there were few economic opportunities back home. In fact, a disproportionate number of the Arab officers in the Turkish Army were from the Baghdad area. This is one reason why Iraq has always been so dominated by the military. When the Ottoman Empire entered World War I, the British enticed many of these Arab officers to defect in return for freeing the area from Turkish rule and establishing an Arab nation.

When the nation of Iraq was established in 1932, it consisted of the three provinces of Baghdad, Mosul, and Basra. There was some dispute with the new Turkish Republic, as the Mosul Province (and the Kirkuk oil fields) were more Turk and Kurd than Arab (because of the largely Kurdish population). The British gave the area to Iraq anyway, partially to reward their Arab allies for World War I services and partially to ensure that the Turkish Republic did not have future oil wealth with which to entertain ideas of reestablishing another Turk Empire. In hindsight, this proved to be a big mistake, as the forward-looking Turks turned Westward in their thinking and have been a staunch ally of the Western democracies ever since. Moreover, the Iraqis were only given Mosul with the understanding that they would allow the (largely Kurd) population the opportunity to vote on their political destiny.

As a final political touch, a prince was imported from the ruling (then and now) Hashemite family in Jordan. At the time, the Hashemites also ruled western Saudi Arabia, but that did not last beyond the 1920s. Providing all these jobs for Hashemite princes was another means of repaying the Arabs for aiding Britain in World War I. But the Baghdad members of this family of imported aristocrats were lined up against a wall and shot when the Iraqi Army took over in 1958. Before that happened, the British had to take over the country again during World War II when a large number of Iraqi Army officers sought an alliance with the Nazi Germans. Iraqi and Nazi officers apparently had a lot in common, at least in terms of politics and attitudes toward Jews. After World War II, the British left once more, leaving the Hashemite royalty to their fate.

In 1958, with the Hashemite royal family dead and the army in control, a civil war began. While the army was a potent political power, it was overshadowed by the Arab nationalist Baath (Renaissance) party. The party was organized in the 1930s and 1940s by a Christian Syrian intellectual (Michel Aflag) and like-minded fellows in Damascus. The Iraqi branch was founded in 1949, partially as a reaction to the creation of Israel. Initially, the Baath wanted to overthrow the monarchies and unite all Arabs from Iraq to Morocco into one powerful state. This ideal soon faded nationalist pressures. The Syrian Baath wanted a "Greater Syria" (Syria, Palestine, and Jordan, for starters) and eventually all Arab states united under Syrian control. Baath took over Syria in 1963, followed by a bloody purge of any potential opposition. Also in 1963, Baath (and non-Baath) army officers took control of the military government in Iraq. At that point, Syria and Iraq began to move apart.

In 1968 the non-Baath Iraqi Army officers were purged, and Baath had sole control of the army, and Iraq. At the time, the second in command of the Iraqi Baath party, and the real power in the country, was thirty-one-year-old Saddam Hussein. Saddam waited in the shadows until he could take complete control of the country.

Meanwhile, Iraq sought a Baath-controlled unification with largely Sunni Arab Syria as a way to solve its minorities problem. There was one catch, and that was that the Baghdad Arabs of Iraq would then be an even smaller minority in the united nation, and the more numerous (and nearly as bloody-minded) Syrian Sunni Arabs would run the whole show. Syria also had a minorities problem, but not as severe as in Iraq. The Syrian Baath party members were not gentle people, and dealt harshly with real or imagined opposition. Thus began the ongoing blood feud between Baath factions in Iraq and Syria over, essentially, which wing of Baath would control the other.

Oil had also changed the relationship. Iraq has lots of oil; Syria doesn't. Excluding oil, Syria is a richer nation than Iraq. The Syrians are also better educated and more productive.

Both Syria and Iraq have dangerous neighbors to worry about. Syria has Israel, Iraq has Iran. Syria has never been able to defeat Israel militarily, and is never likely to accomplish this. Iraq was able to fight Iran to a standstill in the 1980s, gaining great prestige among Arabs. And then there are the local opportunities. Iraq has the oil-rich and population-poor Arab Gulf states to the south as potential conquests. Syria has only strife-torn Lebanon and poverty-stricken Jordan as potential victims. Thus Iraq sees itself as the more equal of the two Baath states. Syria does not agree, and the feud between "Damascus and Baghdad" continues (as it had done for centuries before the Baath party came along).

The problems between the two countries reached a new watershed in 1979 with the emergence of Saddam Hussein as the sole ruler of Iraq. He was by no means a new player in Iraqi politics, having first appeared on its political scene in 1958 when he tried to assassinate the (non-Baath) general then ruling Iraq. Saddam failed (even though he was something of a professional assassin at that point), was wounded himself, and found refuge in Syria. He returned and joined in the eventual Baath takeover in Iraq. Saddam has not got as far as he has alone. He is one of the "Tikrit clan." Tikrit is a region (since expanded to province status with a population of several million) of a few hundred thousand people a hundred miles north of Baghdad. While Baghdad contains several warring "clans," the Tikrit group has remained fairly united, in no small part due to the skill and ruthlessness of Saddam.

In 1979, Saddam persuaded his mentor (and cousin), and nominal head of Iraq, to retire. In the same manner as other modern dictators such as Stalin and Hitler, Saddam was quick to consolidate his power with the gun. With the sickly al-Bakr departing the scene, Saddam immediately executed dozens of senior officials and purged the army and government of any he suspected of disloyalty. This was all done in secret, as he had no desire to create public martyrs. Saddam learned quickly and became a skillful user of the media, presenting himself to the people as a great leader. This combination of carrot and stick has kept him in power for over twenty years.

Assassination squads were sent abroad to kill Iraqi exiles who might form a resistance movement. This terror has not been without personal cost to Saddam. He has averaged one assassination attempt a year since he took power in 1979, and lives furtively in the expectation that yet another disgruntled Iraqi will try to eliminate him. Many Iraqis despise Saddam, and over a million have fled the country since he came to power (mostly Kurds, however). Even at home, Saddam is armed to the teeth and surrounded by real and imaginary enemies.

The bottom line: Iraq is a multi-ethnic police state run by one man with the aid of about 10 percent of the country's population, a group comprised of the members of the Baath party and their families. Fewer than 100,000 disciplined (and terrorized) key Baath party members serve as the bedrock of party power. Terror is doled out in large measure, privilege less so.

Saddam and the Tikrit clan provide a classic example of a patronage operation, similar to that found in the former Communist regime of Nicolae Ceausescu in Romania. Before Sadaam took over as sole leader of the Iraqi Baath party (and Iraq), he was in charge of party (and national) security. He employed many family members in these key security jobs. When one of these kin proved too inept, or gave the least hint of disloyalty or timidity, the errant relative would be put aside for a few months or years. Sometimes this would be internal exile, sometimes it would be in a foreign post. The normal family gossip and secret-police reports enabled Saddam to keep tabs on the offender, and usually such family members were given new government positions. At the time of the Kuwait War, a handful of family members were in key positions.

Buying Loyalty

The Baath party members (and Saddam's family) have become the newly rich in the past twenty years. Much of this wealth has come from what Westerners would consider corruption. As a further means of maintaining control, and in recognition of the middle-class roots of the early Baath party members, business opportunities were handed out on the basis of how well one served the Baath regime. The sharp increase in oil revenue after 1973 largely benefited Baath. Between 1973 and the beginning of the Iran-Iraq War, this additional oil income amounted to over $80 billion. All this new money doubled Iraqi's GNP while simultaneously making Baath party members rich.

The flood of oil wealth kept Baath members loyal and the population satisfied and optimistic. Then came the Iran-Iraq War, which cut oil revenue by more than half and increased defense costs by over $10 billion a year. This had the effect of wiping out the gains in oil revenue that Iraq had enjoyed since 1973. To overcome this, Iraq borrowed around $90 billion from other Arab nations (mainly Saudi Arabia and Kuwait) and their primary arms suppliers (Russia, France, etc.). The money that was not spent on weapons went to keeping the population happy. Families of those killed in combat were given substantial payments, plus the return (in most cases) of their loved one's body. This last point was important, as it was rare to get the body of war dead back in this part of the world, much less compensation for the loss. By borrowing all that money, the Baath party was able to afford the war and keep the population happy at the same time.

Throughout all this, the Baath party has not forgotten its own needs. The Baath party has tens of billions of dollars of its own money, separate from the finances of the Iraqi government. These funds were obtained by skimming a percentage off the top of the oil revenues the Iraqi government receives, an arrangement pre-dating the Baath takeover but that Baath allowed to continue. Saddam Hussein currently controls the secret accounts. While of dubious legality—and much of these funds are deposited in offshore hard currency accounts—it gives Saddam even more power within Iraq. Thus, even if the Baath party is driven from power, they would still be there. Money is power, and the Baath has plenty of it. Assuming some amount of party discipline remained, the Baath would still be a formidable opponent to anyone else trying to run Iraq. Under these circumstances, even someone as notorious as Saddam Hussein, or one of his inner circle, would have a chance of making a comeback. Stranger things have happened.

INSTRUMENTS OF CONTROL

Saddam Hussein, and the Baath party, stay in power largely through terror delivered by an overlapping collection of secret police agencies. Foremost among these is the GID (General Intelligence Department), which is actually a part of the Baath party. The government security service, the Amn, also has spies everywhere and also takes care of criminal investigations. The MID (Military Intelligence Department) keeps an eye on army loyalty (as do all the other security agencies) and collects militarily useful information overseas. After the Republican Guard was expanded and sent to the front in 1985 to stabilize the Iran-Iraq War situation, a new security agency, Amn al-Khas (Special Security, or SS), was formed. Primarily a secret-police organization to protect Saddam Hussein, it also has a strictly military component that now has three armored brigades and supporting units. The SS is run by Saddam's most trusted associates, and any coup against Saddam has to get by the SS.

Living, and Dying, Beyond One's Means

The Iraqi strategy of trying to have guns and butter backfired when it became obvious that the large armed forces, the foreign debt, and domestic spending could not all be maintained on the basis of the oil revenue available. Something had to give. The solution was to seek debt forgiveness and larger subsidies (gifts), particularly from the Arab Persian Gulf states of Saudi Arabia and Kuwait, to whom at least half of the foreign debt was owed.

While Iraq had a population of 18 million and a GNP of $35 billion, the largely Bedouin Persian Gulf states had a GNP of $140 billion and a population of 23 million (of which more than half were foreign workers). The Baath party leadership in Iraq (and many Iraqis in general) felt that Iraq had paid too high a price to keep the fanatical Shiite Iranians away from all that Arab oil wealth, and it was only just that the Arabs of the Gulf share some of that wealth to help Iraq get back on its feet.

The Gulf states clearly saw the threat from Iran, but they also

saw a threat from Iraq. While Iran (formerly Persia) had long
maintained domination over the Gulf, which is why it's called
the Persian Gulf, it was felt that the Gulf states' Western allies
would not let the Iranians do anything rash. The Gulf Arabs
believed as well that their Western allies would also keep Iraq
from getting out of hand. Iraq, however, had painted itself into
a corner. Perhaps a less ambitious and paranoid government
than the one led by Saddam Hussein might have cut the armed
forces, renegotiated the foreign debt, and waited a decade or so
for its oil wealth to heal the damage of the Iran-Iraq War. Such
was not the case. After foreign suppliers began to cut off Iraq's
imports in early 1990 because of nonpayment, Iraq decided to
put the squeeze on the Gulf Arabs. The major demand was for
tens of billions of dollars in outright gifts, plus forgiveness of
debts and other concessions. Kuwait and Saudi Arabia de-
murred, without flatly refusing to do anything. Iraq increased
the volume of its threats and demands until, on August 2, 1990,
the Iraqi Army invaded Kuwait.

The Persian Gulf War did over $50 billion worth of damage
to Iraq, excluding over $15 billion in lost oil revenues, and un-
told billions of dollars' worth of damage in the form of lost pro-
ductivity. The war also left Iraq with a reparations bill of over
$50 billion for the damage done in Kuwait. Including Iraq's pre-
war foreign debt, Iraq is now over *$200 billion* in the hole. Even
with a lot of debt forgiveness and aid, Iraq is going to spend a
generation or more recovering from the maladministration of
the Baath party.

Riding the Tiger

Saddam Hussein held the admiration of many common people
(inside and outside Iraq) largely because he's a tough character
(he "beat the Persians," "attacked Israel," etc.). Saddam is also
quick to give cash and gifts to common people, which accounts
for a large portion of the debt the country has piled up through
the 1980s. Much of this generosity also served to keep people
loyal to the bloody war effort against Iran.

Another of Saddam's popularity-building measures has been
a mixed blessing. The Baath call for pan-Arab unity really got
rolling when Nasser kicked the monarchy out of Egypt in 1952.
Egypt is the most populous Arab state, and has long been seen

by many Arabs as a natural leader for all Arabs. Nasser got sidetracked fighting two unsuccessful wars (1956 and 1967) with Israel. His successor, Anwar Sadat, fought another war with Israel (1973) and then made peace. This peace effort put Egypt out of the picture as a leading Arab state for over ten years. Meanwhile, Syria and Iraq tried to fill the vacuum. Through the 1970s, Syria and Iraq (and, to a lesser extent, Libya) vied for leadership of the disunited Arab world. Iraq got a boost, and Syria slipped, when Iraq invaded Iran in 1980 and Syria sided with Iran: Saddam saw the Islamic revolution in neighboring Iran and saw an opportunity to accomplish two goals by going to war with Iran: diminishing Syria as a leader of the Arab world and weakening the traditional Arab enemy, Iran.

War with Iran

The Iraqi invasion was ostensibly about Iraqi access to a seaport. One intransigent Iraqi dilemma has always been access to the Persian Gulf. Another, more important problem was the loyalty of the Iraqi Shiite Arabs, who outnumbered the Sunni Arabs, who were (and generally always had been) ruling Iraq. Both these issues revolved around the Shatt-al-Arab, the deep-water shipping channel from the Iraqi rivers to the Persian Gulf. The Shatt was on the border with Iran, and through most of this century arguments had raged over who should control the eastern (Iranian) bank of the Shatt. The Iranians wanted to control the east bank, and have the border run down the middle of the narrow Shatt. The Iraqis felt they should control the east bank, as the Shatt was their only outlet to the sea. In 1975, the Iranians squeezed an agreement out of Iraq to leave Iran in control of the east bank. This treaty was obtained by promising to withdraw support for the Kurdish rebels in the north. Indeed, the Kurdish revolt did collapse, and has not been able to again achieve its 1960–75 ferocity.

In 1980 Saddam saw Iran going into its second year of intense civil war and internal disorder. This meant Iran was weak, and this circumstance perhaps provided one of those rare opportunities for an Arab nation to take something from the usually dominant Iranians. The Iranian religious fundamentalists were purging the army. Saddam calculated that he could use his lavishly supplied (largely Russian equipped) army to grab the east bank of the Shatt. He also hoped to trigger a rebellion among the Iranian Shiite Arabs just across the border. These Iranian Arabs also occupied some of Iran's most productive oil fields.

The Iranian armed forces were not as weak as Saddam thought, and the Iranian Arabs were not keen on rebelling. The invasion thus turned into an eight-year war that killed over 150,000 Iraqis (and injured more than three times as many). As we have seen, Iraq had to beg and borrow over $90 billion to defend itself against an enraged Iran, with nearly half of this war chest coming principally from Kuwait and Saudi Arabia, much of it as outright gifts. But with the 1988 cease-fire effectively ending the war, Egypt was now on speaking terms with most Arab states once more. In 1989 the socialist world, to which Baath party countries nominally belonged, fell apart. This eliminated some of the economic aid Iraq was receiving, and a lot of its diplomatic and political support. The huge debts Iraq had assumed to fight Iran were now coming due. Some countries were refusing to ship any more goods.

Iraq had other problems. In the last decade, certain Turkish circles began to ponder how nice it would be to get back the oil-rich province of Kirkuk. Iran still longed to possess the holiest shrines of its Shiite religion, which happened to be in an Iraq thickly populated with Iraqi Shiite Arabs. Syria was still keen on making all of Iraq part of "Greater Syria." Saddam had by now been calling the shots in Iraq for over twenty years, and at this point the state of the nation was worse than ever. Saddam's enemies, in high and low places, were beginning to taste blood.

The disastrous aftereffects of the Kuwait invasion have not immediately threatened the Baath party hold on power in Iraq, but they did weaken it. While this weakness may not bring about another government, it does push forward the specter of civil war, or, even more likely, anarchy. No other group is as well organized as Baath, for it has spent the last thirty years quashing any other political organization that appeared to be taking root in Iraq. The result will most likely be chaos.

DATA CAPSULE: IRAQ

Iraq covers 434,000 million square kilometers (about one-fifth the size of Saudi Arabia). It has a tiny coastline (50 kilometer in the south) and largely dry interior. Most of country is flat river plain, with mountains in the north and along the border with Iran. While 70 percent of the land area is desert and mountain, about 12 percent is productive farmland, supported largely by the Tigris and Euphrates rivers. Rainfall averages six to fifteen inches a year (much higher in the north). Temperatures vary by season. Summers average in the 90s (Fahrenheit) with daily highs of 110 or more common. Winters average in the 60s, with subfreezing temperatures at night.

The border with Iran is 1,460 kilometers, with Kuwait 240, with Saudi Arabia 680, and with Jordan 130. The Syrian border is 610 kilometers, and the Iraq-Turkey border runs 330 kilometers in length. Iraq's population is about 18 million. With its high birthrate (the average married woman has seven children), this means the population increases at a rate of 3–4 percent a year. The literacy rate is about 55 percent. The average life span is approximately sixty-five years. Before the 1990–91 war, and particularly during the Iran-Iraq War, there were several million foreign workers. Most of these have now departed.

The population is divided among many different ethnic and religious groups. About 75 percent speak Arabic, although not all of these are the same ethnic group. Many are still tribal in their orientation, particularly in the southern part of the country. South of the Euphrates River, there are over a million Bedouin, many of them still nomadic. Most of the Arab speakers are Shiite Muslim (as are most Iranians). Near Basra are the Shiite "Marsh Arabs," who consider themselves a distinct group. Sunni Arab-speaking Muslims (nearly a quarter of the population) live in central Iraq. This group, focusing on Baghdad and generally considered the "Baghdadis," have long been the dominant group in the region even though they are a minority. Also in central and southern Iraq are the 10 percent of the population that are Christian or non-Arab speakers (Assyrians, etc.). To the north are the 3–4 million Kurds, plus small numbers of Turks, Armenians, and sundry others. The Turks are Sunni Muslim, but ethnically related to the Iranians. The Kurds, who speak an Indo-European language like the Iranians, are also tribal, and share a number of Kurdish dialects.

The annual preinvasion Iraqi GNP of $35 billion was mostly derived from oil and gas. Per capita income was about $1,800. Since the 1960s, the nation has been under Baath party rule, making it eventually a one-party state. Law is based on Sahria (Islamic religious laws) and ancient tribal practices in many areas, with Western-type civil law in other areas.

Iraq has 2,900 kilometers of railroads, and 25,000 kilometers of roads (20 percent hard surface, the rest gravel and such). There are about 1,000 kilometers of waterways.

Service in the armed forces is by conscription. Before the 1990–91 war, armed forces numbered about 740,000; only 25 percent of these were demobilized after the 1988 cease-fire in the Iran-Iraq War. Until recently, about 20 percent of GNP was spent on defense. Most of this defense spending went to the purchase of weapons and manufacturing equipment to enable Iraq to produce some of its own weapons and munitions.

Quick Study 3:
The Desert Kingdom: Saudi Arabia

Arabia was the source of one of the most profound religious, cultural, and military events in history: the rapid expansion of Arab culture, military power, and a new religion, Islam, from the late 600s A.D. to 800. The Arab language was adopted by tens of millions of new converts to Islam, spreading west from Arabia across North Africa to the Atlantic Ocean. The new religion, minus the Arab language, also spread north to Central Asia and east to the Pacific Ocean.

For thousands of years, Semitic nomads (the Bedouin) had wandered the arid wastelands of the Arabian Peninsula. It was a hard life, and it produced a hard people. Basically, the Bedouin followed their herds of camels (mainly females, for their milk), sheep, and goats, going to wherever there was vegetation for the herds. Along the coasts of Arabia, these same Semites were sailors, fishermen, and merchants. In the few areas with water, there were towns and farms where many Bedouin settled down. These sedentary Arabs were not considered Bedouin, yet still had a kinship with the nomadic Bedouin and did business (political and economic) with them. In the south, in Yemen, and the north, in southern Iraq and west toward Jordan, many of these former Bedouin were farmers.

Until earlier in this century, the population of Arabia never exceeded 5 million, with about 2 million in the interior (including the Red Sea coast), another 2 million in Yemen, and the remainder along the Persian Gulf coast and on the border areas of Jordan and Iraq. Borders were never precise, as government was based on family, clan, and tribal affiliations. The tribes would often move, and their "borders" would move with them. The settled areas did have some borders, but rarely went beyond their fields. The "empty spaces" in Arabia were controlled by whichever Bedouin tribe was passing through at the moment.

One could say that Islam was the product of a population explosion. When Muhammad first preached his message in Arabia, the area was suffering from increasing overpopulation. The usual result was a famine and much death from starvation and disease, or migration to adjacent areas. But this time the Arabs were electrified by the call of Islam, and the desert warriors rode off in the thousands to spread the message. While much of Islam's rapid spread in the next three centuries was based on military conquest, there was also an appealing spiritual and cultural element; therefore the peoples the Arabs conquered often considered the Arabs better rulers than the previous crowd (whoever it was). For over five centuries, the Arab-dominated Islamic world was a paradise of good government, cultural progress, and economic prosperity. But then civil war, Western invaders, and Mongol hordes undid the Arab Empire. All that remained was Islam, and its holiest shrines were still in Arabia.

Many Arabs stayed in Arabia, especially the Bedouin. The term "Arab" was now adopted by a wide range of Semites and non-Semites who knew little of Arabia and its harsh deserts. The Bedouin remained poor, and disunited. Although most were now Muslims, they were still torn by tribal disputes and the nomadic mobility that made uniting them difficult.

Eventually, the bulk of Arabia was united by the Sa'ūd clan. Early in this century, Arabia came to be known as Saudia Arabia. Saudi Arabia is the personal fiefdom of the al-Sa'ūd family, one of the many Bedouin clans that have long wandered across Arabia herding, trading, and warring with each other. Ironically, the Sa'ūds themselves are not Bedouin, although they claim descent from one of the Bedouin tribes. The Sa'ūds were, for many centuries, sedentary Arabs, living in the area around Riyadh (the current capital of Saudi Arabia). From this base, they were able to contend with the other politically able clans for the elusive, and dubious, title of ruling all of Arabia.

In the last 200 years, three clans in particular have dominated the Arabian Peninsula, the Sa'ūds, the Rashîds, and the Hashemites. There were also the Ottoman Turks and various European nations, but until oil was discovered in the area, these external powers did not evince great interest in the affairs of the desert tribes. In fact, until then, the only areas of any interest were along the Persian Gulf and Red Sea coast (for fishing, trading, and commerce) and in the relatively densely populated Yemen area to the south, where there was more rain and thus more intensive grazing and agriculture. Another prize near the Red Sea coast were the Muslim holy cities of Mecca and Medina. Muslim custom encouraged believers to make a pilgrimage to Mecca at least once, and each year thousands of the faithful would make the arduous pilgrimage. This traffic became a major source of income for the local Arabs.

Overall, however, Arabia was desperately poor. Were it not for the oil, Arabia would currently have one of the lowest per capita incomes in the world. Yet, power is a form of wealth, and for the last two centuries the Sa'ūds, Rashîds, and Hashemites fought each other for control of all Arabia, not knowing that the winner would gain the world's largest supply of petroleum.

What the Sa'ūds, Rashîds, and Hashemites were really fighting for was the interior of Arabia. The coasts were held by well-established Arab emirs or more powerful foreign nations who could send some warships down the Red Sea or Persian Gulf to thwart any ambitious warriors from the interior.

In the 1700s, the Saudi clan supported a religious revival, Wahhabism, among local Muslims. This alliance provided the Sa'ūds sufficient political leverage to eventually gain control of much of the Arabian Peninsula (although not the Muslim holy cities of Mecca and Medina, the Hejaz area).

Control of the Hejaz brought with it economic benefits, as Muslim pilgrims had money to spend. But the Hejaz was close enough to the coast, and valuable enough as a political and religious symbol, to attract the constant attention of the Turks, who had ruled most of the Arab peoples since the 1500s. As was their custom, the Turks recognized the traditional rulers of the area as long as taxes were paid and Turkish law obeyed. In the case of the Hejaz, the traditional rulers were members of the Hashemite clan (direct descendants of Muhammad). The Turks appointed one Hashemite male to be the emir of Mecca, thus creating a constant competition among the several eligible candidates. This competition took place in Constantinople (Istanbul), the capital of the Ottoman Turk Empire. With the senior Hashemites spending most of their time intriguing in Constantinople, the emir of the moment found himself somewhat out of touch with his subjects in Mecca and the surrounding area. This lowered the standard of government in the Hejaz, giving the Sa'ūds one more reason for taking over. The primary Saudi objective was, however, to protect the Muslim holy places from the less than rigorous standards of piety maintained by the Hashemites and their Turkish overlords.

The dozens of tribes and clans that made up the Saudi coalition were difficult to control, and the Saudis lost much of their power to internecine tribal fighting in the 1800s. But by exploiting the religious fervor of the tribal warriors, the Saudis regained control of central Arabia, and then parts of eastern Arabia in the two decades before World War I.

The Kuwait Connection

Kuwait had been founded in the eighteenth century by several clans of Bedouin fleeing one of the frequent droughts of central Arabia. Although most of Arabia only receives a few inches of rain a year, without even this moisture the already sparse vegetation disappears and the Bedouin flocks waste away. Any nomads must then move to greener pastures, or die. In this case, the path of least resistance led some Bedouin to Kuwait Bay, where the desperate Bedouin ousted the few local Arabs, took over, and built a small fort. The Arab word for fort is *"kut"* and a small fort is called *"kuwait."* One of the clans, the Sabah, provided the hereditary Military leadership for the area, while the other clans concentrated on commerce. Some of this commerce was by sea, some by caravan to the towns of central Arabia. To safeguard these caravans, the Kuwaitis had to cultivate good relations with the powers that be in central Arabia. For much of the time from the 1700s to 1900, the principal power in central Arabia was the Saudis. Thus when the Saudis fell on hard times at the turn of the century, the Kuwaitis took the long view and gave the Sauds shelter. From this secure base, the Sauds soon made a comeback. But this did not guarantee Kuwait's independence from Saudi unification of the entire Arabian Peninsula. That guarantee came from Great Britain's interest in Arabia.

The British Connection

Great Britain never had much interest in Arabia, but the quasi-independent British colonial government in India did. The British had acquired control of most of modern India and Pakistan during the eighteenth century. This was done largely as a commercial venture, and the British government didn't take over until the mid-1800s. Even then, British India was left to conduct its own local affairs, having its own army and diplomatic staff. One area that fell into British India's sphere of influence was Arabia, and during the 1800s British Indian diplomats and troops began to assert themselves in the Persian Gulf. This was all done more as diplomacy than as a military operation. Warships were employed largely to back up the diplomats. Moreover, the Persian Gulf, and Arabia, were a backwater, their only importance to British India being that the area lay astride the vital sea routes between India and Britain.

With the Ottoman Empire the nominal ruler of the area, but with there being so little of value in Arabia, the Turks ruled the area loosely. The Arab emirates on the Persian Gulf, from Kuwait south, were not ruled by Turkish officials, but merely acknowledged the Ottoman Empire as in control of the area. That done, the emirates went about their business. The Turks didn't bother to assume even informal control over the people of interior Arabia.

While the British Indian government had an interest in maintaining some influence over affairs in the Persian Gulf, the British government was more concerned about relations with the Ottomans. At the turn of the century, the Ottoman Empire began to come apart. At the same time, the diplomatic tensions that brought on World War I began to build. The British government was keen to retain Turkey as an ally, or at least a neutral, in any future war. As Germany was rapidly developing a cozy relationship with the Ottomans, the British government was anxious to avoid any actions in Arabia that would antagonize the Turks.

Saudi efforts to unite Arabia, and especially the Saudis' desire to take control of the holy cities of Mecca and Medina from the Turks, caused friction with the British. Then the Turks joined the German cause in World War I, and the British saw it as a good thing to support an Arab revolt. The most likely candidates to lead such an effort were the Saudis, who had been implacable in their resistance to the Turks.

The other two Arab powers, the Rashîd clan and the Hashemites, had always worked with the Turks to one degree or another. But in 1915, the Saudis lost a major battle to the Rashîds and were out of the picture for the duration of World War I. Moreover, many British diplomats felt more comfortable dealing with the Rashîds and Hashemites (both of whom had been accommodating to the bureaucrats of the Turkish Empire) than with the more independent-minded Sa'ūds.

The Arab Revolt began in 1916, led by Hussein, the Hashemite grand sharif of Mecca. In that same year, the British Army began advancing into the Sinai from Egypt and up the Tigris River toward Baghdad from Kuwait. Although the Hashemites had collaborated with the Turks for centuries, they were still Arab nationalists and, as direct descendants of Muhammad, felt a duty to lead a revolt against the Turks to achieve Arab independence, particularly independence for the holy cities of Mecca and Medina. With British assistance (in particular, Lawrence of Arabia), the Hashemite-led revolt succeeded, most of the action taking place along the Red Sea coast and in the Sinai, Jordan, and Palestine. Geographically, the Saudi lands were not involved, and Abdul al-Aziz ibn Sa'ūd (the founder of Saudi Arabia) never met Lawrence. The results of this war are the cause of current distrust between Arabs and the West. Even while the Arabs were fighting and dying in their successful effort to expel the Turks, the British and French were carving up the Arab lands among themselves. While the Arabs had been promised a united Arabia, the end of the war saw France occupying Lebanon and Syria while Britain took control of Palestine, Jordan, and Iraq. More portentous were the Western plans to accede to Zionist demands for a Jewish homeland. This was not realized until after World War II, but the plans were known in the 1920s,

and the Arabs were not happy about it. As Abdul Aziz put
it to one English diplomat, "How would you like it if Scot-
land were given over as a Jewish homeland without your
permission . . . ?" The Arabs felt betrayed, and indeed they
were. Even though it was Western armies that drove out the
Turks, and even though the Western nations eventually granted
the Arab states their independence, the double-dealing during
World War I was never forgotten and plays a major role in Arab
attitudes toward the West to the present.

Saudi-controlled Arabia was untouched by the post–World
War I Western machinations, for the extent of the oil riches
there was not yet known, and the Saudis still controlled the desert interior. Britain still controlled many of the coastal areas,
and the Hashemites held the holy cities of Mecca and Medina.
The Sharif Hussein ruled as the king of the Hejaz. His son
Abdullah was king of Jordan, and his great-grandson would become the current king of Jordan. Another son, Faisal, was installed as king of Mesopotamia (renamed Iraq, which means,
roughly, "where things grow").

In 1924, Sharif Hussein was over seventy years old and men-
tally unbalanced. The Sa'ūds were eager to take advantage of
Hussein, but they were restrained by the risk of losing the annual subsidy they were receiving from the British. But that year
a financially strapped Britain curtailed its subsidies to various
Arab leaders. The Saudis had been receiving over $2 million a
year (in 1991 dollars). With that subsidy gone, so too went any
Saudi restraint. Moving quickly, the Saudis deposed Hussein,
and by 1928 nearly all of present-day Saudi Arabia was under
the control of Abdul Al-Aziz ibn Sa'ūd.

The Lion of Arabia

Saudi Arabia was very much the creation of one man, Abdul al-
Aziz ibn Sa'ūd, born in 1876. His father, Abdul Rahmān
(185?–1928) and the rest of the Sa'ūd clan were driven from the
Sa'ūd hometown of Riyadh in 1891. Taking refuge in Kuwait,
Abdul Aziz led a small band of followers and retook Riyadh in
1902. This pleased his father immensely and Adbul Aziz was
given more power and control over the family's fortunes.

Abdul Aziz not only acted like the founder of a kingdom, he
also looked the part. Standing over six feet tall, he had an ath-

letic build, a hypnotic gaze, and an endearing demeanor. His hospitality, bravery, and diplomacy were legendary. He dispensed justice in a fair and wise manner, becoming the kind of leader the Bedouin had little trouble following. And Abdul Aziz also had a knack for turning enemies into allies.

Most significantly, Abdul Aziz was a devout Muslim. This was his key asset in uniting the many tribes and clans of Arabia. Islam was the only thing all these often antagonistic groups could agree on. The Sa'ūds had been followers of the strict Wahhabi sect of Islam since the 1700s, and Abdul Aziz was strict enough in his religious practices to win the approval of the most orthodox Muslims.

Among the more orthodox was a warrior brotherhood called the Ikhwan, which had been prominent in the early history of Wahhabism until about the late 1800s. While the original Ikhwan was drawn from settled Arabs, those spearheading the movement's revival at the turn of the century were nomadic Bedouin. When the new Ikhwan came to Abdul Aziz's attention, he provided them with money, weapons, and other aid. With the support of the powerful and popular Abdul al-Aziz, the Ikhwan became the Saudi shock troops. The Ikhwan warriors were fierce and disdainful of death. They behaved as if they were reincarnations of the seventh-century Arab warriors who spread Islam from the Atlantic to the Pacific. The Ikhwan provided the glue that kept the Saudi alliance together during the 1920s as the Saudis conquered the remaining independent tribes and clans.

But the fervor of the Ikhwan could get out of hand. The orthodoxy of the Ikhwan rejected most modern devices. Everything that was not mentioned in the Koran was suspect, and subject to destruction by the Ikhwan zealots. The rifle was a curious exception.

Abdul Aziz proved himself once more when it came time to tame the Ikhwan. By 1926 the Saudi forces had defeated all those who stood in the way of Arabian unification (at least in terms of Saudi Arabia's current borders). The holy cities of Mecca and Medina were taken, along with the Red Sea coast; but Abdul Aziz judged it imprudent to attempt the conquest of the more populous Yemen or the British-protected emirates along the Persian Gulf states.

The British also guaranteed (and guarded) the borders of Jordan, Syria, and Iraq. The Ikhwan knew of no such restrictions, so for the next two years Abdul Aziz warred on the Ikhwan, eventually bringing them to heel without leaving lasting tensions in the kingdom. One of the principal means of keeping the orthodox Muslims on his side was to enforce a strict brand of orthodoxy in the kingdom. The "religious police" Westerners hear about are the modern-day Ikhwan. But instead of riding off, rifle in hand, to destroy the nonreligious, the modern-day Ikhwan swing canes at anyone rash, or careless, enough to appear irreligious in public.

In 1932 Abdul Aziz declared the Saudi-controlled lands to be the kingdom of Saudi Arabia. For the first time in over a thousand years, Arabia was, more or less, firmly united. Yemen and the Persian Gulf emirates, protected by the British, were acknowledged as free from any further attempts at Saudi conquest. For the next twenty years, Abdul Aziz prepared his twenty sons (eventually to number forty-three, including those who died as infants) to carry on his work. This work, then as now, consisted primarily in safeguarding the Muslim holy places. Abdul Aziz conquered his kingdom as a religious act, and it was as servants of Allah that the Sa'ūds would continue to hold it. At the official founding of the kingdom in 1932, there was as yet no oil wealth for the Saudis to contend with. The major oil discoveries did not come until the late 1930s, and significant oil wealth did not appear until after World War II. It was up to Abdul Aziz's sons to contend with the mixed blessings of oil riches while still maintaining the religious foundations the House of Sa'ūd was built on.

With Abdul Aziz's death in 1953, the first of several of his sons ascended to the Saudi throne (and, in fact, all of that nation's kings through the present day have been sons of Abdul Aziz). Following the Bedouin custom, each son, in order of birth, first becomes the crown prince (the next king) and then king. The first son, Turki, died as a teenager during the influenza epidemic in 1919. The next son, Saud, became crown prince in 1932 (at age thirty) and king in 1953. Saud had some of his father's traits (he was generous and sired over fifty sons) but little of Abdul Aziz's shrewdness. This awkward situation enabled some of the strengths of the Bedouin government system to assert themselves. When King Saud's inability to rule effectively became more apparent, the next half-dozen or so senior brothers held a series of *"majlis"* (combination dinner party, business meeting, and judicial proceeding common in Bedouin life) to figure out what to do. They also consulted the ulema (a group of senior religious leaders), and a compromise was reached whereby the next in line (Faisal, born in 1904) would assume most of the duties of king while Saud continued as a figurehead. Saud was never comfortable with this, and after years of vacillation was finally persuaded to abdicate in 1963, going into exile with his sons.

Faisal was quite different from his brother Saud. A very exacting person, he exercised a punctuality and precision Westerners do not usually associate with the Bedouin. But, as has regularly been the case with the Sa'ūds over the centuries, he was the right man for that period of the kingdom's development. Unfortunately, he was assassinated in 1975 by a disgruntled nephew during one of his majlis (held to receive petitions for redress from any of his subjects). The next in line, Muhammad, had in fact renounced his place in the succession in 1965. (This was another feature of the Bedouin system. If a son did not feel up to the rigors of being king, he could let it pass to the next in line.) So Khalid, Abdul Aziz's fifth son, succeeded Faisal. He died in 1982 and was succeeded by the sixty-one-year-old crown prince Fahd (two older brothers, Nasir and Saad, had given up their place in favor of Fahd in 1975). The current crown prince is Abdullah (born in 1923).

Who becomes crown prince after that is problematic. The next six princes in line were all born between 1923 and 1928. All will be getting on in years when, and if, their turn comes up. Abdul Aziz's youngest son, Mishaal, was born in 1947 and is a businessman. Beyond that, there are hundreds of grandsons of Abdul Aziz, many of them quite capable. It's up to the senior members of the Sa'ūd family to decide who becomes the crown prince, and the choice will say much about where the kingdom is headed.

The Bedouin Lands and Why Arabs Don't Like Bedouin

The Bedouin, being nomads, never confined their movements to what is now Saudi Arabia. The normal range of the Bedouin was from the Sinai Peninsula north into Jordan and parts of Syria and then into southern Iraq and Arabia proper. All these areas had one thing in common: marginal grazing land that was only useful to a nomad's herds. As we have seen, most of the sedentary populations in these areas are descended from Bedouin who found (or took by force) an area around a water source (usually underground, as in an oasis) and settled down. It was just such a group of settled Bedouin (around Riyadh) that produced the Sa'ūd clan.

The settled Bedouin were no longer considered Bedouin, although they looked similar to the nomads to outsiders and had similar habits. The relationships between the nomads and non-nomads were often violent. The towns almost always had walls, and most adult males within had weapons. The town dwellers also had more time for education and keeping up on world affairs. The frequently desperate lifestyle of the Bedouin left them little time for literacy or study. The Bedouin were (and still are) considered something akin to "country bumpkins." Among other complaints, the nomads are seen as irregular in their religious orthodoxy, tending toward superstition and practices similar to those that the prophet Muhammad worked so hard to eliminate. It gets worse. In Arabia the equivalent of "Polish jokes" are turned into "Bedouin jokes." The Bedouin make the most of their ill-deserved reputation, for while they are considered a bit slow, it is also acknowledged that the Bedouin will drive a hard bargain, and when it comes to the ways of the unforgiving desert, only a Bedouin can get you through it in one piece.

The Bedouin and settled Arabs are also defined by their very separate forms of government and attitudes toward legal matters. The nomad Bedouin traditionally lived by a very personal form of tribal government. The tribal chief (or "emir") was the law in most respects. Problems with other Bedouin or Arabs were often avoided by simply moving away.

Bedouin-style war revolved around mobility in the desert and access to precious water. The larger oases (underground springs) were usually fortified and controlled by settled Arabs. The Bedouin needed the water, the settled Arabs needed access to desert trade routes. Most of the time both sides respected each other's needs. But the primary sport of the Bedouin was stealing other people's camels. The settled Arabs also had camels, as camels were the primary pack animal of the desert for nomad and nonnomad alike. If a Bedouin's camels were stolen, the victims were often able to track and catch the raiders. If this happened, there was usually no bloodshed. The "losers" forfeited their own camels and weapons and had to walk home. Settled Arabs had less recourse, being less adept at tracking and chasing Bedouin through the desert. Worse, the raider often remained unidentified, leaving the Arab wary of any Bedouin.

Bedouin would often join together and raid far from their normal grazing areas. These were major expeditions involving hundreds or thousands of Bedouin. The raiding parties would storm out of the desert, looting caravans and any towns and settlements that were not alerted to defend themselves. The Bedouin would pile the loot on their camels and disappear back into the desert. There was often no way to retaliate against these marauders other than to demonstrate a general hostility toward all Bedouin. From these thousands of years of raids and pillaging came the general antipathy to the Bedouin and the current underlying hostility toward the oil-rich Bedouin of Arabia. The Bedouin may no longer go raiding, but all those centuries of ill will cannot be dissipated overnight.

Most of southern Iraq has been settled over the centuries by Bedouin tribes. The desert to the south is harsh, and in some decades it becomes unbearable even for the Bedouin. In these times, Bedouin tribes would move north, where there was more water, and fight a desperate battle (not always successful) for a piece of well-watered land to settle on. Often these desperate Bedouin were fighting Bedouin who had settled there before them. Had it not been for the discovery of oil, providing the funds to build desalinization plants, this pattern of Bedouin moving north during exceptionally dry decades would have continued.

The House of Sa'ūd's Greatest Treasure

The Bedouin House of Sa'ūd and its personal fiefdom (Saudi Arabia) are unique in other ways. The Saudis are the guardians of the holiest shrines in all of Islam. Every faithful Moslem is obliged to attempt at least one pilgrimage to Mecca, and with increasing wealth and cheaper air travel, many more do so. It is a great honor for the Saudis to guard and maintain the holy places, but they do so largely through enforcing a very orthodox (and puritanical) form of Islam in their nation. The House of Sa'ūd came to rule the holy places partially because the Sa'ūds were more devout than their rivals, and largely because they were more astute militarily and politically. For example, they became allied with the United States because, as they put it, "America is far away and has no designs on Saudi Arabia." This may be less true as the United States becomes ever more dependent on Persian Gulf oil. But the move toward a U.S. alliance is another example of Saudi pragmatism. The Saudis manage to be one of the loudest opponents of Israel (largely because of the Muslim holy places in Jerusalem) while remaining close to Israel's most powerful ally.

The Saudis (and more worldly Kuwaitis) have managed to live well with their "gift of oil." The standard of living of all Saudis has risen spectacularly in the last two generations. The nation's education level has also increased dramatically. Each year, thousands of Saudis pour forth from first-rate universities around the globe. Despite the modernizing effects of wealth and education, the Saudi monarchy and political structure is, however, deeply rooted in ancient tribal traditions. Tradition is often in conflict with the lifestyle of the more educated elements of the Saudi populace. Three generations ago, a bad king would have to face the rifles of unhappy subjects. Today, unhappy subjects can still shoot a king they are dissatisfied with (as happened with Faisal in 1975), but they can also clamor for democracy or any other new idea that catches their imagination.

Democracy, on the other hand, is not necessarily something that would bring immediate benefits to Saudi Arabia. The nation is still a patchwork of religious and ethnic groups further fragmented by still-strong tribal associations. On the coast, there are a substantial number of Shiites, long treated as second-class (and somewhat heretical) citizens in a stronghold of orthodox Sunni Islam. These Shiites are not ignorant of the fact that if they were a nation, the oil under the land they have long occupied would make them the wealthiest people in the Gulf. Instead, they work for ARAMCO (the state oil company) and watch most of the money go to Riyadh. Another 10 percent of the population are the descendants of African slaves. Many are concentrated in nearly all-African villages in Asir Province (southwest Saudi Arabia). While Saudis may be relatively color-blind, few Saudis of African origin have impressive pedigrees by Bedouin standards. But it is the tribal and metropolitan rivalries that are the biggest threat. Because of the nature of Saudi rule, many local disputes are taken directly to the king, who is the court of last resort. A bad ruling can cause problems for generations. Yet the House of Sa'ūd has so far made a successful effort to merge ancient tradition with twentieth century wealth and aspirations.

Two other aspects of Saudi wealth bear significance. The Saudis adhere to the traditional Bedouin (and Islamic) precepts of charity and hospitality. Hundreds of thousands of Palestinians (and other Muslims in need) are direct recipients of Saudi aid. Within Saudi Arabia, no one is allowed to want for anything. Additionally, although millions of foreign workers live in the country, they are well paid and send billions of dollars home each year. But Saudi Arabia is also a very puritanical nation, at least by Western standards. Alcohol and public socializing with women are forbidden (and the prohibitions diligently enforced). Lawbreakers are whipped, mutilated, or publicly beheaded or stoned to death. The practice of any religion but Islam is not tolerated, nor are Jews (normally) allowed in the country. The Saudis, however, are also human, and many of their aristocrats, merchants, and educated elites (up to 10 percent of the population) spend a lot of time outside the country sinning in the Western fashion. But then, Saudi princes were always prone to living it up. Now they can afford to do it away from the scrutiny of the religious authorities, and this helps keep the peace at home.

Such behavior does not, however, keep the peace in other Arab nations. For thousands of years, the Bedouin Arab nomads in the area were considered less civilized and rather inferior to their better-educated Arab brethren living in the urban areas in other parts of the Arab world. The enormous wealth that has fallen upon these "camel herders" seems somewhat unfair to many less fortunate Arabs. There is a lot of resentment, and perhaps even more envy, in the rest of the Arab world. It was for this reason that Iraq had some popular support for its takeover of Kuwait. But the Saudis have had to live with such envy and resentment for a long time. They have made their alliances carefully and, being what they are, put their trust in God and kept their weapons and allies handy.

DATA CAPSULE: SAUDI ARABIA

Saudi Arabia is a large nation with 2.1 million square kilometers (about one-quarter the size of the United States). It has humid coasts and a dry interior. The coastal plain (2,500 kilometers long) quickly rises to a large interior plateau. There are no year-round rivers or streams or lakes. While 60 percent of the land area is desert, most of the rest is pasture (usually quite dry) but capable of supporting nomadic grazing. The nation has about 20,000 square kilometers of farmland, supported largely by underground water sources. Rainfall averages two to three inches a year. Temperatures vary by season. Summers average in the 90s (Fahrenheit) with daily highs in the 120s common. Winters average in the 60s, with subfreezing temperatures at night.

The border with Kuwait is 220 kilometers and 680 kilometers with Iraq. In mid-1990, the population was said to be over 16 million, but no real census has been taken since 1974. About 10 percent of the population are Afro-Asian, most of these the descendants of African slaves. Slaving in Africa had been going on for over 1,000 years, and the children of slaves were generally free. Slavery was outlawed in 1962, and finally disappeared in the 1980s. As with Iraq, there is a high birthrate; the average woman bears six to seven children. Literacy is about 50 percent (the education of girls is a recent trend). There are 3 million foreign workers. GNP is about $80 billion, nearly 90 percent derived from oil and gas.

The per capita income is about $5,000 (less than a third of the United States). Although Saudia Arabia is a kingdom, the government is based on Sharia (Islamic religious laws) and ancient tribal practices. As a consequence, there is very little poverty or crime. Alcohol is officially prohibited (and very difficult to get); there are also severe restrictions on "Western-type" lifestyles (women cannot drive cars or do much of anything without a male relative in attendance).

Saudi Arabia has 890 kilometers of railroads and 74,000 of roads (half hard surface, the rest gravel and such). There are over a million Saudi males fit for military service, with 50,000 males a year becoming eligible for military service (at age eighteen).

Armed-forces service is voluntary. Before the war, armed

forces were believed to number about 74,000. This figure quickly went to over 100,000 after August 1990. Postwar plans are for an even larger armed forces. Conscription is legal, but never used. If the same proportion of population was in armed forces as the United States, Saudi forces would number 130,000. Until recently, about 17 percent of the country's GNP was spent on defense. Most of this defense spending went to construction and made the movement of large U.S. forces into the country much easier.

Quick Study 4:
Kuwait, and the Other Kuwaits

The Persian Gulf contains a number of coastal "city states" that have maintained their independence for centuries largely because they were out of the way and adroit at maintaining their freedom from foreign domination. Kuwait is one of them.

Kuwait has more qualifications for nationhood than Iraq, which is but one of the many ironies in the 250-year history of this tiny state. While Iraq is a recent creation, cobbled together from parts of the Ottoman Turk Empire in 1918, Kuwait has led an independent existence since before the United States was formed. Although a small state, even by Persian Gulf standards, Kuwait was populated by several clans of clever, resourceful, and sometimes battle-hardened Bedouins who, honed by centuries of surviving by their wits in the desert, found a settled lifestyle to be no less demanding but much more rewarding.

The West coast of the Persian Gulf was dotted by these fishing and trading emirates. Each was built up around a seaside fort and good relations with its neighbors. But Kuwait's task was made more difficult by the presence of the city of Basra 150 kilometers to the north and the Persian city of Abadan.

Fortunately, Kuwait was far enough out in the Arabian desert to be of little interest to either the Turkish or Persian empires. Kuwait defended its independence by being inoffensive and diplomatic, and by encouraging all male Kuwaitis to possess arms.

When an infrequent military crisis occurred, the sight of the entire male population of Kuwait standing at the ready within the walls of this fort on the desert coast was sufficient to deter most aggressors. If that failed, Kuwait would call on any number of larger powers that it had cultivated in the past. This approach worked when Iraq invaded during August of 1990.

Life on the Gulf

Like most of Arabia, Kuwait is dry, with little rainfall and no surface water (rivers, streams, or lakes). What water there was showed up in oases, which usually relied on wells to bring up the underground water. As a result, the population could not get very much of it until oil revenue paid for a water pipeline from Iraq and, later, desalinization facilities. Until oil was discovered in the 1930s and pumped for sale in the 1940s, Kuwait's primary source of income was fishing, pearl-diving, and trade (shipping goods in by boat and out across the Arabian deserts by camel). The development of cultured-pearl technology in Japan during the thirties actually forced Kuwait to develop its oil industry, which proved a much bigger revenue producer than pearls ever were.

Several major, and many minor, families (clans, actually) maintain political control in Kuwait. As we have seen, the Bedouin clans that migrated to Kuwait in the eighteenth century chose the Sabah clan to take care of defense and diplomacy while the other clans concentrated on commerce, and for years this arrangement worked out rather well. There was not a government in the Western sense, as major decisions were made by consensus among the major clans. The Sabahs were kept on a short leash because their income came from contributions from the other (commercially oriented) clans. There was no standing army, just a gathering of all adult (and armed) males under Sabah leadership in times of crisis.

The Sabahs proceeded to produce a continuous line of competent, and sometimes brilliant, leaders. Aside from keeping the Turks and Persians at bay, the Sabahs also maintained good relations with the tribes inside Arabia. Recognizing that the nomadic Bedouin tribes were also dependent on trading towns inside Saudi Arabia, and that the caravans going forth from Kuwait needed towns from which to market their goods, the Sabahs also developed good relations with these tribes and towns (although they occasionally tried to conquer some of them, including Saudi-dominated Riyadh). All of this diplomacy within Arabia was not easy, as the tribes and towns were often at war with each other. Yet the Sabahs managed, using words, money, or threats (usually the first two) as needed to keep their commerce with the interior going. During this period, particularly in the nineteenth century, the Sabahs noted the skill and power of the Saud family in Riyadh. The Sa'ūds and the Sabahs were usually allies, and when, in the 1890s, the Sa'ūds fell on hard times and were driven from Riyadh, Kuwait gave the Sa'ūd family refuge. Kuwait once offered more than refuge. The Kuwaitis armed themselves and joined with the Sa'ūds when their foes the Rashîds came to the walls of Kuwait looking for (Saudi) blood. By 1910 the Sa'ūds were back in power in central Arabia. While some members of the Saudi coalition wanted to incorporate Kuwait into the new kingdom of Saudi Arabia, the century-plus relationship with the Sa'ūds was a major factor in keeping Kuwait independent.

While the Sabahs conducted relationships with foreigners, the rest of Kuwait prospered. It was the Sabahs who arranged to have oil prospectors come to Kuwait. So skillful were the Sabahs as negotiators that they managed to have the first Kuwaiti oil well drilled during the 1930s Great Depression when Western oil producers were faced with overcapacity and falling prices. They not only managed to attract attention from Western oil producers but to actually activate something of a bidding war during a very depressed oil market. From this first Sabah-negotiated oil contract, and with the Sabahs' long monopoly on dealing with the British, the Sabahs' power grew. It is the growth of this power and the Sabahs' ensuing independence of financial aid from the other Kuwaiti clans, thanks to the oil, that is the root of the current political problems in Kuwait.

Unlike Saudi Arabia, which continued to see its stewardship of the holiest shrines of Islam as its primary goal, their post–World War II oil wealth turned the Kuwaitis into what they had always wanted to be: very wealthy Bedouin. While still retaining many of the strict prohibitions of Islamic law, the Kuwaitis are also far more predisposed to commerce for commerce's sake than their fellow Bedouin in Saudi Arabia.

The enthusiasm for commercial affairs has led many Kuwaitis

to various forms of excess that caused consternation, and envy, among fellow Arabs. The Kuwaitis also suffer from being Bedouin—descendants of those whom other Arabs have long disdained as low class. The Kuwaitis never tried to distance themselves from their Bedouin origins, and their newfound wealth created a distasteful combination in the eyes of other Arabs, particularly the Iraqis.

The fact that Kuwait had over $150 billion in assets offshore when the Iraqis invaded gives you an example of how aggressively they are engaged in commerce. And Kuwait will need to tap into that wealth, as there is over $20 billion worth of destruction to repair, and it will take several years of expensive reconstruction to get its oil exports back up to prewar levels. The Iraqi invasion, and subsequent destruction, of Kuwait can be expected to bring a lot of expatriate Kuwait high rollers and party animals back to the counting house. In the long run, the disastrous experience with the Iraqis may even help the Kuwaitis, by reminding them that if you don't prepare for the future, you may not have one.

Democracy in Kuwait

There are very few democracies in the Arab world. In fact, the only government in the region resembling a democracy is Egypt's. But in Egypt the "government party" (National Democratic party) dominates the government and everything else in the nation. It's sort of a one-party democracy, with the legislature up for election every five years.

None of the Gulf states is a democracy; all are monarchies, and some are very much *absolute* monarchies. Kuwait's is the exception. The 1962 constitution stipulated that there be an elected assembly that would turn the nation into a constitutional monarchy where, in turn, the emir would still have substantial powers. The emir resisted, which was not easy to do as the arrangement in Kuwait from the eighteenth century was that the Sabah family would "rule" in consultation with the other major merchant families. The merchant families (and the populations in general) had become more educated, wealthier, and more politically active. With one of the highest literacy rates in the region (over 70 percent) and one of the highest per capita incomes, Kuwaitis wanted the power they knew they could handle. Or could they? The fifty-man National Assembly (plus fifteen appointed cabinet members who can also vote) represent only about 80,000 adult males (descendants of males living in Kuwait before 1920). Women cannot vote, nor can hundreds of thousands of other adults who have lived all their lives in Kuwait. There was much else to argue about in the legislature, and as a result, in 1976 the emir shut it down. That raised an even bigger stink. So in 1981 the emir opened up the legislature again.

The tensions of the Iran-Iraq War (among others) caused the emir to again shut down the legislature in 1986. The pressure was building to open it up again when the Iraqis invaded in 1990. An aftereffect of the invasion was a promise by the emir to open the legislature again and let the chips fall where they may. That may be messy. Previously, the ruling Sabah family had access to a lot of money that the government of Kuwait never had to deal with. Before oil came along, running the Kuwaiti government was a relatively hand-to-mouth affair. Following it, there were tens of billions of dollars to play with. Some of it was misused, and if the government now becomes too open, embarrassing questions may be asked. Uncomfortable questions have already been raised about the administration of the nation's defenses before the Iraqi invasion. The Sabahs can only hope that heroic efforts during the reconstruction will allow them to get a constitutional democracy started without too many Sabahs going to prison or into exile in the process.

The Other Coastal Gulf Arab States

The Sa'ūd clan was only able to conquer some of the coastal emirates when it created Saudi Arabia in the 1920s. Most of the Persian Gulf emirates remained independent, and these included Bahrain, Qatar, the seven emirates comprising the United Arab Emirates (Abu Dhaby, Ajman, Fujairah, Sharjah, Dubai, Ras-al-Khaimah, Umm al-Qaiwain), and Oman. To put them all in perspective, compare them to Kuwait, and Saudi Arabia (page 128).

Aside from the above population, GNP, and area differences, all of these Gulf states share many of the same characteristics. All the original populations consisted of Bedouin tribes coming

GULF STATES BY THE NUMBERS

	Population (in millions)	GNP (in billions of dollars)	Size (in square kilometers)	Per Cap (GNP per capita in dollars)
Kuwait	2.1	20	18	9,524
Bahrain	.5	4	.6	8,000
Qatar	.5	6	11	12,000
UAE	2.2	24	84	10,909
Oman	1.4	8	212	5,714
Total	6.7	62	326	9,254
Saudi Arabia	16	80	2,100	5,000
Total	23	142	2,426	6,200

NOTE: Kuwait's GNP will essentially be halved (or worse) for the next ten years or so, reducing it to the level of Saudi Arabia's. Kuwait may also end up with a much smaller foreign-worker population, thus increasing its per capita GNP. Other Gulf states will pump much of the additional oil to make up for Kuwait's lost production, leaving the GNP for the region basically unchanged.

out of central Arabia to settle on the coast. All of these states make their living from the sea (fishing, trade) and by sending caravans to the interior Bedouin tribes. The larger Gulf emirates, particularly Oman, have a fair amount of nomadic Bedouin following their flocks around within their territory. Boundaries are, as they always have been, vaguely defined. To this day, many of the boundaries are still listed as "undefined," and will probably stay that way unless oil is discovered in those areas. Kuwait, for example, historically attempted to control territory only fifty to one hundred miles out from Kuwait City, which resulted in a Neutral Zone between it and Saudi Arabia. This was typical of the coastal Gulf states and resulted in the several "neutral zones" that were established after World War I until more precise boundaries could be established.

These fortified towns had sufficient manpower to defend their walls, but not to keep townsmen riding all over the hinterland behind them to attempt constant control over whatever Bedouin tribe might wander by. The coastal states could not afford to be at war for long with any Bedouin tribe in their vicinity, as a large part of the towns' prosperity depended on the ability to get caravans safely into the interior. The combined shortage of troops and need for safe caravan routes led the Gulf towns to depend on diplomacy more than force. If unruly Bedouins could be bought off, the money was considered well spent. One could always raise the price of the goods transported to the interior. If the town could do a favor for a tribe in distress, this was done, as the tribal Bedouin had a long memory and remembered the good as well as the bad. Prominent townsmen also endeavored to intermarry with key tribes, providing still more links to potentially valuable tribal goodwill.

The Gulf states also managed to avoid domination, or at least direct rule, by any of the local superpowers (the Turkish or Persian empires). This was done with a combination of adroit diplomacy and making the most of their out-of-the-way location. It was rarely worth the effort for the empires to seize and rule these Gulf states, largely because they were not countries but rather a series of small, fortified towns along the sandy Gulf coast. As with the rest of Arabia in pre-oil times, there was simply nothing worth taking. Moreover, the Turks were at the end of a long supply line in their Basra and Baghdad provinces, and up against a usually vigorous Persian Empire. The Gulf Arabs made the most of being in a no-man's-land, and would not hesitate simply to bribe the local imperial governor to report that "there was nothing worth noting" out where one of the coastal towns was located.

Beyond these traditional methods of survival, the Gulf towns discovered a new technique in the nineteenth century. The British Empire desired secure trade routes between Britain and India, and that meant the suppression of pirates who often operated out of Persian Gulf ports. British warships were more powerful than anything the pirates had and the Gulf Arabs proved amenable to making diplomatic and military arrangements with the British. Moreover, the British were powerful enough to keep any Turkish or Persian (Iranian) naval forces (an infrequent nuisance) at bay and protect the Gulf Arabs from pirates. British naval guns provided one more reason for any ambitious Bedouin tribe to refrain from attacking one of the coastal towns. This last advantage proved crucial when the Sa'ūd

clan proceeded to conquer most of Arabia. With British assistance, the Sa'ūds would have conquered more of the Persian
Gulf Coast than they eventually did.

This British assistance did not come without a price. From
their experience in India, the British realized that no single (and
potentially troublesome) power could develop in the Gulf if they
maintained the independence of many small states. And when
oil was finally discovered, this divide-and-conquer strategy assumed commercial significance. By preventing too much oil being controlled by a few Gulf states, Western oil companies had
an easier time controlling the price. When OPEC (Organization
of Petroleum Exporting Countries) finally established a working
cartel in 1973 and more than tripled the price of oil, the mercan-
tile value of this strategic nineteenth-century British practice became even more obvious.

Yet even with OPEC becoming functional in 1973, the multiplicity of small Gulf members soon led to the cartel becoming
less effective. One of the many grievances Iraq held against Kuwait was Kuwait's refusal to abide by the OPEC limit on how
much oil Kuwait could sell. Iraq wanted all OPEC members to
keep within their sales quota so that the price would rise. Kuwait preferred to ship as much as it could, even if this lowered
the price for all OPEC members. Several of the other Gulf
states also played fast and loose with the OPEC quotas. Had
there been fewer of these Gulf states, or none at all and simply
one larger Saudi Arabia, it would have been easier to enforce
OPEC quotas and keep the price of oil up.

While the Gulf states were quite pleased with their independence, the concentration of so much wealth among so few Gulf
Arabs has been a continuing sore point for the more populous,
and less wealthy, Arab states. Together, the small Gulf Arab
states have GNPs equal to Saudi Arabia's ($80 billion a year),
but with a population 9 million smaller (16 million including foreign workers in Saudi Arabia versus a combined Gulf states
population of under 7 million). Compare that to the other Arab
states in the region (economic data is pre-1990 war, the war having made things worse for all the nations shown in the following
chart):

GULF STATES COMPARED TO OTHER ARAB NATIONS

	Population (in millions)	GNP (in billions of dollars)	Size (in square kilometers)	Per Cap (GNP per capita in dollars)
Iraq	18	35	434	1,944
Syria	12	25	184	2,083
Jordan	4	5	91	1,250
Lebanon	3.3	2	10	606
Egypt	56	26	995	464
Total	94	93	1,714	989
Gulf States	23	142	2,426	6,200

NOTE: Iraq's GNP will be reduced to half for five or more years, depending on reparations that are eventually paid to Kuwait and other nations involved in the war.

The differences in populations and GNP clearly show the basis for the hostility between the populous and oil-poor Arab states and the thinly populated and oil-rich Gulf states. The differences are even more striking when you take into account the fact that at least half the population of the Gulf states are foreign workers (often from the less wealthy Arab nations). Note also that the OPEC cartel's sharp increase in oil prices in 1973 was not solely responsible for this situation. Prices before the 1973 OPEC price rises were about nine dollars a barrel (in 1991 dollars). Even at those prices, the Gulf states would have a per capita income nearly three times that of the largely nonoil-producing Arab states in the area.

The Gulf states, and Kuwait in general, have been generous with their wealth. Kuwait regularly gives away more money per capita each year than any other nation in the world. Saudi Arabia has given away over a $100 billion since World War II. The ingratitude of Iraq came as quite a shock, as did the Jordanian, PLO, and Yemeni support for Iraq.

One major result of the Kuwait War is to force the Gulf states to cooperate more closely with each other and their Western allies. For a while, up until 1990, the Gulf states thought that all their wealth had bought them a large degree of freedom.

After experiencing what an envious neighbor is capable of, the Gulf states are discovering that their wealth comes with a lot of strings attached.

Kuwait and the Gulf States in the Later 1990s

Going into the 1990s, the Gulf states will still have their oil wealth, and will have an increased sense of urgency in holding on to it. With Iraq out of the picture for the moment, there will still be Iran, the traditional enemy, to contend with. Having more money than native population, the Gulf states will continue to put their defense spending into high-technology weapons. This will probably result in a "Gulf states" air force of 300–400 high-performance aircraft, and nearly as many attack helicopters and hundreds of expensive tanks like the U.S. M1A1. Saudi Arabia already has a squadron of AWACS air-control aircraft, and will probably maintain this fleet. Naval forces will no doubt increase, to include a lot of expensive small combat ships (European-designed frigates and U.S. Spruance-type destroyers) heavily equipped with antiaircraft and antiship missiles. Ground forces will be expanded, perhaps with more mercenaries from other Muslim nations, to a total of several hundred thousand ground troops (ten or more divisions). To put it bluntly: An invasion won't be so easy the next time someone goes after the Gulf oil.

DATA CAPSULE: KUWAIT

Kuwait is a small nation of only 18,000 square kilometers (about the size of New Jersey). The coastal area is humid (there are 500 kilometers of coastline) and the interior dry. Topographically, the coastal plain becomes more rugged in the interior. There are no year-round rivers or streams or lakes. About 90 percent of the land area is desert, while the rest is mostly dry pasture but capable of supporting nomadic grazing. Rainfall averages five to six inches a year. Temperatures vary by season. Summers average in the 90s (Fahrenheit) with daily highs in the 120s common. Winters average in the 60s, with subfreezing temperatures at night.

The border with Saudi Arabia is 220 kilometers, and with Iraq 240 kilometers. Population (mid-1990) was about 2 million. Only 40 percent of the population are ethnic Kuwaitis, and only 20 percent of the work force is Kuwaiti. About 40 percent of the population is from other Arab lands (largely Palestinian), with the remainder being from the West, Iran, India, and other Asian nations. Kuwait has a relatively high birthrate for such a wealthy nation; the average woman has four children. Literacy is about at 70 percent. There are over a million foreign workers. The GNP is about $20 billion, with nearly 90 percent of it derived from oil and gas. Per capita income is about $10,000. Wealth is concentrated in the native Kuwaitis, although the "guest workers" are well paid by regional standards.

Although Kuwait is a principality run by an aristocracy, the government is based on Islamic law and ancient tribal practices that demand a certain amount of consensus. As a consequence, there is very little poverty, or crime. Alcohol is allowed, and lifestyle restrictions are less severe than in Saudi Arabia to the south. Less than half the population are Kuwaiti citizens, and only those who are male and had a male relative in Kuwait before 1920 are eligible to vote (about 70,000–80,000 voters). Constitutional democracy was established in the 1961 constitution, but suspended during the Iran-Iraq War (1986).

Kuwait has no railroads. There are 3,000 kilometers of roads (all but 500 kilometers hard surface, the rest gravel). There are approximately 100,000 male Kuwaiti citizens fit for military service; 10,000 males a year become eligible for military service (age eighteen). Armed forces service is voluntary. Before the war, armed forces were about 24,000, reconstituted to a force of about 12,000 in Saudi Arabia after August 1990. Postwar plans are for an even larger armed forces. Until recently, about 6 percent of GNP was spent on defense.

PART II

Desert War

The first modern war in the desert, fought as a series of skirmishes and battles throughout the 1920s, pitted British forces against various rebellious Iraqi groups. The British had the armor and the aircraft, the Iraqis didn't, and the Iraqis lost. The basics of desert warfare haven't changed in seventy years. Whoever controls the air controls movement on the ground. Whoever can move a lot of firepower quickly on the ground, such as the combat power of tanks and infantry, wins the battle and the war.

CHAPTER 5

From Shield to Storm:
Beware the Ides of January

"Something happened": a global blitz of electronic communications, a dizzying velocity of shifting perceptions, and a manic transformation from public dread to video euphoria. On the eve of January 16 through January 17, the world moved "from Shield to Storm" and the new century, at least when it comes to war, began a decade early.

It is strange, perhaps, but from the prism of the few short months after the events of mid-January 1991, many seem to have forgotten the debate and dread of the Ides (fifteenth) of January.

"Fifty-fifty," Saddam Hussein had said in mid-December 1990, an even bet on war or peace, or at least what, in Saddam's parlance, passes for peace. On January 15, as the United Nations deadline for Iraqi withdrawal approached, a mixture of dread, anticipation, and doubt fixed a worldwide audience. What effect, if any, would the deadline have? Would Saddam order the withdrawal of Iraqi ground forces from Kuwait? If he did not, would the United Nations coalition act to enforce the deadline? How long, after the deadline passed, would the coalition dawdle? And would there be, in the waning minutes before the zero hour, a flurry of diplomatic activity, a sudden urge to negotiate on the part of Baghdad, a slide to concessions by the UN allies?

Surely, the larger cast of pundits concluded, the weeks after the deadline—after Saddam had showed he would spit in the eye of the United States—would lead to a diplomatic break-through. General Calvin Waller's confidence that American forces wouldn't be ready for battle until mid- or late February pushed the date of combat back another month. Surely, because of the narrowness of the vote in the United States Congress, President Bush would wait in order to show the Democratic doves he had "tried everything" before returning to war. There would be a "decent interval."

These thoughts and feelings crossed the minds of many in the global village, via the new technological grid of satellites, television, and instantaneous communications that bind the "developed world" and the elites in the "less developed" corners of the planet to a common information network. The international audience experienced in common the fog of interdeterminate diplomacy and the *doubt* preceding battle. It is a complex human pall soldiers have always known. Perhaps this was the first time that noncombatants half a world away could experience precombat jitters and dread as a spectator sport.

Dread is an "anticipatory terror" and it is a common denominator bonding soldiers and civilians alike. *The Washington Post* on January 14 quoted a soldier in the 82nd Airborne Division as saying that as the deadline approached, "Some tempers [over here] are a little shorter, a little frayed with stress. There's a little more intensity in the training. Everyone's taking training seriously, no messing around. [The cause is] the uncertainty . . . and also the excitement." One marine lieutenant colonel told the same reporter that soldiers are "the least likely to look forward to war, because they understand the devastating effect of war."

Back in the United States, dread and doubt had indeed been compounded by the congressional debate. Fear of "another Vietnam," of Iraqi chemical and nuclear weapons, of U.S. military inadequacy, of terror by Arab radicals, of "tricks up Saddam's sleeve," and other pundit-promoted catastrophes were echoed everywhere.

But the crescendo of fear had been building for months. Here is a sampling of the commentary of fear:

Senator Clairborne Pell (D-R.I.): "An effort to oust Iraqi forces from Kuwait would, according to estimates, cost the lives of 20,000 American soldiers." (September 20, 1990)

Senator Sam Nunn (D-Ga.): "We'll prevail if there's a war, but it will be bloody. It will be costly." (November 2, 1990)

Rowland Evans and Robert Novak (syndicated columnists): "U.S. intelligence has uncovered a chilling reason for Saddam Hussein's self-confidence in facing the growing menace of the U.S. Persian Gulf buildup: The Soviet Union several years ago may have given him accurate SS-12 missiles with a 750-mile range, capable of carrying nerve-gas warheads." (November 16, 1990)

James Schlesinger (former secretary of Defense and secretary of Energy): "The coalition is likely to prove less durable if combat actually takes place." (November 27, 1990)

William F. Buckley, Jr. (columnist): "What is now predictable is that [George Bush] will not use military force [in Kuwait]." (December 17, 1990)

Edward N. Luttwak (fellow, Georgetown University Center for Strategic and International Studies): "All those precision weapons and gadgets and gizmos and stealth fighters are not going to make it possible to reconquer Kuwait without many thousands of casualties . . . The [United States] Army's armored and mechanized forces can play no offensive role against the vast defensive strength of the Iraqi army." (December 1990)

Senator Paul Wellstone (D-Minn.): "We stand on the brink of catastrophe." (January 10, 1991)

Senator Bill Bradley (D-N.J.): "The conflict would not be like the invasion of Grenada and Panama, or the bombing of Libya, that Americans watched on TV the way we watch Sylvester Stallone in the movies, just one successful gunfight after another." (January 10, 1991)

Representative Richard Durbin (D-Ill.): "I do not know if this is waging war in the age of microwaves or what, but the idea is [that this looming war] is going to be a quick war, and not too many people will get killed and it will be over quickly. I would say that that is really a sad commentary, that many of these people are not leveling with the American people about the scope of the disaster that may lie ahead." (January 10, 1991)

Senator John Kerry (D-Mass.): "In the long run, such a war (as the one being considered) could lead to renewed terrorist attacks on Americans as a result of our having killed innumerable Arab civilians." (January 11, 1991)

Senator Joseph Biden (D-Del.): "Let me just say this, Mr. President: President Bush, if you're listening, I implore you to understand that even if you win today [in the Senate vote] you still lose. The Senate and the nation are divided on this issue. You have no mandate for war." (January 11, 1991)

Representative Barbara Boxer (D-Cal.): "I had a community meeting in my district . . . A thousand people came out. I have never seen anything like it. We voted. The vote was on how they would vote on a resolution to go to war, and 95 percent voted no. That is my district in California." (January 11, 1991)

Representative Lee Hamilton (D-Ind.): "War will split the coalition, estrange us from our closest allies, make us the object of Arab hostility, endanger friendly governments in the region, and not be easy to end, once started." (January 12, 1991)

In some sectors, such as the United States State Department and the Saudi Arabian embassy in Washington, dread took a more concrete scenario: If Saddam slips away, the world may have to face his challenge again. Except that next time he may have nuclear weapons. The Allies' "worst case" scenario, according to several analysts, would be a last-minute pullback by Iraq announced minutes *after* the deadline. Why would this be a worst case? Saddam would have shown the world that he had the power to "take on the U.S. but not the entire United Nations." He would pull back from all of Kuwait except Bubiyan Island and the Rumalia oil field. This would, so this analysis went, split the coalition and keep the Iraqi armed forces intact.

Indeed, doubt did translate into dissension and debate. The Bush administration decided to face the issue squarely. The American armed forces are a true "people's army," and, palsied as it may be, the Congress is the forum of verifying public support. The Bush administration chose not to leave the "strategic flank" of U.S. public opinion exposed. Military commentator Colonel Harry Summers (in *On Strategy*) has argued convincingly that failure to have a genuine congressional debate and war resolution was one of the key strategic mistakes made by the Johnson administration in Vietnam.

With Summers's analysis in mind, the Bush administration's inner circle crafted a war resolution authorizing the president "to use United States armed forces pursuant to United Nations Security Council Resolution 678." Debate on the resolution continued until January 12. As a means of reinforcing public support, the war resolution undoubtedly strengthened the administration's position. The short time fuse, just prior to the January 15 deadline, also served as a means of putting additional pressure on wavering representatives and senators. Senator Robert Dole (R-Kans.) made the tactic quite explicit in debate on the Senate floor: "Let's not pull the rug out from under the President when the pressure is building on Saddam Hussein by the minute."

How close was the January 12 vote on the much debated House Joint Resolution 77 (SJR2), "Authorization for Use of Military Force Against Iraq Resolution"? In the Senate, the vote for the war resolution was: 52 for, 47 against (42 Republicans and 10 Democrats supported the measure). In the House, the margin improved: 250 to 183 (164 Republicans and 86 Democrats for, 179 Democrats, 3 Republicans, and 1 independent Socialist against).

The Bush administration got its war resolution. Did the pressure on Saddam Hussein increase? On January 13, he responded by telling the Iraqi people (and journalists gathered in Baghdad) that Kuwait had to be held "because the issue now is not only a matter of a province which is part of Iraq . . . Kuwait has become a symbol for the whole Arab nation . . . The time for capitulation has gone forever . . . it [capitulation] does not exist in the Iraqi vocabulary."

January 15 may have been an "artificial" deadline date in that any time from January 1 through early February would have served as well as a moment to counterattack Iraq. (The "midnight" January 15 deadline was indeed artificial, since there was some question, at least among the press, whether "midnight" referred to Saudi Arabian time or Eastern Standard Time, a dif-

ference of eight hours. As it turned out, the deadline was midnight EST.) Yet some date and hour in that time frame had to
be the moment of action if the coalition was to confront Saddam
decisively. The Iraqis had been pillaging and looting Kuwait,
slowly driving over 500,000 Kuwaitis into exile. Looming on the
calendar was the Muslim fast month of Ramadan. The "shamal"
windstorms of late February and March could also be expected
to hinder military operations. These were all political and opera-
tional-level military concerns. Time was passing. Would the coalition move from the defensive posture of Operation Desert
Shield to a counteroffensive in order to enforce the UN sanctions?

As the January 15 midnight deadline elapsed and no bombs fell
on Baghdad, the sense of immediate decision slipped. Television
newscasts in the United States and around the globe remarked on
the deadline's passage, while the Bush administration let it be
known that all members of the coalition and the UN were still
looking for signs of Iraqi flexibility.

Indeed, there *was* action on the diplomatic front, from
France, through Arab nations (allegedly Yemen and Jordan),
and through the Soviet Union. The French, up until January 15,
pursued a controversial last-ditch peace initiative that sugges-
tively dangled before the Iraqis the prospect of an international
conference on Palestine and (possibly) some "border adjustments" with Kuwait. (The United States and Saudi Arabia,
galled by the French move, believed it to be a violation of Resolution 678.) The Arab initiatives were more in the realm of rumor and sleight of hand.

The Russians were a different matter. The United States had
maintained contact with Soviet president Mikhail Gorbachev
right down to the deadline. Certainly assuaging the sensitivities
of that wounded Superpower was one factor, but the Russians
had some reason to demand such respect: The Soviets had supported UN sanctions and the use of force. Moscow also maintained reasonably close contact with the Iraqi high command. In
the weeks preceding the deadline, Soviet diplomats had been
busy, repeatedly trying to change Saddam's point of view. According to the Russians, their envoys in Baghdad told Saddam—bluntly—that the Iraqi Army faced certain destruction.
But Saddam ignored the warnings from Moscow. When he had
last visited Saddam in late 1990, Soviet Iraqi-specialist Yevgeni

Primakov had reportedly found Saddam in a distracted state of mind. (Primakov would on February 12 meet with Saddam in Baghdad and try to convince the Iraqi to withdraw from Kuwait before the ground offensive drove him out.) As the January 15 deadline passed Soviet diplomats reported that the Iraqi leader seemed "indifferent." Apparently, the Iraqi dictator wasn't interested in the Soviet proposals. A "Baghdad funk" had set in.

An hour before the first air raids began over Baghdad, Secretary of State James Baker called President Gorbachev and informed him that the Allies were in the process of launching an air attack on Iraq. Gorbachev contacted Baghdad. The Soviets' version of the ultimatum—to get out of Kuwait now because air attacks were about to commence—reached Saddam after the first Tomahawk cruise missiles struck their targets.

In the future, astute foreign intelligence agents will tap the phone lines of pizza shops in northern Virginia. In times of crisis, an enormous number of pizzas are ordered by people working late at the Pentagon. When the rush delivery orders begin, the "balloon" (to use the phrase) is about to go up. Obviously, the Iraqis were not monitoring Virginian pizza deliveries. (Note that one intelligence officer reports his shop brought in their own stash of goodies.) But then, the Iraqis weren't monitoring their air surveillance radars adequately, either.

The first bombs and cruise missiles struck almost nineteen hours after the deadline (5:00 P.M. January 16, EST; 1:00 A.M. January 17, Baghdad time). The first attack, launched under a *"nom de guerre"* of Operation Desert Storm, was delivered by U.S. Army AH-64 Apache attack helicopters. Two ground-control radar stations were attacked "deep" (125–150 kilometers) inside Iraq. Within seven hours, 750 combat sorties had been flown in Kuwait and Iraq. Chief targets were surface-to-air (SAM) missile sites, air-defense control sites, command-and-control centers, communications links ("nodes" in the jargon), air bases, and military emplacements located along air-attack "corridors" (the routes taken by aircraft moving to and from a target) and protecting the air-defense and command-and-control centers.

The evening attack displayed the technology of the first twenty-first-century war—"high-tech" precision guided standoff weapons systems, dazzling electronic warfare, radar-blinding equipment, and radar-evading Stealth aircraft. But those first night attacks also had profound and *immediate* political and psychological effects—suddenly there was a swift shift from dread to euphoria, in part because the overwhelming air offensive of Operation Desert Storm was also dazzling *international television.*

The shift "from Shield to Storm" was heady and enhanced by instantaneous *local* coverage of the attacks on Baghdad. Housed in Baghdad's swank Al Rashid Hotel, three Cable News Network (CNN) correspondents, Bernard Shaw, John Holliman, and the veteran Vietnam War correspondent Peter Arnett, had a ringside view of the attacks. Their intense coverage, by turns frightening and exhilarating, provided an example of the first true "videowar." Real-time, spontaneous televised war coverage was born. If this was the first twenty-first-century war the world was getting, its first peep at its combat would be covered, complete with adrenalinated correspondents panting at the window and ducking under the table. Antiaircraft tracers stitched the night sky. The sound of attacking jet aircraft cracked the TV microphones. The cameras at the Al Rashid, turned toward the horizon, managed to detect the pale, evanescent blisters of exploding iron bombs as they punched Iraqi air bases on Baghdad's outskirts.

But where would the attack lead? What would be the political results? Would Saddam back down once he recognized the Allies' overwhelming military and technical superiority and appreciated their will to use it? And what of those dug-in Iraqi troops? If Saddam refused to back down, could this war be the war that airpower alone could win?

Indeed, the pulse of the Allies worldwide had jumped, pumping hopes for success, at least initially. The weapons did seem to work, almost like magic. Euphoria replaced doubt, bubbling like a hot elixir. And if you didn't believe it, you could see it right there on TV.

But the coalition would soon learn—as the Scuds began to fall—that euphoria was as dangerous as dread.

CHAPTER 6

The Air War: Part 1

Desert Storm's air assault was the kind of decisive air war early twentieth-century air-power advocate General Billy Mitchell envisaged. Not since World War II had there been such a massive and complete air campaign. Never in the history of warfare has airpower played such a determining role in winning a war.

The extraordinarily low casualties suffered by attacking coalition ground forces and the high casualties sustained by defending Iraqi ground-pounders have already put the Persian Gulf War into the believe-it-or-not category of military historical annals. And this is fact: The air war made the lopsided coalition victory—and the lopsided casualty rates—possible.

Between January 17 and March 2, coalition air forces flew over 112,000 sorties and dropped over 88,000 tons of bombs. Air attacks destroyed several thousand Iraqi armored vehicles and even larger quantities of trucks. Air power destroyed most of the occupying Iraqi forces' supplies and isolated them from resupply. Air power cut Iraqi communications. Air domination denied the Iraqi leadership their "eyes": aerial reconnaissance by the Iraqi Air Force. Coalition air forces isolated the Iraqi Army and, to paraphrase Chairman of the Joint Chiefs of Staff General Colin Powell, damn near killed it as well.

Based on early estimates, air strikes alone killed or injured 150,000 Iraqi ground troops. Air power was also the key component in the Allies' psychological warfare campaign: Continuous bombing demoralized the Iraqi Army. When given the opportunity, Iraqi infantry surrendered by the thousands.

High Tech and High Talent

The "high-tech" Persian Gulf air war reaffirmed the lessons of air power in past desert conflicts: Desert wars in this century have typically been won by the side that gains and maintains air superiority.

While the carrying capacity and accuracy of modern bombers are far greater than those used in the desert battles of seventy years ago, the number and "robustness" (ability to sustain some degree of damage) of the targets has also increased. What has not changed is the vulnerability of supply lines in the desert. Water, fuel, ammunition, and food must still move by truck. Even moving by night and hiding by day has not fully protected supply vehicles in the past.

The Gulf air war was notable for its around-the-clock nature, made possible by the large number of Allied aircraft equipped with sensors that allowed pilots to see anything at any time. Many of these same sensors, linked with powerful computers, vastly increased the accuracy of bombing, including so-called "dumb bombs." The iron "dumb bombs" dropped by coalition air forces during the conflict were in many cases nearly identical in design to the iron bombs used fifty years ago, but improved fire-control systems made them vastly more accurate.

Success in the air war was expected; but *why* did the air war succeed so dramatically and prove to be so terribly decisive? High-technology equipment and pilot quality (top talent) are the two primary reasons.

Ever since the end of the Second World War and the start of the Cold War, Western air forces have been preparing to breach a Russian-style air-defense system. Russian air defenses are heavy, with mixes of numerous surface-to-air-missile (SAM) systems plus many more large-, medium-, and small-caliber antiaircraft cannons, and extensive ground-based radar and control systems directing fighter aircraft. Iraq had such a system, and the Allies breached it. This accomplishment, as well as the cautionary messages it provides, says much about contemporary air warfare. Let us examine how it was done in some detail.

The air war was composed of the following distinct phases:

1. The Attack on Iraqi Air-Defense Radars and Air-Defense Control Centers.   Primary Dates: January 17–21. *Types of Missions:*

Electronic Warfare, Precision Bombing, Fighter Escort. *Primary Strike Aircraft:* F-117A Stealth, F-15E bombers, Tomahawk cruise missiles, F-4G, E-6, and F-111 Wild Weasels. All other aircraft participated to one degree or another.

Without their radars and air-defense control centers, the Iraqi SAMs and antiaircraft guns were much less effective. With radar destroyed, SAMs and AAA would be reduced to firing randomly into the air. If radars and control centers are destroyed, attacking air forces would not have to attack all the antiaircraft weapons, especially the thousands of smaller antiaircraft guns. If the antiaircraft weapons could be blinded by destroying their radar, they become essentially harmless.

Air action in the Gulf War illustrated this in spades. Once the radars were destroyed, initial statistical analysis shows that flying combat missions against Iraqi targets was only two to three times as dangerous as flying peacetime training missions.

Iraq had 600 surface-to-air missile sites (with one or more launchers) and over 10,000 antiaircraft artillery pieces (mostly 23–57 mm, and effective up to about 12,000 feet). Interestingly, there were thousands of other fortified antiaircraft positions that didn't have antiaircraft cannons emplaced in them. This was a Russian technique that served to complicate enemy targeting and give antiaircraft weapons a choice of firing positions.

The Iraqis had a chain of over fifty fixed and mobile radars immediately situated on sites covering the border areas and a dozen larger area-surveillance radars located away from the borders. The radars and antiaircraft weapons were controlled by a dozen fortified command posts. Communications between command sites was usually microwave (difficult to jam) and buried land lines (impossible to jam). The Iraqi air-defense system, like its Russian model, was formidable.

But the Allied air forces destroyed all of the major Iraqi radars in the first week of the air war. The radars used by individual guns (not all guns had radar) and missile batteries were destroyed as soon as they were detected. Some radars were hidden and moved around. But once a radar was turned on, a Wild Weasel aircraft carrying HARMs (high-velocity antiradiation missiles) shut them down. The threat of HARM attack soon reduced the time an Iraqi radar could be on the air to about twenty seconds.

These air-defense system attacks were repeated, as needed,

throughout the campaign. But the air-defense system (that is, what was left of it) never got as much attention as it did during the first seventy-two hours of war.

2. The attack on Iraqi Air Bases, Airfields, and Iraqi Aircraft in the Air. Primary Dates: January 17–February 2 (NOTE: These strikes and missions, however, were flown through the entire war). *Types of Missions:* Airfield attack and Combat Air Patrol (CAP flown until final cease-fire). *Primary Strike Aircraft:* Tornado, Wild Weasels, all fighters and bombers.

Once ground-based air-defense weapons and air command-and-control sites are out of the action, enemy aircraft on the ground and enemy air-force support facilities are ripe for destruction. In the case of Iraq, airborne Iraqi aircraft also became more vulnerable to Allied weapons. Why? The Iraqis, like other Soviet-model air forces, were very dependent on their radars to control their fighter aircraft. About 300 of the fighters were specifically equipped and the pilots specially trained for air defense. If the radars are not working, the fighters do not know in what direction to fly in order to intercept attacking Allied bombers. Thus the interceptors were disoriented; coalition "combat air patrols" shot the Iraqi interceptors from the skies.

Coalition attacks rendered many Iraqi air bases unusable and destroyed ground-support facilities for maintaining aircraft. Although the Iraqis stored many aircraft in concrete hangars (Hardened Aircraft Bunkers, or HABs), the aircraft could not fly if the runways were bombed or the refueling equipment destroyed. The Iraqis lost forty planes in air-to-air combat. F-15Cs accounted for most of these air-to-air kills (including one that was maneuvered right into the ground). Navy F-18s got two, and A-10s (using its 30-mm antitank cannon) even got air-to-air kills on Iraqi helicopters. (See Air-to-Air chart.) Air-to-air combat cost Iraq seven MiG-23s, six Mirage F-1s, five MiG-29s, four MiG-21s, four Su-7s, six helicopters, six Su-22s, two Su-25s, two MiG-25s. And, theoretically anyway, the air-to-air kills would have been more numerous if the Iraqis had put more aircraft in the air. As it was, several hundred Iraqi aircraft and helicopters were destroyed on the ground, many inside the fortified HABs (where confirmation was difficult). Based on preliminary estimates some 375 of Iraq's prewar total of 594 HABs received "significant damage," which usually means penetration of, and some evidence of explosion inside, the bunker. An estimated 141 Iraqi aircraft were destroyed in such a manner. Another 140 aircraft fled to Iran, including over 100 combat aircraft.

Once the Iraqi Air Force was shut down, the bombers could go about their work much more efficiently, and many fighters could be transferred to bombing missions. When there are still effective enemy antiaircraft weapons and fighters operating, half or more of the bombing missions can be aborted by enemy action. In the case of the Persian Gulf War, very few bombing missions were aborted due to enemy action. Bad weather or a lack of targets was the most common cause of Allied bombers coming back with unused weapons.

3. The Attack on Iraqi Strategic Command and Communications Centers: Primary dates: January 19–February 15 (though missions were flown throughout the war). *Type of Missions:* Bombing, especially precision bombing. *Primary Strike Aircraft:* F-15E and F-117A, plus Wild Weasels and other bombers as needed.

Military communications networks are usually separate from each other. Army, navy, and air force typically maintain their own networks of radio stations and telephone-equipment centers. There are also different networks for supply troops, combat units, air defense, the high command, and so on. Even a Third World country like Iraq maintained duplicate communications networks for its various military arms.

While multiple communications and command networks are more expensive to maintain, multiplicity makes it more difficult for an enemy to sever all military communications with two or three strikes. Yet the communications networks are tops on a planners' target list once the enemy air defenses have been destroyed or effectively suppressed. The reasoning for this is obvious: If communications are in a shambles, the high command cannot effectively move combat forces around on the battlefield, since information and orders about supplies or damage to units cannot be efficiently transmitted.

In the Persian Gulf War, this strategy also worked when later applied (after January 26) to operational and tactical command-and-control networks. Once their command and communications were destroyed or disrupted, the Iraqi armed forces in Kuwait lost much of their ability to react to Allied moves in the air or, when the time came, on the ground. The sluggish response of Iraqi mechanized units and the entire Republican Guards to the Allied ground attack was in a large part attributable to air attacks on their command and communications networks.

4. The Attack on Scud Missile Sites, Nuclear- and Chemical-Warfare Plants, and Storage Areas: Primary dates: January 18–February 26. *Types of Missions:* Bombing, reconnaissance. *Primary Strike Aircraft:* F-117A, A-6, F-15E, and A-10, plus other bombers as needed. J-STARS useful for spotting Scud launch vehicle movements.

With their air force gone, the most potent weapon the Iraqis still had were their "strategic missile" systems. Theoretically, Scud missiles with nuclear or chemical warheads could disrupt Allied air operations and preparations for the ground offensive. No one outside a tight inner circle in Baghdad knew if the Iraqis had nuclear or chemical warheads for their missiles; abundant evidence existed, however, confirming that Iraq had made strenuous efforts to obtain these mass-destruction capabilities. Iraq had already used chemical weapons, delivered by aircraft spray, aircraft bombs, and artillery shells against Iran (1986–88). Iraq claimed to have stockpiled and bunkered chemical munitions. After the Gulf war, Baghdad would claim that its chemical inventory was still substantial, although much of it was buried under the debris of bombed bunkers and warehouses. Still, as the air battle proceeded, Allied air planners concluded that unless chemical stockpiles and production plants were hit, it was possible for the Iraqis to make a desperate chemical attack.

The same logic applied to attack on nuclear-production facilities. The Israelis had destroyed the Osiraq I reactor in 1981. This new war was an opportunity to eliminate Iraqi nuclear capabilities.

Even though events would prove that Iraq did not possess chemical or nuclear warheads for its Scuds, these intermediate range weapons still presented a problem—a political problem. The Iraqis used the missiles as terror weapons, and as a deadly bait to draw the Israelis into the fray. Western Iraq became a graveyard for any vehicle that looked like a Transporter Erector Launcher (TEL) or a Mobile Erector Launcher (MEL). Many liquid tank trucks, some driven by Jordanians, were destroyed as Allied air forces scoured the desert and wadis for launch sites in what became known as the Great Scud Hunt.

5. *The Attack on Logistical and Support Targets: Primary Dates:* January 26–February 28. *Type of Missions:* Bombing. *Primary Aircraft:* Anything that could carry a bomb. General Colin Powell said Allied forces would "cut off" the Iraqi Army before they killed it. This is because all armies need fuel, munitions, and food. Desert combat requires water, lots of water. The equipment of a modern army requires spare parts and mechanics to install them. Spare parts include items like tires for trucks (and other vehicle parts), batteries for radios, parts for weapons, and clothing for the troops as well as tools and building materials. All of the spare parts and supplies *must* be delivered to one's combat units in a constant flow in order to maintain an army's combat power. As the air campaign began to seriously interrupt the supply of all these items, the Iraqi Army became much less capable of resisting the looming coalition ground assault.

Transportation units and supply dumps were primary targets for Allied air strikes. "Transportation units" means trucks, although Iraq's railroad and waterborne transport nets were also attacked. Since trucks are "soft-skinned" (i.e., nonarmored) vehicles, attacking trucks is largely a matter of locating them. J-STARS and aerial reconnaissance, as well as Special Forces troops watching from behind a sand dune or edge of the wadi, supplied this critical intelligence. Finding Iraqi trucks was a lot easier in the desert, especially since most Iraqi ground units were located a hundred kilometers or more from populated areas.

The electrical power-generating system and grid was also attacked. This was, in some respects, a "strategic attack" on the logistics net, since lack of electricity crippled much of Iraq's military-support infrastructure. The Iraqis had built up a technology-based armed forces that was highly dependent on readily available electricity. Once the power was shut down, there were not enough portable generators to light all the repair shops, run all the power tools, or keep a lot of other electricity-driven equipment going. The loss of electrical power also wreaked havoc with the fuel-distribution system, making it much more difficult to move whatever fuel survived the bombing.

6. The Attack on Iraqi Troops in the Fields: Primary dates: January 26–March 2. *Types of Missions:* Bombing and reconnaissance. *Primary Aircraft:* Anything that could carry a bomb, plus all reconnaissance aircraft.

Allied aircraft hit over 20,000 separate targets. There were also over 100,000 separate ground-forces targets in Kuwait and southern Iraq. Iraqi combat engineers had spent six months digging fortifications for their forty-two divisions in the region. Most of the targets consisted of bunkers and other underground field works, amounting to over 2,000 targets (from the Allied point of view) per Iraqi division. And the engineers were prolific. Most individual tanks and artillery pieces had separate, camouflaged fortifications. The intelligence effort required to locate and identify these dug-in targets was prodigious. Assessment efforts were thorough—they had to be. Thus good intelligence assessment and the precision-bombing capabilities of U.S. aircraft made it possible to destroy individual fortifications once they were located. It took about 1,000–2,000 sorties to render a dug-in Iraqi division largely ineffective because of damaged equipment and demoralization. Army and marine attack helicopters were able assist in this effort by attacking bunkers with Hellfire missiles and other weapons.

7. Close Air Support of the Ground Combat Units: Primary Dates: February 15–March 2. *Types of Missions:* Close Air Support (CAS), Battlefield Air Interdiction (BAI). *Primary Aircraft:* A-10s, F-16s, A-6s, FA-18, A-4s, helicopters, and even C-130s shoving large bombs out the rear cargo-bay door.

Once the ground war started, Allied aircraft found new opportunities, and dangers. The opportunities came from Iraqi units on the move, forced to leave their bunkers in order to counter Allied armor advancing to surround Iraqi forces in Kuwait. Allied aircraft and helicopters would operate together, the idea being to let the aircraft do most of the killing while the Allied tanks moved inexorably into Iraq and behind the Iraqi Army in Kuwait. The danger here was from friendly fire. About 20 percent of the Allied ground troops killed in the war were hit by their own aircraft. To keep these losses down, special paint was ordered (it arrived just before the ground offensive began) to mark all Allied vehicles so they could be identified by the pilots (and their fire-control systems) as "friendly." This only worked at close range, but that was helpful, as pilots are notoriously bad at ground-vehicle identification. Other measures were taken to prevent friendly-fire losses, and more elaborate devices were ordered even though they would not be ready until after the fighting was over.

8. *Reconnaissance and Follow-up Missions: Primary Dates:* August 5, 1990–May 31, 1991. *Types of Missions:* naval, ground, and air reconnaissance, mapping, Battle Damage Assessment. *Primary Aircraft:* E-8s, E-3s, RF-4Cs, TR-1s, U-2R, F-14, P-3, Nimrod, KH-11, and other satellites.

Throughout the air war, reconnaissance aircraft (and satellites) first looked for likely targets and then constantly scanned targets that had been hit to determine if they had indeed been destroyed, or if they had been destroyed and repaired. The Iraqis had learned well from their Russian advisers the art of battlefield deception. A little paint or artfully arranged debris could make a damaged (or intact) target look as if it were destroyed—or at least it could be made to appear so from the air. In addition to several thousand reconnaissance missions, pilots were systematically questioned ("debriefed") about what they saw on the battlefield.

Meanwhile, the American spy satellites kept clicking away. But all this was not enough, as only someone on the ground could confirm exactly what damage was done. Even a blown bridge, with its broken span dipping into the water, can still have a floating pontoon bridge thrown up nearby and kept hidden except when used. The air force did get some support from the Allied Special Forces in obtaining such ground reports. But there were never enough of these troops wandering around in Iraqi-held territory. Reconnaissance, its evaluation, and follow-up bombing always remained as much art as science.

9. *Combat Supply and Support: Primary Dates:* August 2, 1990–May 31, 1991. *Types of Missions:* Local transport of material and personnel, air refueling. *Primary Aircraft:* KC-135, KC-130, C-130 (and even a few Learjets).

There were over 100,000 troops involved in the air war, and only about 5 percent were aircraft crews. The rest were for maintenance and support. Naturally, many of the aircraft served in noncombat support roles. The two most common of these support airplanes were the C-130 transport and the KC-135 tanker. The C-130s moved spare parts (including jet engines, hundreds of which were replaced during the war), maintenance personnel, and anything that had to get somewhere quickly. The KC-135 (and the KC-10 and several other types) tanker was essential for getting the enormous numbers of bombs to distant targets. The F-117A Stealth fighter-bomber was stationed over 1,000 miles from its favorite target, Baghdad, and could not have made it there and back with a meaningful bomb load without the tankers.

The Original Plan

From the beginning, it was accepted that the first goal of the air offensive was to obtain air superiority. This would include attacks on Iraqi air defense, Air Force (including Scuds and nuclear and chemical weapons), and command and communications facilities. This was to take seven to ten days. Most of this was accomplished within three days. The Scuds proved a more elusive target and continued to tie up precious F-15E bombers throughout the war. Following the air-superiority phase, there were to be twenty-two days of attacks on Iraqi ground forces in Kuwait and southern Iraq. These attacks on Iraqi ground forces turned out to be more effective than expected, so this phase was extended for over five weeks. Iraqi ground forces were pounded into virtual ineffectiveness, as was demonstrated by the swiftness of the ground campaign and low casualties among friendly ground troops.

A Sortie Is a Sortie Is a Sortie. . . .

The official number of air sorties (one aircraft taking off on a mission) is around 112,000. But that number accounts for only air force and navy sorties. Not counted are over 30,000 sorties by army helicopters (mainly) and fixed-wing aircraft. Most of the army sorties were support, but nearly a third were combat to one degree or another, and over 20 percent were virtually the same as combat missions flown by air-force aircraft. For example, on the first night of the air war, army air units (helicopter gunships) destroyed two vital enemy radar sites in western Iraq. Yet this army mission is not counted as an air sortie, much less a combat sortie. Note that the air force counts flights by its own helicopters as sorties (although not those by marine or navy helicopters).

Of the 112,000 "official" (by air-force reckoning) sorties, a few aircraft types accounted for most of them. Four combat aircraft (A-10, F-16, FA-18, F-14) flew over a third of them. Nearly a fifth of all sorties were flown by C-130s and KC-135 tankers. On the other hand, some aircraft had an impact far in excess of just the number of sorties they flew. B-52s accounted for not quite 2 percent of all sorties, but dropped nearly 30 percent of all bomb tonnage. The F-117A Stealth fighters flew 1.2 percent of the sorties, dropped about 3 percent of the bomb tonnage, and were responsible for about 10 percent of all effective bombing damage.

Army attack helicopters, whose 6,000 sorties the air force did not count, destroyed over 800 tanks, plus an even greater number of bunkers and other vehicles. So, for the record, a more accurate total count for sorties flown during Operation Desert Storm would be 140,000.

The Allied (mainly American) air forces had over 2,700 aircraft and helicopters in the Gulf by January 1991. Army helicopters and fixed-wing aircraft bring this number up to over 4,000 aircraft. However, because most people are fixated on the official 112,000 sorties, the following analysis covers only that number. Army sorties are about 30 percent combat support (reconnaissance and moving troops into a combat area) and combat (helicopter gunships going out and destroying things).

MISSIONS AS A PERCENTAGE OF TOTAL SORTIES

	% of Total Sorties
1. Iraqi Air Defense	4
2. Iraqi Air Power	5
3. Command and Communications	4
4. SCUDS, Nukes, Chemcials	5
5. Logistical and Support Targets	22
6. Iraqi Troops in the Field	20
7. Close Air Support	6
8. Reconnaissance and Follow-up Missions:	6
9. Combat Supply and Support	28

Many sorties were difficult to classify, especially when hitting Iraqi troops in the field. A bunker thought to contain troops or weapons might contain supplies or a command center, or vice versa. Based on an analysis of the sorties flown, and the types of aircraft flying them, the above chart gives a good idea of how the air power was distributed. Note that the attack missions include a varying proportion of combat-support aircraft, usually including electronic-warfare and fighter-escort aircraft. These last two tasks were needed much less in the latter half of the campaign.

Why Air Power Was So Decisive

Lest air-power proponents push their case too far, one must also note that there were several extraordinary circumstances that made possible the success of air power in the Persian Gulf. Not all of these circumstances were specifically military and not all of them useful in most other parts of the world. Let us examine these items one at a time:

- The terrain in the Persian Gulf is nearly ideal for offensive air operations. This is because it's relatively flat and contains little vegetation for the enemy to hide in. The terrain is also dry, so cutting ground forces off from their supplies has more impact because the loss of water supplies is more damaging than any other supply problem. Ironically, Iraq was the area where air operations in the desert were first tested and perfected by the British Royal Air Force in the 1920s and 1930s.
- Iraqi air defenses were decidedly second-rate. This made it easier to obtain air superiority (or, as the air-force people liked to put it, "air domination"). Bombers can go about their business more efficiently if they are not being furiously contested at every turn. A more effective defense would have made the bombing less effective (although still successful) and the Allied losses much higher.
- Air combat and attack technology had advanced, and matured, since the Vietnam era. Many of the precision-bombing techniques were developed to keep our bombers from having to get too close too often to heavily defended enemy targets. By flying above 12,000 feet, aircraft were immune to enemy air defense guns. When bombing runs were undertaken, they usually involved laser-guided

bombs that kept the bombers away from any antiaircraft fire. The principal reason for these precision weapons was to save pilots and planes. In an environment where the enemy antiaircraft defenses have been practically obliterated, the aircraft can concentrate on their accuracy and obtain over 75 percent hits (compared to under 10 percent with older bombing systems). Again, a more deadly defense would have spoiled the aim of even the precision-bombing systems and shot down many of the aircraft using these systems before they could be used time and again.

- Aircraft have become more "robust" since Vietnam (and since our last major air campaigns in World War II). Mechanical and electronic breakdowns have actually declined markedly every decade since World War II. Aircraft has become more maintainable, with many of the more expensive modern aircraft actually cheaper to maintain than older aircraft (requiring fewer man-hours of maintenance and spare parts). Though the aircraft are more complex and expensive and the pilots take longer to train, they are also tougher and more resilient. Critics tend to gripe more about the rising costs than to acknowledge the good news on performance and reliability.

  Reliability is important in peacetime as well as wartime. It's bad enough to lose a pilot and an aircraft in combat; it's even more painful to see them go down in a training accident. In the 1950s, peacetime training accidents per 1,000 sorties destroyed more aircraft and pilots than 1,000 combat sorties in the Persian Gulf campaign. This robustness does not come without other costs. Modern aircraft require extensive support to keep them in the air twenty to forty hours a week. Part of their robustness is the ease with which many of their components may be replaced. A dozen sorties result, on average, in over a ton of the aircrafts' components being replaced. Without the extensive air-base facilities already present in Saudi Arabia (admittedly built with a contingency such as the Iraqi invasion in mind), parts replacement would have been extremely difficult. Fewer aircraft would have meant more Iraqis in a fighting mood and more Allied casualties, and so it goes.

- Time. Iraqi forces did not keep coming south into Saudi Arabia after they invaded Kuwait. This decision allowed the Allies to quickly bring in enough force to prevent the Iraqis from overrunning many of those large air bases the Saudis had built. In turn, this led to a five-month buildup of aircraft (which were flown in) and support equipment and supplies (most of which came by ship). The Iraqis then sat still while they were pounded from the air for six weeks. Time will not always be on the side of the good guys.
- Better sensors. Okay, your air force may be able to get to the enemy without getting shot down or being grounded for inadequate maintenance. But how do your fly-boys find the target and, more important, how do you find out if what you think you hit was actually destroyed? Part of the answer is to use more powerful sensors. AWACS, J-STARS, LANTIRN, and FLIR (among others) represent fifty years of successful airborne-sensor development that bore spectacular fruit during the Persian Gulf War.

  These more powerful sensors are partially a result of increased computer power and, as such, are not a panacea. More accuracy in finding things that are hot (like vehicle engines, even after they've been turned off for a while), or masses of warm metal underground (a tank in a bunker) made the difference. Sensors and fire-control systems that were just coming into use at the end of the Vietnam War finally got their combat experience. The intervening twenty years of practice and working out the bugs paid off.
- The rehabilitation factor. Vietnam air operations left most people with the impression that U.S. aircraft were ineffective. This was not exactly the case. Vietnam was not the best place to use air power, but air power was not ineffective. B-52 attacks in particular were feared by the North Vietnamese. The jungle, however, provides a myriad of places where enemy troops can move and hide; the desert, over time, reveals all. The success of air power in the Persian Gulf looks much better than Vietnam by comparison. But warfare in the desert is the exception, fighting in jungle and forested areas is the rule.

United States air power came out of Vietnam with something of an inferiority complex and a burning desire to reaffirm its capabilities. The U.S. air forces (the army has more aircraft than the air force, and the navy's air force is one of the world's ten largest) knew they were good and were burning for an opportunity to prove it. (Readers take note: The next war following a dramatically successful war tends to be difficult. Easy victory tends to lull the victor into bad habits.)

- Superior maintenance factor. Only a fraction (less than a third) of available Allied air power was sent to the Gulf, and this made it possible to send a higher proportion of maintenance personnel and material there. The air force normally stocked spare parts and munitions for a worst-case war in Europe against the Russians, which would have involved more than twice the number of combat aircraft and sorties than were used in the Gulf. These large stocks of munitions and spares were used to keep the Gulf air war going. Hundreds of civilian technicians were also brought in. As a result, readiness rates of aircraft were (at 85–95 percent) 5–10 percent higher than peacetime.

It is common in wartime for spare parts and munitions usage to assume a different pattern than predicted by peacetime planners. An example of this was the need for more filters to deal with the sand and dust of the desert. Thus, the large stockpiles for the European air war provided sufficient leeway to provide an adequate supply of spare parts for the Gulf operations. Note that a side effect of this will be reduced readiness and flying time for aircraft stationed outside the Gulf.

The ATO (Air Tasking Order) in the Persian Gulf War

The key to the precision and devastating effect of the Allied air attack was the ability to create an accurate Air Tasking Order (ATO) for all 1,600 combat aircraft and the over 1,000 support aircraft involved in daily air missions.

The ATO is the result of the high command's decisions on what it wants its air power to do on a given day and the air commanders' appraisal of what they would have available and how they could best use it. An interconnected system of computers then figures out all the tedious (and complex) details, such as: where and when each aircraft would fly; how much fuel it would take off with (and where and when it would refuel in the air with a tanker); what weapons would be carried; what targets would be attacked; and which aircraft would fly together in a mission package.

During the Persian Gulf War, the allied ATO was transmitted to the air units in electronic form at least a day before it was to be used (this was a recent innovation). Most people using the ATO only saw it on a computer screen. The AWACS aircraft were the heaviest users of the ATO, as AWACS made sure aircraft in the air were where they were supposed to be when they were supposed to be there.

The ATO controlled all American air force, navy, marine and allied fixed-wing aircraft (in over seventy different major units). Helicopters, with a few exceptions, were not included in the ATO; instead, the nearly 500 attack helicopters in the Gulf were controlled by the ground-combat units to which they were assigned.

The Air War: Major Lessons

AWACS (Airborne Warning and Control System)   This was the first real workout for the airborne-control aircraft concept (although the navy had been doing something like it for years with its smaller E-2 and much smaller number of aircraft). In the Gulf War, three AWACS were up at all times throughout the campaign in order to handle the large air traffic. The number of sorties flown was about half of what was expected in a major war in Central Europe, the kind of war the AWACS was designed for. Peacetime exercises never allowed for so large and sustained a workout for the AWACS, much less against a hostile (although inept) opponent. Much was learned on what the AWACS system was capable of and how best to use it.

Precision Bombing   The war settled the argument between the advocates of expensive precision munitions, precision targeting systems, and expensively equipped aircraft to deliver them versus supporters of the traditional "more tonnage" school. Precision was more effective. Aircraft with laser-bomb guidance equipment (F-117, F-111F, A-6, LANTIRN-equipped bombers, etc.) flew 20 percent of the bombing missions, dropped 8 percent of the bomb tonnage, and did about 30 percent of the damage. F-117s alone, flying 2 percent of the bombing missions, inflicted over 10 percent of the confirmed hits and hit 40 percent of the strategic targets (mostly up north in Iraq). B-52s dropped 30 percent of the bomb tonnage in concentrated carpet bombing and did 40 percent of the damage. The other 62 percent of the bombs that were dropped (not always very accurately) using conventional methods accounted for the remainder.

Precision bombing has become more common since it was first developed in the 1960s, one of the first weapons based on massive computer power. Precision munitions are much more expensive than "dumb" bombs, but with the increasing cost of combat aircraft, the additional cost of bomb-guidance equipment on the aircraft and the bombs themselves becomes, relatively, less of an expense. These higher cost of the aircraft makes it more practical to spend the money for precision-bombing equipment because these bombing systems expose the aircraft to less Iraqi fire and require fewer missions to take out a target. Uncharacteristic bad weather in the Gulf caused 40 percent of the bombing missions to be canceled during the first two weeks of the war. Yet the "precision bombers" were less frequently stopped than the other bombers, another infrequently mentioned advantage of precision munitions.

Further speeding the transition to precision-bombing systems is the availability of better sensors to find targets. Even in the desert, enemy vehicles could hide by literally digging themselves into a hole in the ground and then covering themselves over with sand and dirt. U.S. heat and metal sensors were still able to find these hidden vehicles, and use precision bombing to destroy them.

Bomb Damage Assessment (BDA) The American military's love affair with high-tech sensors produced masses of sensor data on targets, and the destruction wrought on them. But, as we've mentioned, it didn't work out as planned. Aside from the problems with the satellites and recon aircraft, the gun cameras were of such low quality that only half the air-to-air kills recorded could be positively identified. It was worse for ground attack, with the existing cameras incapable, in most cases, of obtaining useful evidence of what was hit and how much damage was done. The F-117A camera system (and a similar one on the F-111) was able to get good assessment photos, but this was not the case with the majority of aircraft dropping bombs. Thus, it was still found necessary to have someone on the ground to confirm what many targets were and what damage was done. The Special Forces scouts were able to perform some of this duty, but it again emphasized the need for friendly eyes in enemy territory. Many deficiencies in sensor effectiveness were also discovered, although many of these problems are expected to be solved by new sensors coming into use shortly. We probably won't have more spies on the ground, just more expensive (and, hopefully, more effective) sensors in the air.

Intelligence wasn't effective enough   Aircraft had become more effective at hitting targets the pilot can see. There is still a problem with finding the targets in the first place. The potential targets had a lot of places to hide, considerable resources to assist them, and a powerful incentive to stay under cover. The most prominent example of this problem was the Iraqi Scud launchers. Allied aircraft never could find all of them. The same was true with more mundane targets like Iraqi tanks, trucks, and bunkers. The elusiveness of the Scuds was more prominent because every day or so several came roaring across the border. Look for this area to get more attention, and to attract some very expensive proposals.

Robotic aircraft are here, and they work   Most of the 288 Tomahawk missiles launched hit their targets, and did it without the loss of any pilots. The Tomahawk doesn't have a pilot, and is literally a robotic bomber. This is the first time the concept has got a workout under combat conditions. Tomahawk worked. In many ways, it works better than a manned bomber. It's smaller than any manned aircraft. It's difficult to detect with radar because of its small size and the low altitude it normally flies at. The next generation of cruise missiles will be entering service this decade and will be "stealthy" and smarter. The Stealth cruise missile will be able to hit several targets by dropping off other guided missiles and then crashing into its final target. There is some resistance from pilots and senior officers to extensive use of cruise missiles. No one likes to be replaced by a robot, but in the case of suicidal bombing missions, exceptions are usually made.

Stealth works, is important, but how important?   No F-117A Stealth bombers were lost to enemy fire. This in spite of the F-117A operating over heavily defended targets. At no point in the war were all Iraqi radars destroyed or shut down, so the stealth concept had some value. But how much? Stealth is expensive, only works well at night, and to be stealthy means the aircraft cannot use any navigation radars. The F-117A carries a small bomb load (two tons) and requires frequent refueling. Despite its "fighter" designation, the F-117A is actually a light bomber. Yet it costs as much as an F-15 fighter-bomber. Without the stealth features, the F-117A would have cost half as much. With shrinking defense budgets and escalating aircraft costs, there will be quite a few arguments over how much stealth is needed.

Night Vision Comes of Age   The first "all-weather" bombers of several decades ago relied on radar to get them through the darkness and stormy weather. Radar could do a lot of things to assist night operations, but it couldn't do everything. It was only a partial solution, and until infrared and light enhancement devices matured in the last ten years, night operations were only partially successful. But now infrared "cameras" provide pilots with sharp black-and-white nighttime pictures of what's out there while light-enhancement goggles turn light into day with the help of starlight. These devices still had serious limitations. The infrared radars have a narrow field of vision and are degraded by rain, clouds, and other atmospheric clutter. The night-vision devices are clumsy and take getting used to. Despite the drawbacks, the current generation of equipment is effective enough to give the air force that possesses them a decisive edge. Look for most future air operations to be on the night shift.

Electronic Warfare Comes First   The Allies won the electronic-warfare aspect of the campaign decisively. But how this was done had some embarrassing moments. Because electronic warfare is not "sexy" (what's there to look at except a bunch of very pricey black boxes?) and constantly gets into trouble with Congress because of cost overruns and performance questions, many aircraft going to the Gulf were not as ready as they could have been to face the electronic defenses of the Iraqi Air Force. Many aircraft had older, and somewhat obsolete, ECM (Electronic Countermeasures) and EW (Electronic Warfare) equipment. The new stuff was due "any year now." But the Iraqis were ready right now. Fortunately, there was such a preponderance of Allied ECM and EW gear available that these deficiencies could be got around. One of the reasons most of the bombing took place at higher altitudes (over 10,000 feet) was because there was not enough ECM gear to deal with all the different missiles the Iraqis had, nor the many radars controlling their thousands of antiaircraft guns. The specialized EW (Wild Weasel) aircraft were used extensively, if only to provide an extra margin of safety.

Bombs travel 90 percent of the way to the target in ships   While it took only an hour or two for an Allied bomber to reach Baghdad and drop its load, those same bombs required a six-week journey by rail and sea from Stateside depots. Many thousands of tons of bombs also came from European-based stocks, which took only half as long. In any event, everyone was reminded that you cannot launch an air offensive without first spending several months moving ships and ammunition about.

Bombers and recon aircraft become one   Many current bombers have better sensors than specialized recon aircraft of ten to twenty years ago. Given that development, it didn't take pilots long to discover that they could combine the reconnaissance (find targets) and bombing (destroy targets) roles in one sortie. While there were not a lot of these lavishly equipped fighter-bombers in the Gulf, those that were available were far more effective than more conventionally outfitted aircraft. In daylight, it's the same story. But then it always has been. A-10 Thunderbolt IIs operated just like their namesakes (P-47 Thunderbolts) did in 1944. Both aircraft roamed the battlefield looking for enemy troops and vehicles to shoot up. The night vision–equipped aircraft prevented the enemy from moving and resupplying under cover of darkness.

Thirsty little devils   There were never enough aerial tankers. On an average day of air operations, over 80,000 tons of aviation fuel would be consumed to carry 2,000 tons of bombs into Kuwait and Iraq. In order to maximize bomb loads, aircraft often took off with half-empty tanks. They took on the missing fuel from the tankers. To extend their range so that targets deep in

Iraq could be hit, bombers would return to the Saudi border with nearly empty tanks and thus would require yet another fueling from the tankers in order to make it home. Although the U.S. Air Force has nearly 700 tankers (90 percent converted B-707s, the rest DC-10s and C-130s), and a third were sent to the Gulf, it wasn't enough. There wasn't a severe shortage, but it pointed out how vulnerable operations were to the availability of the otherwise mundane and unseen tankers.

Friendly fire is still a problem   Friendly fire will not go away. A lot of money and effort will be thrown at the problem, and there will be some improvement. The battlefield is becoming more robotic, as well as more automated. Robots have a harder time telling good guys from bad guys than man-operated machines. The solution will get better, but the problems will get worse. There will always be losses to friendly fire.

Aircraft still can't clear naval mines   In the 1960s, the increasingly powerful aviation community in the U.S. Navy convinced everyone that ships dedicated to clearing mines were obsolute and the future was in helicopters dragging "sleds" in the water to do the job faster and cheaper. That was true as long as mine technology stood still; it didn't, and the United States finds itself playing catch-up in the minesweeper department. Without the specialized minesweeping ships of our allies, we still wouldn't be able to get ships near Kuwait because of all those modern Italian mines the Iraqis planted.

Having Enough of the Right Munitions   Only 8 percent of the munitions dropped were precision munitions because there were only a limited number of aircraft available that could use them. Precision munitions were thus doubly expensive; up to $2 million for fire-control systems on the aircraft plus the munitions themselves costing ten or more times "dumb" bombs. Despite success in the last years of the Vietnam War, most U.S. munitions stocks were "dumb" (unguided) bombs and rockets. However, because even fewer aircraft were available to deliver smart bombs, there was not a shortage of smart munitions. There were shortages of some more mundane munitions, like 5-inch (127mm) smoke rockets used by aircraft to identify ground targets, or even some types of 1,000-pound iron bombs. Generally, however, there were lots of iron bombs available, particularly in Europe, and this is one reason why the 60 B-52 sorties were flown from Europe, and over 1,000 tons of bombs dropped by those British-based bombers. Because smart bombs and missiles weigh less in relation to the damage they unarguably cause, their future is assured. The next opponent may not, like Iraq, allow six months for the munitions ships to arrive with thousands of tons of iron bombs. But then, a C-5A can fly in over 100 Maverick missiles, which can, in turn, be fairly certain of destroying up to two battalions of enemy tanks. This is yet another reason why you will be seeing fewer dumb bombs in the future.

Communications Integration   Not all of the gadgets worked effectively together. A particular shortcoming was the ability to get information on targets found to aircraft that could attack them. Most of the Allied recon aircraft were still using film cameras. The film had to be developed before it could be delivered to the bomber units. Newer electronic cameras, a few were available, allowed target photos to be transmitted immediately. J-STARS demonstrated how this would work (to a lesser extent, so did AWACS). But too much time-dependent intelligence information loitered in the "system" without getting to the troops in time to be useful. The air force needed faster updates, and the status of targets both before and after they were hit. Satellite reconnaissance, the oft-heralded solution to this problem, was misunderstood (or simply oversold) before the war. Coordination between services and within each service was also a problem. Lots of paperwork had to be short-circuited to get things done. Peacetime security measures got in the way of wartime command efficiency. People who should have known about, say, logistics, for planning operations had to (often unsuccessfully) fight to find out what was going on. Nothing like a war to provide a jarring reality check.

More-Flexible Software   When it was discovered that targets could be attacked safely at higher altitudes (to avoid antiaircraft cannon), some of the fire-control systems could not be programmed quickly or precisely enough to maintain accuracy. All of the many computer controlled weapons and equipment are run by sets of instructions called "programs." Increasingly, these computer programs are designed for quick modification. The

Gulf War demonstrated that not everyone involved knew exactly what this meant. Pilots had to discover, and apply, "aiming adjustments" required for bombing from higher altitudes because of less than optimal computer programs. Now everyone understands what flexible software really means.

Traffic Control There were often nearly 1,000 aircraft in the air at one time, and a lot of them were loitering around the several dozen aerial tankers waiting to be fueled. Although U.S. pilots have been using in-flight refueling for decades, techniques for handling several thousand refuelings a day had to be improvised. There were some traffic jams up there initially. Training and resourcefulness did pay off, as a combination of trained AWACS crews, experienced pilots, and a flexible air-force mission-control computer prevented any midair collisions. This was a historical first for air operations of this magnitude.

Nerd Power Many opportunities were found to use electronic-warfare and sensor equipment to deal with Iraqi radar-controlled weapons and mobile radar systems that continued to operate throughout the war. The nerds (crack computer technicians) were in great demand. A lot of these cat-and-mouse exercises could have been investigated and practiced in peacetime. Diddling with the electronics can decrease the effectiveness of enemy air defenses and lower friendly aircraft losses. There were more cliff-hangers in this department than there should have been. Now everyone agrees that the nerds should be allowed to play around a lot more in peacetime.

Flak Rules World Wars I and II demonstrated that flak (a German term for antiaircraft artillery) is lethal. Korea, Vietnam, and the Kuwait War demonstrated that flak continues to be a lethal adversary for low-flying aircraft. Low-altitude antiaircraft cannon, machine-gun and mobile surface-to-air missile fire continued to cause most (actually, all) of the aircraft losses in the Gulf war. Doctrine developed through the 1980s insisted that flying lower (a few hundred feet from the ground) was safer. Such was not the case in the Gulf, and even as you read this, air-force and navy pilots are being retrained. In the Gulf, pilots had to improvise and learn on the spot how to bomb at higher altitudes (over 10,000 feet). In some cases, the fire-control computers could not be reprogrammed to deal with higher-altitude bombing. Aircraft that could sneak in low at night (like the F-117A) remained effective. But if the enemy knew you were in the area, he would open up with every gun in the area, and most Allied aircraft damage and losses were from this random fire. For seventy years, pilots have been hoping that flak would go away, but it won't, ever.

A Return to the Good Old Days   In 1944, U.S. Army M4 tanks and U.S. Army Air Corps (the air force belonged to the army back then) P-47 Thunderbolt fighter-bombers operated as a closely integrated team. The tank commanders and P-47 pilots could talk to each other on the radio, enabling the P-47s to act as armed scouts for the tank units. Even the Germans were impressed. After World War II, the air corps became the air force (a separate service). The flyers didn't just change uniforms, they changed a lot of other things, including radios. It wasn't until the Kuwait War (well, the 1980s, actually) that the tank units and A-10 aircraft (Thunderbolt II is the official name) could easily communicate and operate as their grandfathers did in France nearly fifty years ago. The old ways were better, and there are a lot of army tank commanders and A-10 pilots who will provide testimonials.

Other Aspects of the Air War

Pilot Planning

Pilots don't just attend a briefing, make a few notes, jump into the cockpit, and go busting off on a mission. Individual pilots have a considerable number of items they have to take care of before each mission. The mission briefing (generated by a computer) gives the pilot navigation information that must be followed precisely. Other items pilots must consider include: cruising altitude; way points (where changes in direction take place); how to approach the target (altitude and speed); tactics for attacking the target; weapons carried (which can vary considerably); fuel situation (how many times the afterburner, for emergency high speed, can be turned on); where and when to refuel from airborne tankers; expected enemy defenses (and how to deal with them); and what to do in any emergency (what alternate airfields to use, what to do if you have to bail out).

Once pilots have absorbed all this, they have to contend with working with all the other pilots in the mission package. Even a lone wolf like the F-117A often has to coordinate with other F-117As and with supporting aerial tankers. Flying at night with other aircraft requires skill, discipline, and planning. The same applies for attacking targets, especially over Iraq where small-caliber antiaircraft guns (and some small missiles) still surrounded many targets. Although the Iraqi radar-warning system was destroyed, the first Allied bomber to pass over the target would wake up the gunners. If three or four bombers made low-level runs on the same target, the last one in would get most of the Iraqi ground fire.

A combat sortie is a complex operation, the planning of which has been made much simpler with the use of computers. The pilots use personal computers with programs that sort out a lot of the mission data and perform the many calculations required. The mission data for most aircraft is then transferred to a cassette tape that the pilot takes to the aircraft and inserts into the aircraft fire-control system (which is also loaded with all the pertinent navigation and target information). The pilots who are the most thorough in this preflight planning and checking have fewer problems and are best able to deal with the unexpected problems that do arise.

In-Flight Refueling

In-flight refueling was a major factor in the Allied air victory. The airborne tankers did not go in with the attack groups, but waited just outside enemy airspace to refuel aircraft going in and out. This was particularly true of the bombers going in. Bombers can carry more bombs farther if they take off without all their fuel but with a maximum bomb load. All aircraft have a maximum takeoff weight; bombers can, however, actually remain in the air at a heavier weight. The mathematics is easy: It is possible to top off the fuel tanks of an aircraft that just took off with a maximum bomb load, or add more fuel some miles away when the bomber has used up even more fuel (and left even more room in its fuel tanks). The United States has over 700 tanker aircraft in its air force and navy. Nearly 300 of these tankers were assigned to support the Persian Gulf War, and most of the remainder supported the war effort from U.S. and European bases.

Electronic Security

The United States made extensive use of electronic information collection and electronic warfare. It was learned shortly after the fighting stopped that the Iraqis had not been as inept in this area as was first thought. Russian-trained Iraqi electronic warfare (EW) troops in Kuwait and Iraq monitored much of the Allied radio traffic, of both air and ground forces. Allied pilots began to get sloppy with their use of radio as the air war progressed and it became apparent that the Iraqis were incapable of mounting an effective resistance. But the Iraqi EW units were active and capable, and would have caused substantial damage if they had more well-trained air-defense units. It was later discovered that the Iraqis had determined Allied air tactics from listening to Allied pilots talking freely about what to do next. Allied laxness in changing pilot frequencies, or call signs (for example, the same Allied pilot would call himself "Foxbait 11" for over a week) enabled the Iraqis to easily follow the progress of operations and sometimes warn their ground units to move out of the target area. The result was another sharp, although relatively inexpensive, lesson in the importance of maintaining communications and electronic security during air campaigns.

Air Force Reservists

While the army was reluctant to send reserve combat troops to the Gulf, the air force had quite the opposite attitude, sending over several reserve fighter and bomber squadrons. Typically, these units had the advantage of enormous flying experience among their pilots (usually averaging over 1,000 hours) and, equally important, more experienced maintenance crews. About two thirds of the reserve pilots flew for a living, usually for major airlines. To maintain their proficiency in combat aircraft, they fly their military aircraft six or seven times a month, which gets them the 200 or so hours a year they need to maintain proficiency as combat pilots. Most of these pilots are also former military pilots, so they are simply building on past experience. The maintenance crews are also largely employed doing similar work in their civilian jobs, usually for the same airlines the fighter pilots work for. Unlike their active-duty air-force counterparts, the reserve technicians have many more years of experience in aircraft maintenance, and this can make a difference in combat.

Combat Losses

The Allies set historical records for low aircraft losses during a major campaign. Total Allied aircraft losses were forty-two during six weeks of combat and thirty-three noncombat (accidents, equipment failure, etc.) during six months of operations. Iraqi losses in the air were forty (seventeen in the first three days, nine the first day) and several hundred on the ground.

The Allied losses worked out to a combat loss rate of 31 per 100,000 sorties. Peacetime loss rate due to accidents is about 14 per 100,000 sorties. During the 1966 Rolling Thunder air offensive over Vietnam, the loss rate was nine times higher (350 per 100,000 sorties). Over Iraq the loss rate varied considerably by service and nationality. The U.S. Air Force had the lowest rate, 22, followed by the U.S. Navy with 40, non-U.S. aircraft with 51, and the Marine Corps with 81. The U.S. Army, which put over 500 combat aircraft into the air (mostly helicopters) does not keep sorties statistics the same way the air forces do, but the loss rate was probably even lower than the U.S. Air Force's 22 per 100,000 sorties. Army combat helicopters tend to fly a lot more sorties per day than larger fixed-wing combat aircraft.

AIRCRAFT COMBAT LOSSES BY TYPE

2 UH-60 helicopters. Front-line transports

1 AH-64 helicopter. Shot down by Iraqi ground fire in Iraq prior to the ground offensive and destroyed by a U.S. TOW ATGM so it would not be captured

1 UH-1 helicopter. Older transport, replaced by UH-60.

1 OH-58 helicopter. Scouting helicopter

1 F-14A

4 A-6E

1 F/A-18

2 F-15E

5 F-16A. Did a lot of low-level bombing in Kuwait and took a lot of ground fire.

1 F-4G. Wild Weasel aircraft, attacked antiaircraft units.

1 AC-130H. Special Forces gunship, shot down during battle of Khafji

5 A-10. Constantly operated at low altitude attacking Iraqi ground units.

2 OV-10. Observation aircraft, spotted targets for aircraft attacks

4 AV-8B. Low-flying Marine Corps bomber

6 Tornado GR1 (British)

1 A-4 (Kuwait)

1 Tornado GR1 (Italy)

1 F-5 (Saudi Arabia)

COMPARISON TO HISTORICAL AIR LOSSES

Campaign	Loss Per 100,000 Sorties
World War II (U.S.)	620
Korea (U.S.)	440
North Vietnam 1966 (U.S.)	350
North Vietnam 1967 (U.S.)	300
North Vietnam 1968 (U.S.)	150
Six-Day War 1967 (Israel)	1,400
Yom Kippur War 1973 (Israel)	900
Desert Storm 1991 (Allies)	38

SORTIES AND LOSS RATES

Air Force	% Sorties	Loss per 100,000 sorties	
		All	Combat
USAF	59	22	47
USN	16	40	56
USMC	9	81	90
Allies	16	51	64
Total	112,000	31	52

Notes on the Chart

Combat sorties are different. Some 40 percent of the sorties were noncombat, and most of these were U.S. Air Force sorties. Thus, if we adjust the sortie loss rate to show losses per 100,000 combat sorties, we obtain a higher number but one comparable to previous air campaigns where there were far fewer (and often no) noncombat sorties included in the calculation of sorties loss rates. Even so, the loss rate was a historical low. Current U.S. training losses are about 14 aircraft per 100,000 sorties. These training losses have been much higher in the past. In fact, during

World War I, training and other noncombat losses exceeded combat losses. During World War II, there was stiff opposition until the very end of the war. Most of the losses were due to ground fire, a pattern that has persisted to the present. Korea and Vietnam were unique in that they were "limited" wars. For the air forces, that meant that the enemy air forces and air defenses could not be attacked persistently enough to eliminate them. This kept losses higher than they should have been, for the 1950s and 1960s saw the introduction of more robust aircraft and better-trained pilots.

The Arab-Israeli wars were unique in that Israel had much superior pilots and overall superiority in aircraft quality. But the Israelis had to destroy Arab air power quickly and then provide support for their ground forces without benefit of laser bombs delivered out of ground-fire range. While Israel suffered relatively high aircraft losses, its total personnel losses (ground and air) were low in proportion to the damage it inflicted on its (much more numerous) opponents and the speed with which it did it. The 1973 war lasted only two weeks. The Kuwait War was unique in that the winners' losses were so low, but the Allies also had an enormous advantage in quantity and quality of aircraft and pilots. Exceptional care was taken to minimize friendly aircraft losses, even if it meant targets were not hit. There was such a superiority of combat power that eventually all targets that needed to be destroyed would be destroyed. This takes nothing away from the Allied air victory; it was an exceptionally professional and efficient application of air power. Even against a larger and more effective Iraqi Air Force, the Allies would have prevailed, although with higher—but not that much higher—losses. The Allied aircraft were more capable, Allied tactics and weapons superior, and the Allied pilots were better trained. Most of the air power came from the United States, a nation that had never lost an air battle and once more demonstrated why. It was all of this that has caused so much gloom and consternation in the Russian Air Force.

Confirmed Allied Air-to-Air Kills

There were forty confirmed air-to-air kills. There were probably more, as several could not be confirmed but some were likely to have resulted in a downed Iraqi aircraft.

MiG-29   5 (top Russian fighter with mediocore Iraqi pilots)

Mirage F1   8 (1960s-era French fighter-bomber)

MiG-21   4 (1960s-era Russian fighter)

MiG-23   7 (1970s-era Russian fighter)

MiG-25   2 (1970s-era Russian recon aircraft)

Su-25   2 (Russian equivalent of U.S. A-10)

Su-7/22   6 (1960s-era Russian fighter-bomber)

Helicopter   6 (various types)

Total   40

Shot down by

F-15	35
A-10	2
F-18	2
F-14	1

Weapon Used

Aim-9 (Sidewinder)	13 heat-seeking missile
Aim-7 (Sparrow)	24 radar-guided missile
Cannon	2 A-10 30-mm antitank cannon
Maneuver	1 Iraqi was chased into the ground

Date	Unit	AC	Kill	Wpn
Jan. 17	1st TFW	F-15c	Mirage F1	Aim-7
	33rd TFW	F-15c	MiG 29	Aim-7
	33rd TFW	F-15c	2 Mirage F1	Aim-7
	33rd TFW	F-15c	MiG 29	Aim-7
	33rd TFW	F-15c	MiG 29	Aim-7
	VFA-81	2A-18	2 MiG 21	Aim-9
Jan. 19	33rd TFW	F-15c	MiG 25	Aim-7
	33rd TFW	F-15c	MiG 25	Aim-7

	33rd TFW	F-15c	MiG 29	Aim-7
	33rd TFW	F-15c	MiG 29	ground impact
	36th TFW	F-15c	Mirage F1	Aim-7
	36th TFW	F-15c	Mirage F1	Aim-7
Jan. 24	Saudi AF	F-15c	2 Mirage F1	Aim-9 (both)
Jan. 26	33rd TFW	F-15c	MiG 23	Aim-7
	33rd TFW	F-15c	MiG 23	Aim-7
Jan. 27	36th TFW	F-15c	2 MiG 23	Aim-9 (both)
	36th TFW	F-15c	MiG 23	Aim-7
	36th TFW	F-15c	Mirage F1	Aim-7
Jan. 29	32nd TFGp	F-15c	MiG 23	Aim-7
	33rd TFW	F-15c	MiG 23	Aim-7
Feb. 6	36th TFW	F-15c	2 SU-25	Aim-9 (both)
	36th TFW	F-15c	2 MiG 21	Aim-9 (both)
	926th TFGp	A-10	observation helicopter	30 mm GAU gun
	VF-1	F-14a	helicopter (type unknown)	Aim-9
Feb. 7	33rd TFW	F-15c	2 SU-7[1]	Aim-7 (both)
	33rd TFW	F-15c	2 SU-7[2]	Aim-7 (both)
	36th TFW	F-15c	helicopter (type unknown)	Aim-7
Feb. 11	36th TFW	F-15c	helicopter (type unknown)	Aim-7
	36th TFW	F-15c	helicopter (type unknown)	Aim-7
Feb. 15	926th TFGp	A-10	Mi-8 helicopter	30 mm GAU gun
March 20	36th TFW	F-15c	SU-22	Aim-9
March 22	36th TFW	F-15c	SU-22	Aim-9

1. Maybe SU-17s (SU-7 and SU-17 are externally identical)
2. Maybe SU-17s (SU-7 and SU-17 are externally identical)

Date—Date of operation

Unit—Unit aircraft was from (TFW [Tactical Fighter Wing], or Gp [Group], VFA [Marine fighter squadron])

AC—Aircraft type

Kill—Type of Iraqi aircraft destroyed

Wpn—Weapon used

NOTE: Two air-to-air kills have not been substantiated. The F-14A shooting down an Iraqi plane with an Aim-54 Phoenix is still rumor—loose rumor. An EF-111 Raven may have forced an Iraqi plane to crash by disabling its navigational equipment. That's an Aardvark with a nose for combat.

Cost of the Air War

There were two major cost items. One was lost aircraft, the other was munitions expended.

The total aircraft loss amounted to some $82 billion (at replacement costs). Some of the lost aircraft cannot be replaced because they are no longer being manufactured. The two most expensive individual aircraft losses (below) fall into that category.

- The biggest individual losses were one C-5A transport that crashed ($140 million, which can be replaced by two C-17s at $200 million each) and one EF-111 Raven electronics-warfare aircraft, lost due to noncombat causes ($75 million, which can be replaced by a rebuilt old model F-111 at $60 million).
- The air force lost $650 million worth of planes before the war, and $800 million during the war.
- The army lost over $80 million worth, during the conflict mostly Blackhawk (UH-60), Apache (AH-64), and Huey (UH-1) helicopters.
- The navy had total aircraft losses amounting to $360 million.
- The marines lost mostly Harriers ($20 million each), with a total loss over $120 million.

The other major cost was munitions and operations. Coalition air forces dropped munitions (smart bombs, dumb bombs, missiles) costing over $500 million. Wear and tear on aircraft was substantial, with most fixed-wing combat aircraft flying a year's worth of sorties in five weeks. This, plus battle damage, cost another $400 million for air-force and navy aircraft.

Mission Planning Seventy-five years ago, pilots were told roughly what the situation was, then aircraft would go out individually or in small groups to engage enemy air and ground forces. This impromptu approach rapidly escalated over the next twenty-five years into "mission planning." From the 1950s, the U.S. Air Force used a complex, and largely manual, planning procedure for preparing pilots and aircraft for their increasingly complex missions. This planning includes items like how much fuel can be carried (less fuel means more munitions), where air refueling will take place (if needed), the best approach to the target, the best weapons to carry, and which aircraft will be in what position to the others during the flight and who will do what under different circumstances. Potential enemy opposition is taken into account. In the 1980s, the microcomputer revolution entered the process, and in 1986 the air force began installing computer-based MSS (Mission Support Systems). The air war in the Gulf gave MSS a real workout and proved the worth of this approach. Aside from taking a large workload off the pilots, MSS allows for more effective mission planning and execution. For most aircraft, pilots can work out their flight plan on a computer, take a tape of the PC-generated plan, insert the tape into the aircraft computer, and eliminate a lot of the guesswork and rough calculation.

Through World War II and into the Vietnam War, the assortment of aircraft going out to fight became more elaborate and effective. At first there were just the bombers and (increasingly) their fighter escorts. When surface-to-air missiles were used during the Vietnam War, there arose a need to use electronic warfare to deal with the target detection and tracking radar (on the ground) as well as with the electronics in the missiles themselves. This evolved into the first specialized electronic-warfare aircraft ("Wild Weasels"). The Wild Weasels eventually had fighter-bomber aircraft assisting them in destroying enemy ground radars detected. After Vietnam, the AWACS aircraft were added to orchestrate these flights of hundreds of aircraft into heavily defended enemy territory. The increasing number of aerial tankers (to make sure the bombers had enough fuel to get out and back) also had to be kept track of. The basic mission of all this remained the same, to get the bombers over enemy targets. But for each group of four bombers there would be one or more fighters, at least one Wild Weasel, and one or more tankers. This became the "mission package." The Kuwait War reaffirmed the importance of the mission package and revealed that more flexibility was required in order to develop more effective packages in the face of the new technology of enemy countermoves. Although the F-117A Stealth fighter nominally operated on its own, in practice it was sometimes escorted (at a distance) by F-15 fighters and sometimes followed Wild Weasels that would trigger Iraqi antiaircraft cannon fire. Once the antiaircraft guns had overheated their gun barrels and run short of ammunition, the F-117A would fly in and drop its bombs. In one case, an AWACS noted an Iraqi fighter flying in the vicinity of where an F-117A was supposed to be (the Iraqi aircraft was actually flying around with a searchlight looking for the F-117A). The AWACS directed an F-15 to go after the Iraqi aircraft, and put its searchlight out.

It was also an expensive war for the army, with over 4,000 Hellfire missiles fired, costing $40,000 each ($160 million). Other munitions, maintenance, and spares added another $40 million in cost.

Background: Air Force Organization and Operation

The basic unit in the air force is the squadron, consisting of twenty-four (in some cases eighteen) aircraft, forty to fifty pilots, and several hundred maintenance and support personnel. Three squadrons of the same-type aircraft are organized into an air wing, and three or more wings and independent squadrons are organized into an air division. Spare aircraft are often assigned to an air wing to quickly replace training and combat losses. There are more pilots than aircraft because under combat conditions the stress of flying is harder on the pilots than on the aircraft. So the planes will fly more often than the pilots.

Most of the personnel in an air-force squadron perform

ground support duties. The maintenance required for an aircraft is measured (as a rough guideline) in the number of man-hours of maintenance required for each hour the aircraft is in the air. This value varies greatly by type of aircraft. More modern aircraft, despite their increased complexity, are actually easier to maintain than older aircraft. This is because the more modern planes are designed for ease of maintenance. Even so, it takes an average of twenty hours of maintenance for each flight hour. With over 2,000 sorties a day flown during the campaign (each averaging three to four hours), the maintenance crews had to cope with 200,000 hours of daily maintenance to keep the aircraft flying. Obviously, the maintenance people were up to the task, even with the additional job of repairing battle damage from thousands of Iraqi antiaircraft guns and portable antiaircraft missiles that remained in action to the end of the war. The maintenance load was manageable mainly because the aircraft did not fly as often as they could have and because of hundreds of civilian technicians brought in to augment the regular military technicians. Moreover, in peacetime, aircraft are used about a half to a third as much as they would be in wartime. Aircraft in general, and combat aircraft in particular, are basically a collection of complex components that have to be regularly replaced at intervals based on the number of hours they fly. A jet fighter has been essentially rebuilt several times by its tenth birthday (4,000–5,000 hours in the air). The aircraft are kept in excellent shape in peacetime so that they can be "run down" in wartime, at least for the first days or weeks when getting the maximum number of aircraft into combat is so vital. Worldwide inventories of parts were stripped for the Gulf effort, leaving the two thirds of U.S. combat aircraft that weren't sent to the Gulf much less capable due to lack of spares and mechanics to install them.

Collateral Damage

Beginning in World War II, when large number of bombers became available and attacks on economic targets became practical, civilian casualties unfortunately became common and numerous. Bombing accuracy was a general concept, not a precise art. People lived near the factories and bombing raids were often done at night. Civilians got killed. Accidental bombings of purely civilian targets early in the war begat indiscriminate bombing of cities. As a result of this, over 90,000 British civilians were killed in bombing raids (including German V-2 rockets, the design the Scuds were based on). Germany and Japan each lost over half a million civilian dead to bombing raids. Air raids killed hundreds of thousands more in Korea and Vietnam. The relatively low number of civilian bombing casualties during the Gulf War (under 5,000) then, came as something as a surprise, although not an unexpected one.

Nonetheless, collateral damage became a key political issue when CNN broadcast pictures of a destroyed Iraqi command bunker—or was it a civilian shelter? Likewise, pictures of damage in what appeared to be clearly areas of Baghdad and Basra supercharged an already electric emotional issue. Bomb Damage Assessment (BDA) on the part of the Allies also became something of a political hot potato because few in the media understood the problems of determining the extent of destruction of targets in enemy-held territory. When the smoke, so to speak, cleared, it was obvious that the civilian casualty rate was quite low by historical standards. This was no accident, and there were several reasons for this uncharacteristically low civilian-casualty count.

1. Bombing Accuracy. During World War II, only half the bombs landed more than 3,000 feet from their target. In Korea and Vietnam, half the bombs landed more than 400 feet away. In Iraq, half the bombs landed more than forty feet away. Half of the guided bombs (the ones used most frequently in built-up areas) landed within four feet of their targets.

2. Target Location. Most of the Iraqi targets were located away from populated areas. This was obviously the case with the Iraqi Army in Kuwait and southern Iraq, but many of Iraq's military and industrial installations were deliberately located away from populated areas for "security reasons" (the Iraqi government does not trust the Iraqi people). When bombs were dropped on targets in populated areas, the guided bombs were used.

3. Policy. When the Iraqis began to move military equipment into civilian areas (aircraft, supplies, antiaircraft weapons, etc.) the Allied commanders did not bomb them, even though this put coalition troops at risk.

Thoughtful Destruction

Many factors went into selecting targets for the bombers. Take Iraqi oil facilities. The oil fields were not bombed, but transportation facitities (which could ship about 12,000 tons of oil a day before the war) were. But not all facilities were hit. Most of Iraq's oil was exported via pipelines, either south to Saudi Arabia, southwest to ports on the Red Sea, or north through Turkey to ports on the Mediterranean. The pipeline across Turkey can move about 2,500 tons of oil a day, for which Turkey receives a fee from Iraq of over $100 million a year. Not surprisingly, this was the only Iraqi oil-shipment facility that was not destroyed during the war, even though Allied bombers were based just across the border in eastern Turkey. Moreover, Iraq could probably not fail to note the political side effects of being forced to begin its first shipments of oil through (and payments to) Turkey (a staunch U.S. ally).

Air Force Glossary

ATO—Air Tasking Order. Daily list of missions for all combat aircraft, including target location, air-refueling location and time, and much more. Prepared by computer and electronically transmitted to all units involved.

Afterburner—System to greatly increase the amount of fuel being burned in a jet engine, which also increases aircraft speed and fuel consumption. Only used briefly, as in emergencies.

Armed Recce—Armed reconnaissance mission. Recon aircraft carry some bombs so that if a particularly valuable target is seen it can be attacked immediately. Primary mission is still taking photos.

Bingo Fuel—This is when there's just enough fuel left to get home, or to a tanker waiting outside the combat zone.

BLU—Bomb Live Unit. An old-fashioned "iron bomb" (a steel casing filled with explosive).

FLIR—Forward Looking Infrared Radar. A sensor that detects objects according to how much heat they are producing. Used in many of the more modern fire-control systems to enable the pilot to find and hit targets at night (in particular armored vehicles, which are warmer than their surroundings, even in the desert where the ground cools off rapidly when the sun goes down).

GBU—Glide Bomb Unit. A BLU with a set of controllable fins, a guidance computer and sensor unit attached. Here, the bomber pilot guides the bomb to the target.

HUD—Head-Up Display. Aircraft and target information projected on a see-through display in front of the pilot so he doesn't have to look down for key information.

Kill Box—A box-shaped area on the ground, ten to twenty kilometers on a side, that is carefully reconnoitered and then gone over with bombers to destroy all targets. A kill box was used to destroy dug-in Iraqi ground divisions in Kuwait.

Killer Scout—F-16s (usually) sent out to patrol an area for targets. The killer scout would attack targets, such as moving vehicles, that might get away and call in other bombers to take care of stationary targets (bunkers, supply dumps, etc.).

LANTIRN Scud Box—LANTERN-equipped F-15Es patrol a large box-shaped piece of terrain looking for Scud launchers and destroying any found.

Mission—A group of aircraft going off to do something together.

Mission Package—All the different types of aircraft required to accomplish one mission. A bombing mission would include bombers, fighter escorts, electronic-warfare aircraft, and tankers.

Paveway—Air-force teams for its GBU system used on F-111 bombers.

Pickle—An expression for getting the cross hairs in the bomb sight over the target (as in "pickle the target").

SAM Removal Team—Electronic-warfare aircraft "Wild Weasels" and bombers that go after a surface-to-air missile installation.

Scud Hunt—Any type of aircraft patrolling an area looking for Scud launchers to attack.

SLAR—Side Looking Radar. A radar that is mounted so that it looks out from the side of the aircraft and creates a map of the ground underneath. The map is recorded and used later for planning or intelligence purposes.

Sortie—One aircraft takes off, does something, and lands.

Tank Plinking—An aircraft assigned to attacking tanks and armored vehicles. Usually A-10s or F-16s with Maverick missiles.

Quick Study 5:
Patriots and Scuds

The Gulf War saw the public forcefully reminded of a World War II weapon that has not got much attention in the last forty-five years: the V-2 (A4) ballistic missile. In 1944–45, Germany fired over 2,000 V-2 missiles at Allied targets (mainly London). The V-2 missile was used as the model for all post-1945 ballistic missiles. One of the earliest descendants of the V-2 was the Russian Scud missile. A more accurate missile and with a longer range, the Scud was literally a "son of the V-2," as it was developed in the 1950s using V-2 plans and some of the German V-2 technicians.

The Scud saw no combat use until the 1980s, when Iran and Iraq bought over 1,000 now-obsolete Scuds, and fired most of them at each other. The Russian-backed Communist government in Afghanistan has also fired over 1,000 Scuds at rebel strongholds starting in the late 1980s, and continues to do so.

The Scud was designed to carry nuclear weapons. But its warhead could deliver about a ton of anything with a 50 percent chance of landing within a mile of where it was aimed. Because of this poor accuracy, a nuclear warhead was the only kind that made any sense. That is, unless you wanted to use it as the origi-

nal V-2 was used: as a terror weapon against enemy populations. That's exactly how Iraq and Iran used them against each
other in their 1980–88 war. Although Iraq threatened to use
Scuds with nuclear or chemical warheads during the Persian
Gulf War, neither of these warheads were available. Well,
chemical warheads were available, but their reliability was
highly questionable even by Iraqi standards. So the Scud was
used once more as a terror weapon.

During the 1980–88 Iran-Iraq War, Iraq fired between 250 and
300 Scuds. Each Scud fired caused an average of seventy-five
casualties. In 1988, the Iraqi Scud attacks played a part in Iran
calling off the war. In 1991, the Scuds fired at Israel came close
to getting Israel involved in the Persian Gulf War. Close wasn't
good enough. In 1991, the Iraqi Scuds had to deal with the Patriot antimissile missile. Because of the Patriot, most of the
Scuds fired in 1991 were intercepted and the casualties per Scud
fired were fewer than ten per missile. Militarily, the Scud was
a bust in 1991. Allied countermeasures against the Scud were
impressive. The Allied air attacks against Scud launchers sharply
reduced the Iraqi capability to launch the missiles. On the first
week of the war, Iraq fired thirty-five missiles. On subsequent
weeks, the firings declined sharply (missiles fired on second and
subsequent weeks; eighteen, four, five, six, four). The Scud
looked more impressive than its performance on paper, or in
the news, indicated.

What was also surprising to the Allies was the greater number
of Scud launchers, which greatly complicated the job of hunting
down and destroying them. At the end of the war, there were
still some Scud launchers and dozens of Scud missiles still surviving. There were a lot more Scud launchers because the Iraqis
had figured out how to build their own using flatbed trucks.
These home-made systems became known as MELs, or Mobile
Erector Launchers. MELs are relatively easy to construct, and
the basic operation of a Scud launch was quite simple. The
launcher and fuel truck drove out to the launch point. One of
the two fuels used by the Scud could be loaded before driving
to the launch point. Upon arrival at the launch point, the missile
was erected to a vertical position, the other fuel (nitric acid) was
loaded, and the coordinates of the missile and the target entered
into the missile-guidance system. Once the guidance system was
programmed, the missile was launched, and then, within min-

utes, the launcher could be on its way back to its hiding place.

The U.S. Patriot antiaircraft that consistently intercepted the Scuds did not destroy these missiles; at best the Patriot destroyed or neutralized the warhead and almost always threw the warhead off course, which usually resulted in the Scud warhead landing in a less densely populated area. One unexpected development was the tendency of intercepted Scuds to break up into smaller pieces during their final dive toward the earth.

To reach deep inside Iran during the 1980–88 war, Iraq modified the basic Russian Scud. This longer-range Scud became the principal one that Iraq used in 1991. The Iraqi-modified Scuds were poorly constructed. Moreover, in doubling the range of the original Scud (in the "Al Hussein" version), the Iraqis made the speed of the Scud as it plunged to earth twice what the missile was originally designed for. The additional stresses generated by this greater speed caused most of the Scuds to break up at about the same time the Patriot radar picked them up. Patriot radar operators quickly learned that the radar blip in front of the rest represented the warhead, and that's what the Patriot missile was aimed at.

During the final seconds of a Scud's five-minute flight, it was moving, literally, faster than a speeding bullet. At this point, the missile body and warhead together weighed nearly four tons. As the Scud broke apart, most pieces weighed at least a few hundred pounds. Even if the warhead did not explode, the Scud did great damage to whatever the heavier pieces of it hit. In one case, a Scud with a disabled warhead hit a wing of an unoccupied Saudi high-rise building and demolished the entire structure. In more densely populated Israel, the rain of Scud (and Patriot) parts damaged over 10,000 apartments and injured nearly 300 people (and killed one). Thus, even without the warhead exploding, the Scud was a dangerous falling object wherever it landed.

Ironically, the poor construction of the modified Scuds proved to be an Iraqi advantage, albeit one that a quick Patriot software update partially overcame. Scuds breaking into several parts created the same effect as having several objects showing up on the Patriot radar screen. The Patriot was programmed to find and aim for the warhead of the missile, or one object (the warhead) traveling slightly in front of another (the rest of the missile). Confusion reigned when the Patriot phased-array radar picked up five or six chunks of missile plunging earthward. One Patriot software update, which directed the missile into an interception point in the middle of the broken-apart Scud, and fired more than one Patriot at each Scud, helped mitigate the problem but did not answer it completely.

The Patriot missile was designed to shoot down missiles as something of an afterthought. Patriot began development in the early 1960s as a replacement of the 1950s Hawk antiaircraft missile. The Hawk is still around as the "improved Hawk," mainly because Patriot didn't get to the troops until the mid 1980s. Patriot took advantage of the most modern technology, several times, during over twenty years of development. In the early 1980s, it was noted that the Patriots' fire-control computers were fast enough to spot an incoming missile, then launch and guide a Patriot to an interception. Tests were successfully conducted against U.S. missiles from 1986 on. Another modern feature of the Patriot was that the fire-control software could be easily changed, and several changes were made since 1986 to increase Patriots' effectiveness against missiles. In 1990, a new warhead for the Patriot was issued that increased the probability of disabling an incoming missile. During the Kuwait War, further software changes were made based on combat experience with the Scuds.

The Patriot system (also called a "fire unit" or "battery") consists of a radar controlling eight launchers (each with four missiles.) A Patriot battalion contains six systems, for a total of 48 launchers and at least 300–400 missiles (including reloads). The Patriot missile itself is 17.4 feet long, 16 inches in diameter, and weighs 2,000 pounds. Normal range of the Patriot is up to 60 kilometers and at altitudes of from 400 to 72,000 feet. The Patriot missiles cost half a million dollars each; a complete battery (radars, reloads, training, trucks, R&D, etc.) costs nearly $100 million. Overall, each Patriot launched cost about $1 million. The Iraqis paid about $1 million for each of their Scuds, although the final cost may be even more than double that because of modifications, launching equipment, etc. At least two Patriots were fired at each Scud. Space war gets expensive.

Iraq apparently launched at least eighty-one Scuds (forty-three Scuds were fired at Saudi Arabia and thirty-eight at Israel). Official U.S. Army figures say Patriots succeeded in hitting forty-five of the forty-seven Scuds they went after.

Patriots, according to other open-source figures, attempted to intercept fifty-one of the Scuds and hit forty-nine of them. About half the Scuds were so off target that they fell harmlessly in the desert or water. About 50 percent of Scuds fired at Israel and 90 percent of those fired at Saudi Arabia were intercepted by Patriot missiles.

Why the discrepancies? First, there seem to have been at least two accidental Patriot launches, triggered by the electronics of Allied aircraft or other misidentification. Then there is some uncertainty about the number of Scuds launched. Here are the guesstimates: twelve to fifteen Scuds were fired at Israel before Patriots arrived in that nation. Obviously, they were not intercepted. Apparently ten or eleven Scuds fired at Saudi Arabia and Israel had trajectories that took them out to sea or in the middle of empty desert (or the West Bank?); the Patriot computers decided that they were not a threat and did not attempt to intercept them. Seven Scuds broke up so badly and were not intercepted because the Patriot fire-control systems judged that they were "out of parameters" and not interceptable. Parts of one Scud hit the U.S. Army barracks in Dhahran, which housed the 14th Quartermaster Detachment. Twenty-eight soldiers were killed, and over ninety were wounded in that Scud attack. This last attack, which caused the most casualties, was not fired upon because one of the two Patriot batteries in the area was shut down for maintenance. A Patriot battery is supposed to operate fourteen hours and then stop for maintenance. Some had to stay operational for over 100 hours, including the one that let the Scud hit the barracks. This excessive operating time allowed inaccuracies to build up in the system. The long operating time caused a "drift" in the accuracy of the Patriot's fire-control system. The incoming Scud did not appear as a threat, so it was not fired on. New software was on the way to correct this problem, but it was not yet installed on this batteries' computers. Such problems are common when a system is used in combat for the first time. What surprised most people, in and out of the military, was that the complex Patriot performed with so few of these problems the first time out.

Twenty-nine Patriot batteries were sent to the Middle East. Six operated in Israel (two manned by Israelis and four by the United States), two were assigned to Turkey, and twenty-one were deployed in Saudi Arabia.

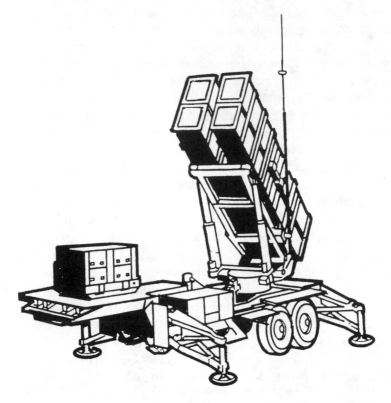

Patriot—Anti-missile missile

AIR DEFENSE GETS SOME RESPECT (FINALLY)

Western, and especially U.S., air-defense troops have never really had a chance to strut their stuff since World War II. In fact, even during the 1941–45 war, American air-defense units, especially those belonging to the ground forces, never had a lot to do.

Since the early 1940s, U.S. forces generally fought their battles with air superiority. American fighter aircraft were the principal antiaircraft weapon, leaving the ground-based antiaircraft to shoot (with good effect) at ground targets rather than the generally absent enemy bombers.

Since 1945, several generations of air-defense weapons have

come and gone without ever being able to demonstrate what they were capable of. The Persian Gulf War finally gave the Army Air Defense Artillery (ADA) troops their moment in the spotlight. Shooting down (or at least deflecting) Scud missiles may not have been exactly what the Patriot surface-to-air missiles (SAMs) were designed for, but it was something. The Patriots gave the coalition enough protection as well as "political cover" to keep Israel on the sidelines and out of the war.

CHAPTER 7

The Air War: Part 2

Aircraft Types and What They Do

An air-force commander has a wide variety of aircraft types with which to fight an air war. Each of these aircraft has a specific job, and all are needed to win the air war with minimum losses.

There were over a hundred different aircraft and helicopter types operating in the Gulf during the Persian Gulf War. Here is a brief list of the most widely used aircraft types, what they do, and how they operated in the theater:

Intelligence and Battle Management Aircraft

These are the eyes and brains of any air operations. These aircraft (and spacecraft) perform three tasks:

1. Obtain Information. Air commanders need information about prospective targets so that the most important ones can be selected. This involves a lot of scrutiny of the enemy territory before an attack to find out exactly where the targets are, how well they are defended, and, if they are mobile (ships, army units, ect.), where they are likely to be when you want to hit them.

2. Keep Track of Information. Commanders need a way to keep track of all friendly and enemy aircraft in action. The Persian Gulf war involved an average of over 2,000 aircraft in the air every twenty-four hours. Frequently, there were hundreds up at once, and you had to keep them sorted out if only to avoid collisions. Moreover, the aircraft assigned to each mission often came from a variety of different bases, and their takeoffs had to be timed so that all aircraft in a particular mission were in the right place when all of them passed over into enemy territory. This was where the AWACS and navy E-2 radar aircraft did most of their work, playing traffic cop in the air war.

3. Verifying Information. Finally, the targets hit have to be checked to see how much damage was done and if another attack is needed. Every bombing mission is not successful, and you are never absolutely sure the target was destroyed until you get to look at it on the ground. This is often not possible, so you have to rely on various types of observation from the air. This reconnaissance has varying degrees of accuracy, making it something of a guessing game as to which targets have to be hit again, and again.

Aircraft (and Spacecraft) Used for Intelligence and Battle Management

1. Satellites—There are several types of orbiting satellites that provided crucial information during the war. There are several dozen in orbit providing support for the air force and ground troops. The principal types are:

- The KH-11 series reconnaissance satellite. There were three KH-11 satellites in orbit (launched in December 1984, October 1987, and November 1988), each equipped with a large telescope and electronic listening devices. Objects as small as three inches can be detected when orbiting at low altitudes. There are also four advanced KH-11 (launched in August 1989, February 1990, June 1990, and November 1990), each with the standard KH-11 equipment but capable of photographing objects at night using an infrared scanner, plus a sensor package capable of detecting some materials used in camouflage. The KH-11 launched in December 1984 is probably no longer working (they first run out of fuel for maneuvering, then start to break down) and one of the advanced KH-11s apparently failed in orbit. This left five KH-11s available for observing the Gulf by the end of 1990. The KH-11 birds move about in orbit and while passing over can observe an area for about two hours. The detailed photos are transmitted via relay satellites to a ground station in Maryland and are then retransmitted or further analyzed. These images could be shown within mintues to U.S. analysts and commanders in Saudi Arabia.

- One Lacrosse radar satellite (launched in December 1988), which can see through clouds and other atmospheric obstructions. This satellite can detect items buried up to ten feet underground to pinpoint missiles and other equipment hidden in trenches and bunkers. This satellite, however, is only available a few hours a day because it circles the earth.
- Two Mentor SIGINT (Signal Intelligence) satellites (launched in January 1985 and November 1989), which sit in fixed orbit and eavesdropped on Iraqi transmissions (communications, radars, etc).
- One Vortex SIGINT satellite (launched in May 1989), which is like the Mentor but more specialized.
- The Defense Support Program satellites (exact number is classified, but an advanced model was launched November 1990 to increase Scud missile-launch coverage). These satellites use large infrared telescopes to locate the hot plumes of missile launches. When Scuds were fired, these satellites could only give a few minutes' warning, but some warning was better than none.
- GPS (Global Positioning Satellite) Systems. Provides precise location information (to within twenty-five meters or less) via a hand-held satellite signal receiver. Not all twenty-four satellites were in orbit when war began, but there were enough up there to give coverage over most of the Gulf except for a few hours in the late afternoon. The importance of this system will often be underestimated by nonmilitary observers. Anyone who has served in the army, as I have, knows all too well how easy it is to get lost while traveling over (the usually) unfamiliar terrain. Maps only appear to add to the confusion, and in desert operations, "navigation" becomes a major matter of life and death. All that was changed in the Gulf War because of the GPS. This system provided precise location infor-

mation to anyone with a battery-powered SLGR (Small, Lightweight GPS Receiver, or "Slugger") unit. The smallest version weighed two pounds, measured nine by four by two inches, with a four-line by fifteen-character LCD display (similar to those found on digital watches) and used six standard AA batteries. The batteries allowed for seven hours of continuous operation, although the unit could be turned off and then take two to three minutes when turned on again to get an accurate location fix. Aircraft traveling faster than the speed of sound could use them, and most were mounted in vehicles with a cable going to an exterior antenna (to pick up the satellite signal). Knowing who (and what) is where on the battlefield is often a matter of life and death. Calling in artillery fire or air strikes depends on the ground observer (who is often not far from the target) knowing exactly where he is so that the shells or bombs hit the enemy and not friendly troops. Reconnaissance is much more effective with GPS, as the location of the target can be recorded with precision. Marking the location of enemy minefields, a common occurrence during the Persian Gulf War, was much more effective with GPS-equipped units. Coordinating the movement of ground units on the featureless desert became more effective when everyone had GPS. If there is one unsung techo-hero of the Gulf War, it's the GPS. On the average, each U.S. Army maneuver company (tank, mech infantry, or armored cavalry) had at least one GPS receiver. Some 4,500 GPS receivers were in the Gulf by the end of February, and another 5,500 were on order. The military expects to have over 30,000 in use by the end of the decade. Receivers also built into aircraft and some weapons. Future models of cruise missiles will replace their expensive-to-make-and-maintain terrain-following systems with cheaper GPS. More combat aircraft will be able to navigate and attack ground targets using GPS. The original GPS receivers for the military were built to handle the encrypted wartime signal, so as to deny enemy nations the advantage of a less accurate, unencrypted "commercial" signal. Because there were few military GPS receivers available (and those weighed, and cost, much more than SLGR), the military signal was not used because thousands of SLGRs could be obtained on short notice. Trimble Navigation Company (of California) snagged most of these contracts (over $40 million worth), much to the discomfort of their usual commercial customers (boat owners, truckers, etc.).

- EC-130—Electronic warfare aircraft. This is a four-engine (propeller) aircraft (C-130), used for jamming enemy communications. The EC-130s would get in rather close behind the bombers and Wild Weasels going in to attack Iraqi antiaircraft installations. It trails a 500-foot antenna with a weight attached. This caused some air-traffic problems, as the EC-130 also tended to fly back and forth along the border while some fighters and bombers were crossing on their way north. Another version of the EC-130 carried an airborne communications center to coordinate operations between ground and air units (the ABCCC, or Airborne Battlefield Command and Control Center). This was the first time ABCCC was used, and it proved very successful in keeping the ground commanders in touch with the bombers overhead.
- P-3 Orion—A U.S. Navy recon aircraft that normally searches for submarines and surface ships. Patrolled the Gulf to keep an eye on Iraqi naval operations (particularly minelaying). Also had some aircraft control capability. An electronic-warfare version (the EP-3) was also used, making it difficult for the Iraqis to use any electronic equipment over the Gulf.
- SARSAT (Search and Rescue Satellite-Aided Tracking)—This bird could receive signals from the emergency radios carried by downed pilots. The satellite passed over the Gulf area (on average) ten times a day for twelve to fifteen minutes at each pass. The times the satellite was over the area was given to pilots each day so that if they were downed, they knew when to broadcast a signal that the satellite could receive. A four-minute transmission by the pilot (by holding down the Talk button for four minutes after identifying himself and his condition) allowed the satellite to determine where the pilot was. The rescue teams could then go get him. The only drawback was that if the Iraqis in the area had any radio-detection equipment, they could find him too.

- SPOT—The French commercial multispectrum satellite. The pictures are sold to the public, and the Allies availed themselves of the images from this source for a wide variety of mapping and planning purposes.
- DMSP (Defense Meteorological Satellite Program)— Three of these specialized weather satellites were assigned to keep an eye on weather conditions. In addition, the DMSP birds had a radar that can do things like check soil conditions. Over 100 satellite receivers for these birds were in use in the Gulf area. Weather satellites belonging to other nations (including Russia) were also used.
- EC-135—Electronic-warfare aircraft. This is actually a converted Boeing 707 civilian aircraft used to spy on electronic transmissions. Unlike SIGINT satellites, EC-135s could stay close to a specific location for hours at a time and get a better fix on enemy electronic capabilities and the location of their equipment. They are also capable of jamming and otherwise compromising enemy electronics, and are also used for command and control (although much of this function has been taken over by the AWACS). A similar aircraft, the RC-135, is primarily used for collecting electronic information.
- E-2 Hawkeye—Airborne Command and Control Aircraft. A two-engine aircraft used by the navy (from aircraft carriers). Israel also uses a version of the E-2 from land bases. They are not as capable as the E-3 (they have a shorter range, and thus can track fewer enemy and friendly aircraft). But the E-2 does the job, and passes data back and forth with E-3s as they share control of other aircraft.
- E-3 AWACS—Airborne Command-and-Control Aircraft. Think of these customized Boeing 707s as a cross between a giant flying radar (which it is), an enormous airport control tower (which it also is), and a military command post for hundreds of combat aircraft. AWACS is yet another creature of the enormous increase in computing power, and the miniaturization of electronic components in the last thirty years. The AWACS's radar has a range of between 300 kilometer (for small aircraft flying close to the ground) to 600 kilometer (for large aircraft flying at high

altitudes). The AWACS can track several hundred enemy and friendly aircraft simultaneously. In practical terms, three AWACS were required in the air at all times during the Gulf War to handle all the Allied air activity. Each AWACS could stay up eleven hours at a time, or twenty-two hours with refueling and extra crew to man the equipment. The AWACS were a combination early warning radar (to detect enemy aircraft) and command center (to keep friendly aircraft sorted out and going in the right direction). The communications equipment on board allows information gathered by one AWACS to be quickly shared with other AWACS in the vicinity and at ground stations.

- OV-1—A slow, propeller-driven U.S. Army aircraft used to scout around the battlefield and provide photo reconnaissance for local army units. These are not armed scouts, but strictly observation aircraft, and therefore have to avoid enemy fire because they are unarmored and quite vulnerable. OV-1s usually operate behind friendly lines, or at least where enemy ground fire is not expected.
- E-8 J-STARS (Joint Surveillance and Target-Attack Radar System)—The "Joint" stems from the fact that it is both a U.S. Air Force and U.S. Army system. An Airborne Command-and-Control Aircraft. Not scheduled for regular troop use until 1993–94. But the two prototype models were undergoing testing at the time of the Iraqi invasion. These two developmental aircraft were quickly brought up to active-service status and sent from Europe (where they were being tested) to the Gulf. Unlike the AWACS, which handles only air operations, the J-STARS's primary job is tracking ground activity and was designed to better integrate air and ground operations by quickly locating targets for our aircraft and coordinating those attacks with friendly ground operations. The radar is built into the underbelly of a B-707 aircraft. The radar has two modes; wide area (showing a 25- by 20-kilometer area) and detailed (4,000 by 5,000 meters). Each E-8 had ten radar displays on board plus fifteen more on the ground with army headquarters units. All the radar displays could communicate with each other. The radar si-

multaneously supported both modes and several different chunks of terrain being watched. While an operator might have to wait a minute or two for an update on his screen, this was not a problem because of the relatively slow pace of ground operations. The radar could see out to several hundred kilometers, and each screenful of information could be saved and brought back later to compare to another view. In this manner, operators could track movement of ground units. Operators could also use the detail mode to pick out specific details of ground units (fortifications, buildings, vehicle deployments, etc.). For the first time in history, commanders were able to see and control mechanized forces over a wide area in real time. During the Persian Gulf War, J-STARS performed its designed mission well and speeded up the development process (and guaranteed the spending of billions of dollars on additional J-STARS aircraft). The two E-8s flew forty-nine missions during Desert Shield and (mostly) Desert Storm, each lasting about eleven hours.

- OV-10—These are slightly different aircraft from the OV-1, but provide the same functions for the air force and marines. Unlike the army OV-1, the air force and marines have lots of fixed-wing jet aircraft that they have to control on the battlefield. The slow-moving OV-10 can linger near ground units and play traffic cop for the faster jet-attack aircraft passing through on their bombing runs. They can be equipped with a laser designator for smart bombs dropped by other aircraft and carry some armament, mainly for self-defense (antiaircraft missiles and machine guns). It was found that using a faster F-16 for this job was more effective during rapidly developing situations and especially when attacking large enemy formations behind the fighting lines.
- RF-4 (Reconnaissance)—These are primary tactical reconnaissance aircraft sent in after air strikes to get photos. They can also do some electronic snooping. The RF-4 is essentially a stripped-down version of old F-4 Phantom fighter. Its navy equivalent is an F-14 outfitted with a recon pod (reconnaissance equipment contained a special detachable carrying container).
- TR-1 (Reconnaissance)—An updated version of the

1950s-era U-2, these aircraft are larger and more capable, flying high to get satellitelike photos of wide areas. They cover enemy territory when satellites are not around. A detachment of modernized U-2s were also brought in to aid the reconnaissance effort.

- Pioneer RPV (Remote Piloted Vehicles, or, as the Pentagon is currently calling them; UAV, or Unmanned Aerial Vehicles)—A small propeller-driven aircraft carrying either a TV or infrared (for night work) cameras and flown by a pilot on the ground by remote control (up to 150–200 km away). Israel has used RPVs for over a decade. The Pioneer is an adaptation of an Israeli RPV first used by the U.S. Navy on its battleships (to spot targets for the big sixteen-inch guns). Pioneer has since been adopted by the marines and the U.S. Army. Pioneer weighs only 420 pounds, has a top speed of 180 kilometers an hour and a usual operating range of 160 kilometers. It can stay in the air about four hours and flies as high as 15,000 feet (out of range of small antiaircraft weapons). It's very difficult to spot on a radar and usually cannot be heard on the ground. During the Gulf War, only about forty Pioneer RPVs were available for use. Two thirds were used by the ground force, mostly the marines. The Pioneers were used extensively, flying 533 sorties, each about three hours long. Twenty-six were damaged (twelve destroyed). Two were lost to enemy fire, the rest were lost to accidents, one from getting thrown out of control by the propwash of a C-130 transport. One ran out of fuel and crashed while shadowing a Scud launcher. Several Pioneers were sent deep into Iraq (well, over 100 kilometers deep) to spot aircraft on the ground and to look for Scuds. Principal uses were looking for enemy artillery positions and troop bunkers. The Iraqis soon got wise to this, and although the Pioneer's engine sounded like a chain saw, it couldn't be heard very well when the RPV was flying at altitudes of 2,000 feet or higher. When the Pioneer did come lower for a better look, the Iraqis got in their licks as best they could. The Pioneer's advantage was that it was under the control of the ground troops and could thus be sent up quickly when the local ground commander felt he needed to get a look at what was going on over enemy territory. In areas where there are a lot of enemy ground troops who could shoot at helicopters, the RPV can go in, look around, and survive. This proved a significant advantage against Iraqi ground units on the Saudi border. The loss rate per 100,000 sorties was high, plus an even higher noncombat loss rate. But then, no pilots were lost, and each Pioneer cost less than 10 percent as much as the cheapest manned reconnaissance aircraft.

- Pointer RPV—A shorter-range RPV under test by U.S. Army troops during the summer of 1990. Although the tests were successful, in the Gulf, it was not as effective as expected. This was due to a short range (one hour, up to five kilometers from the operator, 500–1,000 feet altitude), and lightweight (two 50-pound units, one being the aircraft, the other ground equipment). In the desert, the troops could often see up to five kilometers, and high winds made the Pointer difficult to control. However, had the fighting continued into built-up areas, the Pointer would have been very useful. The light weight had some advantages; it can be taken anywhere by the troops (even light infantry), and as the troops put it, give you a 200-foot-tall observer with binoculars. With only black-and-white TV cameras available in the Gulf, usefulness was limited in the desert. In the future, a color TV model is expected to solve that problem.

Several other RPVs were used in the Gulf, including British and French systems used for artillery fire control. One of the more interesting RPVs deployed was the little-known ExDrone. The marines used about fifty-five of these "Expendable Drones," and details of the systems operations have been kept secret. The system must have worked well, as another 110 were purchased after the war. The TV-equipped ExDrone was used extensively in scouting the way for the marine advance into Kuwait. The marines attributed their fast advance and low casualty rate to timely information from ExDrones.

Electronic Warfare Aircraft

These aircraft accompany the air strikes to detect and jam enemy electronics (particularly radars). Commonly called "Wild Weasels," they have most of their weapons removed and instead carry a number of pods filled with electronic gear to detect and deceive enemy electronics. The most important detectors are for enemy radars. The Wild Weasels are usually two-seat aircraft, and the "guy in the back" is the EWO (Electronics Warfare Officer), who uses dozens of instruments and displays to determine which type of enemy radars are directed at his aircraft, how far away the radars are, and how likely each radar is to have detected him. Aircraft radar signals can be picked up before they become effective, much the way a fuzz-buster detects police radars. Unlike fuzz-busters, Wild Weasels can send back signals to either blind or deceive enemy radars. If the air defenses appear too strong, the EWO can plot a less dangerous approach to the target. Often, the Wild Weasel directs attacks on the enemy radars and antiaircraft weapons. Wild Weasels work closely with the electronic-intelligence aircraft and the AWACS so that the air commanders have a view of the electronic shape of the battlefield, as well as a physical view of where the targets and attacking aircraft are.

- EF-111 Raven—This is the Wild Weasel of the F-111 swing-wing fighter-bomber, and is the top of the line of U.S. electronic-warfare aircraft. It carries several tons of electronic equipment and has fuel capacity to take several strike groups into and out of enemy-defended zones.
- EA-6 (Prowler)—A navy carrier–based Wild Weasel. It uses navy A-6 all-weather attack aircraft, but carries additional electronics in place of weapons. There are actually two versions. The one the marine air wings use is somewhat less capable but has some attack capability.
- F-4G—An older Air Force Wild Weasel (the original, actually), it is still in use, and these were the most numerous Wild Weasel aircraft. The F-4G is a variant of the Vietnam-era F-4 Phantom fighter.
- S-3B—A two-engine navy antisubmarine carrier aircraft that also served in an electronics-warfare role.

Tanker Aircraft

The long distances from Saudi air bases and U.S. carriers required airborne tankers in order to refuel bombers that would otherwise not be able to reach some targets or not get there with a very large bomb load. This works several ways. The most

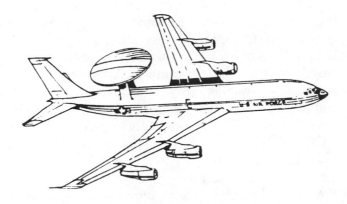

AWACS—Air control aircraft

obvious approach is to send an aircraft on a long-range mission without sufficient fuel to get back. Once the aircraft gets out of range of enemy air defenses, the tanker refuels it so that it can land safely. Another technique is based on the fact that aircraft can carry more weight than while taking off. Bombers take off with a maximum bomb load but with much less than their maximum fuel. Once airborne, these aircraft have their fuel tanks filled up by the tankers. The third use of tankers is particularly for fighters that may have used more fuel than expected in high-speed combat maneuvers (which burn much more fuel than just cruising along). Upon leaving enemy airspace, these fighters often do not have sufficient fuel left to get back to their airfields; thus they need the tankers to refuel from. However, the aircraft they must refuel consume huge quantities of fuel. For example, the maximum fuel load of the F-15 is six tons, the F-16 three tons, the A-6 seven tons, the F-18 five tons, and the F-111 fifteen tons. During the war, American tankers carried 270,000 tons of fuel aloft for in-flight refueling. About a third of the sorties in the air war required in-flight refueling (35,000 of them, averaging over seven tons of fuel for each refueling). Tankers flew about 10 percent of all sorties.

- KC-135 Tanker—The principal tanker in the U.S. Air Force, it is based on the Boeing 707 cargo jet. There are over 500 KC-135s in use worldwide. Although initially

built to support the B-52 bomber fleet, they have increasingly been used to support other aircraft types (including transports). The KC-135 carries sixty tons of fuel on board for refueling other aircraft.
- KC-10 Tanker—This is a more recent tanker model, based on the MD-10 commercial wide-body jet. With nearly fifty available, they can refuel three aircraft at once and also carry a considerable amount of cargo. They carry ninety tons of fuel on board for refueling other aircraft.
- KC-130—The USMC has about a dozen C-130s converted to tanker use. They carry twelve tons of fuel on board for refueling other aircraft.
- KA-6D—The U.S. Navy has some three dozen A-6 bombers converted to carrier-based tankers. These aircraft have limited refueling capability because they can carry little more than seven tons of fuel for transfer (or ten tons of fuel on board for refueling other aircraft if the refueling is done just after the KA-6 takes off from its carrier). Not many KA-6s were in the Gulf because the air force was better equipped to deal with the tanker situation.

NOTE: Most of the other Allied tankers used were various U.S. aircraft fitted out for air-to-air refueling.

Air-Superiority Aircraft

The primary job of such aircraft is to keep enemy fighters out of the air and to shoot down any other enemy aircraft. Once the enemy air force has been largely swept from the skies, there is still a need to escort strike groups. The reason is simple—you never know when you've got all the enemy fighters. This was the case in Iraq, where the Iraqi Air Force kept its head down, leaving the threat that some of its fighters could still get into the air and nail an unprotected Allied bomber. Most Allied air-superiority fighters could also operate as fighter-bombers, or have models of the basic fighter aircraft that specialize in bombing (as with the F-15E model of the F-15 series), although most of them could not operate on night missions or as accurately as the specialized bomber aircraft.

- F-5—An older, simpler fighter sold by the United States to nations without the technical resources to handle the more complex planes. Saudi Arabia still uses this aircraft, and the F-5 is still capable against older Russian models like the MiG-21. The F-5 is also used for reconnaissance by Saudi Arabia.
- F-14 (Tomcat)—These planes were not seen much over Iraq, as they are the navy's principal "fleet defense" aircraft. The swing-wing F-14 was used extensively over the Persian Gulf to insure that no Iraqi aircraft attacked U.S. and Allied ships. Armed with the long-range Phoenix missile, an F-14 may have had the first air-to-air kill with a Phoenix when an Iraqi aircraft was spotted far inland, but still within the range of the Phoenix.
- F-15 (Eagle)—The principal air-superiority aircraft of the U.S. and Saudi air forces. A relatively large, fast fighter that is well equipped with electronics. Long-range, heavy armament and all-weather capability made it the principal air-superiority aircraft of the war. The two-seat "E" version (F-15E "Strike Eagle") was one of the principal bombers because it still had the range and agility of the fighter version with the addition of the latest all-weather bombing equipment.
- F-16 (Falcon or "Killer Bee," when operating as a bomber)—This is the Air Force's "lightweight" fighter. Designed as a fighter for air-superiority missions, it can be used later for precision bombing with the addition of LANTIRN pods and for less precise bombing in daylight. In fact, F-16 pilots generally spend most of their training time practicing for bombing missions. The success of the F-16 in the bombing role (especially with the LANTIRN pods) has caused the air force to emphasize this role more and to consider canceling plans to arm and train F-16s to replace A-10s in the ground support role.
- F/A-18 (Hornet)—This navy carrier aircraft is similar to the F-16, but with two engines. While designed as a fighter, it is used more frequently as a bomber (the "A" means attack).
- Tornado—This European designed and built fighter-bomber is sort of an updated F-14 optimized for bombing.

It is available in four different versions, some for bombing, some for air superiority.
- Mirage 2000—This French interceptor also did some bombing.

Bomber Aircraft

Some aircraft are primarily bombers, with little air-to-air capability.

- A-4—An old U.S. Navy light bomber, it was used only by Kuwait in the Gulf.
- A-6 (Intruder)—The principal U.S. Navy carrier bomber. It has an all-weather and precision-bombing capability.
- F-117A "Stealth fighter" (also known as "Nighthawk," "Black Jet," "Wobblin Goblin," "117" or "F-117")—The F-117A is actually a light bomber with minimal air-to-air capability, but has a state-of-the-art fire-control system that enables it to deliver laser-guided bombs plus all-weather navigation capability. At a cost of $100 million each, the F-117As earned their keep by leading the first strikes against the Iraqi radar and antiaircraft systems. They also did most of the bombing over Baghdad and other targets deep inside Iraq. With the F-117A operating alone and at night, the Iraqis didn't know it was there until the bombs exploded. By then the F-117 was out of range for any antiaircraft guns firing blindly into the night. As a result, no F-117 was hit during the campaign. It was designed to go out by itself, using its Stealth design to get it past enemy radars, and use the very accurate GBUs. An attack by non-Stealth–type bombers would still require as many as two support aircraft (fighter escorts, electronic warfare, tankers) for each bomber. The F-117 was also a marvel of automation, as it had only one crewman, unlike most other ground-attack aircraft, which carry two (the second one to take care of the various weapons systems). With the F-117A operating at night and largely immune to enemy detection (and subsequent attempts to shoot it down), the pilot could concentrate on precision bombing. The F-117 has a complex, automated and highly accurate navigation system that gets it to its

target within seconds of whatever time was previously selected. Because of its "stealth" attributes, it can fly closer
to targets (only at night) than conventional aircraft. Not
only is the F-117 difficult to spot on radar, but its jet engines are quieter. Thus the first inkling that the F-117 is
in the area is when the bomb explodes. The F-117 uses
two infrared radars (which display objects—on a black-
and-white screen in front of the pilot—in terms of how
much heat those objects are giving off). The forward-fac-
ing infrared radar enables the pilot to get the aircraft
properly lined up with the target and to activate the fire-
control computer, which will do more and more of the
aiming and flying as the F-117 gets closer to the target.
When passing over the target, a second infrared radar under the F-117 automatically picks up the target, and
switches on the laser designator for a few seconds before
the glide bomb hits the target, in order to achieve the
pinpoint accuracy you saw on the VCR tapes films of the
infrared radar display in the cockpit. A third of the smart
munitions used in the war were dropped by F-117As, with
over 80 percent destroying their targets. Most of the time,
F-117As carried one of three types of bombs. GBU-10s,
which are Mk 84 two-thousand-pound bombs fitted with
Paveway laser guidance; GBU-10I and GBU-27, which
are I-2000 penetrating bombs with similar laser guidance;
and GBU-12 which are Mk 82 five-hundred-pound laser-
guided bombs. The F-117A weapons bay can only hold
two 2,000-pound bombs, or four 500-pound bombs. No
weapons are slung underneath the F-117, everything must
be stored inside to maintain the Stealth capability.
• B-52 (BUFF, or "Big Ugly Fat Feller"; also called the
  Stratofortress)—This U.S. Air Force heavy bomber is
  generally used for carpet bombing, although it was intended to be used for dropping guided missiles, or even
  laser-guided bombs. This last option was ready to be used
  when the war ended. By then it had been discovered that
  a few aircraft with laser designators acting as "spotters"
  could guide in scores of bombs in one sortie. Normally,
  one B-52 carries either fifty-one 500-pound iron bombs or
  eighteen 2,000-pound iron bombs, which are just dropped
  in a freefall pattern. Using an aircraft below with a laser

designator, a B-52 can carry nearly the same load of laser-guided bombs and have each bomb hit a target precisely (with over 80 percent accuracy). All the current B-52s are at least thirty years old; however, to keep the aircraft operational, the airframes have been rebuilt bit by bit as needed and the engines replaced as they wore out. In the last twenty years, the aircraft have been given the most effective fire-control systems available in any aircraft as well as the most effective ECM (Electronic Countermeasures) system in existence. During Desert Storm, there were only about sixty-five B-52s available for conventional bombing (as the rest are configured for delivering nuclear cruise missiles). Nonetheless, B-52s dropped about 30 percent of all the bomb tonnage during the war. Nearly all were dropped against area targets. The damage was substantial and the psychological effect even more so.

- Jaguar—1960s-era bomber used by the French and British forces, now equipped with smart-bomb capabilities and stand-off weapons.
- Buccaneer—Older bomber used by British forces now used as a laser-targeting designator aircraft.

Ground Support

While all bombers can be used to attack enemy ground forces operating close to friendly troops, some bombers are especially designed for such precision work. These ground-support aircraft are slower, thus able to more accurately sort out the enemy and friendly forces. Some of these aircraft are also built with more robust protection from ground fire.

- AV-8B (Harrier)—A British design used by American Marines, the A-8 can take off like a helicopter and then operate like a fixed-wing bomber.
- A-10 (Thunderbolt II or "Warthog")—A U.S. Air Force ground-attack aircraft based on 1970s technology, but well designed for its task. It has 30-mm GAU automatic cannon with special armor-piercing shells that can penetrate the thin top armor of any tank. The A-10, which also uses guided bombs, was so successful that the air force may not to phase the aircraft out of its inventory (as was

planned before the Kuwait War). What may be phased out is the plan to convert F-16 fighters to perform the A-10 role. The F-16 was successful in its bombing mission but will do more of that using smart bombs. The big advantage of the A-10 in ground-support missions, amply demonstrated in the Gulf, was its ability to get down low, take a lot of punishment, and hang around long enough to find targets.

- AH-1S (Cobra)—The original helicopter gunship, it is still in use with U.S. forces although it is being replaced by the AH-64.
- AH-1W (Sea Cobra, or "Whiskey")—The original version of U.S. attack helicopter customized for USMC use.
- AH-64 (Apache)—The U.S. Army's primary attack helicopter. Over 260 used in the war, and organized into battalions of eighteen or independent companies of six. The Apache normally operates very low (fifty feet or so) and thus is referred to as a "flying tank." Though resistant to a lot of ground fire, it is not nearly as bullet-proof as the lightest armored fighting vehicles. It has a 30-mm automatic cannon, rockets, and Hellfire antitank missiles. A FLIR–based (infrared, "heat-sensing") fire-control system, similar in capabilities to those used in the most advanced air-force attack aircraft. It can spot targets up to 12,000 meters away, and usually launches Hellfire missiles at 3,000–6,000 meters from target. The official "Kill" count for the AH-64 Apache is 500 tanks, 120 armored fighting vehicles, 10 radar sites, 10 helicopters, 10 fixed-wing aircraft, and 4,500 prisoners. No air-to-air kills. This does not include the trucks and bunkers engaged and destroyed by the chopper. The AH-64 also has a unique "look and shoot" helmet for firing the cannon. As the pilot moves his head, the gun automatically moves to fire and hit whatever is in the helmet's cross hairs. Helmet was found to operate better if eyeglass-wearing pilots used contact lenses instead. So 200 such pilots were issued contact lenses. The AH-64 was a more difficult helicopter to maintain than the older AH-1 (the marines used the AH-1W). AH-64s were able to fly thirty-seven hours a month, while the Marines were able to keep their older AH-1Ws up for ninety hours a month. The AH-64 was

much more capable at night, and during the day. But
there was a price to be paid in terms of support required.
- AC-130 (Spectre)—Although fewer than ten of these
  were deployed to the Gulf, the AC-130 is a combat version of the C-130 transport containing a variety of sensors
  and weapons (e.g. automatic cannon).
- OH-58 (Kiowa)—A small, light helicopter used as a
  scout. The OH-58 is armed, but mainly for self-defense:
  Its primary purpose is to find ground targets for the more
  heavily armed gunships (AH-1 and AH-64). OH-58D is
  the AHIP (improved) version.

Transports

The combat aircraft were able to fly to Saudi Arabia, but there
was not much they could do once they arrived without their
ground-support crews and equipment. The fact is that each aircraft requires the constant services of several dozen technicians
and tons of support equipment. Each sortie consumes hundreds
of pounds of spare parts and whatever munitions are expended.
(Even most of the fuel had to be shipped in for, although Saudi
Arabia had plenty of oil on hand, it does not have the refining
capacity to produce the million-plus tons of fuel needed for all
the aircraft involved.) Thus, to get the combat aircraft operational quickly, the support people and their equipment had to
come by air. The air transports played a vital role in the campaign by getting critical items to the Gulf quickly. In the beginning, it was material to keep the combat aircraft combat-ready.
Later on, it was to bring in vital equipment (electronics, spares,
etc.) that were needed fast: As the war progressed, most of the
tonnage for fighting the air and land campaigns came by ship,
but the air transports were always there to take care of emergencies.

During the first month of Desert Shield, the United States
flew in 63,000 tons of cargo. This material came an average of
7,500 miles. Because of the large airlift capability built up over
the years to support a major war in Europe, the United States
was never lacking in airlift capacity to support the Gulf operation. Indeed, less than half of the United States' military airlift
capacity was used throughout the operation as the major limitation in Saudi Arabia was the availability of airports to handle

the large transport aircraft. Only transports that operated within the area had their sorties counted against the theater total. C-130s were the most widely used in this sense, flying over 7,000 sorties.

- C-5—Built, in part, so that it could fly tanks, the C-5 was never able to do this efficiently. What it could do was move large quantities of military material, especially odd-shaped vehicles. Like most military transports, the C-5 is built like a flying garage, with large doors to allow vehicles to be driven in and out. The C-5 was the mover of more military material than any other transport aircraft. Ninety percent of our C-5 fleet was used in the Gulf, operating an average of 10.3 hours a day.
- C-141—Although carrying much less than the C-5, more than twice as many C-141s are available. The C-5 and the C-141 are the only long-range military transports, able to carry large loads long distances without landing (partially due to in-flight refueling capability). Eighty percent of America's C-141s were used in the Gulf, operating an average of 11.9 hours a day.
- C-130—This is the workhorse battlefield cargo carrier. Because it is prop and not jet propelled, it can go slower and land in places jets cannot manage. Saudi Arabia is a large place, and the nearly 200 C-130s sent over there operated 4.7 hours a day, with two or more flights a day the norm. Other coalition forces also supplied nearly 100 additional C-130's.
- C-12—A military version of a two-engine civilian aircraft, used by the air force and army as an airborne pick-up truck, the C-12 moves small numbers of personnel or cargo around the battlefield.
- C-17—Just for reference, this is the next-generation heavy military transport, likely to replace both the C-5 and C-141.
- B-747—The Boeing 747 jumbo jet was drafted in large numbers to assist in the movement of troops and equipment. The 747 comes in several models, including freighters with large doors to allow bulky equipment to be loaded. Most of the troops were flown over, and most of them flew in 747s.

- CH-46—Cargo helicopter used by the marines, mostly for carrying assault troops into battle-zone landing areas. It operates off helicopter carriers.
- CH-47 (Chinook)—A cargo helicopter used extensively by the army, it is the principal mover of troops and cargo within the battle area.
- CH-53D—This is similar in use to the CH-46.
- CH-53E—This is a much upgraded model of the older CH-53D.
- UH-1—The first cargo helicopter widely used on the battlefield (in Vietnam), the UH-1 is still widely used by American forces.
- UH-60—The replacement for the UH-1, this transport has a longer range, a larger carrying capacity, and is more sturdily constructed.

NOTE: There also several dozen special-operations helicopters, designated with an *M,* as in MH-47, MH-53, and MH-60. Some special-operations aviation units employed the Hughes M-500, a highly modernized version of the famous "LOACH" (Light Observation Helicopter, also LOH) of the Vietnam era. These were basically the non-*M* versions with additional electronic equipment, weapons, and other gear added. The helicopter rotor blades are also "silenced." The crews are specially (and intensively) trained for missions like landing Special Forces teams on the outskirts of Baghdad at night without being detected. Many (if not most) of the helicopters lost in the Gulf were the *M* series. You didn't hear much about these helicopters. You weren't supposed to.

Search and Rescue

The U.S. Air Force has several aircraft, mainly helicopters, used in Search and Rescue (SAR) missions to recover pilots who have to bail out. For many years, up until 1989, the air force had given up its rescue function to the army. In the last two years, the air force has been rebuilding its own rescue capability, primarily using its own special forces units and their *M* series helicopters. In the Gulf, if the pilot has to be recovered in enemy territory, whatever aircraft are available from the other services are also employed, including combat aircraft to keep the enemy away from the downed pilots. In the Gulf, army combat and transport helicopters were also used in these rescue efforts, along with Special Forces teams and their specialized heli-copters.

Aircraft Weapons

Aircraft weapons range from the primitive ("iron bombs") to the exotic (most of the guided missiles). These weapons formed a triad with the aircraft and their pilots to produce the stunning aerial victory in the Gulf.

Air-to-Ground Weapons

- BLU (Iron bombs)—Referred to by the air force as BLU (Bomb Live Unit), these are usually metal casings filled with explosive, but some of them are filled with poison chemicals, incendiary chemicals, smoke-producing chemi-cals, land mines, or whatever. There are over a hundred BLU types (such as BLU-34, for a 3,000-pound bomb filled with explosive). The most commond BLUs used were those using just explosives, largely the 500-, 1,000-, and 2,000-pound variety. The ultimate iron bomb used was the "Daisy Cutter" (BLU-82) 15,000-pound bomb. Eleven used, usually dropped in pairs from 15,000–18,000 feet from a specially equipped C-130. Landed within twenty meters of aim point, exploded above ground. Found to kill all unprotected troops within 4,000 meters of explosion. Three were dropped on Failaka Island, off the Kuwait coast. The others were used to clear dense minefields in front of U.S. Marines and British troops in preparation for the penetration of Iraqi fortified lines.
- GBU (Glide Bomb Units)—These are BLUs with a guid-ance unit attached. The guidance system consists of a sen-sor and computer attached to the front of the bomb and a set of fins attached to the rear of the bomb. The air-force Paveway system has a sensor that looks for reflected laser light and uses the computer and fins to guide the bomb toward the laser light, and the air-force GBU-15 system uses TV cameras in the bombs. The GBUs turned out to be the most successful weapon of the war. This was a bonus from the efficient suppression of the Iraqi air

defenses. Normally, GBUs are dangerous to use because they only have an average range of five to nine kilometers, thus bringing the bomber aircraft fairly close to the target. If the target is heavily defended, the aircraft is put at great risk. In the Gulf, this was less of a problem and made the GBU a great success. Some of these bombs were spectacularly effective. The Bunker Penetration Bomb (GBU-27), consisted of 500 pounds of explosive inside a 1,500-pound steel case shaped to penetrate reinforced concrete structures of six feet or more before exploding. The fuse is in the tail, not the nose. The GBU-27s were designed specifically for the F-117As and had not been adapted for any other aircraft. Although the explosive load is relatively small, it does relatively more damage within the restricted confines of a bunker. During the war, the 19-foot-long, 4,700-pound GBU-28 was developed for the F-111. Thirty were delivered, and two were actually used (two others were used in testing). During testing, the GBU-28 penetrated over 100 feet into the earth during one test and twenty-two feet of concrete in another. Two more bombs were used for testing after the war. The remaining twenty-four will stay in the air-force inventory. Each bomb cost $335,000 to make. The cost was kept low because discarded barrels from army eight-inch guns were used as the bomb body. A specially hardened front end was attached, and the bomb was filled with 650 pounds of explosive. Normally, producing such a new weapon takes at least two years. In this case, the elapsed time was six weeks.

• CBU (Cluster Bomb Unit)—A bomb that carries several dozen or several hundred smaller bombs (bomblets). The bomblets are usually either antipersonnel (hand-grenadelike devices to injure troops) or antitank (armor-penetrating devices to penetrate the thinner top armor of armored vehicles), or mines (antipersonnel small devices that will mangle or blow off a person's foot, or antitank, with a large enough charge to destroy an armored vehicle's tracks or blow the wheel off a track). Some of the bomblets would have timers on them so they would self-destruct after a while to allow friendly troops to enter the area. The most common CBU was the CEM (Combined

Effects Munitions), a 1,000-pound bomb carrying 202 2.4-pound bomblets that could penetrate four inches of armor, burn things down, or wound troops in the area. CBUs were not as effective as expected, particularly the mines, because the enemy troops could see the mines and would often effectively take cover when ordinary bomblets were being dropped. Several American troops were injured after the cease-fire by cluster bomblets that had not automatically deactivated.

- Maverick (AGM-65)—A longer-range, laser-guided weapon (up to twenty-four kilometers) and weighing nearly 500 pounds, the Maverick is effective against vehicles (with a 125-pound armor-piercing warhead) or field fortifications (300-pound high-explosive warhead). Essentially a fixed-wing equivalent of the helicopter-fired Hellfire, it is five times heavier and has three times the range. The Maverick can be fitted with three different nose-cone seekers: TV guidance, laser guidance, or infrared. The infrared version can display what its sensor sees on a TV set in the A-10 cockpit, thus turning the A-10 into a crude, but effective, night bomber. Over 50,000 Mavericks have been built, many for foreign customers.

- SLAM (AGM-84E)—This was a rather elaborate guided missile (based on the Harpoon antiship missile) that was just being introduced by the United States Navy when the Gulf War broke out. Its range is about ninety kilometers. Basically, it's a guided missile that is guided, in its final approach, by a human operator viewing what's in front of the missile via a television camera inside the front portion of the missile. Thus the SLAM can be (and was) guided through specific windows in buildings in order to take out very specific targets. As this weapon was still under development when the war broke out, less than a hundred were available and not all were used. Those that were used worked well.

- TALD (Tactical Air Launched Decoy)—This is a U.S. Navy glider system, carried by aircraft like a 500-pound bomb. When launched, this 400-pound glider deploys folding wings and flies ahead (at 500–600 mph) for four to five minutes. Usually carried by the lead aircraft of a strike package, the TALDs look like full-size attack aircraft on enemy radars, causing the radars to stay on to assist the firing of guns and missiles. This in turn exposes the location of enemy defenses to Wild Weasel aircraft, which can then launch HARMs against enemy radars and cluster bombs against missile sites. In at least one instance, Iraqi interceptors were seen searching for a group of TALDs. Many of the U.S. aircraft the Iraqis claimed to have "shot down" were probably TALDs. Over 130 were used during the first three days of the air war, but after that the Iraqi air defenses were so shattered that the remaining 300 TALDs available were not needed. Until the successful navy use of the system in the Gulf, the air force was not much interested in the concept, even though the TALD was derived from a similar Israeli system used with great success against Syria in 1982. The air force felt that its Stealth aircraft would eliminate the need for TALDs. The air force has since changed its mind and is working on a similar system. TALDs cost about $18,000 each; they can be programmed and can drop chaff to further confuse enemy radar.

• Hellfire (AGM-114A)—This is an antitank guided missile used by helicopters (AH-1 and AH-64). Over 4,000 Hellfires were used, with over 80 percent accuracy, resulting in over 3,000 tanks, artillery, vehicles of all types, and bunkers destroyed. The firing helicopter (or another aircraft or someone on the ground) aims a laser at the target, and the Hellfire homes in on the reflected laser light. With an average range of up to 6,000 meters, the Hellfire allowed the helicopters to attack Iraqi tanks outside the range of most antiaircraft weapons. The desert is the perfect place to do this, for there are few places for the tanks to hide. In more built-up, or forested, areas, it's common for the helicopters to be shot down by enemy armored vehicles that are hidden from view. AH-64 can carry up to sixteen 95-pound Hellfire missiles. The Hellfire missile made its combat debut in the Gulf. Its extreme range is 8,000 meters, and hits were often made at that range, and a little beyond. It's normal for the official specifications to be somewhat short of what the weapon can actually do. It's safer for whoever built the weapon to hear that it per-

formed better than it was supposed to than the other way
around.

- TOW—An antitank missile that was used on helicopters
  until replaced by the Hellfire. The marines still used some
  TOWs on their AH-1W helicopters. Most of the 3,000
  TOW antitank missiles that were fired during the Gulf
  War were fired from the 1,600 Bradley IFV (Infantry
  Fighting Vehicles) that accompanied the M1 tanks into
  combat. Many were used to destroy Iraqi bunkers. If a
  bunker showed no sign of life, the Bradley would fire a
  few rounds from its 25-mm cannon at it. If there were
  sparks, the bunker probably had an armored vehicle in it
  and a TOW was used to destroy the Iraqi vehicle in the
  bunker. In most cases, the M1's 120-mm gun was able to
  take care of any targets nearly up to the maximum range
  of the TOW (3,750 meters), the gun getting effective hits
  at up to 3,500 meters.

Over 15,000 guided missiles were used in the war
against ground targets. This was the first time so many of
these weapons were used in such a short period of time
and under such difficult operational conditions. Included
were 5,500 Mavericks, plus over 4,000 Hellfires, over
3,000 TOWs, and sundry more expensive items (including
guided bombs). More than two thirds of these missiles hit
and destroyed what they were aimed at. Because of their
accuracy, long range (which prevented enemy return fire),
and the large number of missiles available, Iraq's 10,000
tanks, armored vehicles, and artillery in Kuwait were
largely destroyed. What was left was vastly outnumbered
by the ground forces, who handily cleared out the survivors and won an unprecedented quick and low cost (to
our side) victory.

Air-to-Air Weapons

These weapons did not get much of a workout in the Persian
Gulf because the Iraqi Air Force largely stayed on the ground.

- Sidewinder air-to-air missile—This is the principal short-
  range air-to-air weapon in the USAF (and most Allied air
  forces). It accounted for eleven of the thirty-nine air-to-

air kills. The 1990 version of this missile is much more capable than the original 1956 design that was widely used in Vietnam. It is 9.5 feet long, weighs only eighty-seven pounds (with a twenty-one-pound warhead), and has a range of eighteen kilometers. Its guidance system takes it toward the closest heat source, which is usually the exhaust of enemy jets. But the current version's heat sensor is capable of picking up the heat from an enemy jet at any angle. Nearly 200,000 Sidewinders have been built in the last thirty-five years.

- Sparrow air-to-air missile—The principal long-range air-to-air missile in the USAF and (most Allied air forces), it accounted for twenty-four of the forty air-to-air kills. The first version (1958) developed a reputation for poor reliability and accuracy; the current version is a much smoother article. Aircraft require a rather powerful radar and fire-control system in order to use the Sparrow. The missile weighs 500 pounds (with its own built-in radar and a 90-pound warhead), is twelve feet long, and has a range of fifty kilometers. It is usually fired at aircraft the pilot cannot see, but has instead spotted on his radar (at ranges of 100-plus kilometers). This has always made pilots nervous that they might shoot down one of their own planes. As the Sparrow has become more reliable in the last thirty years, so have the electronic safeguards and pilots' confidence that they will be able to tell friend from foe electronically. The Sparrow is particularly good at night, when you can't see much anyway and have to use the radar for everything. After being fired, the Sparrow is guided part of the way by the radar of the aircraft that fired it, and makes its terminal approach using its own small short-range radar.

- Phoenix air-to-air missile—Used only by the navy's F-14, this is the longest range air-to-air missile in the world (200 kilometers). It weighs 990 pounds (including a 135-pound warhead and small radar) and is thirteen feet long. The fire-control radar in the F-14 is a complex piece of work, designed to spot and hit cruise missiles several hundred kilometers distant. The F-14/Phoenix combination was designed primarily to defend the fleet against Russian bombers and cruise missiles and served the same purpose in the

Persian Gulf against Iraqi aircraft and Chinese- or French-built missiles.

- Automatic cannon—Most American aircraft carry an automatic 20-mm cannon (M-61 model). These are currently rarely used in air-to-air combat, mainly because air-to-air missiles have got much more effective and reliable. Aircraft fire-control systems (radars and computers) are also more efficient. Cannon had been removed from many fighters just before the Vietnam War for the same reasons. However, that decision proved to be unrealistically optimistic. During the Vietnam War, most fighters got their cannon back and most enemy aircraft brought down were with cannon. Although the Gulf War saw missiles bring down most of the air-to-air kills, it's unlikely that most pilots are willing to part with their cannon just yet—until the recently confirmed reliability of missiles has time to sink in.

AIRCRAFT CHARACTERISTICS

The air war was the crucial component of the Gulf combat, and the aircraft were the tools that did the work. This section gives a concise description of the principal aircraft involved.

ELECTRONIC WARFARE

	Weight (tons)	Range (kilometers)	Max Load
EF-111	44	2,000	10
EF-6	30	1,000	8
EF-4	28	1,200	7

Weight—maximum weight of aircraft on takeoff. *Range*—average operating range, in kilometers. Can be extended (doubled, or more) by carrying extra fuel tanks or in air refueling. *Maximum Load*–in tons. Several tons are electronics, and they also often carry antiradar missiles and other weapons.

AIR SUPERIORITY

	Weight (tons)	Range (kilometers)	Load (tons)	Thrust (ratio)	Max Speed	Year Introduced
F-5	11	1,000	3	1,250	1,840	1972

F-14	34	1,000	6	1,522	2,760	1970
F-15	31	1,500	10	2,488	2,875	1977
F-16	17	900	6	2,871	2,300	1980
F-18	22	1,000	7	2,238	2,070	1982
Tornado	27	1,400	7	1,616	2,300	1980

Weight in tons—maximum takeoff weight of aircraft in tons. *Range in kilometers*—average operational range, allowing sufficient fuel to go the range indicated, engage in combat, and return. Can go about three times the indicated range if just moving from one base to another. *Load*—maximum load, in tons, of munitions (bombs, missiles, cannon shells). *Thrust Ratio*—the higher it is, the more maneuverable the aircraft is. *Maximum speed,* in kilometers per hour, is another indicator of combat capability. *Year Introduced*—how old the technology on the aircraft is. Most aircraft are, however, kept up to date with constant overhauls.

GROUND ATTACK

	Weight (tons)	Range (kilometers)	Load (tons)	Thrust (ratio)	Max Speed	Year Introduced
A-4	20	1,500	3	571	1,058	1960
A-6	27	750	8	984	1,208	1963
F-117A	25	700	5	1,615	1,200	1985
B-52	225	16,000	20	688	1,035	1955
Tomahawk	1.5	2,500	.5	400	880	1983

Weight in tons—maximum takeoff weight of aircraft in tons. *Range in kilometers*—average operational range, allowing sufficient fuel to go the range indicated, engage in combat, and return. Can go about three times the indicated range if just moving from one base to another. *Load*—maximum load, in tons, of munitions (bombs, missiles, cannon shells). *Thrust Ratio*—the higher it is, the more maneuverable the aircraft is. Maximum speed, in kilometers per hour, is another indicator of combat capability. *Year Introduced*—how old the technology on the aircraft is. Most aircraft are, however, kept up to date with constant overhauls.

GROUND SUPPORT

	Weight (tons)	Range (kilometers)	Load (tons)	Thrust (ratio)	Max Speed	Year Introduced
AV-8B	14	800	4	2,192	1,035	1969
A-10	23	500	7	783	644	1977
AH-1S	5	180	1.6	NA	225	1975

AH-1W	7	200	2	NA	250	1982
AH-64	9.5	300	2	NA	300	1985
AC-130	77	1,000	8	NA	800	1982
OH-58	1.4	160	.4	NA	220	1969

Weight in tons—maximum takeoff weight of aircraft in tons. *Range in kilometers*—average operational range, allowing sufficient fuel to go the range indicated, engage in combat, and return. Can go about three times the indicated range if just moving from one base to another. *Load*—maximum load, in tons, of munitions (bombs, missiles, cannon shells). *Thrust Ratio*—the higher it is, the more maneuverable the aircraft is. Maximum speed, in kilometers per hour, is another indicator of combat capability. *Year Introduced*—how old the technology on the aircraft is. Most aircraft are, however, kept up to date with constant overhauls.

TRANSPORTS

	Cargo	Aircraft Weight	Range	Airfield Length	In Use
C-5	120	151	4,800	2,600	96
C-141	41	66	6,400	1,000	240
C-130	34	33	4,600	1,100	540
C-17	59	117	5,200	1,000	2
B-747	75	177	9,000	3,200	300
CH-46	3	10	340	10	280
CH-47	10	23	140	10	430
CH-53D	9	21	160	10	280
CH-53E	16	33	280	10	80
UH-1	1	4	160	10	3,000
UH-60	3	9	200	10	1,200

Cargo—maximum tons of cargo carried. Usually, only two-thirds or half that weight is carried because of bulky cargo (vehicles). *Weight*—maximum takeoff weight of aircraft. When taking off with maximum cargo, less fuel is carried, and tanker aircraft are used to top off the fuel tanks. *Range*—in kilometers, the farthest the aircraft can go on one load of fuel. The C-5, C-141, and C-17 can be refueled in flight. The other aircraft can go a third or more farther if they carry less cargo. *Airfield Length*—in meters, what is needed to land. Aircraft requiring shorter landing fields have more landing areas available to them. *In Use*—number of aircraft type available to American forces.

Ground Attack Fire-Control Systems

The crucial factor in the effectiveness of ground-attack weapons is the fire-control system of the aircraft. During the last fifty years, fire-control systems have got much more accurate. From

World War II accuracies of under 5 percent (of bombs dropped hitting their target), the best ground-attack systems can now average over 80 percent accuracy.

Most modern bombing aircraft have, at minimum, a fire-control system that calculates when the pilot should drop his bombs in order to have the best chance of obtaining a hit. These systems use a computer, a sighting device, and the aircraft's navigational system to calculate when the target the pilot has sighted can most likely be hit by dropping a bomb. These systems do not take into account wind or other climate considerations, nor do they correct for any last-second bouncing around the aircraft will do. Some fire-control systems require the pilot to look down in the cockpit at a display of the upcoming target; others (more expensive systems) use a "head-up display" of target information projected onto a see-through display in the front portion of the canopy. The target comes into view of the fire-control system when the aircraft is less than a minute from the point at which the bombs are released. The pilot maneuvers his aircraft so that the target shows up on the fire-control display and when the cross hairs (or "dot") are on the target ("the target is pickled"), the bomb is released. The pilot usually only has ten to twenty seconds to pickle the target and release the bomb. In aircraft with only one crew member (the pilot) this absorbs his attention for several crucial seconds, a long enough time to be shot at by an enemy missile, aircraft, or ground-based artillery. It's also enough time for the low-flying bomber to fly into the ground. In any event, these systems, at best, average 10–40 percent accuracy for individual bombs. A lot depends on the target. As pilots can usually drop an iron bomb within thirty to fifty feet of the target, large targets (like buildings) can usually be hit. Anything smaller is more likely to be missed, or only damaged.

The preferred way to drop iron bombs effectively is in groups against targets covering a large area. Even a small aircraft like the F-16 can carry two 2,000-pound bombs or, frequently, four or six 500-pound bombs. Built-up areas would be a typical target, such as a military maintenance facility or air base. The fire-control system in the B-52 is accurate enough to put a bomb within two meters of its target for every 1,000 feet of aircraft altitude. For that reason, B-52s practice bombing at low levels, often 1,000 feet or less. To avoid ground fire, the B-52s have to fly at 10,000–15,000 feet, which means an individual bomb may miss the target by ten to fifteen meters. But the B-52 drops several dozen bombs at once and usually does so in a formation of three B-52s. The result is the carpet bombing that trashed spread-out Iraqi bases and terrorized troops on the ground.

Guided Bombs

The most accurate (and expensive, at a cost of several million dollars per aircraft) systems rely on the pilot (or the guy in the backseat; the weapons officer) guiding the bomb or missile to its target. There are two methods for precision guidance for bombs, a laser designator or a TV camera. Some aircraft, like the F-117A, have other sensors to spot the target initially. Most of the time, a target is found with nothing more high tech than human eyesight, often assisted by high-powered binoculars.

- Laser Bombs—The most successful method has been the laser designator. It is a simple system consisting of two components. In the aircraft (or on the ground), there is a laser that is pointed at the target. The laser light reflects off the target, and the missile or bomb has a laser light–seeker in its nose cone that detects the laser light and homes in on it. The laser designator often has an optical system built in that allows the operator to see at night or even through smoke and haze. The major advantage of this system is that it is simple. The bomb, once released, does not need to communicate with the aircraft, so it cannot be jammed by electronic means. The laser designator can be in the aircraft that dropped the bomb, another aircraft, or on the ground. Laser bombs were found to be most successful when one aircraft did most of the laser work while others simply came in and released their bombs as needed. If the target is heavily defended and the aircraft with the laser designator cannot afford to hang around until the bomb hits the designated target, he can LAL (Launch And Leave) by telling the bomb to proceed on the course where it last saw the laser light reflected. This works reasonably well for stationary targets (there is still some loss of accuracy) but is ineffective against moving targets. The Gulf War was the first time for these mature weapons to strut their stuff, and this they did to great and convincing effect. The catch was, because not everyone was sold on laser bombing, there were not a lot of laser-equipped bombers available. The navy also had very few laser-guided bombs in stock. Only about 300 bombers had laser-bombing equipment. These included navy A-6s, air force F-117As, F-111s, and twenty sets of LANTIRN laser-targeting pods that could be mounted on F-15Es (usually) or F-16s (sometimes). Thus, only about 200 aircraft with laser-bombing capability were available on any given day. These aircraft dropped about 200 laser-guided bombs every twenty-four hours during the forty-two-day war. These bombs had an 80–90 percent hit rate. This was in spite of the unexpected change in tactics during the air war. Throughout the 1980s, U.S. bombers had been preparing and training to deliver their bombs from low altitudes (often under 1,000 feet). In the Gulf, pilots quickly discovered two things. First, plain old flak (gun and cannon fire from the ground) was still prolific and deadly. Second, the laser-bombing systems were accurate enough to be used at higher altitudes (over 12,000 feet, out of flak range). Some of the fire-control systems on aircraft were not really adaptable to this higher-altitude bombing, but the pilots made manual adjustments, and the demolition of Iraqi forces continued safely from the higher altitudes. The laser bombers flew over 9,000 sorties and generally carried several bombs, so many of the bombs dropped were not laser-guided. Some were self-guided Mavericks (nearly 6,000 of these were used, each costing over $70,000), although the Maverick was also popular with nonlaser-equipped bombers. The fire-control and navigation systems on the laser bombers were, as one would expect, top-of-the-line, and these aircraft were also quite accurate in dropping unguided bombs, day or night. Against large targets, such as warehouse complexes or parked vehicles, this was about as effective as laser-guided weapons anyway. There was a shortage of laser-guided bombs, but not a serious one. There were so many targets that bombers usually ran out of bombs before they ran out of fuel.

• TV Guidance—This is a more elaborate system that has

a TV camera in the nose cone of the bomb and an electronic link between the bomb and the launching aircraft.
The bomb is released so that it glides in the general direction of the target. The weapons officer sees what's in front
of the bomb on a TV screen and uses controls to move a
cross-hair symbol over the point he wants the bomb to
hit. The bomb will continually head for wherever the
cross hairs are set. The cross hairs are usually placed as
accurately as possible on the target and then "locked,"
meaning the weapons officer doesn't have to constantly
fiddle with the controls while being bounced around in the
back of the aircraft. The fire-control system memorizes
the televised shape of the area the cross hairs are covering
and tries to maintain its position over that area. If the
radio link with the bomb is momentarily lost, the weapons
officer may still be able to get the cross hairs on the target
again.
- Infrared Guidance—This is a weapon that guides itself,
  without the help of a weapons officer, toward the warmest
  object on the ground. Similar technology to that used in
  infrared air-to-air missiles that chase after a jet-engine exhaust, infrared technology has a more difficult time
  against ground targets because ground vehicles provide
  less heat to home in on, and an already destroyed (and
  burning) enemy vehicle is more likely to attract the infrared homing system than a still operational target. More
  powerful microcomputers and more efficient infrared
  homing devices have solved a lot of these problems. Similar guidance systems rely on the image of the target in
  terms of light and darkness and, of course, we end up
  with TV guidance. But to make this type of guidance automatic, it has to be kept simple. Even the most powerful
  computers cannot keep track of an image the human eye
  can easily track. That's why heat (infrared) detection has
  been used so much in the last forty years. Once the infrared sensor (think of it as a "microphone" that is "listening" for heat) detects a heat source and the pilot
  confirms that this heat source is the one the missile should
  head for, the infrared sensor can guide the missile the rest
  of the way without human intervention. The A-10 was
  particularly fond of the infrared guided Maverick missile,

as ground crews rigged small television sets in the cockpits that displayed the Mavericks' infrared sensors' view of what was in front of the aircraft. This gave the A-10 some nighttime capability. The A-10 was not designed as a precision bomber, and this novel use of the Maverick in the otherwise low-tech A-10 shows how flexible high-tech equipment can be. Infrared technology finally came of age during the 1980s and proved itself in the Gulf.

- LANTIRN—This is not a weapon, although it looks like one. The LANTIRN system is two electronic containers (called "pods" by the troops) that look like bombs and are slung under an F-16 or F-15 just like a pair of bombs. LANTIRN (Low Altitude Navigation and Targeting Infrared for Night system) was originally developed as a cheaper way to obtain more high-performance bombers without building all that expensive electronics into fighter aircraft that would spend some of their time operating as fighters and some as bombers. The U.S. F-111 and F-117A already had LANTIRN capabilities built in. Putting all this capability into two pods proved a formidable undertaking and took most of the 1980s to accomplish it. In fact, LANTIRN had not yet officially been placed into service when the Kuwait War broke out. A dozen LANTIRN sets were undergoing final testing, and eventually twenty sets shipped to the Gulf, where they went into service and performed admirably (much to the manufacturer's relief). One of the LANTIRN pods uses terrain-viewing radar that allows the aircraft to fly low and fast at night or in bad weather. This enables the aircraft to avoid most enemy radar and antiaircraft weapons, although the terrain-viewing radar can be detected. This was not a problem in the Gulf, where most Iraqi air defenses were destroyed after the first week. The second pod, the targeting one, did most of the work. It enables the pilot to see his target 5,000–15,000 meters (twenty to sixty seconds' flying time) away. The target can be magnified six to fifteen times and accurately "painted" with the weapon-systems laser. Maverick missiles or laser-guided bombs can then "see" the laser-painted target, memorize its location, be released, and go after the target while the aircraft flies away or picks out another target. Videotapes of some of these missions were shown, and the press was suitably impressed. The downside of LANTIRNs is that they are expensive. Each pod costs over $1 million, and they tend to break down, on average, every fifty hours of use. If the breakdown occurs during a bombing run, the target usually doesn't get hit. Fifty hours isn't all that bad, as the original objective was 108 hours, and that is expected to be achieved eventually. Another limitation of LANTIRNs (and similar systems used on other aircraft) is that they only provide a limited view of what is in front of the aircraft. This severely limits what the pilot can see and puts a heavier workload on the pilot. LANTIRN worked, but it's not quite "turning night into day." Not yet, anyway.

THE TARGETS

The types of targets attacked during the air war changed as the campaign shifted from destruction of Iraqi air and antiaircraft power to preparations for the Allied ground offensive (See Map 2). During the first week of the air war, bombing attacks were actually a minority of the sorties; most aircraft were flying support sorties (electronic warfare and fighter escort). Once the Iraqi air-defense system was out of the way, the Scuds, nukes, chemicals, and command centers were disposed of. By the first and second weeks of February, most of the action had moved to Kuwait and southern Iraq. By that time, the two E-8 J-STARS aircraft were in use, and their highly detailed images of what was on the ground provided detailed and timely target lists, often directing aircraft to ground targets that were currently moving and being observed by the J-STARS radar. Satellite and aircraft taking pictures also added to the targeting effort. The U.S. Air Force coordinated all the combat missions into a daily 250–300-page "Air Tasking Order" (ATO). A typical list of targets during the second week of February include:

1. A mechanized infantry battalion dug-in within a trench system

2. A moving formation (about 1,000 meters in diameter) of armored vehicles
3. Trucks moving along a specific stretch of highway
4. Heavy-equipment transporters (perhaps carrying tanks; J-STARS could tell what size vehicle it saw, but not what it was carrying) moving on a highway
5. A self-propelled artillery battalion moving across the desert
6. Various supply dumps, identified by the type of bunkers and the truck traffic to and from them
7. A fuel dump, identified by the bunker layout and the number of tanker trucks coming in and out
8. Certain highways were known to have traffic most of the time, and the location of the well-traveled sections was given so the aircraft could cruise along them at night to pick off any vehicles they found

And then there were the Scud hunts. The ATO would also include a list of locations where the Scuds were likely to operate, and aircraft were sent out to patrol the likely Scud operating areas. F-15Es were sent out at night, because they had fire-control systems that could spot targets in the darkness, while A-10s went out at first light to attack any Scud launchers returning to their hiding places or to destroy identified Scud positions. Typically, one or two dozen F-15E sorties were launched per day and one dozen to three dozen A-10 sorties. A typical Scud-targeting order, listing suspected Scud positions and other information, would cover the following items.

1. Fixed Scud-launch sites that were suspected of still being used because of Iraqi activity near them. These sites contained a lot of bunkers and nearby support installations that were only identified and destroyed over time. New launch sites were also detected (by the nature of entrenchments, objects lying about, and vehicle traffic) and watched or scheduled for a visit from the bombers.
2. AWACS and satellites could spot Scud-launch activity, and waiting F-15E or A-10 aircraft in the vicinity were directed to the launch site to destroy the launch vehicles or, if they were lucky, Scuds that had not launched yet.
3. Scud patrols were scheduled, usually pairs of F-15Es or

A-10s (depending on how deep into Iraq the patrol area was). The F-15Es took care of far-distant western Iraq. The A-10s, especially on moonlit nights, were able to cover southern Iraq even after the sun went down.

HANDOFF

A tough problem encountered when using fighters as bombers is the short amount of time the pilots have to identify their ground target, position their aircraft for a bombing run, and, finally, accurately drop their bombs. When supporting ground troops, the bombers' targets are either moving enemy vehicles or enemy positions just discovered by the friendly ground forces in need of support. For a long time, the solution was to have slower spotter aircraft, or trained personnel on the ground, guide the bomber in. A more efficient solution got its first real workout in the Gulf War. This is the ATH (Automatic Target Handoff) system first developed by the army so that smaller scout (OH-58) helicopters could automatically pass target information to (larger, more vulnerable, and more valuable) attack helicopters. The target-position data picked up by the scout helicopter was automatically passed to the attack helicopter's fire-control system. The air force began equipping its F-16s used for ground attack with OTH systems. The 174th Tactical Fighter Wing (a National Guard unit) was so equipped and was guided in by scout helicopters, hit its targets, and got away before taking any enemy fire. The scout helicopters were difficult for the Iraqis to see in the first place, and the fast-moving F-16s were there and gone (leaving their bombs behind) before there was any time for the Iraqis to react.

Quick Study 6:
How to Fight in the Persian Gulf: Strategy and Tactics

After the initial panic following Iraq's invasion of Kuwait, military analysts took a fresh look at the situation in the Persian Gulf. The best concluded that while Saddam talked a tough

Strategic Air Targets

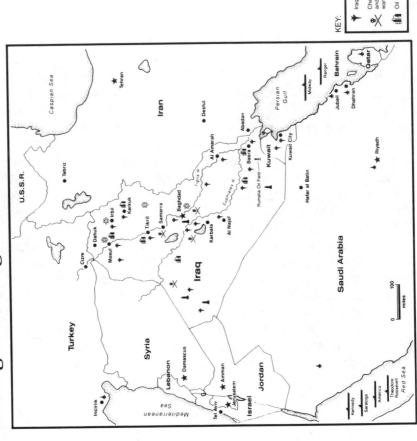

KEY:

Iraqi air bases

Chemical and biological warfare factories

Oil refineries

Nuclear facilities

Scud launch areas

Coalition air bases

game, Iraq was behind the eight ball. Indeed, from August 5, 1990, on the Iraqis' military and political situation became increasingly grim. While initially fielding numerous ground troops, as the Allies' mobilization swelled, Baghdad's forces were completely outclassed in the air and at sea. Many Iraqi officers suspected—correctly, as events would demonstrate—that U.S. and coalition troops would outclass them on the ground as well. While Iraq's ground forces were numerous, most of them were infantry, who are formidable only if they dig in (which they are good at) against an enemy who obliges by attacking these fortified troops head-on. The Allied ground forces were not about to oblige the Iraqis.

Iraqi Strategic Concerns in the Kuwait Theater of Operations

A quick look at the map of southern Iraq and Kuwait focuses the military mind: Basra and Kuwait City had to be defended. Centering on those two cities and retaining forces in the Euphrates River Valley would leave a 500-mile wide-open flank to the west. So the Iraqis decided to dig, fortifying Kuwait and creating a huge "hedgehog" defensive position. The dug-in forces and the complementary minefields, tank traps, fire trenches, and other calculated horrors of trench and bunker warfare would become the "political concrete" of Saddam's attempt to frighten and convince the coalition that attacking the Iraqi forces would produce politically unacceptable casualties in Europe and the United States. This was the gambit.

Kuwait did not contain sufficient ground water to support all of the 400,000 or so Iraqi troops in Kuwait and in the surrounding desert. Allied air planners knew this. To "cut off" the Iraqi Army would begin to "kill it." Without food, fuel, and ammunition coming down from Iraq, the troops defending Kuwait would quickly lose their effectiveness. This is precisely what happened.

Ironically, the Iraqi "eco-destruction ploy" of releasing millions of gallons of crude into the Persian Gulf exacerbated the already delicate water situation. As the water-desalinization facilities around Kuwait City were shut down because of the oil Iraq released into the Gulf, water shortages developed. Eventually, this would have caused deaths from dehydration among, first, the Kuwaiti civilians, and then the Iraqi troops in Kuwait.

Because of the potential civilian deaths, the desalinization plants were not attacked by Allied air forces. Instead, Allied fighter-bombers and B-52s concentrated on the Iraqi Army's transportation networks and supply lines in order to confine the damage to enemy troops.

Simultaneously, that "open flank" always gaped. The open desert flank, when screened by Allied combat aircraft and helicopters, gave Allied armored forces vast space for maneuver—maneuver around the hedgehog.

The Iraqis were ill prepared to meet the Allied mobile force in the desert, and when they attempted to do so, they fought under severe handicaps. Basic lack of information (tactical, operational, and strategic intelligence) was a major constraint on Iraqi military efforts. Allied air superiority kept Allied ground forces informed and Iraqi ground forces in the dark. Without its own air force in the air, Iraqi ground commanders were blinded. Intelligence was limited to what could be gleaned from Allied television and radio broadcasts, what a few Bedouin spies *might* be able to report, and what the Iraqi ground forces could see directly in front of them (when they crawled out of their bunkers and peeked).

Allied air superiority also meant that any Iraqi ground forces moving were subject to air attacks before they even came to grips with Allied tanks and infantry. Air superiority, even at its minimum, slows ground forces. In the Persian Gulf War, Allied air domination translated into near-total disruption and destruction of Iraqi ground forces.

This intelligence advantage, however, was the product of much more than air superiority. United States, Western European, and Japanese research in the 1980s had produced a wider array of devices ("sensors") for spying on the enemy. Besides the reconnaissance aircraft and satellites carrying cameras, there were also sensors for detecting heat, metal, and other signs of troop activity. This negated the strenuous efforts by the Iraqis to hide their ground forces from observation by digging in, providing long networks of communications trenches, and camouflaging everything.

The Iraqi troops proved to be deft at camouflage, but deft was not good enough. It took a few weeks for the Allies to refine their techniques in using all these sensors, but after that the Iraqi losses of tanks, APCs, and artillery rose dramatically. Allied photo-intelligence interpreters schooled their "Mark 1" eyeballs on computer-enhanced images of dug-in tanks and detected the warmer metal in the armored vehicles, which did not cool off as quickly at night as the surrounding desert.

With control of the air and mobile ground forces, the Allied forces could either force the Iraqis to attack at a disadvantage or dig in around key areas while Allied forces rampaged throughout Kuwait and Iraq.

Operational and Tactical Problems in Desert War

Desert warfare has its own peculiar characteristics. Here are some key considerations for desert fighters:

- Lack of water—This is the key factor in desert warfare. A desert is not completely without water. In fact, most deserts are not completely barren, but receive a few inches of rain a year and have some vegetation at least during spring or the rainy season. There are also some underground sources of water, usually found around oases. But for large numbers of troops, there is not sufficient water, and the water needed for the troops and equipment must be obtained from somewhere. A minimum of several pounds of water per day per soldier are needed to avoid losing troops and equipment to dehydration. Troops can survive without food for days, or even weeks, but a few days without water and you are dead.
- General lack of resources—The lack of water means there is generally not much of anything else large numbers of troops need, such as lumber for fortifications, shelter, and warmth or food and other supplies from local civilians. The lesson is direct: When you are out in the desert, what you don't bring with you, you don't have.
- Harsh conditions for troops and equipment—Unlike areas where large surface water resources (lakes, oceans, etc.) help moderate temperatures, deserts are warmer during the day and colder at night. This means that even in tropical deserts, you need heavy clothing in order to survive the nights. The prevalence of sand makes the troops un-

comfortable and causes some health problems (the eyes and respiratory system are commonly affected). The sand is even more damaging to equipment, where it clogs air intakes and jams moving parts. Deserts also tend to have an abundance of animal life, particularly insects and reptiles. Many of the insects are poisonous or carry diseases. Water and food go bad in the desert, and when that happens, the troops often get sick. While there is little rain, there is a lot of wind, and this produces sandstorms that blind and choke both men and machines. The desert is not a healthy place for armies.

• Few civilians—The lack of civilians has benefits and disadvantages. Civilians in a combat zone often get hurt; therefore, most armies divert some resources to care for the local populace. With few civilians in the desert, armies have one less thing to worry about. However, civilians also have their advantages, particularly for information and labor.

• Few built-up areas—Towns and cities are rare in the desert, although they do exist. For the most part, there aren't any, and this eliminates one of the major causes of delays and casualties. Fighting in towns and cities takes longer and causes more casualties than fighting out in the open.

• Few natural obstacles—In most parts of the world, a major obstacle to armies is, well, natural obstacles. These are usually water obstacles in the form of rivers, streams, lakes, swamps, and so on. Given that there is little water in the desert, there are few water obstacles. The exception here is the presence of underground water. In some places, the "underground rivers" run close to the surface and turn the ground the watercourse is running beneath swampy or simply difficult to get across. There are also areas of deep, soft sand that act as a dry "quick sand" and will slowly swallow vehicles that try to cross it. The desert also has fewer of other types of obstacles, such as forests. Deserts still possess obstacles such as breaks in the ground (ravines, ridges, and the like) and the ever-popular sand dunes. But generally, an army will encounter far fewer natural obstacles operating in Arabia versus some place like Belgium.

• Lack of cover and concealment—"Cover" is the military's

term for something to hide behind that will protect you from enemy fire, while "concealment" will just give you somewhere to hide. Lack of water means lack of vegetation. While brush is not bullet-proof, it does conceal troops, and forests can stop some firepower and provide a bit of protection. This is particularly important for protection against enemy aircraft. If the Iraqis were attacked in an area with more vegetation, they would have lost fewer troops and vehicles and would have destroyed and damaged a lot more Allied aircraft, especially helicopters. Helicopters fly low and slow and are most vulnerable to unseen enemy forces on the ground. Unseen Iraqi troops in the bush would have been more encouraged to open fire, given the feeling that the helicopters could not see them and shoot back. Buildings and other man-made structures can also provide some protection. In the desert, with little vegetation and fewer buildings, there are few places to hide. The desert is not totally lacking in cover and concealment, however. The surface of the desert is not totally flat but contains numerous depressions and gullies plus occasional low hills. The troops quickly learned to make the most of these terrain features.

Strategy and Tactics in the Desert

Fighting in the desert consists of using the following time-tested techniques:

1. *Control the Water.*   In times past, this meant getting to the water source (oasis) and defending it against your opponents. If your enemies did not take the water from you, they would often die of thirst, or surrender on your terms. The Allies controlled the water by attacking Iraqi supply vehicles bringing water out to their troops in the dessert.

2. *Get There First with the Most.*   The desert, although not the perfect ground to move over, is generally much easier to maneuver across than any other region. This enables the faster army to concentrate more of its combat power against smaller portions of the enemy army, and this is the classic pattern of successful desert warfare. If you don't move fast and decisively in the desert, you won't win. The Allies fully exploited their mobil-

ity, with some divisions moving over 200 kilometers in twenty-four hours. This high rate of speed was achieved by units practicing moving the entire division several days at a time before crossing into Iraq and Kuwait. This was an important factor, as entire divisions rarely move around together during peacetime. For one thing, it's expensive, costing up to half a million dollars a day just for fuel. The desert terrain could also be an ally for those who knew how to use it. In August 1990, Allied forces deployed their meager forces against the Iraqis in Kuwait to take advantage of the *"Sbakhas"* (wet tidal flats), which presented a movement problem in northeastern Saudi Arabia and southern Kuwait. This was particularly true along the coastal road from Kuwait into Saudi Arabia. The ability to see long distances also proved to be an advantage for the Allies. Line of sight in the KTO is typically five kilometers. The occasional rolling "slope" (low desert ridges), however, creates "reverse slope" situations where line of sight is 300 to 800 meters. Oil-well fires during the war frequently reduced visibility to near zero. Even in daylight, flashlights were needed to read thermal sights and maps. Light-amplification scopes and goggles would not function in these conditions. The Iraqis were aware that the Allies might try to take advantage of the vast maneuver room in the desert. The Iraqi troops took what they considered prudent measures to deal with this. Generally, the Iraqis tried to camouflage their defensive positions by "staying low"—building only to ground level and not raising a berm or parapet. Iraqi trenches were typically 1–1.5 meters deep and strong enough to allow tanks to roll over them without causing collapse. Bunkers were cut in between the trench systems. Marines reported that many of these "bunkers" consisted of little more than sand and galvanized-tin roofs. Defensive positions were built with few alternative or supplementary firing positions, and one USMC report found few positions that allowed Iraqi tankers to pull into total defilade. The Iraqis, strangely, did little to prepare for an active (mobile) defense. If Allied forces broke through and attacked them from the rear, Iraqi defenders had few options. The Allies exploited the "disadvantages" of the desert, while the Iraqis became victims of these same conditions.

3. Information Superiority.   Before aircraft were available, the desert army with the most effective scouts had a tremendous advantage. Information superiority allowed you to avoid a superior enemy or quickly destroy an inferior one. Since the introduction of aircraft, the scouts have become airborne. Moreover, aircraft also provided another dimension to combat. Aircraft can not only keep an eye on the enemy, they can also prevent your own forces from being observed, as well as be used to attack your opponent and keep him away from water. Thus, information superiority in the age of aircraft also enhances combat superiority directly. The Allies also used scouts on the ground and computers and extensive communications systems to control and distribute the gathered information in a timely fashion. For example, the military took a lot of heat during the last few years for buying $7,000 fax machines (that were rugged enough to function under desert conditions). Updated intelligence maps could be faxed immediately to commanders in the field and enable the information to be quickly exploited.

4. Experience in Desert Operations Counts. American forces had more experience with desert fighting than just about any other army in the world, except perhaps Israel. Most of our major training areas are in the desert, and U.S. combat units train under desert conditions a lot. The Iraqi Army had never operated much in the desert, and this contributed to a fatal ignorance of the key problems of desert warfare. This ignorance led to the rapid defeat of Iraqi forces operating in the Kuwaiti desert.

The Downside

The desert also held perils for the side with most of the advantages. The Allied forces operating against Iraq had several major obstacles to overcome before they could fully apply their advantages. The primary obstacle was to provide sufficient logistics to make the most of their advantages. Moving large mechanized forces around in the desert requires enormous quantities of liquids. For every two tons of fuel needed by the armored vehicles and trucks, a ton of water is required. In other words, machines, as well as troops, require water in the desert. An armored or mechanized division can gulp over 2,000 tons of fuel a day, another 1,000 tons of water, plus at least 1,000 tons of ammunition, food, and other supplies. For all the oil underfoot, there were times during the ground war when the fighting troops were literally out of juice. And not just the petroleum kind. The logistics planners had not anticipated how much the troops would use things like batteries. There were a large number of battery-powered devices, including GPS receivers, fire-control systems, radios, and so on. During the ground war, many pieces of equipment were inoperable because batteries (those types found anywhere in the civilian economy) were simply not available. More conventional fuels were also in short supply. The 24th Mechanized Division, in its 220-km race to the Euphrates, found most of its units stationary on the riverbank, out of fuel, for three hours. Not that the fleeing Iraqis even noticed. Ammunition supply can vary enormously. If your division is maneuvering in the vast spaces, out of contact with the enemy, ammunition requirements would be minimal. As desert battles tend to be brief and violent, daily ammunition use tends to be lower than in other types of terrain. Only about 12 percent of 120-mm antitank shells carried on U.S. M1 tanks were fired in combat. The Allied tank crews were quite accurate, rarely needing more than one 120-mm shell to demolish an Iraqi target. The 2,000 M1 tanks carried a total of eighty thousand 120-mm shells, with only 10,000 of them fired at the Iraqi targets surviving the air bombardment. In the final analysis, most of the substantial quantities of supplies needed in the desert will thus be liquids, to keep the machines and troops working.

While movement for tracked vehicles (tanks, etc.) is relatively easy, wheeled vehicles had more problems. The desert surface is strewn with rocks and spotted with patches of fine sand. Truck tires get cut up by the rocks, or otherwise had their undercarriage damaged. Wheels also had a more difficult time getting traction in the sand. There are three solutions to this problem:

1. *Identify most passable routes.* If you had Bedouin on your side, as the Allies did in the Persian Gulf, you had access to intimate knowledge of which routes are more easily driven over by various types of vehicles. Special Forces ground patrols also went into Kuwait and southern Iraq to take soil samples that, upon analysis, would show what kind of traffic that area could support. American weather satellites also proved useful in identifying passable routes.

This will still leave some routes that contain difficult terrain. It will therefore be necessary for:

2. *Bulldozers (and other engineer equipment).* These are
needed to create or finish routes. Tanks or engineer vehicles with bulldozer blades go over rough routes to
smooth them out for the trucks. Even tracked vehicles
benefit from this.

3. *Accurate navigation.* Knowing where the trafficable terrain is was one thing, finding it and staying on it was
another matter. Until the advent of the U.S. hand-held
GPS (satellite navigation device) came along, navigating
the treacherous terrain of the featureless desert was very
difficult. A compass and map still needed soldiers who
could use both with a high degree of skill. Such was not
always the case. The GPS saved many Allied units not
containing a number of skilled navigators.

The Iraqis had a different view of the above problems, and
they considered them insurmountable. Most senior Iraqi officers
considered a movement by large forces through the southern
Iraqi dessert impossible. Allied preparations and GPS proved
them wrong and provided a decisive advantage.

The Limitations of Fortifications and Deception

The Iraqis had been trained well by their Russian advisers in
the art of fortification and deception. They expected these skills
to enable them to punish their Allied opponents. Such was not
the case. More accurate sensors enabled Allied aircraft and
ground units to find camouflaged Iraqi bunkers and to determine
which ones were empty and which contained something worth
attacking. Three key Iraqi techniques for dealing with Allied
ground forces were significant failures. The first of these was the
placement of Iraqi tanks behind sand walls, leaving just enough
of the tank exposed so that it could use its gun. U.S. M1A1
tank fire-control systems were accurate enough to detect and hit
the small portion of the Iraqi tanks that showed above the sand
wall. Moreover, the M1A1's 120-mm gun was powerful enough
to penetrate the sand wall and still destroy these tanks.

The Iraqis also had dummy tanks behind some of the sand
walls, but again, U.S. sensors and tank fire-control systems were

capable enough to determine, in most cases, which was real and which wasn't. The Iraqis also planned to use smoke and fire pots to confuse Allied aircraft and tanks. Once more, U.S. sensors and fire-control systems came out on top. The Iraqis were good, as they demonstrated against the Iranians between 1980 and 1988. But in 1991 the Allies were better.

Logistics: The Key to Victory

Iraq lost its war in the Kuwaiti desert; the Allies won theirs. The Allies also won the logistic battle by being able to move enormous quantities of troops and material quickly and on time. On average, the Allies moved over 30,000 tons a day into Saudi Arabia. Iraq, even with land access, was never able to move more than 20,000 tons a day into Kuwait. After two weeks of bombing, the daily flow of supplies into Kuwait had been cut from 20,000 tons a day to 2,000 (ten to twenty pounds per man, barely enough to sustain what troops were there and not enough to reinforce or replace material or personnel losses).

The scope of the Allied logistics achievement was enormous.

While the combat troops grabbed most of the headlines, the work of several hundred transportation specialists and the expenditure of billions of dollars on logistics equipment during the 1980s made it possible to keep the Iraqis at bay until significant ground forces arrived. Consider the timetable of events during the first weeks of August 1990. Though troops, were moving, the final decision to assist Saudi Arabia and Kuwait militarily was not made until August 7. In the next two weeks, the following U.S. troops movements were made. The F-15Cs from the 1st Tactical Air Wing and the 82nd Airborne Division's lead brigade (2nd Brigade) arrived between August 7 and 9. The 1st Tactical Fighter Wing moved forty-five aircraft to Saudi Arabia in fifty-three hours. The first U.S. Marine units to arrive moved into positions north of the Saudi town of Al Jubail. By August 15, over 30,000 marines had been flown into Saudi Arabia and, after a week's steaming from the tiny island of Diego Garcia 2,500 miles to the south, 10 MPS (Maritime Prepositioning Ships) arrived in Saudi ports. The marines unloaded their trucks, tanks, and artillery, which had been stored in the ships' air-conditioned holds. The equipment, which was checked regularly, worked. Marine pre-crisis training included unloading some of the ships and actually using the equipment. The ships also carried thirty days' worth of food, medical supplies, and ammunition for the marines. On August 19, eighteen F-117A Stealth fighters arrived. At this point, the Iraqis lost any chance to advance out of Kuwait into Saudi Arabia. Iraq had fewer than 200,000 mechanized troops in Kuwait and southern Iraq. Its air force was now outnumbered by the much higher quality U.S. and Saudi aircraft.

By mid-August, the army had already flown in over 10,000 paratroopers, armed with light weapons and some antitank missiles.

The first heavy army division to arrive would have to come from North America, 8,700 sea miles distant. For this purpose, the navy had years earlier purchased eight high-speed cargo ships, especially built to carry heavy vehicles (like tanks). The first of these ships arrived at a U.S. port on August 11, and arrived in Saudi Arabia on August 27 with its load of trucks and armored vehicles for the troops of the 24th Infantry Division that had already been flown over. Seven of these fast cargo ships could move one army tank or mechanized division (these are organized almost identically) every thirty-one days. And this they did, including side trips to Europe to get the U.S. 7th Corps and to replace most of the M1 tanks previously delivered to Saudi Arabia with the more powerful M1A1.

The U.S. Navy maintains two dozen ships loaded with ground combat gear (mainly for the marines, but any trained ground-pounder can use it). Also held in readiness are two hospital ships and two aviation-support ships, to provide maintenance support for over 1,000 land-based Marine Corps aircraft and helicopters that were flown into the combat zone.

Before Desert Shield and Desert Storm were over, more than 200 merchant ships were used to move all the ground and air units to the Persian Gulf. These included over 7 billion tons of cargo, a third of which was fuel. Although Saudi Arabia is awash in oil, it does not have refineries to produce all the fuels the combat units needed. Worse yet, in January half of Saudi Arabia's refining capacity was knocked out by a fire.

The smoothness of the shipping effort was no accident. Since the 1960s, planning and preparation had gone forward to resupply U.S. and NATO forces in Europe from North America. Since the 1970s, plans had been made for a similar effort in the

Persian Gulf. During the 1980s, special ships were bought and legal and financial arrangements made to get control of merchant ships to take cargo into a combat zone. Some 20 percent of the cargo arrived in foreign-flag ships. These ships served when called upon, and the legislation already enacted allowing the U.S. government to requisition foreign-flag (but U.S. owned) ships. They did not have to be used.

These efforts paid off. Without all this behind-the-scenes work, the ground forces would had taken months more to get there, and the aircraft would have had fewer bombs to drop and less fuel and fewer spare parts to get them into the air. The war wouldn't have been such a world-class and low-casualty effort without the behind-the-scenes logistical planning and preparations.

To support the war effort, the Allies moved 7 million tons of material to Saudi Arabia. Most came by sea from U.S. ports, while 900,000 tons from U.S. armed forces stocks in Europe. This was largely stocks of the U.S. 7th Army stationed there since World War II. But the air-transport effort was also huge, with over 15,000 flights by military and civilian aircraft. These delivered nearly 600,000 troops. By March 25, 1991, over 590,000 tons of cargo had been shipped in by air. Within Saudi Arabia, short-range transports (mainly C-130s) made over 7,000 flights carrying troops and equipment. Some 65 percent of the personnel and 20 percent of the cargo came in by commercial airliners. Getting the troops out after the war saw commercial airliners moving 85 percent of the personnel and 45 percent of the cargo. At its peak, 110 commercial aircraft were being used for Gulf operations. Because of the tempo of operations (aircraft in use over fifteen hours a day), four crews were required for each aircraft, and often this was not enough.

Throughout the air war, each sortie used up over ten tons of fuel, munitions, and spare parts (in that order). That's nearly 200,000 tons a day when you include the supplies to support the 130,000 air-force personnel.

FACTS AND FIGURES: WAR BY THE NUMBERS

The total of goods shipped to the Gulf in support of the war effort exceeded 7 million tons when Arab military shipments and civilian goods (later purchased for military use) are added.

FUEL USED BY U.S. AND NATO COALITION FORCES
JANUARY 15 THROUGH MARCH 10, 1991

Jet Fuel	4.1 million tons*
Diesel (Marine)	.9 million tons
Diesel (Ground)	310 thousand tons
Gasoline	53 thousand tons

*Includes coalition Arab air units.

TONNAGES TRANSPORTED TO U.S.
CENTCOM AREA OF OPERATIONS
AUGUST 7, 1990, THROUGH MARCH 10, 1991,
BY U.S. AND NATO ALLIES.

Airlift	538,606 short tons	(15,893 missions)
Sealift	5,035,387 short tons	(441 shiploads)

To support the ground war, 2.8 million tons of material were moved by truck to the interior of Saudi Arabia. Cargo aircraft within Saudi Arabia (primarily C-130s) moved 127,000 tons of material.

To prepare for an extended ground war, army engineers were laying a planned 420 km of portable oil pipelines and field storage for 140,000 tons of fuel when the cease-fire was declared at the end of February.

HETs and the Army of Excellence

To supply and support Desert Shield—and to make Desert Storm's armored "Hail Mary" possible—took far more HETs (Heavy Equipment Transporters) than the U.S. Department of Defense had on hand. In August 1990, DOD had only 480 HETs available. Desert Shield and Desert Storm would require over 1,200.

How do you handle a trucking problem? One hundred eighty-two HETs were leased or borrowed from U.S. trucking companies. Foreign nations provided another 715 HETs.

Saudi Arabia: 330 (leased)
Germany: 189 (donated)
Egypt: 100 (loaned)
Italy: 60 (donated)
Czechoslovakia: 40 (purchased)

In this shortfall lurks a strategic scandal that *this* time the United States had the chance to overcome. Like the shortfall in the navy sealift capabilities and the air force's airlift assets, the HETs shortage reveals the weakness of the so-called "Army of Excellence" organization, which cut combat support (CS) and combat service support (CSS) structures from the active army and moved it to the National Guard and reserve forces. In some cases, CS and CSS units were eliminated and their equipment sold. Naturally, a general, given a budget choice, will take a tank over a truck, and an admiral will buy an aircraft carrier rather than a high-speed troop transport. The U.S. Navy is especially aghast at doing something to help the U.S. Army. This bias on the part of the brass plays right into the way the U.S. Congress has decided to run the procurement business. Military trucks aren't sexy in Washington. What is lost in this trade-off is the ability to move and sustain combat forces. Weakening combat-support structures ultimately *destroys* a modern army's ability to fight and win a war. In the case of Desert Storm, the United States had the time and wherewithal to call up reserves and acquire missing equipment. The Saudis' modern maritime and air-transport facilities gave Desert Shield a first-class support infrastructure—unusual for a war.

The army, air force, navy, and marines shipped thousands of smaller trucks to the Gulf, and there were never enough.

Deception

Any trained staff officer (including many Iraqis trained at Russian staff schools) could see that the most likely plan of action was a march around the open Iraqi western flank. The Allies were openly shipping armored units to Saudi Arabia, and the Iraqis were beginning to move more units to the west of their dug-in infantry on the Kuwait-Saudi border.

So the Allies developed a deception plan that worked. The United States 1st Cavalry Division made many aggressive raids across the Kuwait border in the days before the ground offensive began. A radio deception plan was carried out in the same area consisting of radio operators generating a lot of radio traffic that would be typical of several divisions preparing to advance. The Iraqis, who had radio-intercept units operating in this area, picked up the radio traffic and believed, until it was too late, that the Allies were not going to try an advance through southern Iraq.

CHAPTER 8

The Ground War: AirLand Battle in the Sand

The ground war did not begin on "G-Day" (February 24) or in the days immediately preceding the twenty-fourth when marine and army recon units crept ahead, probing for Iraqi weaknesses: The ground war began on August 2, 1990, when Iraq invaded Kuwait. Nor did the ground war involving coalition troops last one hundred hours as the mythmakers maintain. Even accounting for the two sharp battles fought between March 1 and March 4 with wayward Iraqi units, the ground war did not end with the cease-fire, but continued when United States Special Forces (10th SF) entered northern Turkey to help establish Kurdish refugee camps, and other U.S. forces, including army reservists, went to Turkey to support the Kurdish relief effort.

The ground war consisted of eight stages:

1. The initial Iraqi buildup and invasion of Kuwait (July 15 through August 2)
2. The "Saudi panic" (August 3, 1990, through August 5 or 6)
3. The initial Allied build-up (August 7, 1990, through late September)
4. The defensive stage (early October to November 5)
5. The shift to "full offensive capability" (November 6 to January 16)
6. Desert Storm, Phase 1 (January 17 through February 12)

7. Desert Storm, Phase 2 (February 13 through March 4, "the 100-Hour War" of February 24–28 and its immediate aftermath)
8. After the Storm (March 5 through mid-July 1991)

1. Initial Iraqi Buildup and Invasion of Kuwait

Between the first week of July and August 2, Iraq began to move elements of eight "elite" divisions into positions north of Kuwait and west of the Iraqi city of Basra. The sensitive Rumalia oil-field region already had portions of at least two reinforced motorized Iraqi Army infantry divisions sitting in defensive positions. Apparently, the Iraqi Army had been building up logistics dumps at least since early June. The new divisions included (from the Republican Guards Force Corps, or the RGFC) the Hammurabi and Medina Armored Divisions, and the Tawakalna Mechanized Infantry Division. The Iraqi Army's 10th (Saladin) Armored Division was also brought into the region. Elements of the RGFC Special Forces Division reinforced by other Iraqi Special Forces units were interspersed throughout the divisions. Saddam Hussein made it clear that security and reliability were very important in whatever the "impending operation" would entail.

By July 23, American intelligence estimated that Iraq now had over 130,000 troops in positions near the Kuwait border, a figure agreeing with Kuwaiti Army intelligence estimates. Air activity had also increased over Southern Iraq. The Kuwaitis concluded, however, that the buildup was another Iraqi bluff.

The Iraqi invasion on August 2, 1990, began with a quick motor march by the Republican Guard Force Corps from assembly positions west of Kuwait and north (the Safwan area). The Iraqi Army launched a helicopter-borne air assault (using elements of two "paracommando" battalions) directly against Kuwait City. These units flew from near the Iraqi port of Umm Qasr. Helicopters also ferried troops into strategic points (road junctions and airfields) west of Kuwait City.

Iraqi tank units crossed the eighty kilometers of desert from the west in eight to twelve hours. Initially, the attack was unopposed, but all apparently did not go well. The tank units began to straggle, just as they had in the invasion of Iranian Khuzistan in 1980. All this was seen by a Kuwaiti radar system (suspended from a balloon) that clearly displayed the Iraqi armored vehicles crossing the border. The radar operators fled as they saw the Iraqis approach their ground station.

Despite their radar, however, the Kuwaiti Army was not prepared. Paramilitary, police, and a small forward detachment near the border disappeared as Iraqi brigades headed toward Al Jahrah and as the Iraqi Air Force struck Kuwaiti Army installations and airbases. Elements of one Kuwaiti brigade engaged the Iraqi Republican Guards' Medina Armored Division on the main highway north of Kuwait City and pulled back. Medina continued to roll south. (At least one company that shot at the Medina Division would succeed in escaping across Kuwait into Saudi Arabia.) Elements of two Kuwaiti brigades (amounting to perhaps a full battalion) tried to take up positions northwest of Kuwait International Airport, but within hours they were bypassed and overwhelmed. During this time period, the Kuwaiti Air Force succeeded in escaping to Saudi Arabia. At least one Kuwaiti A-4 strafed an advancing Iraqi column and Kuwaiti SAMS shot down ten to twenty Iraqui planes.

By late August 3, an Iraqi tank division (possibly the Saladin) had pulled within five kilometers of the Saudi border near Mina Sa'ūd. At that point, the fear factor in Saudi Arabia and the rest of the Arab Gulf states hit its highest peak. Was the Iraqi division preparing to continue the attack south, or was it in a blocking position, closing the armored trap on any retreating Kuwaiti units?

Meanwhile, the Kuwaiti Army had not entirely disappeared. Sniper resistance continued in several suburbs of Kuwait City. Kuwaiti mechanized infantry battalion based in southeastern Kuwait slipped across the border into Saudi Arabia to provide the kernel of the Kuwaiti Army-in-exile. Dribs and drabs of Kuwaiti tank units, their soldiers stumbling into the barracks and depot areas, began to move south to escape across the border. The Iraqi armored units stringing out along the Saudi-Kuwaiti border did a poor job of blocking escape routes.

Though the Iraqi attack was overwhelming in numbers (effectively attacking Kuwait with a 20 to 1 advantage), the attack was not finely coordinated. Kuwaiti soldiers continued to escape south for a week after the invasion. This poor performance by the "best" Iraqi Army units was noted by U.S. intelligence analysts.

Within three weeks, the Iraqi high command began to replace its elite mechanized and armored units strike with Special Forces infantry divisions ordered to police the Kuwaiti population. Regular infantry divisions followed and deployed into positions along the Saudi border.

2. The Saudi Panic Stage

This "phase" lasted roughly from August 3 through August 8, 1990. "Roughly" is an important term: The Saudis really didn't begin to regain confidence until mid-August.

It wasn't that the Saudis were caught totally by surprise. The Saudi Air Force was on alert and was ready. The Saudi Army, however, did not begin to mobilize until August 3. Several sources suggest that at best the Saudis could rely on three mechanized brigade groups and elements of one National Guard brigade (about 15,000 troops) to cover the Kuwaiti border from Hafir al Batin to Safaniya. With so few troops, the critical coast road to Dhahran lay open to an Iraqi armored blitz. The Saudis began to shift units from Tabuk and western Saudi Arabia, but these units were weak and in disarray. A small lead element of the 5th U.S. Special Forces Group arrived in Saudi Arabia on August 5.

3. The Initial Allied Buildup Phase—August 7, 1990, Through Late September
(See maps on pages 248 and 249.)

Napoleon said that God is on the side of the biggest battalions. The Lord must also have a place for logisticians and air-transport commands. At this point in the conflict, putting troops on the ground (U.S. troops) was all-important, and it was imperative that these forces avoid the situation of "fighting their way off the airplanes onto the airfields." On August 7, the lead elements of the U.S. 82nd Airborne Division began to arrive in Saudi Arabia. The lead brigade left Fort Bragg, North Carolina, on August 6, and arrived in Saudi Arabia eighteen hours later.

While American airpower could delay an Iraqi armored attack, it was necessary to get more tanks and infantry on the ground. The Saudis were strung-out along the line and were still experiencing mobilization problems. The ground units would serve as a "fixing force," a force the Iraqis would have to account for in their attack.

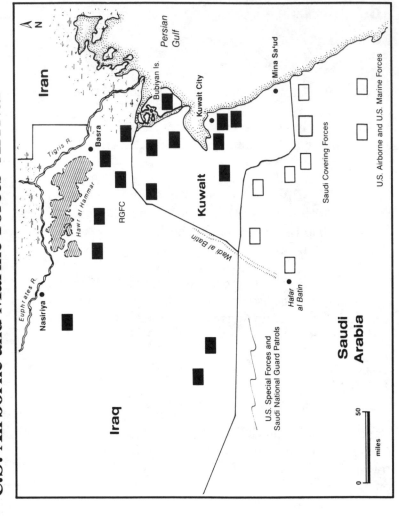

August 1990:
U.S. Airborne and Marine Forces' Arrival

Mid-September to Late October 1990: The Initial Buildup

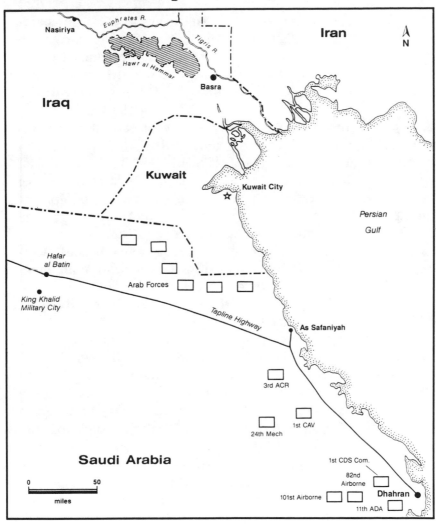

Iran

N

Nasiriya

Euphrates R.

Tigris R.

Basra

Hawr al Hammar

Iraq

Kuwait

Kuwait City

Persian Gulf

Hafar al Batin

Arab Forces

King Khalid Military City

Tapline Highway

As Safaniyah

3rd ACR

1st CAV

24th Mech

Saudi Arabia

1st CDS Com.

82nd Airborne

101st Airborne

11th ADA

Dhahran

0   50

miles

The 82nd Airborne was the lead unit in CENTCOM's 18th Airborne Corps. Elements of 3rd and 5th Special Forces followed. The next wave of transports shuttled in troops from the 101st Airborne (Airmobile). Most of the 101st's helicopters, however, would come by sea. A fast naval convoy composed of all eight Algol-class fast sealift transport in the U.S. merchant-marine inventory left Savannah, Georgia, during the third week of August carrying the equipment of the 24th Mechanized Infantry Division. Troops from the 24th Mech would ferry to Saudi Arabia by air-force and charter aircraft. (The Algol-class transports can ferry tanks to most ports on the globe within fifteen days.) Two 3rd Corps units were also set for early deployment. The 3rd Armored Cavalry Regiment (3rd ACR) began to send its tanks from its post at Fort Bliss in El Paso, Texas, to coastal ports by the third week of August. The 1st Cavalry Division (a heavy armored division) shipped its tanks and heavy equipment during the first weeks of September, and its troops began the airlift to Saudi Arabia between September 25 and October 1. The 1st Cavalry's tanks arrived between October 16 and October 25. (Several of the merchant ships that took on equipment in the Texas Gulf coastal ports were taken out of the mothball fleet. Not surprisingly, some of these merchant ships had engine and serviceability problems.)

Lead elements of the 1st Marine Expeditionary Force arrived in August and early September. Much of the Marine Corps' equipment was prepositioned on a dozen transport ships located at the American base at Diego Garcia. The marines took up positions north of the east-coast Saudi ports, beefing up defenses between the Kuwait border and the critical naval and logistics facilities in the Dhahran area.

The arriving forces aligned themselves opposite the Iraqi positions, with the U.S. forces well behind the screen of Saudi and Gulf Arab units. (See maps on pages 248 and 249.) The marines covered the coast, and the army covered the interior. Even at this early date, the marines publicly discussed amphibious operations and conducted amphibious training for Iraqi eyes. The threat of a marine amphibious assault was expected to make the Iraqis less eager to try a lunge for the Saudi oil fields. Once again, the marines' reputation was as militarily significant as their combat power.

British and French formations also began arriving in the theater. The units included a French Foreign Legion battalion and lead elements of the British 7th Armored Brigade.

On the other side of the border, Iraqi infantry continued to enter Kuwait. Iraqi combat engineers dug fire trenches and built bunkers along the Kuwait-Saudi border. In Iraq, just north of Kuwait, the Republican Guards and Iraqi mechanized units also began to fortify their positions. The Republican Guards moved into several bunker complexes that had been built between 1988 and early 1990. One of the huge bunkers, which could hold up to 600 men, was of German design. This bunker had a two-inch steel blast plate laid across the concrete-and-steel bunker. The blast plate was designed to dampen the effects of near misses.

U.S. TROOP AND EQUIPMENT BUILDUP

(The numbers that follow are estimated from open sources. The Pentagon says they have the real numbers, but they aren't talking.)

	Troops#*	Combat Aircraft	Main Battle Tanks	Warships
August 1	0	60	0	8
August 15	15,000	120	5	14
September 15	75,000	300	110**	40
October 15	220,000	360	350	51
November 15	280,000	590	580	61
December 15	340,000	760	900	62
January 15	580,000	1,140	1,500	64
February 15	600,000	1,420	2,300	68
March 1	610,000	1,440	2,300	68

*# Includes naval forces
**From this point on, MBT total includes approximately 54 light tanks

4. The Defensive Stage: Early October to November 5

The conflict entered a defensive stage—for both sides. The Iraqis spent the month of October improving their defensive positions as well as forcing more and more Kuwaitis into exile. Part of the

Iraqi strategy was to empty Kuwait of Kuwaitis, making it that much easier to incorporate the nation into Iraq. The Iraqis built an extensive defensive system running south from Kuwait City along the coast, then across the border to the tip of Kuwait and Saudi Arabia. Just west of Kuwait, in part of the old Saudi-Iraqi Neutral Zone, the bunker line turned and edged north. (See map on page 248.)

Iraqi Deployment of Fortified Defenses

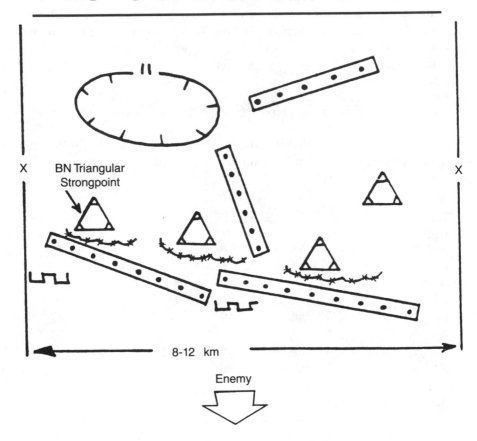

The Iraqi fortifications were classic examples of Soviet-inspired position defense. Typically, an infantry brigade (2,000–3,000 troops) would occupy eight to twelve kilometers of front and from three to five kilometers in depth. (See diagram above.) The troops and combat engineers would sow two to five long minefields along the front, each running from 100 to 300 meters in depth. "Fire trenches" (trenches filled with flammable liquids) and other obstructions would be built to reinforce the minefields. "Spider holes" for Iraqi antitank infantry teams (armed with portable antitank weapons or antitank missiles) were also dug. Company-sized defensive positions, consisting of bunkers and slit trenches, lay within the minefields. Behind the minefields, the engineers typically constructed company- and battalion-sized "triangular" strongpoints of 2,000 meter-long berms on each side. (See diagram on page 254.) An antitank ditch covered at least one of the sides. The angles of the huge triangle contained secondary company and platoon strongpoints—smaller versions of the large triangular fortification. The bunkers in these areas generally contained food, shelter, and firing positions. Armored personnel carriers, tanks, and artillery were positioned in the middle of the triangular strongpoint. The APCs and tanks could exit through a vehicular "drive through" in order to conduct counterattacks. Behind the triangular strongpoints, the Iraqis deployed a mobile reserve (usually a battalion of mechanized infantry and a company of tanks). These units took cover in the strongpoints or smaller "local" bunkers during air attacks.

While the Iraqis improved their fortifications, U.S. and other coalition forces continued to arrive in Saudi Arabia. Once the 1st Cavalry and the Tiger Brigade of the 2nd Armored Division received their tanks, the coalition had a minimal offensive capability. With air support, the coalition now had the forces necessary to defend Saudi Arabia from Iraqi attack.

Though the front remained quiet, the Allies were particularly worried about the Iraqi superiority in artillery. Possessing M-46 FG Soviet 130-mm field guns and South African G-5 and also some Austrian GHN-45s, the Iraqis outranged coalition artillery. The G-5 in particular is a monster. South Africans in Angola reportedly engaged Cuban and Angolan targets at distances of up to 41 kilometers with this 1980s gun. The weapon was designed by Dr. Gerald Bull, the designer of the Iraqi 900-mm "big gun" (Babylon Project) which was allegedly designed to fire nuclear rounds at up to 300 kilometers.

5. The Shift to "Full Offensive Capability" Stage—November 6 to January 16

During this time frame, the coalition concluded that Iraq would not succumb to economic sanctions—or at least Saddam Hussein would not find starvation and industrial rot sufficiently convinc-

Detail from Iraqi
Fortified Defenses
(BATTALION-SIZE
TRIANGULAR STRONGPOINT)

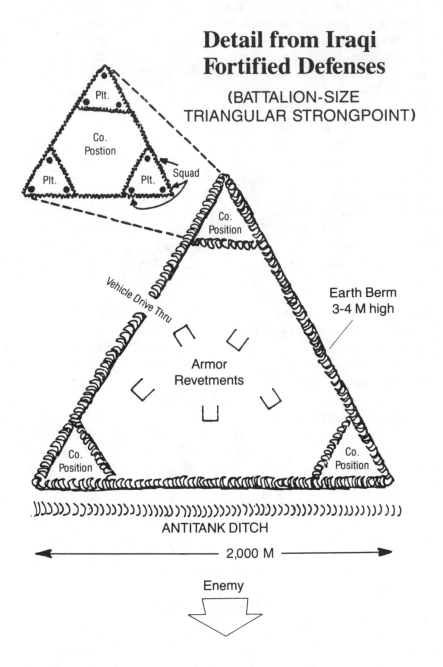

Plt.

Co.
Postion

Plt.   Plt.   Squad

Co.
Position

Vehicle Drive Thru

Earth Berm
3-4 M high

Armor
Revetments

Co.
Position

Co.
Position

Co.
Position

)))))))))))
ANTITANK DITCH

←———————— 2,000 M ————————→

Enemy

ing reasons to pull out. Saddam would rely on "inevitable Arab-Western friction" to pull the coalition apart politically.

In November, the British agreed to double their troop contingent, adding another armored brigade and expanding that force into the 1st British Armored Division. Simultaneously, the United States decided to move its 7th Corps from Germany. This potent armored corps would give the Allies an overwhelming ground-offensive capability, and in fact turned out to be one of the key military and political decisions of the entire campaign. NATO leaders judged that the end of the Cold War gave them the flexibility to deploy over half of the U.S. Army in Europe to the Middle East. (The U.S. 5th Corps and the Bundeswehr, supported by French and other NATO contingents, it was determined, would be more than enough to maintain deterrence in Europe. In this sense, the Germans did participate in the war, by picking up more of the defensive burden in Europe. But this shift only came two to three years sooner than planned. One of the U.S. Army Corps would have been deactivated by 1994, anyway.)

Lastly, during this phase the American logistics effort hit high gear. The United States built a string of supply dumps just behind the front-line coalition forces. New dumps were located near Hafir al Batin and to the west.

6. Desert Storm, Phase 1: "Cut It Off and Kill It."—January 17 through February 12

Apache helicopters from the 101st Airborne Division (Airmobile) were the first aircraft to launch an attack in Operation Desert Storm. Apache AH-64 attack helicopters raided two ground air-defense command-and-control sites deep inside Iraq (125 to 150 kilometers). This "Task Force Normandy" blew a ten-kilometer-wide hole in the Iraqi antiaircraft defense network, allowing Allied bombers to fly through undetected, and kicked off the counterattack against Iraq. This was a classic example of "joint combined arms combat." The entire thrust of AirLand Battle doctrine is to use the appropriate weapons system and the appropriate troops at just the right time. The AH-64s were well suited for the mission. The pilots used night-vision equipment. The attacks were over in two minutes and two radar sites were destroyed. Neutralizing the radar sites helped ensure that the first USAF air strikes would slip

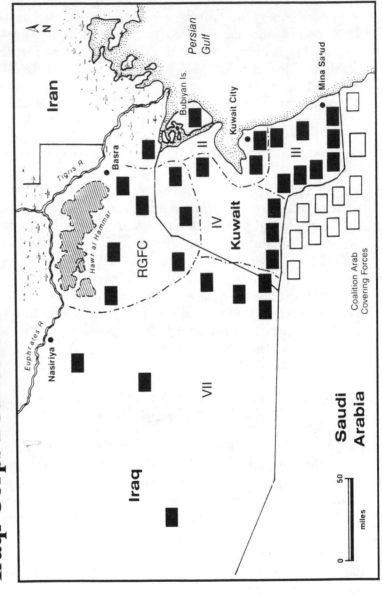

November 1990 to January 16, 1991:
Iraqi Corps Boundaries

January 17 Through February 12, 1991: Logistical Buildup in the West

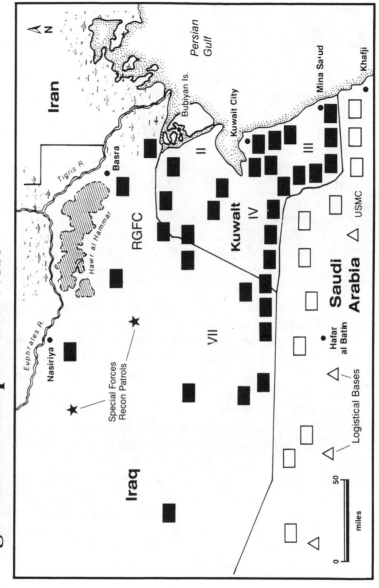

undetected through these gaps in the Iraqi radar warning system. None of the Apache pilots had fired a Hellfire in combat. So why send Apaches? The helicopters could give assured results and immediate intelligence. They could linger on the objective and shoot the targets up with their automatic cannon and rockets if the missiles failed. Immediate confirmation and reattack capability plus the ability to go in low enough to avoid radar detection were crucial advantages. Refueling, the Achilles heel of helicopter operations, was a touchy problem. A supply helicopter with extra fuel had to accompany the Apaches. Going in deep necessitated refueling in enemy territory.

"Task Force (TF) Normandy" consisted of the following aircraft:

9 UH-64 Apache U.S. Army–Attack Force
1 UH-60 Blackhawk U.S. Army–Support
1 CH-47D Chinook U.S. Army–Fuel
4 CH-54E Pave Low U.S. Air Force–Navigation/Support

The crews rehearsed with sand-table, dry-run, and live-fire exercises. During the training, the pilots were not told what their actual objective would be. Task Force Normandy flew 720 miles from the 101st base in eastern Saudi Arabia to the western Saudi Arabian staging base on February 14. On the fifteenth the pilots were given the details of their mission. The CH-54Es would guide the Apaches to and from target and provide rescue for any downed aircraft. Each AH-64 had four Hellfires, thirty-four 70-mm rockets, 1,100 rounds of 30-mm cannon shells, and one 230-gallon external fuel tank. Normally, for missions of this distance, two external tanks would be used. Just before 1:00 A.M. on the seventeenth, the "Red Team" (four AH-64s and two CH-53Es) took off. Seven minutes later, the identically equipped "White Team" followed suit. The remaining choppers took off but remained inside Saudi airspace. While still in Saudi Arabia, TF Normandy was fired on with at least two portable SAMs—apparently fired by Iraqi Bedouin scouts. At roughly 2:00 A.M. the two teams crossed the border in two separate areas. Some Iraqi troops on the border fired into the air at the sound of the helicopters, but hit nothing. At 2:27 A.M., brief radio messages were exchanged by the two teams so that weapons strikes would be simultaneous. At 2:38 A.M., the first Hellfires were launched. By 2:42 A.M., the Apaches had expended their missiles, rockets, and 30-mm cannon shells on the destroyed radar sites. While still inside Iraq, the Apaches landed and refueled. By 4:00 A.M., TF Normandy was heading south. More small-arms fire was taken, but it did no damage. Several portable SAMs were fired and one hit the CH-47 tanker helicopter ("bladder bird") and smashed the landing gear. After flying back to its Saudi Arabian staging area, TF Normandy flew off to its main base, eastern Saudi Arabia, and arrived back at 4:00 P.M., completing a fifteen-hour mission.

The Allied ground forces had already crept north toward the battle zone. On January 17, U.S. Army forces began to move up to the front under the cover of darkness. At least two divisions slipped their armored cavalry squadrons (battalion-size units of infantry and tanks) to within fifteen kilometers of the Saudi-Iraqi border.

Though some of the actions took place before the air offensive began on January 17, the air assault was greatly aided by the reconnaissance missions and raids conducted by Allied special operations forces (SOF, i.e., British SAS, U.S. Special Forces, navy SEALS). Dozens of teams (five to ten men) played a significant but little publicized role in the Gulf War. The British SAS (Special Air Services, an elite commando unit) raided an Iraqi SAM site, stole electronic components, and took prisoners.

U.S. Special Forces reconnoitered troop concentrations, operating with Saudi National Guard and special-operations personnel from frontier forts called *"mazekas."* The Green Berets, some moving in Hummers with grenade launchers, antitank guided missiles, and machine guns, literally lived behind the Iraqi lines. These were classic "SOF" sneak-and-peek missions. Manned by small groups of highly trained troops, special-operations "high value, high risk" missions are often intertwined with intelligence operations. (See map on page 257.)

Typically, the deep missions inside Iraq were conducted by LRS-Ds (long-range surveillance detachments) and LRRPs (long-range reconnaissance patrols). Entering Iraq either by parachute or helicopter, Green Berets used hand-held laser designators to target Air-delivered laser-guided smart bombs. SF recon teams disabled Iraqi communications, blew up bridges, and lasered Iraqi Scud launchers.

While searching for Scuds in Iraq, two SF recon teams were detected. One engaged in a six-hour-long firefight, the other shot it out for three hours before breaking off the action and "exfili-trating," (getting out) and fortunately there were no SF casualties in either fight. One of the engaged SF recon teams was more than 250 kilometers inside Iraq. Helicopters from the 160th Special Operations Regiment, operating from a site along the Saudi border, flew into Iraq and pulled the SF recon team out in a daring daylight extraction. The 160th SAR rescue helicopter rarely rose more than five meters off the ground during the entire operation.

The Green Berets also provided liaison and contact teams with Arab coalition forces. In fact, the Special Forces considered their primary mission in the Persian Gulf War to be "coalition warfare"—supporting Allied contingents as trainers and liaison. For example, an SF "A" Team (ten to twelve men) from the 5th U.S. Special Forces Group manned posts along the Syrian 9th Armored Division's flank. From that point, the Green Berets coordinated the Syrians' tie-in with flanking American armored units. All of the "A" Team spoke Arabic. They even directed close-air support for the Syrian units. The U.S. Army Special Forces provided 106 three- and four-man liaison teams to Allied and coalition units.

The British SAS (Special Air Services commandos) conducted several missions inside Iraq. Most of those involved taking something back with them, either an Iraqi prisoner or a piece of equipment. One SAS mission didn't quite come off as it turned out, because of their own impregnable security. In late January, an SAS minisubmarine was hiding under some Iraqi ships in Kuwait Harbor in a plan to land teams from the sub in order to check out Iraqi defenses in Kuwait. Allied bombers, not knowing there was an SAS sub in the harbor, bombed the Iraqi ships and forced the SAS sub to depart the area. The mission became a case of damage from friendly fire. SAS personnel allegedly wore Bedouin garb as they conducted "close reconnaissance" in the Iraqi and Kuwaiti deserts. Lawrence of Arabia lives.

The extensive air campaign during this time period began to isolate and reduce the Iraqi ground forces. On January 24, the 4th and 5th Marine Expeditionary Brigades and Amphibious Task Groups 2 and 3 conducted an amphibious exercise in the Arabian Gulf. The exercise received a great deal of media attention. It was supposed to. The Allies also conducted numerous seaborne exercises (such as Exercise Imminent Thunder), all intended to draw Iraqi attention to the water's edge. (And, in turn, the Iraqis did respond by beefing up their coastal defenses.) With the elimination of the Iraqi Air Force as an effective combat arm, Iraqi intelligence capabilities were further reduced. The Iraqi high command, beyond a handful of Bedouin spies (watched by the Special Forces) and what their troops could see, was blinded. As General Schwarzkopf would later remark of Saddam, when the coalition air forces had driven the Iraqi Air Force from the skies "[We] took out his eyes."

Then, on January 26, the air campaign began to shift from strategic interdiction to "battlefield preparation" for AirLand Battle.

Khafji

While Allied ground forces moved toward the border, Iraq suddenly decided to launch its own attack. On the night of January 29, elements of an Iraqi armored division moved south from southeastern Kuwait and attacked in Saudi Arabia. The main attack was launched against the Saudi town of Khafji, just across the border from the Kuwaiti town of Mina Sa'ūd. (See map on page 257.) The attack had four probing columns, and possibly a fifth was planned for, but was stopped in its assembly area in southern Kuwait by air attack. One mechanized "unit" (it began as a brigade but by the time it reached American lines, it was about 1,000 men, or two battalions) attained U.S. Marine positions at Umm Hujul. Eleven marines died, and two Light Attack Vehicles (LAVs) were destroyed. Seven of the marines and a LAV were destroyed by a U.S. Maverick missile launched by either an A-10 or an F-16.

A subsidiary probe took place on the right flank of the Iraqi attack at Al Wafra, on the Saudi-Kuwaiti border southwest of Mina Sa'ud where an Iraqi tank battalion stumbled into U.S. marine positions and was thrown back. Allied air support destroyed dozens of Iraqi tanks and vehicles.

A third attack took place when a mixed force of Iraqi tanks, personnel carriers, and recon vehicles engaged a reinforced Saudi National Guard company twenty kilometers west of the town of Khafji. The skirmish was brief. This attack may have been a recon "probe" to find out what forces lay to the west of Khafji.

A fourth attack, which proved to be a main effort, took place when an Iraqi brigade with between 80 and 100 tanks (mostly modified T-55s and T-62s) crashed through a Saudi border outpost manned by Saudi National Guardsmen and headed into the abandoned town of Khafji twenty kilometers to the south. Elements of the Iraqi armored unit followed the initial brigade and took up a position straddling the border berm. The first Iraqi tanks had approached the Saudi outpost with their turrets turned around—the tanker sign for surrender. The Iraqis then cranked the turrets around and sprayed the Saudi positions as they drove past. The Saudis returned fire and later spread the word that Iraqi surrenders were not to be trusted.

This would make it harder for future Iraqi surrenders, which may have been part of the intent.

By the early morning hours of January 30, the first three Iraqi probing attacks were clearly over and the Iraqi units, licking their wounds, had withdrawn to their original lines. Not so with the Iraqi mechanized infantry battalion that made it into Khafji. They held the city.

The attack on Khafji became a notorious event, both for the Iraqis and the Allies. Clearly, the attack on Khafji was a political maneuver by Saddam—he had taken a town in Saudi Arabia despite the U.S. presence and he proceeded to trumpet that "victory."

A U.S. marine forward-observer team (comprising eleven men) hid inside Khafji. The Iraqis took up positions in the town and set up an observation point on a water tower. Their BMPs covered all of the approaches.

Saudi National Guard troops from the Abdul Aziz Brigade (named after their patron, the founder of Saudi Arabia), supported by a battalion of Qatari AMX-30 tanks, counterattacked before noon. U.S. Marine artillery and Allied aircraft supported the attack. The Iraqis attempted to support their mechanized battalion with artillery fire, but coalition counterbattery fire and air attacks silenced the Iraqi artillery. Indeed, if Iraqi artillery barked, it was sighted and often attacked within ninety seconds, something the Iraqis had never experienced even in their long artillery duels with the Iranians.

Still, the Iraqis vigorously resisted the Saudi-Qatari attack, as if to show the world that Iraqi morale was high and unimpaired by the air onslaught. But by 1400 hours on January 31, after some intense house-to-house fighting and nerve-racking cat-and-mouse played by the pinned-down American Marine artillery observation team, the Saudi guardsmen declared Khafji secured except for intermittent sniper fire.

The Qatari tank unit shouldered its share of the combat, engaging in what would prove to be one of the war's more dramatic (and more or less even) tank battles. Four Qatari AMX-30s met five Iraqi T-55Ms. After the brief battle, four Iraqi tanks were destroyed and the other abandoned. In the fight at Khafji, four Saudi troops were killed. Thirty-three Iraqi bodies were found, and 430 Iraqis surrendered. The Saudis captured eighty-five armored vehicles, including eleven tanks.

Saddam called it a victory. Indeed, from a naïve political perspective, Iraq had scored. Yes, the fight took place under Allied-ruled skies, and the Iraqis had seized something of the combat initiative. But Khafji was an Iraqi military disaster. Iraqis drove through a position manned by at most two dozen Saudis in Land-Rovers. Khafji was an abandoned city, occupied by eleven U.S. Marines who hid out in houses and cellars while the Iraqis controlled the town. The entire Iraqi force was destroyed, either killed or captured. The Iraqi mechanized unit covering the attack on Khafji, the one at the berm, was devastated by Allied air attacks, and the remnants were driven back into Kuwait.

On February 1, as Saddam continued to tout his victory in Khafji, Iraqi tanks fired on a U.S. outpost along the Saudi-Kuwaiti border, and U.S. artillery returned fire. The Iraqi "attack," if indeed one was intended, was snuffed.

Khafji did do one important thing: It illustrated the problem of "friendly fire"—accidental self-destruction of one's own forces. Usually the cause is misidentification, and death and injury caused by one's own troops' weapons have been a problem for as long as there have been battles.

7. Desert Storm, Phase 2: AirLand Battle—February 13 Through March 4

AirLand Battle

Operation Desert Storm, both in the air and on the ground, was a textbook example of "synergistic combat"—all weapons systems and troops working together and complementing one another so that speed and firepower overwhelm the enemy. The enemy, colloquially, is "outrun and outgunned." In fact, Air-Land Battle provided the template for the entire campaign in the Persian Gulf War.

What is AirLand Battle? After the end of the Vietnam War, the U.S. Army and Air Force began to develop a "warfighting method" (a "doctrine"). Combined "AirLand" combat was the key. Do not forget to capitalize the "L." The words collapse into one another because the air and land components of the doctrine are intimately linked: One reinforces the other. If the air and ground wars became disjointed, U.S. planners believed their forces would lose. The AirLand Battle concept also impressed upon the army and air force the critical requirement to coordinate battle plans. Both services have in the past exhibited a tendency to develop battle plans without closely integrating their operations.

AirLand Battle was not precisely designed with Iraq in mind; rather, the Soviets had been seen as its primary opponent, their forces in Europe in particular. Some commentators, in fact, criticized AirLand Battle as being designed solely to deal with multiple waves of Russian divisions pouring into Western Europe. Design for Europe, however, did not mean that AirLand Battle would be ineffective against an opponent fighting in a desert.

As the Persian Gulf War demonstrated, AirLand Battle is a recipe for mobile, *comprehensive* warfare. Ground forces coordinate their operations with the air forces so that both services' efforts complement the other. AirLand Battle doctrine stresses four basic tenets: initiative, agility, depth, and synchronization.

Initiative in AirLand Battle means executing operations that make the enemy react to what American forces are doing. In Europe against the Russians, this meant deep air, missile, and helicopter strikes to disrupt Soviet advances and supplies. In Iraq this meant deep air, missile, and helicopter strikes to destroy Iraqi supplies and pin down forces. It also meant helicopter, artillery, and ground raids to keep the Iraqis confused and off-balance.

Agility means the ability to execute rapid and bold maneuver. Bold maneuver characterized the Allied ground campaign.

Depth in AirLand Battle is a bit more perplexing. Depth is not simply a matter of distance, but a means of seeing the battlefield as nonlinear; that is, everybody isn't lined up facing one another. In modern battle, dozens of weapons systems can strike at, and thus shrink, what was once a tactical unit's relatively safe "rear" territory. Airmobile troops and helicopters can strike, land, conduct an attack, then leave. With ATACMS missiles, MLRS, and airstrikes, enemy forces are engaged at long range, and then split into small, uncoordinated, and easily defeated subunits. In other words, firepower and troops are "distributed" over the whole of the battlefield, up to 150 kilometers behind the enemy's forward forces. And because the battlefield has no real "front," depth also means retaining the ability to fight (and defend) in any direction.

Synchronization is a sophisticated way of describing what it means "to put all of the pieces together" in a continuous combat operation. Each unit and weapon contributes to AirLand Battle. The fire of each weapon system complements the other. All maneuver is coordinated. Interlocking firepower and maneuver become "comprehensive"—the enemy encounters a constantly moving, mutually reinforcing combined-arms operation. For example, MLRS fires and suppresses enemy air defenses so that air-force A-10s can attack enemy artillery and tanks behind the front line. As the air force destroys and suppresses the enemy, airmobile infantry and attack helicopters land in the enemy's rear areas. Engineer, armored, and mechanized units, supported by artillery and heavy air strikes, break through the enemy's front and link up with the airmobile infantry. All of the enemy's troop dispositions and movements are monitored by J-STAR aircraft, which inform the air and ground commanders. AWACS aircraft keep a deep watch for enemy air activity. Air-superiority fighters (F-15s) fly combat air patrol and are there to deal with any enemy aircraft.

There is one other aspect of AirLand Battle that is always part of good military planning: Do not assume success. Combat plans should be flexible enough to adapt to changes in the battlefield situation. The U.S. Army in particular stresses that planners should recognize and develop contingencies in case the original plan does not succeed.

In its general outline, what is AirLand Battle to a historian? Basically, the doctrine is a "hyper" form of the blitzkrieg ("lightning war") developed by the Germans during the 1930s. The blitzkrieg was a combination of fast-moving motorized ground units cooperating with combat and reconnaissance aircraft. American troops became quite adept at blitzkrieg tactics during the later stages of World War II, but shortly after the war, the U.S. Army Air Corps became the separate U.S. Air Force, and nuclear weapons caused the army to forget about blitzkrieg. After Vietnam, it was again realized that the blitzkrieg was the best way to fight a ground war. The missing link was cooperation with the air force, which since 1945 had gone farther and farther away from one of its principal missions: ground support. Many air-force officers realized this, too. So blitzkrieg was reinvented as AirLand Battle. The new name was more a political device to get recalcitrant air-force leaders to go along with the idea. Perhaps silly, but it worked. The "who's the army?" crowd in the air force is still a powerful clique, and early in 1990, they approached the army with the idea of turning over their A-10 ground-support aircraft to the army so that the air force could concentrate on "air force concerns." The idea was rejected. One of the untrumpeted achievements of the war was to affirm the value of close cooperation between ground and air forces. Such close and effective cooperation had not been seen since 1945. AirLand Battle worked well in Phase 2 of Desert Storm. Thank goodness—for on February 13, 1991, the ground war began in earnest.

The 400 Hour War

The coalition's ground offensive kicked off not on February 23, but during the first week of February, and ground fighting began in earnest on the thirteenth, when 1st Cavalry Division tanks punched through the forward Iraqi defenses (the wall of sand along the border) and advanced on Iraqi-occupied bunkers and trenches concentrated in the Wadi ("dry river bed") al Batin (near the Iraqi, Kuwaiti, Saudi tri-border area). The Iraqis deployed troops in the Wadi al Batin because they saw it as a likely invasion corridor. It was, and the 1st Cav's job was to make them think that CENTCOM thought so too. Seen from that perspective, the Iraqi dispositions make sense.

Two 1st Cav task forces (reinforced tank and mechanized infantry battalions) reconnoitered Iraqi positions on both sides of the wadi. On February 15, two brigades of the 1st Cavalry (actually armored) Division attacked the Iraqi positions. The following day, these brigades moved up the wadi, the brigade on the left flank entering Iraq. The 1st Cav's company teams (employing both tanks and mechanized infantry) drove straight at Iraqi positions and toward the fire trenches, making every effort to convince the Iraqis that the M1A1s and Bradleys would drive straight through Iraqi defenses and fight into the bunker systems. Apache helicopters attacked in front of the company teams to set off the fire trench. One task force started to move around the fire trench, but the brigade commander ordered it to stop. Under no circumstance were the Iraqis to see U.S. ground forces maneuvering around obstacles. The fighting and skirmishing went on for several days, the primary purpose being to make the Iraqis believe that American forces would attack frontally, as the Iranians had done during the 1980–88 war.

Further to the east, U.S. Marine units conducted similar attacks. These attacks stressed the use of tanks, artillery, and air power (particularly helicopters). Attacks occurred regularly from February 15 through February 21. Lots of artillery was used. Allied casualties were light; Iraqi losses were much heavier. In addition to several thousand dead and wounded, over a thousand Iraqi prisoners were taken during these actions. Most of the Iraqi casualties were caused by air attacks. The Iraqis were left with the impression that American forces would attack into the Iraqi lines. This maneuver (and the USMC coastal exercises) "sold" the Iraqis on the idea of a U.S. attack into the teeth of their defenses. Iraqi reserves (mechanized and armored divisions) thus prepared to move south instead of west to meet this "main allied attack." The importance of the feint operations cannot be underestimated. The ruse worked, as the Iraqis continued to prepare for Allied frontal attacks, which made the "swing to the west" all the more effective. (The official start date of the "100 Hour War" was February 23, when the major movements and attacks began. But the "official" isn't accurate—it's political, a nice soundbite. Four-hundred hours of ground war from the start of the feints to the ceasefire is a better figure, and that doesn't allow for the ground fighting in early March. In one of the post-ceasefire battles, Allies forces destroyed the better part of an Iraqi division. The ceasefire notwithstanding, the fighting was not over until all Iraqi units had fled the area or been destroyed.)

Between February 10 and February 15, other American forces, including the marines, began a series of combat patrols to the border and beyond. Some of the marine recon units used "dune buggies" armed with antitank weapons, grenade launchers, and machine guns. Offshore, SEAL commandos conducted beach and island recon missions. The Iraqis would have reason to think the marine units afloat on ships in the Persian Gulf might launch an amphibious attack. Artillery and air attacks struck Iraqi units dug-in north of Khafji.

From February 16 to February 20, the intensity of ground operations increased. American and British artillery battalions began firing heavier and heavier artillery barrages into the Iraqi lines. Again, part of the purpose of the artillery preparation was to convince the Iraqis that the U.S.-led forces, like the Iranians the Iraqis had faced in the past, would shell the Iraqi fortifica-

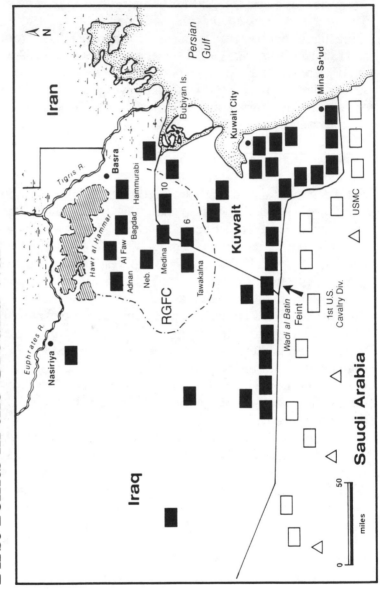

February 13 Through February 23:
First Feints in the Ground War

tions, then drive forward in a frontal assault. But the artillery raids also added to the physical and psychological toll wreaked by the air raids. MLRS (rocket) units proved to be particularly effective in flattening Iraqi artillery. The 24th Mechanized Infantry Division began to shift its units farther west, while other sporadic ground engagements continued. U.S. Army units began to use Vulcan 20-mm automatic antiaircraft cannon as bunker-busters. The high rate of fire by the 20-mm cannon "seemed to encourage" Iraqi troops to surrender.

Yet in places along the front, Iraqi morale had not yet collapsed. On the nights of February 18 and 19, the Iraqis "thickened" the defense in their 3rd Corps sector near Wadi al Batin by bringing over three battalions of additional field-artillery pieces (about 50–100 guns), presumably because they believed a ground attack in the area was likely. Then, the next night, the 1st Cavalry Division moved twelve kilometers up Wadi al Batin into Iraq and Kuwait and encountered an elaborate bunker complex. A ten-minute firefight ensued, with the Iraqis springing an ambush that hit two Bradleys and a Vulcan before the U.S. attack destroyed the bunker complex. The Iraqis replied with heavy artillery fire. A-10s dealt with the Iraqi artillery.

Still, the Iraqis in the Wadi al Batin area showed a strong will to resist. In other sectors, however, the Iraqi ground forces were already near collapse. Another combat action on February 20 illustrated just how devastated the front-line Iraqi forces really were. A helicopter team of two OH-58 scout helicopters and two Apaches from the 101st Airborne Division attacked a nest of Iraqi infantry bunkers. The Apaches, firing Hellfires and cannon, destroyed fifteen bunkers. Four hundred fifty Iraqi infantrymen then surrendered to the hovering helicopters. U.S. infantry, flown into the area on CH-47 (Chinook) transport helicopters, herded the Iraqi POWs into a group and disarmed them. The Iraqis and their captors were then flown back to Saudi Arabia in the Chinooks.

Potential Iraqi use of chemical weapons remained the biggest concern of the Allied commanders. The troops prepared for the worst. Bulky chemical protective suits were seen all over the battlefield. The Allied command, however, used a political stratagem. The Bush administration warned that if Iraq used chemical munitions, the coalition's objectives would change. The UN would hold Saddam personally responsible and march on Baghdad. One senior Arab official told the *Los Angeles Times,* "If Saddam does not use chemical weapons I think people will squeeze him out of Kuwait and lock him into Iraq." But, the official continued, "If Iraq uses chemical attacks to blunt a ground war, the Allied forces could hunt down and kill Hussein." Leaflets were dropped by Allied aircraft warning Iraqi troops that they would face war-crimes trials if they used chemical weapons. Nonetheless, in the actions on February 20, the front-line forces engaged in the deception and probe operations in the Wadi al Batin area wore chemical-protective suits and had their gas masks ready.

Though chemicals presented a potentially major problem, the fundamental Allied consideration in the ground war was, as General Schwarzkopf noted in his final briefing, numbers. On paper, at least as of January 16, 1991, the Iraqis outnumbered the Allied forces six to five in manpower, and considering that the Allied forces' total manpower included a large number of support troops, the readjusted numbers show the Iraqis outnumbering the Allies two to one in combat troops. The tank figure was 4,700 Iraqi tanks to 3,500 Allied.

By February 23, the official beginning of the ground war, fourteen of the forty-two Iraqi divisions in Kuwait and along the Kuwait-Iraqi border had been blasted to less than 50 percent strength. In some of these units, defections and desertions may have sapped 10 to 25 percent of the personnel. Eleven Iraqi divisions were at 50–75 percent strength, nineteen divisions (and one separate armored brigade), the Allies estimated, still were at 75 percent strength or better.

Politically, the Iraqis were given a noon Eastern Standard Time deadline for beginning a withdrawal from Kuwait. Yevgeni Primakov, the special Soviet envoy to Iraq, tried to persuade Saddam to comply with the United Nations Security Council resolutions and avoid a decisive ground battle. On February 23 (2:00 A.M. Moscow time, 6:00 P.M. February 22 Eastern Standard Time) the Iraqis told the Soviets they would pull out of Kuwait. But the pullout statement was hedged and fudged with dozens of other issues and a demand that the UN revoke all Security Council Resolutions after Resolution 660.

In Washington the noon deadline passed. And Iraqi forces remained in Kuwait.

"Hail Mary"

Logistical preparation and rapid, audacious maneuver keyed the coalition ground offensive. The Allies, for the most part the United States, had reinforced the logistics bases and supply dumps well to the west of the critical point on Wadi al Batin where the Saudi-Kuwaiti-Iraqi borders intersected. (See map on page 257.) The Allies had lugged enough fuel, ammunition, spare parts, water, and rations out west to support sixty days of heavy combat. This preparation reflected AirLand Battle contingency planning: If the Allied offensive bogged down in a slugfest, General Schwarzkopf was prepared to win that battle as well. The coalition could make these preparations because it controlled the air and the United States had assembled the greatest military logistical support and combat service support forces that have ever existed. Bar none. Historical superlatives are usually highly suspect, but this is one that is deserved. The United States can "outlog" any opponent—as long as its economy remains healthy.

In the past, however, the United States has been very iffy when it comes to maneuver. America has had its Pattons, but it has also had its Grants. In this instance, however, Schwarzkopf's "Hail Mary play" coupled with the extensive tactical and operational deception plan, completely unbuckled the already sagging Iraqi defenses.

In football a Hail Mary play is usually a desperation play. All of the offensive team's receivers go to one flank and run down the field. The quarterback then lofts the ball toward the end zone, hoping one of his receivers will catch the ball. The Allies' situation was not so desperate, though rapid maneuver would limit casualties and overrun Iraqi artillery and munitions stockpiles, thereby limiting the opportunity for the Iraqis to use chemical weapons.

The "Hail Mary" reflected AirLand Battle's concepts of initiative and agility.

The Iraqis were incapable of reacting to the quick move to the west. They lacked an air force that could see and impede the HETs (Heavy Equipment Transporters) which hauled coalition tanks deep into desert-assembly areas. Way out west, the extensive Iraqi defensive barrier petered out into sand. Again, another superlative is applicable: As General Schwarzkopf later trumpeted, at no time in the annals of military history had so large a force (particularly an *Allied* force) moved such an extended distance (up to 250 kilometers) and gone immediately into a major ground offensive.

AirLand Battle, a 1990s blitzkrieg, was ready to roll.

The Offensive

On February 23, U.S. 101st Airborne Division (Airmobile) began deep reconnaissance operations in preparation for what would be the largest helicopter assault since Vietnam. At 8:00 A.M. on the twenty-fourth, the air assault began. Helicopters moved troops and supplies 120 kilometers into Iraq. The 101st's objective was to cut off Iraqi forces to the east and disrupt any Iraqi operations in the Euphrates River Valley to the northwest of Kuwait. The 101st established "Cobra Zone" as a refueling and rearming point for its helicopters and air-assault troops preparing to drive further into the Euphrates Valley.

The Cavalry Goes First

The 3rd Armored Cavalry Regiment (ACR) scouts had been in a firefight on January 22, in one of the war's first ground actions since the Iraqi invasion of Kuwait. They had killed two Iraqi soldiers and captured six. Two troopers had been wounded in the skirmish. The "Brave Rifles" of 3rd Cav expected resistance from the Iraqis when they began moving into southern Iraq in late February.

The 3rd ACR began berm-busting on February 22, knocking seventy-three gaps in the berm north of its positions. The 3rd Cav kicked off its attack at noon on February 24 in a diamond formation, with 2nd Squadron in front and 1st and 3rd Squadrons on the flanks. The "regimental wedge" had a fifteen-kilometer front and was ten kilometers deep. Instead of Iraqi resistance, however, the 3rd ACR ran into bad weather, poor visibility, and a few Bedouin, and in less than twenty-four hours it was 125 kilometers into Iraq, waiting for the rest of 24th Mech to catch up. On February 26, the 3rd ACR overran two airfields and began picking up POWs. On February 27, after encountering haphazard Iraqi artillery fire, 3rd ACR completed its sweep to block retreating Iraqi forces and stopped close enough to Basra to see the city's lights. Ironically, 3rd ACR's biggest firefight occurred in the hours after the cease-fire took effect. Disoriented Iraqi forces attacked the 3rd ACR near the Rumalia

Southwest Airfield. In an hourlong firefight, 3rd ACR destroyed and scattered elements of an Iraqi brigade.

Officially, on the morning of February 24 (Saudi time), the Marine Corps, accompanied by the Tiger Brigade of the Army's 2nd Armored Division (1st Brigade, 2nd Armored Division), started to do exactly what the Iraqis thought they would do—attack into the heavily defended "bight" of Kuwait. We say officially, because on February 22 marine ground patrols had reconnoitered the Iraqis' forward minefields, and on February 23, the 1/3rd U.S. Army Field artillery, the Tiger Brigade's 155-mm self-propelled artillery battalion, had moved across the border.

At 4:00 A.M. on February 24, the 1st and 2nd Marine Divisions sprang toward the Iraqi defensive belts. Of the 84,000 marines in the Gulf, 66,000 were ashore and most were involved in this operation. The marine divisions did a superb job executing a classic breaching of a tough minefield, barbed-wire obstacles, and fire trenches. The marines attacked the barriers as if they were attacking a defended beach (breaches instead of beaches). The marines moved on three axes: Red, Green, and Blue, cutting two lanes in each breach zone. The 1st Marine Division, on the southeast flank and the 2nd Marine Division, on the north side of the attack zone, both moved slowly and methodically. The minefields and barriers were extensive. They quickly crossed the first barrier and then blasted the second line with artillery fire. The Iraqis pumped intense artillery fire on the forward marine infantry units, which were moving on foot. Marine Corps F/A-18Ds and Allied artillery replied. The 2nd Marine Division took nine hours to clear the Iraqi lines. Some of the mine plows attached to their tanks to speed the process did not arrive until days before the battle. The marines suffered fewer than fifty casualties, and less than ten vehicles were lost in breaching the Iraqi defensive positions. Both divisions then moved through the breach. After that the pace of Iraqi artillery fire rapidly diminished.

Iraqi front-line infantry began to crawl out of their bunkers, soon surrendering in large numbers when they saw their "impregnable" defenses so easily crossed. The 2nd Marine Division took 700 to 800 prisoners in the morning hours. The numerous Iraqi POWs who had to be cleared and sent to the rear began to impede the rate of advance.

At exactly noon on February 24, the 1st Brigade, 2nd Armored Division, under the operational control of the marines,

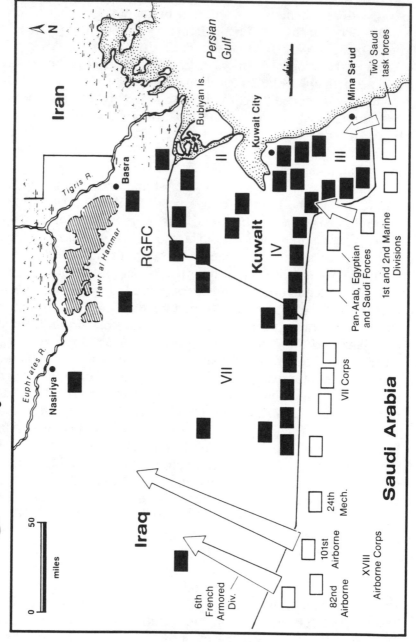

Morning, February 24

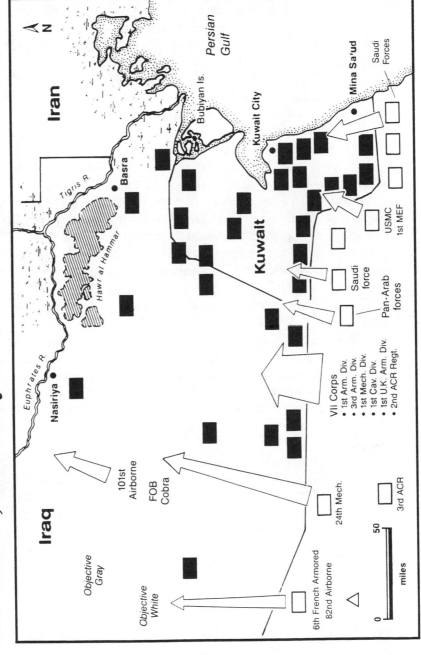

Afternoon, February 24

entered the breaches. The Tiger Brigade became the Marine Corps' exploitation unit. (Remember, AirLand Battle means using the appropriate unit and weapon at the appropriate time.) The Tiger Brigade was heavily reinforced, with a USMC Light Armored Infantry (LAI) battalion under its operational control. The marines provided the army brigade with an ANGLICO (Air and Naval Gunfire Coordinating platoon) and other support. The armored brigade swung east, turned north, then swung northwest to push up the boundary between the Iraqi 3rd and 4th Corps. The Tiger Brigade pushed units west, trying to link up with coalition Arab forces (Syrian or Egyptian) who were to advance along the Marine Corps' left flank.

Behind a wall of artillery fire, the USMC divisions headed north toward Kuwait International Airport and Kuwait City. The marines reported thousands of Iraqi surrenders.

To the east of the marines, two Saudi Arabian armor and mechanized infantry task forces, accompanied by other Gulf Arab contingents, launched a penetration attack up the coast road north of Khafji. U.S. battleship sixteen-inch gunfire supported the Arab forces.

With the pace of Iraqi surrenders accelerating, the biggest problem seemed to be the weather. The weather conditions got worse, the low clouds limiting air support and making helicopter operations more difficult. Additionally, Kuwaiti resistance fighters and special-operations forces in Kuwait reported an increasing number of atrocities being committed by Iraqi Special Forces units in Kuwait City.

On the afternoon of February 24, Egyptian and Saudi forces entered southwestern Kuwait and attacked headlong into the defensive barriers, precipitating thousands of new Iraqi surrenders. The Iraqi prisoners, many of them reserve officers from Baghdad, told their fellow Arabs that the Regular Army officers had quit their units as early as a week before the ground battle started. The Iraqi reservists said that with the Special Forces and Baath party members gone, they had planned to surrender at the earliest opportunity. Syrian forces and the Kuwaiti Martyrs Battalion entered Kuwait and headed toward Kuwait City. The Tiger Brigade of the 2nd Armored Division made contact (several times) with the advancing Arab coalition forces.

Some 300 kilometers to the west, the 6th French Light Armored Division plus the 2nd Brigade of the 82nd Airborne Division (325th Airborne Infantry Regiment) moved north from the Rafha area on a mission to overrun the As Salman Iraqi airfield and then moved into a flank-screening mission. The fast-moving, light French ARC-10 armored recon vehicles, supported by helicopters, were ideal for the screening mission. The French forces moved over 100 kilometers north on the February 24.

The Republican Guard

With the advance going so rapidly, the Allied high command decided to throw the Sunday punch. On February 24 and 25, the 101st Airborne made a second helilift toward the Euphrates River Valley. The Iraqi Army in the KTO (Kuwait theater of operations) was indeed about to be cut off. Now was the time to kill it, and especially kill the Republican Guard. J-STARS intelligence data showed that some of the Iraqi mechanized forces and the Republican Guard were beginning to come out of their fortifications. Allied air forces reacted rapidly.

On the ground, the U.S. 7th Corps entered the action. The U.S. 1st Infantry Division breached border minefields and bulled into southern Iraq, followed by the British 1st Armored Division. The U.S. 1st and 3rd Armored Divisions just moved around the Iraqi barrier. The 2nd U.S. Armored Cavalry Regiment (ACR) swung wide to the west, circumventing the Iraqi defenses, and churned up the left flank of the corps. The 2nd ACR immediately engaged Iraqi mechanized units emerging from their defensive positions. A sharp firefight ensued at "73 Easting" with 2nd Cav's M1A1s destroying Iraqi bunkers and armored forces.

The Battle of 73 Easting

After two days of leading and then screening 7th Corps' advance into Iraq, the U.S. 2nd ACR (Armored Cavalry Regiment) ran into the Republican Guard's Tawakalna Mechanized Infantry Division. Or perhaps history will show it was the other way around. The Battle of 73 Easting (named after a positioning line marked on desert maps) proved to be one of the bitterest fights of the war. On February 26, the 2nd Squadron 2nd ACR and the rest of the regiment, some 125 kilometers inside Iraq, had swung east toward the Kuwaiti border. The 2nd ACR began to encounter dug-in Iraqi tanks and troops along a ridge "east of 73 Easting." The 2nd Squadron's scouts and tanks began to infiltrate and engage the dug-in line. Suddenly, it became clear that G ("Ghost") Troop (about twenty tanks and Bradley armored vehicles) had run into more than it had bargained for—at least a reinforced brigade (about 100 tanks and lighter armored vehicles) of Republican Guards. Ghost Troop took several casualties. In one of the rare instances of Iraqi offensive action, a reinforced T-55 tank battalion (over fifty tanks and APCs) attacked Ghost Troop's positions. Artillery and cavalry tank fire stopped the attack cold. In a firefight that lasted six hours, wave after wave of Tawakalna's tanks and motorized infantry struck the 2nd Squadron. Why the Iraqi attacks? The 2nd Squadron had rolled into a choke point below the ridge where Iraqi units (Tawakalna and the 12th Armored Divisions primarily) were retreating. Said one cavalry trooper, "If the rest of their [Iraq's] army had fought as hard as the Tawakalna fought we would have been in trouble."

The 2nd ACR covered both the left flank of the 7th Corps and the right flank of the 24th Mechanized Infantry Division.

The biggest move, however, was further to the west, where the elite U.S. 24th Mechanized Infantry Division raced nearly 250 kilometers in twenty-four hours, driving into the edge of the Euphrates River Valley.

The 24th's recon unit, the 2/4th Cavalry Squadron, led the mechanized charge across Iraq. The initial move on February 24 and 25 had brought the 24th Mech in position to cut off all Iraqi units in the developing "Basra Pocket."

Meanwhile, the 24th Mech encountered elements of "a large Iraqi infantry unit" and began a direct attack toward the Euphrates at 2:30 P.M. on February 26. At 4:40 A.M., February 27, elements of the 24th Mech (1/64 Armor Battalion and 2/4 Cav are given credit for being the first) reached the Euphrates. This was a record-breaking movement for a mechanized ground force in the twentieth century.

[All of the previous record moves were against light or minimal resistance and over fairly flat terrain. It's ironic to note that one of the previous records was held by a British force (mainly cavalry with some armored cars) advancing against the Turks in the Middle East during World War I.]

At 6:00 A.M. of February 27, the 24th Mech executed a huge right turn and began to attack east into the Basra Pocket. The 24th Mech crashed through scattered elements of two Republican Guards infantry divisions (and possibly a third) in battles at the Tal'il and Jalaba airfields, where resistance was minimal.

PREVIOUS FAST-MOVING MILITARY RECORDS

Force	Location	Year	Distance	Time	Per Day
24th Inf	Iraq	1991	368 km	4 days	92 km
Russia	Manchuria	1945	820 km	10 days	82 km
Britain	Megiddo	1918	167 km	3 days	56 km
Israel	Sinai	1967	220 km	4 days	55 km
Russia	Russia	1944	400 km	8 days	50 km
Germany	France	1940	368 km	12 days	31 km
Germany	Russia	1941	700 km	24 days	29 km
Allies	France	1944	880 km	32 days	28 km

The 24th Mech then encountered retreating elements of the Hammurabi Armored Division.

The French 6th Light Armored Division with the 2nd Brigade 82nd Airborne Division and the 101st also closed in on the river valley. Less than two Iraqi brigades lay between the French forces and Baghdad. The French armored division had forces as close as 130 kilometers from Baghdad. Elements of the 101st Airborne were only 150 kilometers from Baghdad. The 2nd Brigade of the 82nd Airborne operated under the control of the 6th French Light Armored Division. Most of the 2nd Brigade of the 82nd Airborne Division advanced behind the 6th French Light Armored Division, ready to deal with situations as they developed. Among these situations was the collection of prisoners and moving supplies to troops deep inside Iraq. As the 82nd had very few armored vehicles, most of this movement was by truck, with a few armed paratroopers in the back. In true paratrooper fashion, many of these small convoys found themselves sprinting ahead of the official lead combat elements. This led to some confused encounters between lightly armed paratroopers and more heavily armed Iraqis who, fortunately, were usually inclined to surrender to the first Americans they encountered. The 3rd Brigade had a follow-up mission. If the French and the 2nd Brigade ran into trouble on the flank, the 3rd Brigade was to serve as a reinforcement and enveloping force. The 1st Brigade remained in positions in Saudi Arabia along the Tapline Road near Jallibh, serving as another airmobile reserve.

On February 25 and 26, the forces in the eastern sector continued to push north, with the marines and the 2nd Armored Divi-

February 25 to 28: The Final Days

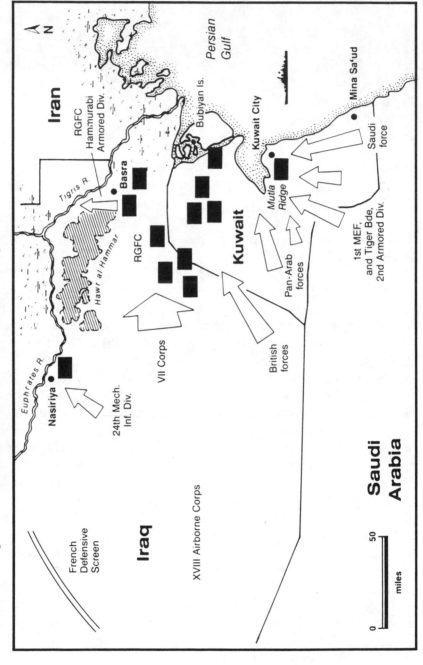

sion's Tiger Brigade investing Kuwait City and its suburbs and the Saudis and Kuwaitis entering the city itself. Here, again, the marines reported that the mass surrenders of Iraqis slowed their advance.

To the west, deep inside Iraq, the French settled into flank guard positions.

In part of its run around Kuwait City, the Tiger Brigade drove north along the Iraqi 3rd and 4th Corps boundary. Several M1A1s in the brigade destroyed Iraqi tanks at ranges of over 3,000 meters (3,320 was the longest confirmed kill, made with an XM900 120-mm sabot round. Several kills up to 3,500 meters are fairly certain). In one engagement, the brigade's M1A1s engaged and destroyed three Iraqi tanks, all at a range of 3,000 meters. Within minutes, another unit from the Tiger Brigade swept in among the destroyed Iraqi tanks and took the surviving Iraqi tank troops as prisoners. One of the Iraqi POWs was an English-speaking lieutenant. He asked his captors what kind of hyperfast antitank missiles they had used to destroy his platoon. When told he had been engaged with tank cannons, he was incredulous. "No tank cannon exists that kills tanks at that range!" he exclaimed.

The Tiger Brigade's ultimate objective was the Mutla Ridge, behind Kuwait City. (See map on page 280.)

Meanwhile, in the Wadi al Batin area, 1st U.S. Cavalry Division pulled back to the south as the British 1st Armored Division cut in behind the two dug-in Iraqi infantry divisions that had been facing the 1st Cavalry. The British overran the infantry divisions' rear areas and smashed into Iraqi mechanized forces. The Iraqi mech units began to surrender.

But the major action was 7th Corps' drive on the Republican Guards. The armored corps drove north, then wheeled east, the British 1st Armored Division cutting below the rest of the corps and driving on dug-in Iraqi mechanized positions in Kuwait. By 6:00 P.M. on February 26, the Allies had destroyed over twenty-one Iraqi divisions. By midnight the 18th Airborne Corps' 24th Mechanized Infantry Division had hit the Euphrates River in force, blocking the last major avenue of escape. The 3rd ACR, under the operational control of 24th Mech, moved into a screening operation. The 1st Cavalry Division swung west and began to chase the rest of 7th Corps. The 1st Cav made a 100-kilometer march in twelve hours.

February 27 found a solid wall of 7th Corps supported by 18th

Airborne Corps attacking east into the Republican Guard.

The Guard's divisions were dug-in as follows: Tawakalna Mech, Adnan, Nebuchadnezzar, Al Faw infantry divisions, Media and Hammurabi armored divisions, and the RGFC Special Forces Division supported by an Iraqi armored brigade next to Basra. Air strikes had completely destroyed Tawakalna. The 2nd ACR and elements of the 1st U.S. Armored Division continued to battle Tawakalna's scattering troops.

Arab forces officially entered Kuwait City on February 26, though in fact substantial Arab coalition forces did not enter the city until February 28. By February 27, the 1st Marine Division held the area around Kuwait City International Airport, and the 2nd Marine Division blocked escape routes on the west and north side of the city.

Still, nearly 40,000 Iraqi troops tried to flee Kuwait City. They headed north, in what Saddam claimed was a "withdrawal." It was a strange withdrawal, with trucks filled with loot and Kuwaiti hostages and Iraqi mobile antiaircraft guns firing at Allied planes. U.S. troopers began to refer to the withdrawal as "the Great Bug-out." The Allied aircraft shot up the retreating columns just south of the Mutla Ridge.

Tiger Brigade, 2nd Armored Division, attacked across the ridge, overrunning the Ali Al Saleem Airfield and pushing toward the coast road. The Tiger Brigade put a "cork in the bottle," destroying thirty-three Iraqi armored vehicles and taking the "Police Station" near the main highway after a fierce firefight that included a dismounted infantry assault. The Tiger Brigade found between 3,000 and 4,000 Iraqi vehicles, many of them stolen civilian cars and trucks, destroyed by Allied air attacks along the "carnage corridor" south of the ridge.

By noon of February 27, Allied intelligence estimated that the battle had rendered thirty-three Iraqi divisions ineffective.

Fighting continued west of Basra as the 7th Corps shot up the remnants of the Republican Guard. All of the armored units of the 7th Corps, the 1st and 3rd Armored Divisions in particular, began to converge on the "Basra Pocket." The 7th Corps moved like a huge armored mallet, swinging north, then east, crushing the Iraqi divisions with air, artillery, and tanks. The 2nd Brigade, 1st Armored Division, got in a firefight with elements of both the Medina and Hammurabi Republican Guards Armored Divisions. The 3rd Armored Division made a 200-kilometer move during the night, with not one of its 320 M1A1s breaking down during the long tactical march. The U.S. 1st Mechanized Infantry Division closed on Safwan, Iraq. The Iraqi forces were shattered; the ground war was over.

The cease-fire took effect at 8:00 A.M. on the twenty-eighth. Elements of six Iraqi divisions, including a substantial portion of the RGFC Hammurabi Armored Division, escaped across a pontoon bridge on the Hawr al Hammar just northwest of Basra. Later, this would prove to be a controversial decision. The Hawr al Hammar is a long lake ringed with swamps. The bridge could have been easily interdicted, either by air or ATACMS missile fire.

Still, Iraqi ground-offensive capabilities had been destroyed and the UN mandate—to rid Kuwait of its Iraqi invaders—had been fulfilled. America agreed to abide by the United Nations resolutions and not operate independently. All the UN could agree on was the liberation of Kuwait. Moreover, within the densely populated river valleys of Iraq lay the potential for another bout of Vietnam. American politicians and soldiers wanted nothing to do with that. While "getting Saddam" was a worthy goal, the UN would not authorize it, and American public opinion would not sustain the number of dead American soldiers required to do it.

In 100 hours of ground combat, the Allies destroyed the combat capability of the Iraqi ground forces. The Allies took 85,000 Iraqi prisoners. Iraqi POWs reported to their Allied interrogators that over 100,000 soldiers had deserted between January 17 and February 23, and many more had disappeared before the bombing began.

Two other sharper engagements, both leading to the destruction of what amounted to trapped Iraqi brigades, would be fought after the initial cease-fire took effect. In one of them, units from the 24th Mechanized Infantry Division would destroy over eighty Iraqi vehicles in a ten-minute-long firefight.

But for all practical purposes Desert Storm had subsided.

8. After the Storm, March 5 Through August

The war waged by the Kuwaiti resistance fighters against Iraqi snipers and "sympathizers" was a small version of that waged by surviving Republican guardsmen against the Shiites in southern Iraq and the rebelling Kurds in the north. Likewise, American forces occupying southern Iraq had to contend with occasional snipers and lots of minefields. United States troops (primarily marines, Special Forces, and combat support personnel) supported the establishment of Kurdish refugee camps in northern Iraq. The Special Forces, along with U.S. Marine and British infantry contingents supported by elements of the Turkish Army, created "safe haven" camps for the Kurds. Iraqi paramilitary and police units were forced out of the zone. By the end of this phase, the Turks were back to tangling with their own Kurdish guerrillas. Likewise, the United States prepared contingency forces to deal with Iraqi reluctance to comply with UN sanctions on chemical and nuclear weapons.

Tactical Analyses

Armored Brigade Maneuver

Both the "armored wedge" and "armored V" (reverse wedge) formations were used by advancing American armored brigades. The armored wedge is, in some ways, easier to control. The standard wedge formation has one battalion task force, usually a mechanized infantry battalion in Bradleys reinforced with tanks, leading the formation. Tank battalions follow on the flanks, ready to reinforce the mechanized battalion or envelop the enemy. A "reverse wedge" puts two battalion task forces in the front and one to the rear. This is used when combat is expected and more firepower is needed up front. Generally, a deployed armored or mechanized brigade moves in a nine-kilometer-long by nine-kilometer-wide box. The direct-support artillery battalion (twenty-four self-propelled howitzers) is "tucked" behind the lead battalion.

WHO DESTROYED WHAT

The ultimate goal of the ground operation was to regain control of Kuwait, and to do this Iraqi ground forces in the area had to be neutralized, which usually meant being destroyed. The core of Iraqi military power was in three weapons systems: tanks, artillery, and combat aircraft. Iraq began the war with 5,500 tanks, of which 4,600 were in the KTO. Four thousand tanks were destroyed or captured. About 1,000 tanks were destroyed by A-10 aircraft, 1,700 by other aircraft (F-16s, FA-18s, etc.) and another

Armor Brigade in "Wedge" Formation

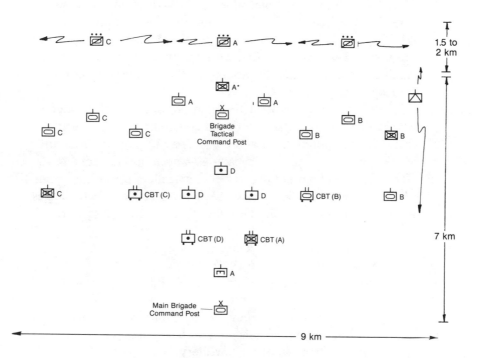

"Brigade Wedge" consisting of A, B, and C maneuver
battalions and D artillery battalion. Cavalry troop with 3 platoons
conducts reconnaissance in forward area.

* = Lead vehicle has GPS

600 by helicopters (mainly the AH-64). Over 400 were destroyed by Allied tanks in the ground war, and 300 were captured.

There were 3,500 artillery pieces and rocket launchers, of which 3,100 were in the KTO. The Allies destroyed 2,100, most by aircraft, although the most crucial counter-battery (artillery destruction) during combat was performed by Allied artillery and tanks.

Of 500 Iraqi combat aircraft, at least 40 were destroyed in the air, over 140 in their shelters, 40 captured on the ground, and 115 fled to Iran. This left Iraq with about 150 combat aircraft in varying degrees of readiness. Some of these were used in March 1991 against Iraqi rebels.

While much was made of the quantity and superior range of Iraqi artillery, it was the quality and competence of U.S. artillery that made the difference. For the past sixty years, American artillery has been the most technically advanced and effective in the world. This lead has not diminished, as artillery operations in the Gulf demonstrated. Several new American artillery technologies got their first work out in the Gulf War. Among these were:

- MLRS—The highly accurate, long-range (40-kilometer) multiple rocket launcher.
- Artillery Spotting Radar—Been around for a while, but the current (early 1980s) Firefinder radar, supported by electronic warfare equipment to ensure that the Firefinder's own broadcasts do not attract enemy fire, can spot the location of enemy artillery, and pass the data to friendly guns (or MLRS) before the enemy shells have hit the ground. If the enemy guns do not move immediately after firing one round, they are doomed.
- Meteorology—In other words, local weather conditions (heat, humidity, winds, etc.). This data is used to adjust fire and make it more accurate. U.S. artillery now has an automated system that keeps all artillery units supplied with accurate information and ensures that first-round fire is on target.
- Fire Control—Now computerized and highly automated. Data goes automatically from Firefinder radars, meteorological stations, and forward observers to the guns. Things happen in seconds rather than in minutes, and this makes an enormous difference. Current equipment is of the laptop personal computer variety.
- Survey—Most of the world's artillery units still use con-

ventional surveying methods to locate where the guns are so that they can accurately fire at distant targets. The United States used GPS receivers in the Gulf, doing in seconds what used to take much longer.

- Training—Probably the best-trained artillery troops in the world. Constant training and experienced leadership gave the U.S. artillery a decisive edge.
- Ammunition—the DPICMs (shells filled with flashlight–battery–sized bomblets) were used for the first time and proved highly effective. A 155-mm shell carries 88 bomblets, an 8-inch shell 180, an MLRS rocket 644, and a larger ATACMS rocket 950 (of a different-model bomblet). The 100-kilometer–range ATACMS rocket is fired from the MLRS launcher (taking as much space as six MLRS rockets). The bomblets were released when the shell was still in the air and rained down on a wide area, where the explosions killed or injured any troops out in the open.

The net result was a slaughter of the highly touted Iraqi artillery. The DPICM was particularly devastating. The Iraqis called it "Steel Rain," and once the word got around (helped by Allied propaganda leaflets), Iraqi troops (particularly artillerymen) abandoned their weapons and fled. Dozens of Iraqi artillery positions were later found with few, if any, dead soldiers in the vicinity and often no damage to the guns. But the trucks and the rest of the troops were gone, having fled after the first taste of steel rain.

Even the best-trained and equipped Iraqi artillery units, those belonging to the Republican Guard, were wiped out once they went into action against Allied artillery.

PSYCHOLOGICAL OPERATIONS

Psychological (propaganda) warfare played an important role in the Persian Gulf War. The Saudis were particularly clever in directing leaflets and radio broadcasts at "fellow Arab" Iraqi soldiers. In some ways, it was easy—Saddam Hussein wasn't popular to begin with, and his religious appeals were easily blunted by the Saudis.

CENTCOM's (Central Command) "psyops" warriors also used leaflets and radio broadcasts, but in particular they liked to play up B-52 carpet bombings. Even when the iron rain from B-52s didn't strike their targets, the morale hit taken by the soldiers suffering from the attack was devastating. B-52 attacks could be heard at least 100 kilometers away, and at times the ground tremors could be felt 200 kilometers away from the target area. So U.S. Army psyops specialists prepared and distributed by airdrop a leaflet with a picture of a B-52. The leaflet gave, in Arabic, the date and time the next wave of B-52s would "visit" the Iraqi troops in the target zone. The B-52s arrived as prophesied. Suddenly, the psyops leaflets had a newfound credibility and encouraged many Iraqis to surrender before, and after, the ground offensive began.

Armored Fighting Vehicle Reliability

The high reliability rates of the M1A1 Abrams tank and M2 Bradley infantry fighting vehicles made possible the extraordinary plunge and hook of the 7th Corps and the 24th Mechanized Infantry Division's gallop to the Euphrates. One U.S. armored brigade made a 300-kilometer march, arriving with 116 of its 117 M1A1s and all of its 60 Bradleys. The one M1A1 that did not make the march did not start the move.

No Bradleys reported transmission problems during the offensive, even though transmission problems had plagued Bradleys during training exercises (but that's what training is for—to work out the kinks). Overall, Bradleys had a 90 percent or better readiness rate prior to and during combat.

Some commanders reported that the two days of rainy weather during the offensive may have given them a bit of a break since that kept the sand down on the ground and out of their vehicles' engine filters. But the importance of keeping engines ready had been drilled into the troops by the weeks and months of training in the dust.

Refueling

On the average, seven to eight M978 HEMTT (Heavy Expanded Mobility Tactical Truck) tanker refueling vehicles (with a 2,500-gallon fuel capacity) accompanied each tank battalion. The tanks needed them. The M1A1s' 1,500-horsepower turbine engines gulped fuel. During the 1st Cavalry Division's 100-

kilometer twelve-hourlong march into Iraq, the tanks in one battalion required 300 gallons of fuel each. That works out to five gallons to the mile. Other units experienced fuel-consumption rates of six to seven gallons to the mile.

Some tankers advocate looking at M1A1 fuel expenditure as a function of time, if the "tactical idle" is employed. When the "tac idle" is operating, the M1A1 burns almost as much fuel sitting as it does moving. Tac idle does have its uses: It gives the tank immediate speed.

Most tankers prefer to run on diesel (DF2), though in Saudi Arabia the M1A1s often ran on JP1 and JP4 (airplane fuel) and occasionally JP5. Tiger Brigade, 2nd Armored Division, was able to refuel USMC AH-1W Sea Cobra attack helicopters with JP5 fuel they had in their M1A1 tanks. The 2nd Armored was also able to give the marine helicopters TOW ATGMs.

More Logistics on the Move

The use of Heavy Equipment Transporters (HETs) to schlep M1A1 tanks way out west in preparation for the "Hail Mary" attack by 7th and 18th Airborne Corps showed what combat service support does for an army. The HETs consist of a truck tractor and seventy-ton-load semitrailer. The HETs can haul the sixty-seven-ton M1A1 tank on highways, unimproved roads, and, as the ground offensive showed, cross-country if need be. Using the HETs to move the tank to the armor unit's combat assembly area saves on tank wear and tear and allows for rapid rear-area movement of tank forces. Such rapid redeployment of a tank force can make for a very surprised enemy, and in the case of General Schwarzkopf's Hail Mary, did. Typically, a HET can move on a road at 30 mph with an M1A1 aboard the semitrailer.

Other facts make the logisticians' triumphs in Desert Storm even more dramatic. A typical U.S. armored division (16,000 troops, 320 M1A1 tanks, 210 Bradleys, 72 M109A3 self-propelled 155-mm howitzers, and a battery of MLRS) in a rapid ground offensive will consume daily over 1,800 tons of fuel, 1,000 tons of water, and 5,000 tons of ammunition. The troops will consume 48,000 meals and use tons of spare parts and other items. That's over 8,000 tons a day for each of ten U.S. divisions. Sometimes when the move is so rapid, the logisticians can skimp on the meals: The troops don't have time to eat. But meals are lightweight compared to lugging water, fuel, and ammo.

This is why chief CENTCOM logistician Lieutenant General William G. "Gus" Pagonis opted for forward-supply bases and highly mobile forward-supply units located just behind the front lines. But this solution would not have been possible if the Allies had not had complete control of the air. Even with air domination, it was a calculated risk, but one that paid off. Pagonis began the war as a major general. He got his third star during the operation. He deserved it.

Combined Arms Scouting

Even with air superiority, there are never enough aircraft to keep all the terrain in front of advancing units covered. Enemy troops could still move around undetected and, when encountered without warning, increase the chance of friendly casualties. This was largely avoided due to the use of many forms of scouting. Traditionally, faster, more lightly armored vehicles acted as scouts. Several U.S. commanders interviewed for this book agreed that the best ground cavalry scout units in the desert were a mix of wheeled vehicles (HMMVs with grenade launchers and TOWs) and M2 Bradley fighting vehicles and M3 Bradley Cavalry fighting vehicles. Units needed armored scouts that could take fire from the enemy, return fire, then disengage. Wheeled scouts were great for quick screens on the flanks. In the Gulf there were more resources available, and several new systems were used for scouting. These included J-STARS, RPVs, and helicopters assigned to major ground units. Electronic warfare (EW) units proved very useful, for if the Iraqis wanted to use their radios, the EW detachments could locate where the transmission was coming from. On the move, the helicopter was the preferred scout. But to provide thorough and twenty-four-hour coverage, a combination of systems was used. Backing up all this scouting capability was a lot of firepower. One of the two U.S. armored cavalry regiments moved into Iraq with one attack helicopter (18 AH-64s) and three artillery battalions (over eighty guns and rocket launchers). The AH-64s could carry over 200 Hellfire missiles on an average sortie (plus rockets and 30-mm cannon). Because the Hellfire hit what it was fired at most of the time, this sortie means that several battalions of any tanks were gone, if they could be found. Any Iraqis that survived would get hammered by the artillery before running into the regiments' 120 M1 tanks. The 7th Corps divisions used similar methods, while the units advancing through the Iraqi

fortifications in Kuwait relied more on RPVs and scouts in armored vehicles. J-STARS had a bird's-eye view of the battlefield,
but it could not always tell friend from foe, nor could it get a good
fix on exactly what that glowing blob on the screen consisted of
(one time it was just a hundred miles of barbed wire swaying in
the wind). When the situation calls for it, like watching a key road,
individual scouts (or Special Forces) will be placed in an observation post. These posts, however, require a lot of resources, as you
must always have helicopters or ground units ready to go in and
get the scouts out if they are discovered.

Iraqi Surrenders

The incessant air attacks broke the morale of the dug-in Iraqi
infantry. Several Iraqi soldiers even surrendered to unarmed
journalists. One U.S. mechanized infantry unit reported firing
one 25-mm round at a single Iraqi (holding a pair of binoculars)
three kilometers away. Well beyond effective range, they
watched the tracer flash toward the soldier. The round hit the
man a split second after he began to raise his arm. What had
he been doing? Moments later, the infantry platoon saw 400 soldiers stand up. The unit began to surrender en masse.

Sometimes would-be POWs weren't so lucky. The marines
pushed a rolling artillery barrage in front of their advancing infantry. Some reports suggest that a score of Iraqi troops were
killed by the artillery fire as they were preparing to surrender.
That is part of the "fog of war"—it is difficult to determine intentions when the high explosive is falling. Others were killed
when Allied engineer vehicles and tanks crushed their bunkers.
The CENTCOM directive was to minimize Allied casualties. In
the latter stages of the Allied ground offensive, however, one
army brigade commander decided to stop using indirect artillery

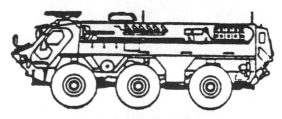

*Fox NBC recon vehicle. Detects the presence of chemical warfare
agents. Sixty of these were donated by the Federal Republic of
Germany to Coalition forces*

fire because, he concluded, "the Iraqis couldn't surrender to an artillery round." The fight was clearly over.

Iraqi Desertions

Many Iraqi soldiers deserted before being sent to the "southern front." Iraqis knew, if not by personal experience then by ancient reputation, that the Arabian desert in August was a most unpleasant place to be. Somehow the large number of deserters was not detected by U.S. intelligence analysts, even though they were monitoring Iraq's communications. Perhaps the Iraqi military commanders did not discuss the topic for fear of getting shot by Saddam. Perhaps the extent of the desertions was not believed, or was suppressed, by American analysts in order to keep coalition troops on their toes. Whatever the case, the desertions increased through mid-January, as Iraq continued to grant troops in Kuwait leave to make short visits home. Many troops on leave did not return. When the air war began, many could not return because of the air attacks on transportation targets. At that point, the Iraqi Special Forces security troops began to clamp down on troops found away from their units, and the stories of Iraqi "death squads" began to circulate.

There were apparently forty-two Iraqi divisions sent to Kuwait and southern Iraq. At full strength, with normal support and supply units, this would have amounted to over half a million troops. But most of these divisions apparently arrived understrength to begin with, and suffered continuous losses from desertions right up to the end of the war, particularly toward the start of the air war. The "missing" 100,000 troops apparently never left Iraq or got back to their homes as soon as they could via the simple expedient of going home on leave and never returning to their units in the desert.

U.S. ARMY WEAPONS SYSTEMS DEPLOYED
JANUARY 15 THROUGH MARCH 10, 1991

M2 Bradley	1,047	Infantry carrier
M3 Bradley	597	Scout vehicle
M1 Tank	116	Older version

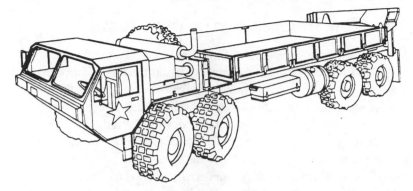

HEMTT—U.S. Army 20-ton supply vehicle

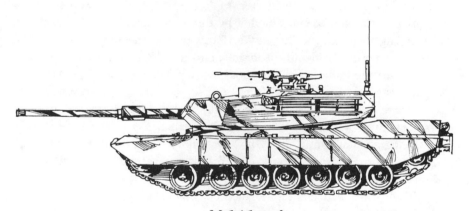

M-1A1 tank

M1A1 Tank	1,837	Latest model
M-109 155 mm (SP)	617	Principal artillery weapon
M-9 ACE	27	Armored Engineer Vehicle
MLRS	181	Rocket launcher
AH-64	267	Attack helicopter
UH-60 Blackhawk	329	Light transport helicopter
CH-47	142	Heavy transport helicopter

THE WEAPONS OF THE GROUND WAR

M1A1 Tank: This armored vehicle exceeded all expectations and put aside for good all the old stories of its shortcomings. The biggest bugaboo was readiness. As previously mentioned, during the U.S. 3rd Armored Division's 200-kilometer road march at night, not one of the 320 M1s involved had a breakdown. Overall, through the campaign, readiness of the M1A1 tank exceeded 90 percent. Most of the meaningful damage to M1s was from mines (two were disabled). Of nearly 1,900 M1A1 tanks in the theater, one was destroyed, four were permanently disabled, and four were damaged. Only seven M1A1 tanks were hit by T-72 fire. None of those hit were seriously damaged. Only a few dozen tank crewmen were injured in combat. Offensively, the M1's thermal sights allowed the tank to destroy T-72 tanks hidden by the worst climatic conditions, including the thick oil-fire smoke. Even though the thermal sight couldn't positively identify a target at over 1,000–1,500 meters, it could see the target as a "hot spot" at over 5,000 meters. The M1 gunners simply fired at the target until something blew up (usually no more than three rounds), and a large "hot spot" from the resulting explosion showed up on their thermal sight. The armor-piercing ammunition of the M1A1 was more lethal than expected. In one case, the frontal armor of a T-72 was penetrated by a 3,500-meter shot (that is, over two miles).

M1A1s survived hits at 400 meters. One revealing incident occurred when an M1A1 was stuck in the mud. The unit (part of the 24th Infantry Division) had gone on, leaving this tank to wait for a recovery vehicle. Three T-72s appeared and attacked. The first fired from under 1,000 meters, scoring a hit with a shaped-charge (high explosive) round on the M1A1's frontal armor. The hit did no damage. The M1A1 fired a 120-mm armor-piercing round that penetrated the T-72 turret, causing an explosion that blew the turret into the air. The second T-72 fired another shaped-charge round, hit the frontal armor, and did no damage. This T-72 turned to run, and took a 120-mm round in the engine compartment and blew the engine into the air. The last T-72 fired a solid shot (sabot) round from 400 meters. This left a groove in the M1A1's frontal armor and bounced off. The T-72 then backed up behind a sand berm and was completely concealed from view. The M1A1 depressed its gun and put a sabot round through the berm, into the T-72, causing an explosion. Other U.S. units arrived. They tried to pull out the M1A1 but couldn't get it out, even with two M88 tank retrievers pulling together. So the order came down to blow the tank in place to avoid capture. As there were no explosives available, a handy platoon of M1A1s decided to fire on the bogged-down tank. Two rounds did not penetrate the turret. The third round did penetrate the turret and caused the onboard ammunition to explode, but this blew out through the roof blow-off panels. At this point more recovery vehicles became available, and they decided to try again to pull it out, and were successful. Just for the sake of a test, they loaded up the 120-mm gun and fired it. It worked although the sights were now damaged from the ammo explosion. The tank was taken back to the repair yard, the turret was replaced, and the tank is back in its battalion.

Many of the M1s were put out of action by the perennial nemesis of armored vehicles, the land mine. One of the more underrated and ubiquitous weapons of this century, land-mine losses have increased steadily since their first widespread use in World War II. In peacetime, despite the large number of mines held ready for combat use, the problems of clearing enemy mines tends to get overlooked. Such was the situation when U.S. forces went to the Persian Gulf. It was known that the Iraqi Army made heavy use of land mines, and this was confirmed from August on when Iraqi troops were observed planting hundreds of thousands of mines on the Saudi border.

There was one other tank in the Gulf that matched the U.S. M1. This was the British Challenger. Not as agile as the M1, the Challenger has, in some respects, a superior long-range fire-control system. The longest confirmed kill by a tank was a 5,100-meter (over three miles) shot by a British Challenger. The Challenger's 120-mm gun is of a different design than the American gun, and the British ammunition is made to even more exacting standards. The results speak for themselves.

M1A1 120-mm Tank Gun: This gun on the U.S. M1A1 tank got its first workout in southern Iraq and exceeded expectations. As an example, in one case an armor-piercing round from a M1A1 hit the turret of a Russian-made Iraqi T-72 tank, passed completely through the turret, and hit (and destroyed) a second T-

72. Even penetrating the thinner side turret armor of a T-72 and having enough punch left to penetrate the side armor of a second T-72 is an impressive performance. These T-72s do not have the same armor as Russian T-72s, as Russia does not export the best versions of its weapons. Instead, it exports what weapon experts call "monkey models" that lack many advanced features, such as in the case of the T-72s, additional armor in both conventional and "reactive"—explosive—versions.

M2 Bradley Fighting Vehicle: The Bradley Fighting Vehicle got less of a workout during the ground phase of the war, although the vehicle proved just as reliable as the M1. The gunsights of the Bradley's 25-mm gun were effective even in oil-fire smoke and sandstorms. The 25-mm Bushmaster cannon was more lethal than expected, easily demolishing all targets except tanks (and even there, some serious damage was done). Of 1,600 Bradleys in action, three were disabled, including one by friendly fire. Several dozen Bradleys sustained damage from artillery and direct fire, but they were not the "coffins ready to burn" many critics said they would be.

M270 MLRS: The MLRS system (an updated version of the Russian "Stalin Organ" multiple-rocket launcher first used on the Germans to great effect in late 1941) made its combat debut in the Gulf. Allied units had 140 MLRS launchers available. Criticized for being more expensive than a "cheap" rocket launcher is supposed to be, the MLRS proved its worth. One reason for its expense was the precision positioning system built into the launcher, exacting construction of the missiles (and its expensive cluster-bomb warheads), all for the purpose of delivering a salvo of twelve rockets accurately at ranges exceeding twenty miles. The MLRS carrier is built on an M2 Bradley chassis. The launcher has two canisters, each of which has six rockets.

U.S. troops later discovered evidence of the MLRS' value when they came upon the scenes of death and destruction where the missiles had landed. The marines were so impressed that they have suggested using MLRS as their *only* artillery (replacing conventional guns). The big advantage of multiple-rocket launchers had always been the surprise of all those rockets arriving at once. With regular artillery, the first shells to hit give the survivors time to head for cover, thus greatly reducing the effect of all the subse-

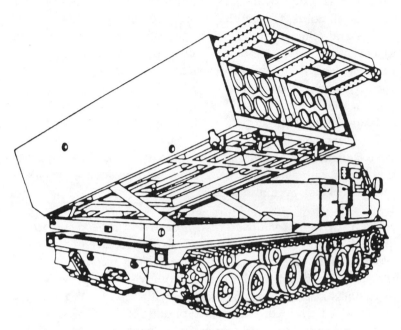

*MLRS—U.S. multiple rocket launcher (also used to launch
ATACMS missile*

quent shells. The hundreds of bomblets raining down from a
dozen MLRS rockets fired from a single launcher will kill or injure over half the troops in an area roughly 700 by 100 meters.
Films of these rockets hitting a target zone presents a terrifying
vision of an expanding zone of closely spaced small explosions.
Each of these small explosions has the effect of a large hand grenade, meaning anyone within ten or twenty yards of each explosion is liable to be hit by fragments. The bomblets fall close
enough together to expose a soldier to fragments from more than
one explosion. This is not at all like normal artillery fire, where
a much smaller number of larger explosions is the norm. Interviews with Iraqi prisoners indicated that these attacks were
deeply demoralizing. The Iraqis learned that if they saw and
heard a few little pops a hundred or so meters distant, they had

a few seconds to find protection, or get torn to pieces. The word
got around among Iraqi troops that this weapon gave little warning and was lethal over a large area. The MLRS attacks were
made at all hours, leaving the Iraqi troops in a constant state of
anxiety and reluctant to leave their bunkers for any reason, even
to bury their dead comrades. Advancing Allied troops found
acres of dead Iraqis where the victims had been caught in the
open by massed rocket fire.

Over 10,000 rockets (at $16,000 each) were fired from MLRS
at Iraqi artillery, antiaircraft units, troop and vehicle concentrations, command-and-control and logistics facilities. From the
same launchers, over thirty of a hundred available ATACMS missiles (each with three times the range and payload of standard
MLRS rockets) were also fired.

HMMWV (High Mobility Multipurpose Wheeled Vehicle) Truck:-
The "Hummvee" (or "Hummer") is the replacement for the
World War II–era jeep and three-quarter-ton truck. In general,
they performed well in the Persian Gulf War and proved to be
mechanically reliable. Hummers are highly mobile. Whereas the
World War II jeep could carry 800 pounds on its eleven-by-four-
foot frame, the Hummer carries 2,500 pounds on a fifteen-by-
seven-foot frame. This makes it a foot wider than your average
civilian vehicle. The Humvee is actually lower than the jeep, six-
ty-nine inches versus the sixty-seven-inch-tall Hummer. Built to
excel at cross-country travel, the wider Hummer is much less
prone to tip over and has more ground clearance (sixteen inches).
The Hummer has a 150-horsepower V-8 engine and gets six miles
to the gallon (with a 25-gallon-capacity tank) cross country, about
twice that on good roads. It can go from zero to thirty miles per
hour in seven seconds and has a governor that limits road speed
to sixty-five miles per hour (troops who have disabled the governor have attained maximum speed of up to eighty miles an hour).
It has special tires that are designed to be shot-up and still take
the vehicle at least thirty miles farther at thirty miles an hour.

The Hummer weighs 5,200 pounds and is flexible enough to
replace two longtime standard army vehicles, the jeep and the
three-quarter-ton truck (a small pickup that could carry
1,500–2,000 pounds). Because of its greater capacity and agility,
the Hummer can also serve as a combat vehicle. A turret ring
can be mounted in the back to support a TOW (antitank) missile

launcher, heavy machine gun, or Stinger antiaircraft missiles. Some of these combat models had up to 100 pounds (or more) of mounted Kevlar panels. This is the same material used in flak jackets and provides protection against small-arms fire and shell fragments. Used as a light truck, the Hummer can carry eight troops in the back or eight wounded troops plus two medics. The heavy-duty suspension, in addition to making for exceptional cross-country performance, allows the mounting of electronic equipment and workshop shelters in the back. There is also a military police version with a Kevlar top. Actor Arnold Schwarzenegger was allowed to buy one to drive around Los Angeles. He can afford it; the army pays up to $54,000 for each Hummer. Thus encouraged, the manufacturer began selling to civilians in the fall of 1991; at about $40,000 per vehicle.

AH-64 Apache: Another much maligned high-tech weapon, the AH-64 Apache helicopter gunship performed much better than many of its critics predicted. Operational readiness ended up at 90 percent, far in excess of even the army's standard of 70 percent. The principal weapon of the Apache was the Hellfire missile, of which over 4,000 were fired (at $40,000 each). The Apache/Hellfire proved too fast and too far away to get hit by Iraqi tanks, and the Hellfire's range and accuracy were lethal at maximum distances (of over three miles). At least four army helicopters were engaged by Iraqi infrared (heat-seeking) and radar-guided missiles, but no helicopters were lost. As previously noted, the defensive systems on the helicopters gave warning of the radar-guided missiles, and heat-suppression devices on the engines confused the heat seekers. This allowed the helicopters to evade the missiles or caused the missiles to miss.

In one battle the 101st Airborne Division's 4/229 attack helicopter battalion destroyed fifty Iraqi tanks with Hellfires. Hellfires were also used against antiaircraft emplacements on oil platforms in the Persian Gulf.

OH-58D (AHIP) Kiowa Warrior: Unarmed OH-58Ds provided laser targeting for artillery-fired Copperhead 155-mm shells and Hellfire missiles fired by Apaches and USMC AH-1Ws. Fifteen armed OH-58Ds participated in the war, attacking oil platforms with Iraqi antiaircraft and antiship missile installations and attacking Iraqi minesweepers.

Copperhead: Ninety 155-mm laser-guided Copperhead rounds were fired during the war. Initial reports indicated at least 75 scored direct hits. One armored-brigade commander reports engaging three Iraqi T-55 tanks with three Copperheads during one hourlong period. An OH-58D scout helicopter provided the laser designation. Two of the tanks were destroyed by direct hits, and one was disabled. That's three for three.

ATACMS: The Army Tactical Missile System (ATACMS) saw its first action in the Persian Gulf War. One hundred five of these "deep strike" missiles were sent to Saudi Arabia, and about three dozen were fired. (As of January 1991 the army had only 170 of these missiles on hand.) The ATACMS is fired from a launcher similar to the MLRS (two ATACMS fit in the same space taken up by twelve normal MLRS rockets) but has a range of up to 150 kilometers (the exact range is classified). The missile packs a payload of 950 M74 baseball-sized antipersonnel/antimaterial bomblets. Targets engaged by ATACMS included SAM sites, Iraqi logistics sites, howitzer and rocket batteries, and tactical bridges. J-STARS aircraft provided targeting information for ATACMS. ATACMS is a preprogrammed missile capable of changing altitude and direction as it nears its target. In one instance, an ATACMS was launched at a suspected Iraqi Scud position. Initial battle-damage reports indicated that ATACMS either destroyed or rendered inoperable all of its targets.

The Infantry War

About 1,200 coalition infantry platoons saw action during the ground war, and these platoons contained some 50,000 troops. While there were at least as many support troops close by the tank and infantry platoons, these combat units operated the 2,200 tanks and 2,800 other armored vehicles that led the charge into and around the Iraqi lines. The 60,000 front-line ground troops and pilots (less than 12 percent of the total) took most of the casualties, as is normal, and inflicted most of the damage on enemy forces.

Desert Boots

United States Army troops experienced some basic problems with a very basic but essential item of equipment: the boot. The standard-issue black leather boot and the Vietnam-era jungle boot have holes that tend to fill with sand. The Army Material Command (AMC) put in a rush order in early January 1991 for 500,000 desert boots. Of course, most didn't start to arrive for distribution until around April 1 (a wry sort of April Fool's joke). The boots feature a "thermal heat barrier" to keep heat from the sand from being transferred inside the boot. The heel and toe of the desert boot are made of suede tan leather.

The Flying Truck

One of the unsung heroes of the ground war was the CH-47 Chinook cargo helicopter. Normally, it carries about ten tons of cargo about 100 miles. But to establish the 101st Airmobile Division's advance base 140 miles deep in southern Iraq, the CH-47s flew with cargoes of fuel, so they could be refueled at the advance base for their return trip. The night before the ground war started, the CH-47s of the 101st were in constant motion, many of the helicopters making over a dozen round trips a day. One of the aviation battalions of the 101st flew 338 missions during this period.

The Mighty Land Mine

Most of the U.S. M1A1 disabled during the war were victims of that perennial nemesis of armored vehicles: the land mine, one of the more underrated and ubiquitous weapons of this century. Land-mine losses have increased steadily since their first widespread use in World War II. In peacetime, despite the large number of mines held ready for combat use, the problems of clearing enemy mines tends to get overlooked. Such was the situation when American forces went to the Persian Gulf. It was known, for instance, that the Iraqi Army made heavy use of land mines, and this was confirmed from August on when Iraqi troops were observed planting hundreds of thousands of mines on the Saudi border.

Nonetheless, U.S. Army and Marine Armor units have been deploying a significant countermine capability since the late 1980s. A few years earlier, the army's Armor School realized that Russian mine-warfare capabilities would gum up the new American mobile-warfare tactics (the AirLand Battle Doctrine) unless U.S. mechanized units had an effective and fast obstacle-breaching, mine-clearing, and mine-breaching capability. Starting in early 1989, the army began deploying the Armor Organic

Countermine System (AOCS). The Marine Corps has also adapted some of the army system to its needs while creating additional equipment for what it sees as uniquely marine requirements. Significantly, the mine-plow portions of the system were manufactured by the Israeli firm Ramta Structures and Systems, which meant at least one Israeli military system played a key role in the Gulf ground war.

The Armor Organic Countermine System (AOCS) consists of a Mineroller Set, three Mineroller Mounting Kits (each tank fitted with one of these kits can use the mineroller set), three Track Width Mine Plows (TWMP) and one Clear Lane Marking System (CLAMS).

One reason for sending the German-based U.S. 7th Corps to Saudi Arabia was that these were the only units in the American Army with modern mine-clearing equipment and some experience in using it. Some of the equipment was sent to Saudi Arabia separately.

Mine-Clearing Use and Effectiveness

There are basically three types of antipersonnel and antitank mines to clear. The most common mine is the "scatterable" mine that is basically a cluster-bomb bomblet. It weighs from a few ounces (antipersonnel) to five pounds (antitank, the "trackbuster" that immobilizes the tank by damaging its track and running gear). The scatterable mine is cleared quickly with the plows, and can also be destroyed by rollers, explosives, or small-arms fire. Both antipersonnel and antitank mines are buried. In this case, there's more variety. Some antitank mines are double impulse: that is, they don't go off until a second tank has gone over them. This is to make them effective against mine rollers. For this reason, you have to clear a minefield twice to make sure you've got everything.

Mine plows will clear 95 percent of all types of surface and buried mines (including the double-impulse variant). A chain stretched between the plows detonated tilt-rod fused mines. This type of mine lets the pressure of the vehicles' track detonate a mine that is a foot or more away, so the explosion will do more damage against the thin bottom of the tank and not just the running gear (wheels and tracks). However, there will still be a two-foot lane left between plows that may contain buried or surface mines. In addition, the rate of advance depends on soil type and plow-depth setting. Average speeds are 80 to 250 meters a minute. Higher speeds can be used if the plow is not digging too deep and you want to move quickly. Often, this is a reasonable tactic if you are pretty sure all you are facing is a bunch of scatter mines dropped by rockets or an aircraft.

The plows used on U.S. Marine AAPCs are not used to do an initial clearing, but merely to "proof" a lane cleared by other means. This is because the lighter AAPC is too vulnerable to damage from mines the plow may explode.

As mentioned previously, the mine roller used by the army and marine armor units clears 95 percent of all mines that the roller actually goes over. Still, up to 40 percent of the mines may remain in the space between the two rollers. The rate of advance with rollers is 150–200 meters a minute. Dual-impulse mines, of course, are designed to destroy tanks pushing rollers, so rollers are generally used to "proof" lanes already cleared by plows or explosives.

Explosive charges are 95 percent effective against surface mines and 75 percent effective against buried single-impulse mines. Most double-impulse mines will still have an impulse left, so you have to use rollers or plows to clear them out.

The plows and rollers described above come in sets of two, one in front of each tank track. This still leaves an uncleared lane in between the two cleared lanes. As more and more armored vehicles move through the cleared tracks, they wear down the cleared areas (depending on the soil composition) until the "raised" central lane is so high that the vehicles get stuck. Engineer units have full-width plows, but these are heavier, and there are fewer of them available. The point of having mine-clearance equipment with the tank companies is so that an advance is not halted while someone calls up the engineers.

Yet Another Tactical Use of Mine Plows

The Tiger Brigade (1st Brigade, 2nd Armored Division) and the 1st Mech Infantry Division used mine plows on M1A1 tanks as bunker-busters. (The Tiger Brigade had 27 mine-plow tanks among its 122 M1A1 tanks.) The mine-plow tanks would flank the resisting Iraqi position then charge through the obstacle-belt, smashing into bunkers and firing pits. Some Iraqi soldiers would be crushed—the survivors usually surrendered after the morale-destroying demonstration. This tactic saved Allied lives as well as ammunition. Ultimately, it saved Iraqi lives. Pounding bunkers with artillery and bombs would have killed everyone.

Call Out the Reserves

Much was made during the war of the failure of the 48th and 256th U.S. Army National Guard Infantry Brigades and the 155th National Guard Armor Brigade to complete their training and deploy to the Persian Gulf. The 48th Brigade (drawn primarily from the Georgia National Guard) was the "round-out" brigade of the 24th Mechanized Infantry Division, and had reported to the Mech Division that it could be combat-ready in forty-eight to fifty days. The officers in the 48th Brigade were both overly optimistic and overly ambitious. It took ninety-one days to reach combat readiness.

Actually, getting a brigade of part-time soldiers ready for Air-Land Battle in three months is quite a feat. Three months is about the minimum amount of time it takes to get battalion- and brigade-sized units up to snuff. (The Israeli experience is unique—Israel has essentially been at constant war for forty-five years, and middle-aged Israeli reservists have more combat experience than many Israeli regulars.)

If World War II is a guide, most National Guard and reserve units took 180 to 300 days of training to even begin to reach a combat-ready level of proficiency. The truth is, Desert Shield and Desert Storm would have been impossible without reserve personnel. U.S. Navy, USAF, and USMC reservists all participated in the war effort. Nearly 150,000 Army Reserve and National Guard personnel were activated for the conflict. This included around 20,000 Individual Ready Reservists (IRRs), who are not assigned to reserve units, and Individual Mobilization Augmentees (IMAs), who are assigned to "fill out" Regular Army units and staff positions. A total of 1,050 different Army Reserve and National Guard units and detachments were activated. The list includes:

- Over 165 port and transportation units activated in the United States and Saudi Arabia
- Forty reserve and National Guard engineer units deployed to Saudi Arabia (seventeen percent of the total engineer missions in Southwest Asia were handled by reservists.)

- Eleven chemical-warfare units sent to Saudi Arabia
- Two National Guard artillery brigades (the 196th and 142nd), deployed in Saudi Arabia (The MLRS battalion in the 142nd fired over 900 rockets.)
- Fifty combat-support units, three combat service-support headquarters, nine ordnance units, twenty water-handling units, and nine petroleum-handling units activated (Reservists provided 65 percent of the petroleum-handling capacity and 59 percent of the water-handling capacity in Southwest Asia).

U.S. Army Reserve units alone contributed the following percentages of units in the Army's Persian Gulf War effort:

89 percent of prisoner-of-war–handling units
39 percent of field medical units
63 percent of psychological-operations assets
94 percent of civil-affairs units
33 percent of chemical-defense units
21 percent of maintenance units
31 percent of transportation units
69 percent of postal handling and administration units

Quick Study 7:
Training Coalition Ground Forces

Although most U.S. ground forces have been primed for a major battle against Russian forces in Europe for the last forty years, the last twenty years have seen extensive preparations for combat in the desert. There are several reasons for this:

- The Israeli Factor—The performance of Israeli ground and air forces during the 1967, 1973, and 1982 nonwars has had a profound effect on American officers and military planners. The Arab-Israeli wars have been the only major mechanized wars fought since World War II. Because Israel is a United States ally and recipient of enormous amounts of aid, American forces obtained detailed information from Israel on how these wars were fought. In addition, since the early 1980s, American preparedness has been enhanced by its annual field exercises with Egyptian forces.

- U.S. Training Areas—The teaching of armored and mechanized units requires large training areas, and most of the big ones, as we have indicated, are in the American West, in the North American desert. Dusty, sandy, dry, and with temperatures over 110 degrees, these areas are similar to deserts anywhere (including Arabia). American troops thus had a lot of experience operating under desert conditions.
- The NTC (National Training Center)—In the early 1980s, the U.S. Army began training battalions at a desert training area in California under very realistic conditions. Using "Laser-Tag" equipment and a well-trained "enemy force," combat battalions obtained a two-week introduction to realistic fighting conditions. The lessons and experiences of these operations read like a historical account of battles. Indeed, the "lessons learned" sound just like the reports of historical battles. But probably the most significant benefit obtained has been to identify those officers and noncommissioned officers *not* capable of operating under combat conditions and getting them out of the way. (This is usually a process that takes place—painfully and expensively—during a unit's first weeks in combat.) The NTC experience has allowed America to field its most effective peacetime army ever. The air force and navy have been running similar programs for their pilots since the 1970s, and the marines have always instilled a realistic battlefield frame of mind starting with boot camp.
- The "Persian Gulf Fire Brigade"—Since the 1973 oil embargo, the U.S. military has been preparing for possible deployment to the Persian Gulf. Much training, staff planning, and logistical preparation has gone into this effort.

In effect, the war in the Persian Gulf was the first war in American history that its armed forces were actually trained and prepared for. All of America's previous wars, right back to the Revolution, were *ad hoc* affairs. This one was different, beginning and ending with the effectiveness of American troops.

CHAPTER 9

The Naval War

Naval operations were a vital part of the Allied coalition's Persian Gulf Campaign, though when compared to air and ground operations, a somewhat invisible, misunderstood, and not adequately appreciated component of the war effort.

Yet naval forces were intimately involved with all aspects of the conflict. The U.S. Navy's Middle East Task Force (METF) and the British Armilla patrol, though small naval forces, provided an immediate political show of force even as Iraqi forces plunged into Kuwait. Naval forces were also vital to the economic war. Ultimately, Allied navies (the American Navy in particular) were responsible for maintaining the naval embargo and isolating Iraq from the outside world. The U.S. Navy and Marines, after deploying half a dozen aircraft carriers in the region, contributed about a quarter of the combat air power used in the air war. The USN's marine troops constituted about 20 percent of the U.S. ground forces, and the surface warships and amphibious craft threatened the Kuwait coast and tied down at least half a dozen Iraqi divisions.

When Iraq invaded Kuwait on August 2, 1990, the only major military forces the United States had in the area were naval. These ships quickly became the nucleus of the embargo force that succeeded in shutting down Iraqi imports and exports by the end of that month. The navy quickly moved more of its aircraft carriers, as well as its marines, into the area. Years earlier, the marines had stockpiled heavy equipment (tanks and artillery) on the island of Diego Garcia, 4,000 kilometers south of

Saudi Arabia. This equipment was immediately shipped north to positions near the Kuwait border.

While the USAF quickly flew combat and transport aircraft, and the U.S. Army landed light airborne and airmobile infantry to defend Saudi Arabia, the U.S. Navy and Allied naval forces (such as Great Britain's Armilla patrol) provided a crucial additional force at sea. If the Iraqis had advanced into Saudi Arabia and overwhelmed Arab and American forces on the ground, the U.S. Navy would still have been off shore and ready to lead the reentry into the Arabian Peninsula.

The Naval Role in the Embargo

The United Nations–mandated economic embargo of Iraq was not a trivial exercise. Iraq had a small navy, but a substantial air force and a proven air-to-surface-missile capability (French-built Exocet missiles). Iraq also had a substantial stock of naval mines and, as subsequent events would demonstrate, the capability to get over a thousand of these mines into the water. The American-led naval embargo required that participating warships be protected by carrier aircraft and constant vigilance against potential Iraqi attacks. Iraq ultimately proved unwilling to oppose the embargo with force. This was a logical move, as Allied naval forces outside the range of Iraqi aircraft (or mine-laying capability) could still stop any ships trying to enter or leave Iraqi ports. But Allied naval units could not take this reasoned behavior as a given. Moreover, Saudi Arabian oil-loading terminals were within range of Iraqi aircraft and missiles; thus the fleet had to defend these as well. As a result, the embargo force was in a constant state of tension as it operated within range of Iraqi air power.

While enforcing the naval embargo, Allied navies (primarily U.S.) intercepted nearly 8,000 merchant ships, and boarded about 12 percent of those. Nearly seventy merchant ships had to be diverted for trying to run the embargo. Over 90 percent of interceptions were in the Red Sea, 30 percent performed by non-U.S. ships. When Desert Storm started, there were 120 American and fifty Allied ships on hand. Iraq was shut off from outside assistance, except for what could be flown in (until the air embargo in December) and what was smuggled across the Jordanian, Turkish, Syrian, and Iranian borders. Much of the smuggling was on pack animals, led by Kurds who had long been doing this sort of thing and saw no reason to stop just because there was a war going on. In any event, over 95 percent of Iraq's normal imports were stopped by the embargo.

Royal Navy in Action

The Royal Navy (RN) proved to be the bane of Iraq's tiny fleet, and the RN's missile-firing Lynx helicopters, the chief killer. The RN fired twenty-six Sea Skua antiship missiles and sank twelve Iraqi patrol ships. Iraqi coastal defenses didn't have much luck either. When the Iraqis fired a Chinese-made Silkworm antiship missile in the general direction of the battleship surface action group, an RN Type 42 destroyer on antiaircraft duty shot it down with a Sea Dart surface-to-air missile.

Naval Aviation and the Air War

Ultimately, half a dozen American aircraft carriers were committed to the campaign. In addition, there were two Marine Corps air wings. Overall, the navy and marines contributed over 1,000 aircraft and helicopters to the Allied air effort.

Yet the primary purpose of aircraft carriers is to protect the fleet (namely, the aircraft carriers and their escorts) and secondarily to attack enemy ships. The third mission of carrier aviation is to attack land targets, and for this reason a smaller portion of carrier aircraft were available for bombing missions than the land-based air-force aircraft. Only about a third of the navy and USMC sorties were used for attacking enemy targets. Another third were assigned to fleet defense and another third were allocated for various forms of support (supply runs, refueling, electronic warfare, etc.). The navy portion of attack sorties would have been even smaller had it not been for all the marine aircraft, which were largely used for supporting the marine ground units.

Carrier Aircraft Operations

U.S. carriers typically have sixty-six to eighty-six aircraft and helicopters (there are some variations because of two smaller carriers and ongoing reorganization). There are twenty F-14s, which are the primary "fleet defense" aircraft as they carry the long-range Phoenix antiaircraft (and anticruise missile) missiles; and there are twenty F-18s, which can be used either as light bombers or as interceptors. On some carriers the F-18 replaces the F-14. The principal bombers are the twenty A-6 aircraft, which carry a large load and are able to operate in all types of weather (on some carriers these are replaced by the newer, and less capable, F-18). One carrier on-station during the war (the *USS Kennedy*) still deployed the older A-7 bomber, which was in the process of being replaced by the F-18 when the war broke out. Beyond these sixty combat aircraft, there are four to five EA-6 electronic warfare ("Wild Weasel") aircraft and four to five E-2 early-warning radar aircraft (smaller versions of the air-force AWACS), plus ten S-3 antisubmarine aircraft (some are used for electronic warfare) and six SH-3 antisubmarine helicopters. The antisubmarine aircraft were useless during the campaign (and did not accompany some carriers to the Gulf) while the E-2s were used to control carrier aircraft over the water before passing them off to the air-force AWACS that were running the air show. Thus, about 20 percent of America's available carrier aircraft stayed out of the action.

When attacking land targets, a carrier would launch "strike packages" of twenty to thirty aircraft. Depending on how far the aircraft had to fly, a carrier could launch three or four of these strike packages a day. In addition, several dozen sorties would be flown in defense of the carrier itself. Overall, each carrier managed to average 150 sorties a day, except for one or two days a week when the ship would be busy taking on supplies. (Carrier aircraft take off with a lot of fuel and munitions and bring very little back with them.)

During the war, carrier aviation operated under three major restrictions, aside from having some aircraft that were not suitable for the campaign. First, most had to operate far away from Iraq. It was at least 1,200 kilometers from the safer Red Sea to most Iraqi targets and 800 kilometers from Persian Gulf locations. Missions flown from the Red Sea area took about five hours, while Persian Gulf operations required about half as much time. The Red Sea missions required heavy use of (USAF) tanker aircraft.

Second, the naval aviation did not have procedures worked

out to efficiently integrate their operations with the air force–led air campaign. The U.S. Air Force and the other NATO air forces had developed elaborate procedures (using computers and high-speed communications equipment) for controlling large numbers of aircraft in combat. These procedures did not include carrier aircraft because no one had considered this a likely scenario. Thus, the navy did not have the computer and communications equipment needed to have its 300 attack aircraft work efficiently with the 1,300 land-based attack aircraft. This is surprising, as planning for a major war in the Persian Gulf began in the early 1970s. At that time, it was known that any campaign would involve large numbers of air-force and carrier aircraft and that these forces would have to work together. Chalk it up to another instance of interservice rivalry: While many such problems had been solved by 1990, this case reminds us that there is still more to be done.

The third problem was supplies. Carriers have limited space on board for fuel and bombs, or for maintenance and operations in general. To sustain the high level of sorties needed for the air war, the carrier crews had to work at a killing pace. Supply ships were constantly coming alongside to replace fuel, munitions, and spare parts used to carry on the bombing. As a result of the distance and supply restrictions, naval aviation was able to generate fewer sorties per aircraft than land-based planes. During the last two weeks of the air war, more of the navy carriers moved from the Red Sea to the Persian Gulf, allowing the carriers to generate more sorties as closer proximity more than halved flight time. The land-based Marine Corps air wings operated at about the same rate as other land-based aircraft, but the carrier-based sorties were a crucial addition to the air campaign even if there could not be more of them. The navy also lacked much laser bombing equipment.

As it was, the navy was able to contribute only 20–25 percent of the sorties flown. There is some dispute between the air force and the navy over the exact percentage, as the air force counts its air-defense sorties flown over Saudi Arabia while not counting the navy air-defense missions flown over the fleet. The number at issue involves 6,000–7,000 sorties, so it is not an inconsequential issue. Overall, navy and marine aircraft flew nearly 30,000 sorties during the war.

Marine Corps Air Wing Operations

The 159 aircraft of an air wing are equipped and trained to support marines fighting on land. During the Persian Gulf War, these aircraft included (for one air wing): 48 F-18s, 40 AV-8 Harriers (vertical takeoff jets), eight EA-6 Wild Weasels, twenty-one forward air-control aircraft, eight RF-4 reconnaisance jets, twenty A-6 bombers, and twelve KC-130 tankers (which spent a lot of their time supporting the distant carrier aircraft). A marine air wing also had 156 helicopters, including 108 heavy transport choppers, twenty-four lighter UH-1s, and twenty-four AH-1 gunships. The marine AV-8s and helicopters could also operate the several amphibious carriers present in the Gulf.

SUMMARY—U.S. NAVY AND MARINE CORPS COMBAT AVIATION IN THE GULF

	F-14	F-18	A-6	A-7	E-6	A-8	AH-1
USS Saratoga	20	20	10		5		
USS Kennedy	20	20		10			
USS Midway		30	20		5		
USS Ranger	20	20	10		5		
USS Roosevelt	20	20			5		
USS America	24	24	10		4		
Navy Total	104	134	50	10	24		
USMC Total		96	40		16	80	48
Total	104	230	90	10	40	80	72 =
							626

Naval Ground Forces

The Marine Corps put the equivalent of two mechanized infantry divisions on the battlefield. Both the 1st and 2nd Marine Divisions deployed over 300 aircraft and helicopters with them and sufficient amphibious ships to send eight infantry and tank battalions across a beach on the Kuwaiti coast. The major contribution of the navy to the Gulf fighting was with the Marine Corps troops.

Other Aspects of Naval Operations

The Threat of Amphibious Operations   In addition to the troops on the ground, the marines were still able to keep over 17,000 troops off-shore on amphibious ships to tie down Iraqi coastal-defense divisions. This made the ground fighting easier as the Iraqi divisions on the coast were largely left alone by Allied aircraft so that the bombing could be concentrated on enemy divisions on the Saudi border and the armored divisions (mainly the Republican Guard) held in reserve.

Naval Mines   The United States Navy has long neglected the danger of naval mines and paid for this lapse during the Gulf War by having its in- (close to) shore operations restricted and two major ships heavily damaged by mines. Although the United States began building new minesweepers in the 1980s, the first of these boats was still being readied for service when the Gulf War broke out. Those that were available dated back to the 1950s. But the United States had not abandoned mine-sweeping technology entirely, and had developed a number of helicopter-based minesweeping techniques. These involved the towing of sleds through the water that contained various devices for detecting and clearing mines. The problem with the sleds was that the technology that could be carried on them was not able to keep up with the emerging technology of the naval mines. Other nations, particularly those in Europe, continued to develop state-of-the-art minesweepers, and these went into the Gulf to clear many of the more difficult to find and clear ("sweep") mines.

They had their work cut out for them. The Iraqis put over 1,200 mines into the Persian Gulf. Most of these were of the ancient (last-century) contact type. These were simple enough to be made in Iraq and consisted of a steel container that floats just beneath the surface and is anchored by a chain and anchor to the ocean bottom. Sensors protrude from the mine in all directions, so that when a ship hits one of these sensors, the mine detonates (which is why they are called "contact mines"). One of them blew a large hole in an amphibious aircraft carrier (carrying marines, helicopters, and AV-8 jump jets). It was suspected that this mine was cut loose from its chain, either deliberately or on purpose, by the Iraqis. These "free-floating" mines are more difficult to detect and sweep because they are constantly moving. Usually, mine fields are set up with groups of mines, sometimes hundreds, to insure that the maximum number of ships will be hit and that it is unlikely that a ship will get through the field unhurt. Free-floating mines are usually encountered singly and in unpredictable locations. Given the water-flow patterns in the Persian Gulf, free-floating mines will eventually wash out into the Indian Ocean, after about twenty years of making their way down the coast with the slow-moving currents.

More modern mines, available from Italy and Russia, do not float but sit on the sea bottom. For obvious reasons, these are called bottom mines. They are also called influence mines, because they detonate as a result of more subtle effects than a ship's banging up against them (as with the older contact mine). Three different influences are used: sound, water pressure, and magnetism; and sometimes two or three of these are combined, in the same mine. To make matters more complicated, the mines are equipped with microcomputers and memory so that only certain degrees of influence (ships of a certain size) will set off the explosive charge. Another favorite trick is to program the mine to turn itself on only at certain times, or to let a certain number of ships go by before detonating under the next ship. All these tricks make sweeping bottom mines very difficult.

Contact mines are much simpler to sweep. The term "sweep" itself comes from the earliest antimine technique of having two small ships with an underwater cable strung between (and in front of) them move slowly through a minefield snagging ("sweeping") the moored mines on the cable, bringing the mines to the surface and detonating them with gunfire (or hauling them aboard for later disposal or reuse). The United States' switch to helicopter-pulled sleds made this sweeping procedure much quicker, but sweeping was much less effective against bottom mines.

Bottom mines can sometimes be fooled ("foxed") by a sled equipped with noisemakers, magnetic devices, or a combination of both. Pressure mines are more difficult to fox, as it is a complex procedure to simulate the water pressure of a warship passing over a mine. The most effective technique for clearing bottom mines is to use a minesweeper with a powerful sonar that literally maps the bottom of the ocean (usually a shipping channel), and then goes through the channel, each time you want to check for mines, and compares the sonar "pictures" from the earlier passes. The bottom mines are often designed to blend in with the ocean bottom, thus requiring the powerful sonar to get a good look plus a small remote-control submarine that can take a close look at suspicious objects with a TV camera and, if a mine is found, leave behind a small explosive charge to destroy the mine.

The Persian Gulf is ideal for bottom mines because these mines cannot be under too much water. The Gulf is rarely more than 100 feet deep, and is therefore well suited for bottom mines. (Contact mines, on the other hand, can be anchored by chains in several hundred feet of water.)

One American cruiser set off a bottom mine and demonstrated another aspect of these nasty little devices. Bottom mines do their damage by forcing a mass of water violently against the ship. This does not normally cause a hull breach, but it does usually rearrange the insides of the ship. In this case, the cruiser was, literally, bent out of shape. This twisting of the ship's frame damaged the vessel's propulsion and steering systems as well as weakening the internal water tightness of the compartments (which would cause a hull breach to sink the ship). The cruiser had to be taken out of service and required some very expensive repairs.

Many reasons were given for the lack of a U.S. amphibious landing on the Kuwaiti coast. One obvious reason was that it was unneeded given the huge success of the ground war and the opportunity to avoid the casualties the marines might have taken going through mine-filled coastal waters and over defended (and fortified) beaches. In addition, the officially stated reason, however, was the desire to engage in an operational deception. A "faked" landing would make the Iraqis think there would be a beach assault and thus force many Iraqi divisions to stay by the beach and out of the battle. Still another reason to avoid amphibious assault was the difficulty of clearing out the mines so that the landing craft could even get close to the coast. The number of Iraqi naval mines and the extend of the minefields were not known with sufficient accuracy. Dozens of amphibious ships, making close to shore for an assault, would be at risk. The fact that a large helicopter carrier and a cruiser got hit by mines reinforces the minesweeping obstacles being faced. By mid-March, fewer than a quarter of these mines had been cleared, which gives some idea of how formidable the mine threat was.

Naval Mine-Clearing Operations: The Numbers

Between February 17 and April 13, 1991, Allied naval Mine Countermeasures (MCM) forces swept up 422 mines. (Another 200 had been swept and destroyed prior to February 17.) This chart illustrates the severity of the problem posed by naval mines. They could not be cleared quickly enough to prevent unacceptable losses during an amphibious landing. Thus, there never was any serious consideration of an amphibious attack.

Dates	*# mines swept*
February 17–23	22
February 24–March 2	2
March 3–9	18
March 10–16	11
March 17–23	47
March 24–30	85
March 31–April 6	159
April 7–12	78
53 days	422

On February 18, in areas thought to be clear of mines, the U.S. amphibious ship *Tripoli* was hit by a turn-of-the-century type mine, which blew a large hole in the ship's hull. This was repaired in the Gulf. But a few hours later, the U.S. cruiser *Princeton* was hit by two pressure mines that nearly broke its back. The *Princeton* was put out of action for the duration.

Iraqi coastal defenders laid about 1,200 mines. Though they did not sink a coalition naval ship, the mines did influence the battle and, in the case of the cruiser *USS Princeton,* put her out of action. The *Princeton* had passed over an Italian-made Manta influence mine and limped away with her hull cracked. The Manta is a 500-pound (235-kilogram) shallow-water mine of modern design. The Manta's sensors detect a ship overhead by the pressure the ship creates as it passes through the water.

The Iraqis seemed to have preferred linear naval minefields. The entrances to Kuwait's harbor featured rows of influence mines laid about a mile apart. The Allies were not prepared to deal with the number and sophistication of the Iraqi minefields, and this was a major reason why the marines did not attempt an amphibious landing.

Naval Special-Operations Forces: U.S. Navy SEALs   The navy's commandos (the Sea Air Land troops) operated along the coast in cooperation with U.S. Army Special Forces and the British SAS commandos. The navy maintains a force of 1,300 special-operations troops, including six SEAL teams (plus two converted nuclear ballistic-missile submarines for delivering them) and several other support units. There were only a few hundred SEAL troops involved, but they played a crucial role in gathering intelligence along the Kuwait coast.

Naval Gunfire Support   Two U.S. battleships were in the Persian Gulf. Each of them had nine 16-inch (406-mm) guns and 32 Tomahawk cruise missiles. The sixteen-inch guns have a maximum range of about 40 kilometers, but the maximum reach inland is about thirty kilometers. The firepower these two ships represented backed up the amphibious assault threat, did a lot of damage to Iraqi installations in the coastal areas near the Saudi border, and (along with the nearby carriers) made it possible for the Saudi/Kuwaiti ground forces to advance quickly up the coast once the ground fighting began. (A ban on live firings of sixteen-inch guns was lifted September 11, 1990, a lingering aftereffect of the 1989 turret explosion on the battleship *Iowa*.)

The battleships *USS Wisconsin* and *USS Missouri* fired over 1,000 tons of shells in support of Operation Desert Storm (which is around 4,300 Mk-82 bomb equivalents, or roughly the bomb tonnage delivered by 550 A-6 fighter-bomber missions). The sixteen-inch guns were the primary weapons, though the battleships also pack several batteries of five-inch (127-mm) guns.

Thirty-one of the eighty 16-inch missions were preplanned missions or missions that were not spotted. Eight (10 percent) of the missions were spotted by ground or air observers. Forty-one (52 percent) of the missions were spotted by the battleships on or-

16-INCH GUN MISSIONS

	16-inch missions fired	16-inch rounds fired
USS Wisconsin	33	324
USS Missouri	47	759
Total:	80	1083

ganic Unmanned Aerial Vehicles (UAV). Bomb damage assessment (BDA) was not available for thirty-nine of the eighty 16-inch strikes. Lack of spotters or smoke and haze prevented assessment. Of the forty-one missions with BDA reports (fired against sixty-eight targets), 32 percent sustained light-to-moderate damage, 26 percent heavy damage, 10 percent of the targets were neutralized, and 32 percent were completely destroyed.

Submarine Support   There was really no need for nuclear submarines in the Gulf War, but they participated anyway. The navy had developed submarine-launched Tomahawk cruise missiles, and this was a chance to try some of them out. Several U.S. nuclear attack submarines fired twelve Tomahawk cruise missiles at ground targets inside Iraq. The navy commented that the submarine launch was a success.

A Carpet of Bombs   The U.S. Navy and U.S. Marine Corps dropped over 38,500 Mk-80 series bombs (approximately 15,000 of the 89,000 tons dropped) over Iraq and Kuwait. The navy alone dropped 22,000 bombs.

Quick Study 8:
Orders of Battle

An "Order of Battle" is a list of troop units and where they are assigned. An "OB" is how the generals, admirals, and historians sort out who is who. This Quick Study gives the reader a real feel for the number of troops involved in the war. By country, it lists in fair detail the major military units used in the campaign and where they were during various phases of the war.

Iraqi Order of Battle

NOTE: Iraq entered the war with seven corps (numbered 1 through 7) and the Republican Guard Force Corps. A "reserve" 8th Corps may have been created to coordinate Reserve units and rear Service units being brought into southern Iraq.

- Republican Guard Force Corps (RGFC)
- 1st Armored Division Hammurabi (350 tanks)
- 2nd Armored Division Medina (350 tanks)
- 3rd Mechanized Division Tawakalna (220 tanks)
- 4th Motorized Division Al Faw (100 tanks)
- 5th Motorized Division Baghdad (150 tanks). This unit was once part of Saddam's bodyguard. It had sported four or five brigades and additional support units.
- 6th Motorized Division Nebuchadnezzar (100 tanks)
- 7th Motorized Division Adnan (100 tanks)
- Republican Guards Special Forces Division (3 brigades of Special Forces troops and some support troops). This may be considered the Corps' security force.

In 1980 the Republican Guards consisted of two brigades devoted to defending the Baath regime. By 1986 the RGFC had expanded to seven brigades. At the end of the Iran-Iraq War, twenty-eight brigades were listed as Republican Guards units.

The Baghdad Republican Guard Division served as the Baath "regime maintenance" unit—a tough and politically reliable formation dedicated to fending off military coups. When back in Baghdad, the division was responsible for watching the RGFC Special Forces brigades. The Baghdad Division, contrary to many reports during the war, did deploy to the Iraq-Kuwait border (just northeast of Kuwait). It was smashed by coalition air strikes and the 7th Corps' ground attack. Still, it appears that at least a brigade of RGFC forces remained in Baghdad. The RGFC Special Forces Division was essentially equipped as a motorized infantry division with a mix of armor, mechanized infantry, and truck infantry units. The RGFC Special Forces Division was dug-in immediately southwest of Basra. Several of its battalions escaped from the U.S. 7th Corps' attack by fleeing into Basra. At least two other Republican Guard Divisions were being formed in mid-March 1991. One of the divisions has been identified in the Western press as the "Abu Nidal Republican Guard Infantry Division." This division probably has the strength and manpower of a single large brigade.

Deployment of the Iraqi Army by Corps

The Republican Guard Force Corps took up dug-in defensive positions just north of Kuwait and inside Iraq. They were in position to act as a mobile reserve—and keep the Iraqi Army from retreating into Iraq. (See the map on page 256 for details.)

Iraq divided its occupation forces into four corps areas. The RGFC was also assigned to the theater. The four corps were (clockwise on map) the 2nd Corps, 3rd Corps, 4th Corps, and 7th Corps (in southern Iraq and west of Kuwait). Estimates suggest that Iraq committed a total of forty-two Iraqi ground divisions in the Kuwait and southern Iraq area, and that the army comprised twenty-five infantry divisions, three mechanized infantry, and six armored divisions, with the RGFC providing the remaining eight divisions. There appear to have been at least two separate brigades assigned to the area, including the 54th Armored Brigade in 3rd Corps' area; a third separate Iraqi Army tank brigade (53rd) may have been located southwest of Basra, dug-in with the RGFC Special Forces Division. Elements of this brigade may have been destroyed west of Kuwait City. A "Palestinian Division" (of dubious military value) was raised in Kuwait City. The 54th Armored Brigade was destroyed by the 1st Brigade 2nd U.S. Armored Division (Tiger Brigade) during its drive on Kuwait City.

2nd Corps: This unit, responsible for the Al Faw Peninsula in Iraq, northeastern Kuwait, and the Kuwaiti Islands (including Bubiyan and Failaka islands) consisted of four infantry divisions and parts of an infantry brigade. The 53rd Separate Armored Brigade, elements of which were identified west of Basra with the RGFC, may also have originally been assigned to 2nd Corps. Three of the 2nd Corps infantry divisions were destroyed in the Allied air and ground attack.

3rd Corps: Eleven or twelve divisions were assigned to 3rd Corps and occupied southeastern Kuwait. The 11th Special Forces Infantry Division operated in Kuwait City and may have been part of this corps. More likely, the 11th operated under separate command. This unit may account for some differences in orders of battle that identify twenty-six rather than twenty-five Iraqi infantry divisions in the theater of operations. The Iraqi 3rd Armored Division, 1st Mechanized Infantry Divisions, and 5th Mechanized Infantry Division were in the 3rd Corps zone on February 23, 1991. This corps also deployed at least seven infantry divisions. The 15th, 18th, 19th, and 20th Infantry Divisions were operating in the southeastern sector of the corps, while the 7th, 14th, and 29th operated in the corps' western sector. (Another infantry division may also have been part of this corps.) The 54th Armored Brigade (which had 45 T-72 tanks) operated in the 3rd Corps area. Most of this corps was destroyed in the Allied ground attack or by air attack as they attempted to retreat from the Kuwait City area.

4th Corps: The 4th Corps occupied southwestern Kuwait, where at least six divisions were also located. The 6th Armored Division was assigned to 4th Corps, while the 10th Armored Division (sometimes called the Saladin Division and at one time considered to be an elite Iraqi Army unit) appears to have been dug-in on the northern edge of the 4th Corps zone, near the Republican Guards. It may not have been under the direct command of the 4th Corps, but may have been part of the 7th Corps or operating as part of the RGFC. The 21st Infantry Division and 36th Infantry Division were two of the four infantry divisions assigned to the 4th Corps; and all of the divisions in the 4th Corps area, including the 10th Armored, were destroyed in the Allied ground attack. The forward-deployed infantry divisions of 3rd and 4th Corps were hit particularly hard by the Allied air offensive.

7th Corps: The Iraqi 7th Corps was deployed in southern Iraq just west of Kuwait. Twelve divisions were assigned to it, including two armored divisions and one mechanized (the 52nd Mechanized Infantry Division). The 12th Armored Division was located in this zone, covering its flank with the Iraqi 4th Corps (where it was destroyed by the 1st British Armored Division). Nine infantry divisions were assigned to the corps, including the 45th, 47th, 48th, and 49th Infantry Divisions. All of the divisions were destroyed in the Allied ground offensive.

1st, 5th, and 6th Corps: These Iraqi corps were "hollowed out" during the course of the conflict to provide troops for the Kuwaiti theater. Units were shifted out of the 1st Corps after the air war began on January 17. At the end of the conflict (February 28) only one mechanized infantry brigade (which may have been Republican Guards or the Presidential Guard Brigade) and a pair of Special Forces brigades remained in the Baghdad area. The Iraqi 1st Corps commanded units roughly situated from south of Mosul to north of Baghdad. The Baghdad area nominally fell in the 2nd Corps area, and apparently some 2nd Corps units remained there during the war (though most of the 2nd Corps was deployed in Kuwait and Basra). The Iraqi 6th Corps covered Iraq from south of Baghdad to the northern boundary of the Kuwaiti Theater of Operations (KTO). It was responsible for covering the important Majnoon Island area north of Basra and had a dedicated "swamp command" (Marsh Forces) as part of the corps. The Iraqi 5th Corps covered the northern (Turkish and Syrian and western Iranian) border areas. Evidence suggests it deployed throughout the crisis nine to ten infantry divisions. This means the Turks and Kurds tied down between 100,000 and 120,000 troops. Some of these divisions were special-operations divisions charged with keeping Kurdish rebels suppressed.

As mentioned above, a temporary "reserve corps" sited in southern Iraq may have been called the 8th Corps. This headquarters coordinated reserve units, militia units, and support formations. Some analysts have published orders of battle referring to an 8th Mechanized Corps that controlled the 10th Iraqi Armored Division. We can find no hard evidence for existence of this corps. This corps and its support formations may well be one of the bones of contention between competing intelligence estimates of Iraqi strength in the Kuwaiti Theater of Operations.

What was the total strength of Iraqi forces in the KTO? Initial estimates of 450,000–550,000 *effective* troops were much too high. The morale effects of Allied bombing and desertions, the difficulty of estimating losses from air strikes, and poor Iraqi record-keeping of personnel assignments all contributed to the overestimates. By May 1991, U.S. intelligence experts had lowered the figure to 400,000–450,000 in the area as of February 23. From 325,00 to 375,000 Iraqi troops seems to be a much finer figure for Iraqi strength in the KTO by that time.

Iraqi Air Force

The Iraqi Air Force entered the war with some 730 front-line attack aircraft, including 370 fighters and 360 fighter-bombers and bombers. Only about 500 of these combat aircraft were operational, and, unless otherwise noted, all equipment was Russian.

- Bombers—20 Su-24, 8 Tu-22, 8 Tu-16, 4 Chinese H-6D
- Fighter-Bombers—70 MiG-23, 64 French Mirage F-1, 45 Su-20, 30 Su-25 (Russian version of the A-10)
- Fighters—40 Chinese J-6, 150 MiG-21, 40 French Mirage F-1, 10 MiG-25, 24 MiG-29

Iraq also started the war with 50 to 60 transport aircraft.

Preliminary figures suggest that the Iraqi Air Force was not so much destroyed as it was suppressed or forced into exile. Iraq entered the war with about 600 hardened aircraft shelters (also called Hardened Aircraft Bunkers, or HABs).

Nonmobile Antiaircraft Defenses

- Missiles—160 SA-2 launchers, 140 SA-3 launchers (both 1960s technology), 100 French Roland launchers (short range)
- Guns—Over 10,000, most 23 mm and 57 mm, some heavier caliber. About a third were deployed around Baghdad.
- Mobile antiaircraft defenses—Largely with army units. Three hundred mobile missile launchers (SA-6 and SA-8); hundreds of mobile and towed antiaircraft guns.

Iraqi Navy

Nine ships of about 1,000 tons, each armed with guns and missiles. Eight smaller missile craft. Six torpedo boats, twenty patrol craft. Eight minesweepers and six amphibious craft.

Allied Air Order of Battle

Avail is the number available in the Gulf. There were over sixty different aircraft and helicopter types used. The most-used 25 percent of aircraft types, in terms of sorties flown,

AIRCRAFT SORTIES BY AIRCRAFT TYPE

Aircraft Sorties	Aircraft Type	# Avail	Percent of Total Sorties
18,910	F-16	288	14.4
12,768	A-10	192	9.7
12,544	C-130	280	9.5
9,828	KC-135	180	7.5
9,408	FA-18	224	7.2
8,729	F-15	144	6.6
6,160	AH-64	267	4.7
4,032	AV-8B	90	3.1
3,898	F-14	116	3.0
3,640	Tornado	130	2.8
2,300	F-15E	48	1.8
2,156	F-4G	40	1.6
2,016	RF-4	36	1.5
1,848	A-6E	60	1.4
1,680	B-52G	60	1.3
1,613	F-111	36	1.2
1,600	F-117	42	1.2

are shown above. These aircraft flew more than 75 percent of the sorties.

The official sortie count was not released as of late 1991. So, the above is calculated from many independent bits of information. It's probably pretty accurate. You'll be able to check it out yourself when the official numbers eventually get released. In any event, it's clear that a few aircraft did most of the work. Note that the air force did not count the army AH-64 helicopter sorties. Here we have done so, and the AH-64 was one of the top five combat aircraft in terms of sorties flown (and destruction inflicted). Note also that the KC-135 tanker and C-130 local transport were also way up there. The air campaign could not have been fought without all those tanker sorties, nor without all the movement of supplies locally by the C-130s.

U.S. Air-Force Units

Most of the air-force units identified are "wings." An air-force wing is roughly equivalent to an army brigade. A wing contains 20–100 aircraft, and the largest ones have three or four squadrons (equivalent to army battalions), each with 12 to 24 aircraft. Just to totally confuse you, the air force has yet another unit type (usually temporary), the "group," which varies in size between that of a large squadron and a small wing. The air force also forms two to five wings into air divisions and two or more divisions into an air force (equal to a field army).

Fighter and Bomber Units: B-52G 1708th, 801st, 806th, 4300th Provisional Bomber Wings; F-15C/D 1st, 36th, 33rd Tactical Fighter Wings; F-15E 4th Tactical Fighter Wing; F-16C/D 363rd, 401st, 50th, 347th, 388th Tactical Fighter Wing; F-111 306th Strategic Air Wing, 48th Tactical Fighter Wing; F-117A 37th Tactical Fighter Wing (Stealth); A-10 354th, 23rd, 10th Tactical Fighter Wings.

Wild Weasel: EF-111 20th Tactical Fighter Group; 366th Tactical Fighter Wing; F-4G 35th, 52nd Tactical Fighter Wings.

Tactical Air Control: OV-10 507th Tactical Air Control Wing; OV-10/RC-12 5th AEB Electronic Warfare and FAC; OA-10 23rd Tactical Air Support Wing, 602nd Tactical Air Control Wing.

Miscellaneous: C-20 CINC Theater Commander transport; C-12 U.S. Embassy (Saudi Arabia) EMBASSY Light Transport; USSOCOM CENTCOM: Special Operations Unit (various helicopters and aircraft); EC-130 193rd SOG Psychological Warfare; 1st Special Operations Wing—55th Squadron (MH-60); 16th Squadron (AC-130H); 9th Squadron (HC-130 tankers); 8th Squadron (MC-130E transports); 20th Squadron (MH-53J).

Electronic Combat: E-8A J-STARS detachment: 4411th J-STARS Squadron (E-8); E-3A 552nd Airborne Warning and

Control Wing (AWACS); EC-130 41st Electronic Combat Warfare Squadron; RC-135 1700th SRS Electronic Warfare; RU-21 138th AVN Electronic Warfare (RU-21); RC-12 (etc.); 2nd AEB Electronic Warfare.

Air Reconnaissance: TR-1A; U-2R 17th Reconnaissance Wing; 1704th Strategic Reconnaissance Squadron; RF-4C 152nd Tactical Reconnaissance Group.

USAF Air Refueling Units: KC-135 1700th, 1701th, 1702nd, 1703rd, 1705th, 1706th, 1707th, 1712th, 1713th, 4300th Air Refueling Squadron.

USAF Airlift and Air Transport (MAC):   C-12 2nd AVN Light Transport, C-12 USMTM Light Transport; C-29 375th MAW Light Transports; C-130 1620th, 1630th, 1640th, 1650th, 1660th, 1670th, 1675th TAW Theater Transport Wings; other elements drawn from the 435th, 317th, and 314th Tactical Airlift Wings.

Base Support: 820th Red Horse Civil Engineering Squadron; 823rd Red Horse Civil Engineering Squadron.

U.S. Marine Corps: 3rd MAW (Marine Air Wing); Marine Air Groups 11, 13, 16, 26, 38, 37; includes F-18, AV-8, AH-1W, and transport aircraft and helicopters.

Allied Air Forces

Arab: Bahrain AF (1 squadron F-5); Qatar AF (20 aircraft, Mirage F-1); UAE Transports (total of 70 aircraft, C-130, fighter-bombers); Saudi Arabian Air Force (total of 220 aircraft, F-5, F-15, Tornado, KC-130, AWACS); Kuwaiti Air Force (total of 35 aircraft, Mirage F1, A-4).

Great Britain Royal Air Force (total of 85 aircraft):   Joint Helicopter Support Unit (Pumas and Chinooks); Tornado F-3 Squadrons: Squadrons 5, 11, 43; Tornado Group 1 Squadrons: elements Squadrons, 9, 14, 15, 20, 31, 617; Jaguar Squadron: 41 (with elements from Squadrons 6 and 54); Buccaneer Squadron (15 aircraft): elements from Squadrons 12 and 208; Nimrod Squadrons: elements from Squadrons 51, 120, 201, 206; RAF

Regiment (airbase defense): Squadron 20 (Air Defence/Rapier); Squadron 34 (Ground Defence).

Canada (24 CF/A-18 and support aircraft) initial unit: Squadron 409 (CF/A-18s), replaced in December 1990 by Squadron 439; Squadron 439 was reinforced in January by elements of Squadron 416.

French Air Force   (total of 60 aircraft): Mirage 2000, Mirage F-1, Jaguar, support aircraft.

Italian Air Force: 1 squadron of 8 Tornadoes, transport aircraft.

Allied Naval Order of Battle

Ships Deployed to the Persian Gulf and Near East Regions

Ship Type Abbreviations (the numbers after ship types are for identification purposes and are usually painted on the side of the ship): AD—Destroyer tender; AE—Ammunition ship; AFS—Salvage and rescue ship; AGF—Command ship; AKE—Cargo/ammunition ship; AOE—Fast combat-support ship; BB—Battleship; CG—Guided-missile cruiser; CV—Aircraft carrier; DD—Destroyer; DDG—Guided-missile destroyer; FF—Frigate, FFG—Guided-missile frigate; LCC—Amphibious command ship; LHA—Amphibious assault ship; LKA—Amphibious cargo ship; LPD—Amphibious transport dock; LPH—Amphibious assault ship (helicopter); LSD—Dock-landing ship; LST—Tank-landing ship; MCM—Mine countermeasures ship; MSO—Minesweeper-ocean; SSN—Nuclear attack submarine, T-AH—Hospital ship; T-AVB—Aviation logistic supply ship; USS—United States ship.
[date] = dates this major warship deployed
[Mediterranean] = indicates this submarine operated in the Mediterranean Sea

Persian Gulf Region
The numbers after ship names are for identification purposes and are usually printed on the sides of ships, or on the flight deck of carriers.

USS Blue Ridge (LCC-19), flagship, 7th Fleet/U.S. Naval Forces; *USS LaSalle* (AGF-3), flagship, Middle East Force; *USS Missouri* (BB-63) [January 1–March 24].

Amphibious Group 2 and the 4th Marine Expeditionary Brigade: *USS Nassau* (LHA-4); *USS Iwo Jima* (LPH-2); *USS Guam* (LPH-9); *USS Raleigh* (LPD-1); *USS Shreveport* (LPD-12); *USS Trenton* (LPD-14); *USS Portland* (LSD-37); *USS Pensacola* (LSD-38); *USS Gunston Hall* (LSD-44); *USS Manitowoc* (LST-1180); *USS Saginaw* (LST-1188); *USS Spartanburg County* (LST-1192); *USS LaMoure County* (LST-1194); *USS Wisconsin* (BB-64) [August 18–March 13]; *USS Worden* (CG-18); *USS Antietam* (CG-54); *USS Horne* (CG-30); *USS MacDonough* (DDG-39); *USS David R. Ray* (DD-971); *USS Leftwich* (DD-984); *USS Reid* (FFG-30); *USS Jarrett* (FFG-33); *USS R. G. Bradley* (FFG-49); *USS Nicholas* (FFG-47); *USS Vandegrift* (FFG-48); *USS Ford* (FFG-54); *USS Barbey* (FF-1088); *USS Avenger* (MCM-1); *USS Leader* (MSO-490); *USS Adroit* (MSO-509); *USS Impervious* (MSO-449); *USS Wright* (T-AVB-3); *USS Curtiss* (T-AVB-4).
　　USS Mercy (TAH-20) and *USS Comfort* (TAH-19), moored off Manama, Bahrain.

Amphibious Ready Group 3 and the 5th Marine Expeditionary Brigade (MEB): *USS Tarawa* (LHA-1) [January 12–May]; *USS Tripoli* (LPH-10); *USS New Orleans* (LPH-11); *USS Mobile* (LKA-115); *USS Vancouver* (LPD-2); *USS Denver* (LPD-9); *USS Juneau* (LPD-10); *USS Anchorage* (LSD-36); *USS Mount Vernon* (LSD-39); *USS Germantown* (LSD-42); *USS Peoria* (LST-1183); *USS Barbour County* (LST-1195).

Also in Region: *USS Tuscaloosa* (LST-1187); *USS Harry W. Hill* (DD-986); *USS Rentz* (FFG-46); *USS Kidd* (DDG-993); *USS McInerney* (FFG-8); *USS Shields* (FF-1066).

Thirteen SSNs (nuclear attack submarines) were deployed in the region. These included: *Louisville* (SSN 724) [January 18–January 30]; *Chicago* (SSN 721) [February 7–March 7]; *Newport News* (SSN 750) [Mediterranean]; *Philadelphia* (SSN 690) [Mediterranean]; *Pittsburgh* (SSN 720) [Mediterranean]; and *Birmingham* (SSN 695). (Seven others were undisclosed).

Red Sea (When Operations Commenced)

USS Belknap (CG-26), flagship, 6th Fleet; *USS Biddle* (CG-34); *USS Philippine Sea* (CG-58); *USS Sampson* (DDG-10); *USS Spruance* (DD-963); *USS Thomas C. Hart* (FF-1092); *USS Detroit* (AOE-4); *USS Yellowstone* (AD-41).

The aircraft carriers *USS Independence* and *USS Eisenhower* were deployed in early August and later withdrew. What follows are the official dates of deployment for the task forces (groups of ships operating together). The most common task force is an aircraft carrier and all its escorts and support ships.

USS Independence (CV-42) [August 5–November 4]; *USS Eisenhower* (CVN-69) [August 8–August 24]; *USS Saratoga* (CV-60) [August 22–September 21; October 23–December 9; January 6–March 11], with Carrier Air Wing 17—2 F-14A squadrons, 2 FA-18 squadrons, 1 A-6E squadron, support aircraft (total of 70 aircraft); *USS Belknap* (CG-26), flagship, 6th Fleet; *USS Biddle* (CG-34); *USS Philippine Sea* (CG-58); *USS Sampson* (DDG-10); *USS Spruance* (DD-963); *USS Thomas C. Hart* (FF-1092); *USS Detroit* (AOE-4); *USS Yellowstone* (AD-41).

USS John F. Kennedy (CV-67) [September 14–March 12], with Carrier Air Wing 3—2 F-14 squadrons, 2 A-7E Corsair II squadrons, 1 A-6E squadron, support aircraft (total of 70 aircraft); *USS Mississippi* (CGN-40); *USS Thomas S. Gates* (CG-51); *USS San Jacinto* (CG-56); *USS Moosebruger* (DD-980); *USS Samuel B. Roberts* (FFG-58); *USS Seattle* (AOE-3); *USS Sylvania* (AFS-2).

USS Midway (CV-41) [November 2–March 14], with Carrier Air Wing 5: 3 FA-18 squadrons; 2 A-6E squadrons, support aircraft (total of 66 aircraft); *USS Mobile Bay* (CG-53); *USS Bunker Hill* (CG-52); *USS Sterrett* (CG-31); *USS Hewitt* (DD-966); *USS Oldendorf* (DD-972); *USS Fife* (DD-991); *USS Curts* (FFG-38); *USS Kiska* (AE-35); *USS Sacramento* (AOE-1).

USS Ranger (CV-61) [January 13–April 19], with Carrier Air Wing 2: 70 combat aircraft (attack heavy air wing with 2 F-14 squadrons and 2 A-6 squadrons); *USS Princeton* (CG-59); *USS Valley Forge* (CG-50); *USS Paul F. Foster* (DD-964); *USS Francis Hammond* (FF-1067); *USS Kansas City* (AOR-3), *USS Shasta* (AE-33).

Amphibious Ready Group Alpha, 13th Marine Expeditionary Unit—(Special Operations Capable): USS Okinawa (LPH-3); *USS Fort McHenry* (LSD-43); *USS Durham* (LKA-114); *USS Ogden* (LPD-5); *USS Cayuga* (LST-1186).

Arabian Sea, Gulf of Oman, Persian Gulf

USS *Theodore Roosevelt* (CVN-71) [January 14–April 20], with Carrier Air Wing 8: 2 F-14 squadrons, 2 F-18 squadrons, support aircraft (66 aircraft total); USS *Leyte Gulf* (CG-55); USS *Richmond K. Turner* (CG-20); USS *Caron* (DD-970); USS *Hawes* (FFG-53); USS *Vreeland* (FF-1068); USS *Santa Barbara* (AE-28); USS *Platte* (AO-186).

Red Sea to Arabian Sea (February 13–14)

USS *America* (CV-66) [Janaury 15–April 3], with Carrier Air Wing 1: 1 A-6E squadron, 2 F-14 squadrons, 2 FA-18 squadrons, support aircraft (86 total aircraft); USS *Virginia* (CGN-38); USS *Normandy* (CG-60); USS *Prebble* (DDG-46); USS *Willaim V. Pratt* (DDG-44); USS *Halyburton* (FFG-40); USS *Kalamazoo* (AOR 6); USS *Nitro* (AE 23).

Eastern Mediterranean

Amphibious Ready Group 3-90 with the 26th Marine Expeditionary Unit–Special Operations Capable: USS *Inchon* (LPH-12); USS *Nashville* (LPD-13); USS *Newport* (LST-1179); USS *Fairfax County* (LST-1193); USS *Barnstable County* (LST-1198).

Additional Naval Forces: 67 ships of various types activated from the Ready Reserve Fleet; Prepositioning Squadron 2 (Diego Garcia) and Prepositioning Squadron 3 (Guam); 13 to 17 Maritime Prepositioning Ships (ships with equipment and supplies for ground forces prepositioned for quick support; Diego Garcia had 13 of these in its harbor prior to July 1990); P-3C Naval Patrol detachment (Seeb and Masirah Island); P-3C Naval Patrol detachment (Diego Garcia).

Ships in theater that returned to U.S. (partial list): USS *England* (CG-22) [July 31–November 3]; USS *Scott* (DDG-995); USS *O'Brien* (DD-975); USS *Taylor* (FFG-50); USS *Elmer Montgomery* (FF-1082); USS *Reasoner* (FF-1063); USS *Tattnall* (DDG-19); USS *Brewton* (FF-1086); USS *Dubuque* (LPD-8); USS *Goldsborough* (DDG-20); USS *J. Rodgers* (DD-983).

Great Britain (Royal Navy) 22 ships (total) included in RN deployments in area January 1991: HMS *Gloucester* (D96, Type

42 destroyer); *HMS Cardiff* (D108, Type 42 destroyer); *HMS London* (F95, Type 22 frigate); *HMS Brazen* (F91, Type 22 frigate); 7 support ships; 5 mine countermeasures ships; 4 landing ships.

Other Allied ships: Argentina—2 frigates; Australia—1 guided-missile frigate, 1 destroyer, 1 supply ship; Belgium—2 minesweepers; Canada—2 destroyers; Denmark—1 corvette; France—18 ships, 1 carrier with helicopters; Greece—1 frigate (Red Sea); Italy—4 ships; Netherlands—2 frigates, mine warfare ships; Norway—1 cutter, 1 supply ship; Oman—12 fast attack and patrol ships; Qatar—9 coastal patrol ships; Saudi Arabia—15 ships; Spain—2 corvettes, 1 destroyer; Turkey—2 frigates in Persian Gulf.

Allied Ground Order of Battle

The following types of units are listed in the Ground Order of Battle. The standard abbreviation for each major type of unit—e.g., Battalion (BN)—is given in parentheses. The number of troops for each is approximate. U.S. Marine units are usually heavily reinforced with various support units (engineers, armor, artillery, etc.).

Battalion (BN)—400 to 1,000 troops
U.S. Armored Cavalry Squadron—800 to 1,100 troops
U.S. Marine Expeditionary Unit (MEU)—900 to 1,300 troops
Brigade (BDE)—2,000 to 5,500 troops
U.S. Marine Brigade—5,000 to 8,000 troops
Group (GP)—1,500 to 4,000 troops
Regiment (RGT)—2,000 to 3,000 troops
U.S. Armored Cavalry Regiment (ACR)—4,200 to 5,000 troops

Division (DIV)—10,000 to 20,000 troops (usually two to five brigades)

U.S. Division—15,000 to 16,000 troops. U.S. armored and mechanized divisions are organized almost identically, the major difference being that armored divisions have one more tank battalion and one less infantry battalion than mechanized infantry divisions. Combat power of both types of divisions is virtually identical. Divisions are normally composed of three ground combat brigades, an aviation brigade, an artillery brigade, and a support command. A U.S. armored division had 350 M1A1, 330 M-2/3, 72 M109, 8 MLRS. Mechanized infantry divisions had 60 fewer tanks and 50 more M2s.

U.S. Marine Division—18,000 to 20,000 troops

1st British Armored Division—17,000 to 18,000 troops (two very large brigades)

Note that some armies (France and UK) call battalion-size units "regiments." U.S. battalions are referred to by two numbers, as in 2/5. This stands for the 2nd Battalion of the 5th Regiment. Although U.S. forces no longer have regiments as such (the armored cavalry regiments and the 160th Aviation Regiment are exceptions), this naming system is used to maintain historical linkage with older regiments, some of which go back to the Revolutionary War. This has meaning to soldiers (who always ask each other, "What outfit were you with?").

In Saudi Arabia, many nations fielded a variety of formations labeled as "brigades." In the case of one small Gulf Cooperation Council nation (Qatar), one of its "brigades" initially contained only one full-strength battalion (about 800 men) and some support units (for a total of around 1,100 troops). This unit was later combined into the Peninsula Shield Force. On the other end of the spectrum are U.S. Marine Corps Marine Expeditionary Brigades. The 5th MEB showed up with nearly 15,000 troops. Most marine brigades were later organized into regiments and divisions.

In the case of U.S. divisions, "Division Troops" (those not directly assigned to brigades) are listed separately.

In some cases, for more "perplexing" units (corps Support Commands, which contain supply and service personnel, aviation brigades, the Bangladeshi Brigade, and the like), the approximate number of personnel serving with a particular unit is given in parentheses after the unit name. The size of some units fluctuated while in the Kuwaiti Theater of Operations (KTO).

U.S. Army armored units were equipped with the M1A1 Abrams tank. When known, the type of tank serving in non-

U.S. tank units is given in parentheses after the unit (e.g., the Qatar Tank Battalion deploys French-made AMX 30 tanks. AMX 30 appears in parentheses).

U.S. field artillery battalions that deploy the Multiple Launch Rocket System (MLRS) are designated.

ONE FURTHER NOTE: Several nations, the United States among them, "task organize" their ground forces. Elements of various units are brought together for a purpose (a task). In U.S. military parlance, a "task force" of ground forces is usually a battalion, which combines infantry, tanks, engineers, etc. A "team" is a company-sized unit (90 to 150 troops) that has a similar mix of arms. Some of the battalion-sized units listed on the OB are *permanent* task forces. For example, several of the tank and mechanized infantry battalions in the 1st Cavalry Division are in fact mixed task-force units. Tank and mechanized infantry companies are assigned to the same battalion. The Omani Combined Arms Battalion serving in the Peninsula Shield Force is also a permanent "task force."

OTHER NOTES: C = Cavalry regimental designation (e.g., 2/5C Mech is a mechanized infantry battalion that traces its history to the U.S. 5th Cavalry Regiment); DU—special armor.

United States Central Command *(Troop Strength in Parentheses)*

(Subordinate Command: United States 3rd Army, Arcent)

Units Under Direct 3rd U.S. Army Command or CENTCOM Control

> 3rd U.S. Special Forces Group (1,500 troops)
> 5th U.S. Special Forces Group (2,500)
> 160th Aviation Regiment (Special Operations Regiment, SOR) (2,500)
> 4th Psychological Operations Group
> 112th Special Operations Signal BN
> 528th Special Operations Support BN
> 416th Engineer Command
> 52nd Engineer BN
> 96th Civil Affairs BN
>
> 11th Aviation Brigade (2,000) with 2/6 Cav and 4/229 Avn BNs (AH-64)
>
> 12th Combat Aviation Brigade (3,000) with 2/229 and 5/6 Cav Avn BN (AH-64)

18th Aviation Brigade (2,500) with 1/159 and 2/159 Medium Avn BN

Army Aviation
   The U.S. Army has over 8,000 aircraft worldwide, all but perhaps 500 of them helicopters. Of these, about 2,000 are combat helicopters (although many of the transport types can carry and use weapons). Each army division has an aviation brigade containing several hundred helicopters and a few fixed-wing aircraft. The principal combat helicopter is the AH-64 Apache, which is as capable, and expensive, as many fixed-wing ground attack jets. Over 200 AH-64s were deployed in the Gulf, organized into battalions of 18 aircraft or into companies of six as part of reconnaissance battalions. Working with the AH-64 (and the older AH-1, of which over 1,000 are still in use) is the lighter OH-58 scout helicopter. But most of the helicopters are transports, primarily the UH-60 Blackhawk (or, as the troops dub it, in typically macabre fashion, the "Crashhawk"). The older UH-1 ("Huey") of Vietnam fame is rapidly being replaced by the more efficient and robust UH-60. About 500 CH-47s do most of the heavy lifting. The typical aviation brigade contains one or two combat battalions (AH and OH types) and two or more UH (transportation) types. In addition to all the aviation brigades and separate, there is one special unit, the 160th Special Operations Aviation Regiment. This unit contains over 120 modified UH-60s, CH-47s, and OH-6s (an older and smaller observation helicopter). The principal modifications allow the 160th's choppers to fly safely at night, fly farther, and refuel in the air. Naturally, their principal mission is to deliver and retrieve rangers and Special Forces troops deep in enemy territory. Most of the 160th was sent to the Gulf and that is what they did.

11th Air Defense Artillery Brigade (5,000): 2/1 Air Defense BN (Hawk); 2/52 Air Defense BN (IHawk); 2/7, 2/43, 3/43, Air Defense BNs (Patriot); 1/2 Air Defense BN (Chaparral); 5/62 Air Defense BN (Vulcan/Stinger).

Special Companies: Fort Sill (Oklahoma) Operational Test Battery, U.S. Army ATACMs (Army Tactical Missile

System; approximately 200 troops). One company of 1/75th Ranger Regiment (one special-operations–capable airborne Ranger infantry company deployed as special rapid strike force under CENTCOM command; approximately 180 troops).

Support Troops: 7th Medical Command (12,000); 22nd Support Command; elements 1st Corps Support Command (28,500); elements 13th Corps Support Command (28,500); CENTCOM Joint Military Police Command, CENTCOM Joint Information Bureau (JIB–Public Affairs).

CENTCOM Theater Reserve (Under Direct Control of 3rd Army):

1st U.S. Cavalry Division (Armored): 1st Cavalry Division began the war as theater reserve; it was later assigned to 7th Corps in the last stages of the ground offensive; 1st Brigade, 1st Cavalry: 2 tank BNs (3/32 Armor, 2/8C Armor), 1 mech BN (2/5C Mech); 2nd Brigade, 1st Cavalry: 2 tank BNs (1/8C Armor, 1/32 Armor), 1 mech BN (1/5C Mech); Division Artillery: 1/82, 3/82, 1/3; 2 MLRS batteries: (A/ 21, A/92); Division Troops: 1–7 Cavalry Squadron, 8th Engineer BN, 4/5 Air Defense BN, 1–227 Avn BN (AH-64).

Saudi I Corps (serving under CENTCOM; assault task forces noted in parentheses): Saudi National Guard Division (4 infantry brigades equipped with armored personnel carriers and trucks); King Saud Infantry Brigade; 2nd National Guard Motorized Infantry Brigade (TF Abu Bakr); 1st Mech Infantry Brigade, Prince Mohammed bin Abdul Rahman Infantry Brigade.

Peninsula Shield Force (10,000 Gulf Cooperation Council troops deployed in Saudi Arabia): Units assigned to Peninsula Shield Force: Qatar Tank BN (AMX-30) (TF Omar); Qatar Mechanized Infantry BN (TF Abu Bakr); Omani Combined Arms Motorized Infantry BN (TF Omar); UAE Combined Arms Motorized Infantry BN (TF Omar); Saudi Peninsula Shield Support Force (Joint Forces-East).
    NOTE: Another 40,000 GCC troops served elsewhere in

the Persian Gulf. Among these were Bangladeshi Brigade (1,500 troops); Pakistani Brigade (8,000 troops); Afghan Mujahidin (300 serving with Saudi forces).

Saudi 1st Armored Division: Saudi 20th Mechanized Brigade (Joint Forces—North); Saudi 4th Armored Brigade (AMX-30) (Joint Forces—North); Saudi 8th Armored Brigade (M-60A3).

The Free Kuwaiti Army: 35th Brigade Group (5,000 troops, elements Shaheed Bde and Al-Tahrir Bde; tanks include Yugoslav M-84s (a T-72 clone), British Chieftains; Kuwaiti Martyrs BN (1,000 troops; may be part of Al Fatah Brigade or 35th Brigade Group); Kuwaiti Exile Infantry Brigade Group (2,000 troops); Free Kuwait Army Helicopter Squadron; Haq Brigade; Kulud Brigade.

The African Brigade: Moroccan Mechanized BN (from 6th Regiment Royal Moroccan, Mechanized Infantry Regiment; total of 2,000 troops); Senegalese Infantry BN (500 troops); Niger Infantry BN (450 troops guarding shrines in Mecca and Medina).

Other Saudi forces: 8th Mechanized Brigade (TF Othman); 10th Mechanized Brigade (TF Omar).

Egyptian Army Corps: Egyptian 4th Armored Division: 2nd Tank Brigade, 3rd Tank Brigade, 6th Mechanized Brigade; Egyptian 3rd Mechanized Infantry Division: 10th Mechanized Brigade, 22nd Mechanized Brigade, 23rd Mechanized Brigade; Egyptian Ranger Regiment (Commando Brigade) (2,500 troops); elements Egyptian 7th Mechanized Infantry Division: 8th Tank Brigade, 11th Mechanized Brigade, 12th Mechanized Brigade; Syrian 9th Armored Division (serving with Egyptian Corps but not under Egyptian command): 43rd Mechanized Brigade, 52nd Tank Brigade, 53rd Tank Brigade; elements 33rd Tank Brigade; elements of the Syrian Parachute Brigade; elements of the Syrian Para-Commando BN from 45th Commando Brigade.

French Army (assigned to CENTCOM): French 6th Light Armored Division, assigned to 7th Corps for ground operations (Note that French regiments are in fact Bns); 1st Foreign Legion Armored Regiment (1 REC); 1st Regiment de Spahis (1 RS); 4th Dragoon Regiment; 2nd Foreign Legion Mechanized Regiment (2 REI); 21st Marine Mechanized Regiment; 3rd Marine Mechanized Regiment (3 RIMA); French Expeditionary Provisional Combined Arms Regiment (3 RHC); 68th Marine Artillery Regiment; 11th Marine Artillery Regiment; 5th Antitank Helicopter Regiment; 1st Transport Helicopter Regiment; 1st Infantry Regiment; Engineer Company from 6th Foreign Legion Regiment (120 troops); Air Defense Artillery Battery with Mistral SAM (150 troops); "several" French "Special-Forces–type units" from French 11th Airborne Division (200 troops).

U.S. 18th Airborne Corps

18th Corps Aviation Brigade (4,000 troops); 20th Engineer Brigade (37th Engineer BN, 27th Engineer BN); 36th Engineer Group; 16th Military Police Brigade; 18th Airborne Corps Artillery; 75th Field Artillery Brigade: 3 BNs: 1/17, 5/18, 6/27 (MLRS); 212th Field Artillery Brigade: 3 BNs: 2/17, 2/18, 3/18, 18th Field Artillery Brigade: 4 BNs: 3/8, 5/8, 1/39, 3/27 (MLRS).

24th Mechanized Infantry Division: 1st Brigade: 2 mech BNs (2/7, 3/7), 1 tank BN (3/69); 2nd Brigade: 1 mech BN (3/15), 2 tank BNs (1/64, 4/64); Division Artillery: 3 BNs, 1/41, 3/41, 4/41 Artillery BN (from 197th Mechanized Infantry Brigade); A Battery 13th FA (MLRS); 197th Mechanized Infantry Brigade, ("The $1.97"), attached to 24th Mechanized Division during Desert Storm; 2/69 Armor BN; 1/18 Mechanized Infantry BN; 2/18 Mechanized Infantry BN; Division Troops: 2/4 Cavalry Squadron, 3rd Engineer BN, 1/5 Air Defense BN, D/4 Cavalry Troop (from 197th Mechanized Brigade); 299th Engineer BN, 1/24, 3/24 Avn BN (AH-64); 3rd Armored Cavalry Regiment (under the command of 24th Mechanized Division during the ground war): 3 heavy cavalry squadrons (1/3C, 2/3C, 3/3C), 1 attack and recon helicopter squadron (4/3C Aviation).

82nd Airborne Division: 1st Brigade: 504th Parachute Infantry Regiment (1/504 Inf BN, 2/504, 3/504); 2nd Brigade: 325th Airborne Infantry Regiment (1/325 Inf BN, 2/325, 4/325); 3rd Brigade: 505th Parachute Infantry Regiment (1/505 Inf BN, 2/505, 3/505) (Although organized as brigades, the paratroopers use their World War II–era regimental designations. Thus the 1st Brigade is called the 504th Parachute Regiment; the 325th is "airborne" since it traces its lineage to a WWII glider infantry regiment.); Division Artillery: (1/319, 2/319, 3/319) [towed 105-mm artillery BNs]; 82nd Airborne Division troops: 3/73 Light Tank BN (Sheridan light tanks), 307th Engineer BN, 1/17 Air Cavalry Squadron, 3/4 Air Defense BN, 1–82 Avn BN (AH-64), 2–82 Avn BN (Assault). Note that the 2nd Brigade of the 82nd Airborne Division was assigned to support the French 6th Light Armored Division during the ground war.

101st Airborne Division (Air Assault): 1st Brigade: 327th Air Assault Regiment (1/327, 2/327, 3/327); 2nd Brigade: 502nd Air Assault Regiment (1/502, 2/502, 3/502); 3rd Brigade: 187th Air Assault Regiment (1/187, 2/187, 3/187); 101st Combat Aviation Brigade: 1/101, 2/101 Avn BN (AH-64), 4/101, 5/101, Avn BN (Air Assault), 7/101 Avn BN (medium helicopter); Division Artillery: (1/320, 2/320, 3/320) [towed 105-mm artillery BNs], Division Troops: 2/17 Air Cavalry Squadron, 326th Engineer BN, Air Defense BN (2/44).

U.S. 7th Corps

7th Corps Artillery: 42nd Field Artillery Brigade: 3/20 Field Artillery BN (155 mm), 1/27 (MLRS), 2/29 (155 mm—attached from 8th Mechanized Infantry Division); 210th Field Artillery Brigade: 3/17 Field Artillery BN (155 mm), 4/27 (MLRS), 2/41 (155 mm—attached from 3rd Mechanized Infantry Division); 142nd Field Artillery Brigade: 1/142 Field Artillery BN (8 inch), 2/142 (8 inch), 1/158 (MLRS); 196th Field Artillery Brigade: 1–201 Field Artillery BN (155 mm), 1–181 (8 inch), 1–623 (8 inch); 7th Engineer Brigade.

3rd Armored Division: 1st Brigade: 1 tank BN (4/32), 2 mech BNs (3/5C, 5/5C); 2nd Brigade: 2 tank BNs (3/8C, 4/8C), 1 mech BN (4/18); 3rd Brigade: 2 tank BNs (2/67, 4/67), 1 mech BN (5/18); Division Artillery: 3 BNs (2/3, 2/82, 4/82), MLRS

Battery (A/40); Division Troops: 4/7 Cavalry Squadron, 3/5 Air Defense BN, 23rd Engineer BN, 2/227, 3/227 Avn BNs (AH-64); 4/34 Tank BN (from 8th Mechanized Infantry Division).

1st Armored Division: 1st Brigade: 1 tank BN (1/37), 2 mech BNs (6/6, 7/6); 2nd Brigade: 3 tank BNs (1/35, 2/70, 4/70), 1 mech BN (1/7, from 3rd Mechanized Division); 3rd Brigade: 2 tank BNs (3/35, 4/66, from 3rd Mechanized Division), 1 mech BN (4/7, from 3rd Mechanized Division); Division Artillery: 3 BNs (2/1, 3/1, 6/41, from 3rd Mechanized Division); MLRS Battery (A/94); Division Troops: 1/1 Cavalry Squadron, 3/1, 2/1 Avn BNs (AH-64), 1 transport helicopter BN, 6/3 Air Defense BN.

1st Mechanized Infantry Division: 1st Brigade: 2 tank BNs (1/34, 2/34), 1 mech BN (2/16); 2nd Brigade: 2 tank BNs (3/37, 4/37), 1 mech BN (5/16); Division Artillery: 2 artillery BNs (1/5, 4/5), 1 artillery BN, attached from 2nd Armored Division Forward (4/3), 1 MLRS Battery (B/6); Division Troops: 1/4th Cavalry Squadron (less one troop in Europe), 2/3 Air Defense BN, 1st Engineer BN (less one company), D/17 Engineer Company, 1/1 Avn BN (AH-64), 1 transport helicopter BN; 2nd Armored Division Forward Brigade (3rd Brigade, 2nd Armored Division, served as a brigade of 1st Mechanized Division during the war); 2 tank BNs (2/66, 3/66), 1 mech BN (1/41), 1 cavalry troop, 1 engineer company.

2nd Armored Cavalry Regiment (during part of the ground offensive, the 2nd ACR served under the command of the 1st Mechanized Infantry Division): 3 heavy cavalry squadrons (1/2C, 2/2C, 3/2C), 1 air cavalry and combat helicopter squadron (4/2C).

1st British Armored Division: 7th (British) Armored Brigade: Royal Scots Dragoon Guards (57 Challenger tanks), Queen's Royal Irish Hussars (57 Challenger tanks), 1st Staffordshire Infantry (45 Warrior Infantry Fighting Vehicles), 40th Field Regiment RA (24 M109 SP howitzers), 21st Engineer Regiment (BN), 21st Engineer Regiment RE (BN), 664th Helicopter Squadron, 10th Air Defense Battery (Javelin SAM), "A" Squadron 1st Queen's Dragoon Guards, 1st Armored Field Ambulance RAMC; 4th (British) Armored Brigade: 14/20 King's

Hussars (43 Challenger tanks), 1st Royal Scots Infantry (45 Warrior Infantry Fighting Vehicles), 3rd Royal Fusiliers Infantry (45 Warrior Infantry Fighting Vehicles), 23rd Engineer Regiment (BN), 46th Air Defense Battery (Javelin SAM), 2nd Field Regiment RA (24 M109 SP howitzers), 1st Coldstream Guards (Infantry BN), Royal Highland Fusiliers (Infantry BN), King's Own Scottish Borderers (Infantry BN); Division Troops: 16/5 Queen's Royal Lancers Recon BN (24 Scorpion, 24 Scimitar, 12 Striker), 4th Army Air Regiment (helicopters, consisting of 654, 659, and 661 Squadrons), 32nd Heavy Artillery Regiment (16 M109, 12 M110), 39th Heavy Artillery Regiment (12 MLRS), 12th Air Defense Regiment (24 tracked Rapier SAM), 32nd Armored Engineer Regiment, 1st Armored Division Transport Regiment RCT; British Forces Support Elements: 30th Signals Regiment, 39th Engineer Regiment, 7th Tank Transporter Regiment, Gurkha Transport Regiment, 22nd Field Hospital, 33 Field Hospital.

British Army Serving with Royal Navy: 21st Air Defence Battery (from 47th Field Regiment RA).

U.S. Marine Corps—serving under Central Command

Note that the marines arrived in the Gulf organized into brigades, but these units were reorganized as divisions by the time of the ground offensive. A unit referred to as the 2/24th Marines is the 2nd Infantry Battalion of the 24th Marine Regiment.

1st Marine Expeditionary Force

Support units: 4 SeaBee construction battalions, 1st Raider BN 24th Marine Regiment (rear area security), 2/24, 3/24 Marines.

1st Marine Division: 1st Marine Regiment (Task Force—TF Papa Bear), 1/1, 3/9 Marines, 1st Tank BN (M60A1), Assault Amphibian BN; 3rd Marine Regiment (TF Taro), 1/3, 2/3, 3/3 Marines; 4th Marine Regiment (TF Grizzly), 2/7, 3/7 Marines; 7th Marine Regiment (TF Ripper), 1/7, 1/5 Marines, 1st Combat Engineer BN, 3rd Tank BN (M60A3); 11th Marine Regiment (Artillery) 1/11, 3/1, 5/11, 1/12, 3/12 Marines; division troops; support units, 1st LAI (Light Armored Infantry) BN, 1st Recon BN.

2nd Marine Division: 6th Marine Regiment: 1/6, 3/6, 1/8, 2/2 Marines, TF Breach Alpha; 8th Marine Regiment: 2/4, 3/23 Marines, TF Breach Bravo; 1st Brigade (Tiger Brigade), 2nd Armored Division (U.S. Army, served as part of the U.S. Marine Corps during the ground offensive. The Marines Corps commander, General Walter Boomer, treated the unit as his mobile "exploitation force." Fought at the Battle of Mutla Ridge outside Kuwait City [see map "February 25–28: The Final Days"]); 2 tank BNs (1/67, 3/67), 1 mech BN (3/41), 1 Field Artillery BN (1/3), B Battery 4/5 Air Defense BN, support units; 10th Marine Regiment (artillery), 2/10, 3/10. 5/10, 2/12 Marines; division troops; support units, 2nd LAI BN, 2nd Tank BN (M1A1 DU), 8th Tank BN (M60A1), 2nd Combat Engineer BN, 2nd Recon BN.

Marine Amphibious Force (on ships in the Gulf): 4th Marine Expeditionary Brigade: 1/2, 3/2 Marines, 1/10 artillery, miscellaneous armor units; 5th Marine Expeditionary Brigade: 2/5, 3/5, 3/1 Marines, 2/11 artillery, miscellaneous armor units; 13th Marine Expeditionary Unit: 1/4 Marines (this unit trained for commando operations).

Marine units were organized somewhat like army troops, but with different types of armored vehicles. Their amphibious assault vehicles carried twenty-five troops, and they had hundreds of LAVs (wheeled armored vehicles). Artillery was towed. There were 84,000 marines in the Gulf, 66,000 of them ashore. Unlike the army, marine aircraft units (including the fixed-wing F-18 and AV-8) were part of the marine force. Most of the logistical support was provided by the navy.

Other Allied Units (serving in Saudi Arabia or in a Gulf Cooperation Council nation) Saudi Royal Guard Regiment (located in Riyadh, 3 infantry BNs); 12th Saudi Armored Brigade (located in Tabuk); 6 Saudi Mechanized Infantry Brigades (covering Yemeni border); Saudi Parachute Brigade (located in Riyadh and Hafir al Batin); Saudi Hijaz Infantry Brigade (serving in western Saudi Arabia); Pakistani Mechanized Infantry Brigade (serving in Hafir al Batin). Czechoslovak chemical decontamination company; Czechoslovak Hospital Detachment; Polish Field Hospital Detachment; French 1st Hussars (a light reconnaissance company with about 200 troops deployed in the United Arab Emirates); Dutch Army field hospital also deployed to Saudi Arabia.

Postwar, June 1991

The 11th Armored Cavalry Regiment (assigned to Kuwait) was to be relieved, or augmented, by a brigade of the 24th Infantry Division in late 1991.

U.S. Army Europe (USAEUR)

No order of battle listing units that participated in the Persian Gulf War would be complete without including at least one battalion of the U.S. Army 10th Special Forces Group, which spent the war in southeastern Turkey. At least that was where it was supposed to be. The authors suspect the 10th SF crossed the border on reconnaissance missions and perhaps to aid downed flyers. Certainly, the 10th SF entered Iraq after April 10, 1991, when United States forces began overtly aiding Kurdish refugees. Germany also assigned one squadron of Alpha jets to Turkey. Eighteen Dutch F-16s were also assigned to Turkey.

The Dead

From early August to early March, the United States armed forces suffered 355 dead in the Gulf. Eight of them were women. There were 148 combat dead and 496 wounded. Noncombat accidents accounted for 207 deaths. This is about normal for peacetime operations, where one out of every thousand people on active service die each year to training accidents and, well, just accidents. Of the 148 that died in combat, most were killed in the ground war, which is normal. Friendly fire caused thirty-five of the combat deaths and seventy-two of the wounded. About 140 children lost one of their parents. This was an exceptionally low death toll for such a large combat operation. It was the first U.S. war in this century that had more dead from noncombat causes. Between 20,000 and 30,000 Iraqis died, mostly from combat action. Noncombat losses may have been higher, but the Iraqis were not keeping accurate records.

PART III

War Myths, War Games, and War Correspondents

How the war was reported, or misreported, is almost as interesting as the war itself. Iraq made the media a part of its arsenal, as did the Allies. Press releases and soundbites were used as weapons, and they did have an effect.

This section examines the miscellany of politics, analysis, and journalism that surrounds every international crisis. The Persian Gulf War became the first war covered by a global information network.

Likewise the general public experienced a tidal wave of military and political analysis, to include war games and other analytical methods, which attempted to examine and even predict the ins and outs of the crisis. All of this created perceptions and misperceptions, both the foundations for what became the immediate mythology of the war, a mythology often at odds with the reality.

CHAPTER 10

Myths, Misconceptions, and Revelations

The Persian Gulf War produced a range of military, political, and historical surprises. Saddam Hussein may have been the most surprised at the coalition's startling victory, but he was one among many. Ignorance and delusion and faith in their own bitter calculations may have blinded Saddam and the Revolutionary Command Council. No doubt the same factors affected many newsrooms around the world as well. Actually, the military's need for secrecy and ever-present misunderstandings about how the military actually works further tangle the subject matter. While it is entertaining to expose these misconceptions, it is also educational. There will always be problems arising out of fast-moving and momentous events.

Here, then, are some of the choice myths and misconceptions of the Persian Gulf War, offered as a smorgasbord of extended soundbites for the "television generation."

The Iraqi Army

The Iraqi armed forces were initially described in the press (Western and otherwise) as a "battle-hardened desert army," when, in actual point of fact, before the war the Iraqi Army would have been more accurately described as battle-weary. Significantly, the Iraqi Army was not an army experienced in desert warfare. The Iran-Iraq War was essentially a swamp and mountain war, with most of the battles being waged in the swamps, marshes, and salt pans of the Shatt-al-Arab and in the mountains of Kurdistan. The media could have "demythified" the myth of a desert army by a cursory look at an atlas and a little knowledge of where most of the battles of the Iran-Iraq War were fought.

Iraqi Army performance during the war clearly bears out these observations. Iraq had nearly 20 percent of its military-age manpower killed or wounded during the Iran-Iraq War, and the performance of Iraqi troops had not been inspiring. During that war, entire Iraqi brigades surrendered, and entire divisions were smashed. What happened to the Iraqi Army in February 1991 had ample precedent. Despite its battlefield successes in 1986 and the Al Faw offensive in 1988, Iraq did not really "win" that war; rather, it was simply Iran that decided to stop fighting. The greatest achievement of the Iraqi Army was that it was able to stay in the war for as long as it did.

The Iraqi Army that Saddam poised on the border of Kuwait in July 1990 was indeed a large army. To its credit, it had remained intact through eight years of attacks by more enthusiastic Iranian forces—but it had fought a largely static war, not a war of maneuver in the desert.

Sorting Out the Numbers in the Air War

Air-force combat operations are intensely technical, not only in the complex equipment deployed, but also in the design of the operations themselves. The aircraft do not just take off, fly to an enemy target, and drop their bombs. In fact, fewer than half the aircraft involved in "combat missions" actually drop bombs. Running a modern air campaign is more like conducting an orchestra. There are always at least four "flavors" of aircraft in a "mission package." There are fighters (to protect the bombers), electronic-warfare aircraft (to warn of enemy defenses and help defeat them), tankers (to refuel aircraft), and bombers (to drop bombs). Before, and after, a mission, reconnaissance aircraft go out to see what to hit, or what got hit. So those 2,000 missions a day, as briefed to the media in Riyadh, only translated into 700–800 planes with bombs going out. As each target was often attacked by more than one bomber, a typical day's work would only see a few hundred targets hit (less those missed because of bad weather or mechanical problems on some of the aircraft). Not all the targets hit would be effectively hit, even with the more accurate "smart" bombs and electronic bombing systems. So the average 2,000-sortie day would see only perhaps 200–300 targets effectively destroyed or damaged. This figure is about what the air-force planners and pilots expected, but most spectators saw the total number of sorties and assumed that that was the number of bombers hitting targets, or even the number of targets hit.

The films of successful bombings (especially those of "smart weapons" shown early-on in the air campaign) further muddied perceptions. Naturally, the air-force people did not want to feature the near (or total) misses, and it's an even bet that near misses were more numerous than the direct hits. As noted earlier, while bombing has got much more effective since World War II, where the average bomb landed as much as 3,000 feet from its target, the current average of misses measured in tens of feet is still enough to leave a target still functional. Put another way, during World War II, only about 3 percent of the bombs dropped hit their target (although many of the misses hit something else worth hitting). That success rate didn't really start to change until the 1970s and is now approaching 50 percent. This makes a big difference. Yet nothing approaching 100 percent accuracy can be expected any time soon. Consider that pilots are zipping along at 400–500 miles an hour, often while being fired at and frequently aiming at something obscured by smoke or haze. The pilots have learned to live with these conditions and consistently get the number of hits they expect. Somehow, many observers seemed to expect more.

The U.S. Intelligence Advantage

Since Vietnam, and especially since America's last large-scale mechanized war in World War II, the effectiveness and scale of intelligence work had increased enormously. Until quite recently, efficient intelligence work was close examination of aerial photos and data stored on three-by-five cards. During the 1980s, satellites, multiple sensors, and computers created a revolution within the intelligence community. While it is still possible for the enemy to hide information, it is now a lot more difficult. Cloud cover can still degrade data collection, but weather can no longer completely stop intelligence gathering. Even before Iraq invaded Kuwait in August 1990, American intelligence agencies (there are several) were taking closer, and more frequent, looks at Iraq.

Despite these efforts, the most important phase of the intelligence effort went almost completely unnoticed. Before the bombing began on January 16, intelligence personnel had been collecting massive amounts of information on what the Iraqis were doing. This included not just photos from satellites and high-flying aircraft, but even larger amounts of electronic data. The SIGINT (signal intelligence, from radars and the like) and COMINT (communications intelligence, listening to Iraqi military communications) data was even more massive, and was a key factor in identifying what was on the photographs. All this information enabled the initial air strikes to paralyze Iraq and the Iraqi armed forces. The thousand-plus coalition aircraft that headed for Iraq the first night of the war needed precise information about what their targets were (buildings, bunkers, bridges, radars, etc.), where the targets were (and what was in the vicinity, such as tall buildings, hills, rivers, etc.), and how they were defended (if at all). Depending on the construction of targets, different types of bombs, and different ways to drop them, were required. If there were hills, tall buildings, or power lines around the targets, the pilots had to know this so they could find the target in all the clutter, or at least avoid flying into an obstacle. How well the target was defended dictated what type of aircraft would attack and how many supporting aircraft would be required. Beyond this technical information, the entire target list had to be arranged in order of priority, as there are never enough aircraft to hit everything at once. None of this "targeting" work could be done without the efforts of the intelligence crew.

The Reconnaissance Advantage

While intelligence work is nothing without reconnaissance, reconnaissance is a battlefield tool all by itself. Allied air supremacy denied the Iraqis any meaningful information about Allied forces while at the same time keeping the Allied commanders better informed about Iraqi forces than most Iraqi commanders. Technically, reconnaissance is just the act of obtaining battlefield information, usually during a battle. In this respect, the Allies had a tremendous advantage. When the ground war began, Iraqi commanders had only a fragmentary picture of what was going on. The Iraqi communications system, both radio and telephone, was in a shambles. There were no Iraqi recon aircraft, or any aircraft that could even get commanders to front-line units. When the U.S. 7th and 18th Corps showed up to the west of the Republican Guard, it was something of a shock to the Guard units. They had heard very little, except that the ground war had started, and for many Iraqi soldiers, most of their information was coming from news broadcasts over the radio. U.S. troops reported that most of the Republican Guard tanks were hit before the Iraqis even knew American tanks were in the area. Often the Iraqi tank crews were asleep next to their tanks, where they were taken prisoner after scrambling away from their burning T-72s. On the Allied side, air and satellite reconnaissance provided the big picture, while swarms of helicopters and recon vehicles moved ahead of the armored divisions to let the Allied units know what they were going to encounter. This was also the first war in which satellite and aircraft reconnaissance photos were faxed to some commanders at the front. The Allies could see; the Iraqis were blinded. It was a case of a boxing match where one fighter was blindfolded and hit up side the head with a baseball bat just before the fight began. Such were the stunning effects of air power.

Electronic Warfare

Allied jamming shut down most Iraqi radios once the ground war began. This was a quickly noted effect of electronic warfare (EW) before news of the ground war got out, because some of the jamming also affected civilian radio frequencies, and reporters soon learned of it. Beyond that incident, most electronic warfare was conducted in the shadows. During the first night of the air war, similar jamming shut down Iraqi radar and radio networks. When the electronic-warfare people were not jamming, they were listening to detect which frequencies and types of electronic equipment the Iraqis were using. As the Iraqis changed the way they used their electronics, the Allied EW units changed their methods to meet the challenge. To defend against Iraqi EW, special radio equipment was used, as well as air-force bombers directed at any Iraqi jamming efforts (jamming transmitters).

Special Operations Forces

The Special Forces (or SOF, as they are now known) are normally thought of as a bunch of commandos operating behind enemy lines blowing things up. While there was some of this going on in Iraq and Kuwait, most of the U.S. Special Forces personnel were assigned the more vital task of accompanying allied Arab units to insure smooth coordination with other Allied units (Arab and non-Arab). This, more than commando raids, is what U.S. SOF troops are trained to do.

There were a number of problems in the Arab contingents that the Special Forces troops had to address. The most obvious one: The Arabs needed access to American Air Force and Army artillery support. But there was also the problem of teaching Arab commanders how to use something as unfamiliar (to most Arab armies) as abundant and efficient air power. Arab commanders were also unfamiliar with operating in division-size operations. A shortage of funds for large-scale training operations (plus the potential political problems of a division-size force turning a division-size training exercise into a government takeover) made this the first opportunity many Arab commanders had ever had to command such a large unit in the field. The SF troops had to show the Arab officers how to plan and execute various types of large-scale offensive and defensive operations.

While U.S. Special Forces are trained primarily to advise and coordinate with foreign (usually irregular and guerrilla) forces, other "Special Operations Forces" perform more traditional roles. These include the SEALs, Delta Force, and the British SAS (Special Air Service) troops, who are primarily commandos and who all operated with U.S. Special Forces on commando-type missions. These included reconnaissance into Kuwait and Iraq (although many of these missions were also performed by special long-range recon teams from U.S. divisions) as well as working with the Kuwaiti resistance. SF and SAS teams also crossed Iraqi lines to capture prisoners, equipment, and, during the opening stages of the air battle, to use laser designators to mark Iraqi air-defense targets for attacking bombers. As part of their recon mission, the Special Forces also tapped into the Iraqi wire-communications system and, at the onset of the ground war, severed the wire (landline) communications between Baghdad and the Kuwaiti front. Special Forces operations also went deep into Iraq, including the north of Iraq and the Kurdish areas.

Deception

There was not a lot of deception, or at least not as much as the American command alleged. The knowledgeable never doubted that there would be a major attack around the Allied left flank, as that was the textbook solution to the problem. This strategy was discussed openly in the Western media months before even the air war began and scores of Iraqi commanders who studied the operational art at Russian military schools would have recognized the "left hook" as the most efficient way to destroy their forces. That the Iraqis moved increasingly large numbers into their open flank in southern Iraq indicates how much they recognized this danger. Once Iraqi forces moved to the Kuwait-Saudi border in force and built their fortifications, they were in a hopeless position because of the several hundred miles of open desert to the west, which they did not have enough divisions to cover. Still, the feints of the 1st Cavalry Division up Wadi al Batin seem to have suckered the Iraqis into thinking that the "left hook" would be a short one.

The U.S. amphibious invasion, which didn't take place and was touted as a deception, was (as we have seen) actually considered too dangerous because Allied forces found they were not able to clear all of the Iraqi naval mines. Nevertheless, the presence of the marines in the Persian Gulf did keep substantial Iraqi forces looking seaward until it was too late to move against the Allied flanking movement.

Iraq Was Not Vietnam, and Vietnam Was Not Iraq

Kuwait provided the perfect battlefield for the type of armed forces created and maintained by the United States since World War II. The desert's arena of "pure" war is the ideal environment for air forces and mechanized forces. Unlike Vietnam, which was a civil war fought in jungles and urban areas, or Korea, which was fought in constricted mountainous terrain, the Persian Gulf desert offered few impediments to the application of massive U.S. firepower.

More important, the generals were given straightforward orders ("Liberate Kuwait") and then left to do it in the most efficient manner they could devise. Unlike Vietnam, there was not a lot of petty interference and second-guessing from Washington.

High-Tech Weapons

The American press frequently excoriates high-tech weapons development for going over budget while not performing as advertised. The budget problems are real enough. Nevertheless, most such weapons do eventually perform well. Most of the high-tech weapons used in the Persian Gulf were not recent designs, but technology first conceived and deployed ten and twenty years ago. The "smart bombs," for example, were first used during the closing stages of the Vietnam War, where they performed well (65 percent hits). The M1A1 tank, while new, was just another development in a long line of functional tank designs. The same applies to helicopters, communications gear, and other systems. Some items that saw first combat use in the Persian Gulf were already available on the civilian market, which insured that they were workable. One of the better examples of these civilian items was the GPS (Global Positioning System) receivers. The GPS receiver displays the user's location and eliminated one of the major problems of desert warfare: getting lost. Also seeing wide use in the Gulf were over 20,000 microcomputers, which automated many administrative tasks. There were computers, fax machines, and cellular telephones all over the place. The military is a reflection of the society that creates it, and this was represented by the degree of functional technology U.S. forces deployed in the Gulf.

Chemical and Nuclear Weapons (Gas and Rads)

Iraq used chemical weapons against Iran during the 1980–88 war and even used the noxious weapons against its own rebellious Kurdish citizens. Iraq was also well on its way toward developing nuclear weapons when the war broke out. Iraqi research on biological weapons had produced stocks of anthrax and botulism agents. All of these items had greater mental than tangible effect. Chemical weapons have not been used extensively since their heyday in 1915–18. The reasons are simple: Chemical weapons are not all that effective, and they have a tendency to slow down operations on both sides. They make the troops more miserable and perhaps even less inclined to fight. Thus, for over seventy years, there has not been a single verified instance of one nation using chemical weapons on another that could immediately reply in kind. This is not to say that the Iraqis were not tempted to use them. There is some evidence that attempts were made to arm aircraft with chemical or biological weapons and attack the Allies. But the Iraqis didn't (or couldn't because the aircraft and artillery that would otherwise be used to deliver them were largely destroyed) and thus continued a long tradition of "restraint." This was further encouraged by U.S. declarations that if chemical weapons were used, America would hunt down Saddam Hussein and the officers involved and prosecute them as war criminals. Worst of all, from the Iraqi point of view, they only had crude means of delivery—artillery shells or spray canisters on helicopters or aircraft. Chemical warheads for Scuds were still in development; these warheads are difficult to make and to make work. Just to be certain, the Allies attacked the known Iraqi chemical and biological production and storage facilities, carefully. If the wind was too brisk, or blowing toward populated areas, the attacks were called off. In the first months after the war, several bombed areas in Iraq were not safe to enter. The chemical and biological agents had to degrade.

Nuclear weapons are another matter, as they are more complicated to build and Iraq had not quite solved all the technical problems by August 1990. The coalition air raids in January 1991 destroyed much of Iraq's nuclear-weapons research. The Iraqi nuclear program turned out to be more extensive than first thought, but the January raids slowed it down for the moment. The Iraqis made some noises about threatening to explode a "radioactive device." This "device" could have been a normal bomb with radioactive material added. This would have produced a small area full of radioactivity but little else. This threat sounded worse than it actually would have been if carried out.

Biological weapons, on the other hand, had never been used in modern warfare but were known to exist. There are several serious problems with biological weapons, however. First, as they have never been used on the battlefield, no one is quite sure how effective they would be. Second, it is easier to create and duplicate these nasty little bugs than it is to manufacture the antidote. It's also very difficult to keep most biological agents alive until they can be delivered to the target. This put the Iraqis at a big disadvantage, as they not only had problems creating the biological weapons but also with manufacturing large quantities of the antidote. Iraqi nerve gas also has a short, 30- to 60-day, shelf life. Thus, any Iraqi use of biological weapons would have likely hurt Iraqis more than anyone else, unless they could have delivered them deep into Allied rear areas. This is because even the simpler forms of biological warfare—agents like anthrax or botulism—can have a devastating effect. Thousands of these generally nonfatal cases (involving, say, pneumonia or persistent fever) would swamp medical facilities. In the case of the Iraqis, whose medical facilities were substandard to begin with and whose source of medical supplies going to the troops was interrupted by Allied airpower, many of these curable cases would result in death. The Iraqis were aware of this situation, or at least some were, which goes to show how desperate and depraved the political situation in Iraq was, and still is.

What Airpower **Can** *and* **Cannot** *Do*

The good news was that Allied air losses were lower than expected. The bad news was that the air assault was not as effective as everyone (except the Allied air-force commanders) expected. Combat aircraft look quite impressive, but their capabilities against ground targets are much less so. Less than half the combat sorties were aircraft carrying bombs. Each aircraft usually attacked one target. Often the target was not a combat one, but a support installation. The first two weeks of the war saw air strikes directed at things like buildings (containing everything from offices to electronics gear to supplies). Bridges, airfields, railroads, and even roads were other "noncombat" targets. Moreover, many of these targets had to be hit several times either because the bombers missed (even smart bombs aren't perfect) or because the Iraqis repaired the damage. The only combat weapons hit initially were surface-to-air missile sites and aircraft. Iraqi aircraft were hidden away in concrete shelters and were generally reluctant to get off the ground and into harm's way. The Allied air forces consequently had to continue flying over 10 percent of their sorties to protect against possible attacks by these withheld (and often hidden) Iraqi aircraft.

The misinterpretation of the effectiveness of air power is primarily a misunderstanding of mission priorities. The air force immediately attacks enemy command-and-control capabilities. The public thinks that it is more logical to tackle the combat units. Historical experience shows that it is more effective to go after the noncombat (command-and-control) targets first. This makes the enemy's combat units less effective right away by preventing effective communication and interfering with movement and resupply, and makes it eventually easier to attack the enemy ground units and defeat them.

Another factor in correctly interpreting the results of air attacks is having a general idea of what aircraft can do to ground units. What, for example, will 1,000 air sorties do to an enemy tank division? Render it ineffective, yes; but note that the average citizen will not have any clear idea what *any* number of sorties will do to a tank division. Most members of the media will be likewise in the dark, and their guesses will further cloud the issue.

Actually, in the final days of the air campaign, the coalition air forces began to use pinpoint targeting techniques and smart weapons on the dug-in Iraqi ground forces. The psychological effects of the extended air campaign on Iraqi ground troops and the increased targeting accuracy began to cut deep into Iraqi ground-unit capabilities. The Air had set up the Land in Air-Land Battle.

Battle Damage Assessment

As mentioned earlier, for most of the war, there was much confusion over "BDA" (battle damage assessment, sometimes called bomb damage assessment when referring strictly to air strikes). BDA is the normal process by which the air force attempts to discover what damage its air strikes actually did. This is a difficult process, complicated by the need to rely on aerial photographs and (recently) other sensors. The enemy on the ground has an incentive to deceive the aerial attacker by making bombed targets look more damaged than they actually are. The Iraqis learned their deception techniques from the Russians, who are quite good at it. But what made all the difference in BDA, particularly out in the desert, was the quantity and quality of U.S. sensors. In addition to the customary photography, there were several types of radar and other sensors that can spot heat and different quantities of metal. You can entrench tanks in the desert, you can use camouflage and dummy tanks, but it's difficult to deceive three or four different types of sensors at once. Thus, the Allies were pretty sure they knew where the Iraqi armored vehicles and artillery (and other equipment and supplies) were on the desert battlefield. These same sensors were almost (but sufficiently) effective against destroyed equipment, which is almost as important as finding the stuff in the first place (otherwise the attacker will waste a lot of attacks on already destroyed equipment).

The reason for keeping the BDA from the press was obvious to anyone with a military background. The Iraqis did not know what the Allies knew about their deception measures, or even the true state of their own forces. If the BDAs were released, the Iraqis would know and could use that information against us. For example, if they found that some forms of deception worked a bit better than others, they would switch to the more effective techniques and make the Allies' job that much harder. The Allied sensors were not perfect, and about 20 percent (or more) of the time the Iraqi deceptions worked. The important point was preventing the Iraqis from finding out where the Allies were having trouble with their deception. Many of the U.S. sensors were being used under combat conditions for the first time, so the entire effort became very much a learning experience. Also, during the course of Desert Storm coalition aircraft engaged over 200,000 individual targets. Most of the post-attack recon was done with aircraft using conventional cameras (film, not electronic images). And the weather was frequently bad. Ironically, the weather was not so bad that it prevented fire-control systems from finding targets to bomb, but the weather was bad enough to make damage assessment difficult. To say that stressed the BDA system is an understatement.

Fuel Air Explosives

For a while, the press (and much of the public) latched on to the idea that fuel air explosives (FAE) in the hands of the Iraqis gave them a terrible, and perhaps decisive, weapon to use against coalition forces. What was forgotten in all this flurry of excitement was that the FAE had been around for thirty years, was used extensively during the Vietnam War, and, essentially, had never worked all that reliably. Imagine the enormous damage of a natural-gas explosion—that gives a good picture of what FAE can do and what its principal limitations are. FAE is used out in the open and must perform two operations very quickly, subject to atmospheric conditions. The FAE first dispenses a large quantity of flammable vapor and then, within a second, ignites the cloud of gas. This explosion uses up all the oxygen within the cloud and in the immediate area as it explodes. The result, under ideal conditions, is an explosion two to three times more powerful than a conventional bomb of the same weight. The major problem is that a high wind, or even the wrong humidity, can greatly decrease the FAE's effectiveness. It is also difficult to make a device that efficiently disperses the gas, and the FAE often misfires. There are other problems, primarily the difficulty of using FAE in artillery shells or many types of bombs. It was discovered in Vietnam that the best way to deliver FAE is by dropping it out of a helicopter or a slow-moving transport aircraft. This method was again used in the Gulf to clear minefields. Much research and development has been put into FAE since the 1970s, but there is not a lot to show for it. FAE is one of those "weapons of the future," and probably always will be.

The Iraqi Republican Guard Force Corps (RGFC)

A reputation can be made in the media, and the Iraqi Republican Guard is a prime example of myth creation. Starting out in the 1970s as a battalion of bodyguards for the Iraqi leader, it grew to a brigade in 1980 and to several divisions by 1988. When Iraq invaded Kuwait in 1990, the Republican Guard had grown to eight divisions, and after the invasion the Iraqis attempted to expand the Guard still further. The Republican Guard immediately caught everyone's imagination (military, public, and the press). Although the Guard had first pick of the latest military equipment and was supplied with chemical shells for its artillery, it was more a political symbol, patronage machine, and insurance policy for the ruling Baath party. The troops were paid twice as much as the regular soldiers and derived great prestige from being members of the Guard.

The reality was quite different. Despite all their material advantages, the Guards' reputation for battlefield performance was less than stellar. One joker said the Republican Guards turned out to be McGovernite Liberal Democrats. During the Iran-Iraq War, for example, the Guard troops made four attempts to recapture the Al Faw Peninsula. They made it on the last try, although the Regular Army 3rd Corps did most of the work while the Guard got most of the credit. Moreover, the Guard was not normally kept in front-line positions. This allowed more time for the Guard troops to train with their equipment. Keeping the Guard out of the lethal battle zones did wonders for the morale of the Guard troops, and they could be depended on to be rather more unflinching than Regular Army troops when the Guard was committed to combat.

That the Guard troops in 1991 became a priority target for Allied aircraft was recognition of their status as the primary guardians of the Regular Army's loyalty, protector of the Baath party, and one of the best-equipped units in the Iraqi Army. When the ground war finally came, the Republican Guard did turn out to be one of the few units that put up a fight, but it caused few casualties and was rolled over by the tanks of the Allied 7th and 18th Corps.

Iraqi Fortifications

Iraq managed to fight Iran to a standstill during the 1980–88 war, despite Iran having three times the population and a lot more enthusiasm. One major reason for Iraq's survival was the extensive use of fortifications. The Iraqis learned, as soldiers have known for centuries, that the shovel is a potent weapon. After Iraq invaded Kuwait, the Iraqis began to prepare numerous fortifications along the Kuwait–Saudi Arabia border. It immediately became popular to imagine these fortifications as some kind of impregnable barrier, a deadly killing zone that no Allied infantry could possibly cross without massive casualties. It was often mentioned that Iraq had planted a million land mines in this border area and prepared three lines of fortifications, one behind the other. Over a dozen divisions of troops manned these lines (which extended along the coast to defend against amphibious attack and, after January, west into southern Iraq). A little simple arithmetic, however, would have revealed a different picture. The fortified lines were about 250 kilometers long, or about 9.9 million inches, which works out to one mine every foot and a half. Minefields are not laid out like that, but rather in lines, sort of like a chessboard, with only the red squares having a mine in them. The point is, there was not a minefield stretching across the entire front. The Iraqis normally build several lines of fortifications, but with only 100 infantry battalions and 250 kilometers of front, each battalion has 2,500 meters to cover. Moreover, each battalion has two or three lines. So the battalion's 500 or so troops end up being distributed in bunker complexes (often triangular, one to two kilometers on a side) with a kilometer or more of undefended desert on each side. In the Russian style, the Iraqis built several sets of bunkers and trenches for each battalion, in two to three lines. Nearly 100,000 separate positions were built, from well-protected bunkers to slit trenches and foxholes. Not all of these positions were manned, obviously, but that was the point. The redundant bunkers provided more targets for the Allied bombers and artillery but reduced the chance that all this firepower would actually hit Iraqi troops.

When several battalions of coalition troops (tanks and infantry), backed up by over 100 artillery and aircraft, attack on a front of two or three kilometers, how much of an obstacle could these Iraqi fortifications have been? These Iraqi-style defenses worked against the Iranians because Iraq did not have to cover so wide a front with so few troops. Against Iran, Iraq was often able to build its fortifications in swamp, marsh, and mountains. Iraq had air superiority during the war with Iran, and Iran did not have several thousand modern tanks and well-trained crews to man them. During the Iran-Iraq War, Iraq had more mobile (motorized) divisions and a better road network behind its lines. When the Iranians attacked, they often destroyed the front-line Iraqi battalions. But even so, this process slowed down the Iranians enough to allow motorized Iraqi divisions to drive to the threatened sector and man (or build) another defensive line.

The situation was altered in Kuwait. Without air superiority, Iraq could not move mobile forces (tanks and infantry in APCs) to the portion of their line under attack. Moreover, the Allies could move as much equipment and manpower as they wanted to the point of attack. The Iraqi fortifications, and defensive system, sounded impressive in the news, but a little calculation, and reflection on what these fortifications would have to resist, revealed that the Iraqis were not in a very advantageous position. After suppressing Iraqi flak, the Allies bombed the minefields (often using helicopters and transport aircraft carrying fuel air explosives) and destroyed them. The Allied superiority in artillery-targeting and artillery-spotting radar made Iraq's large number of artillery pieces nearly useless. Allied engineers were able to move close to Iraqi fortifications to clear lanes for the advance of Allied mechanized units. Mine-plow "bunker-busting" tactics further reduced the forts. Consequently, the Iraqi fortifications turned out to serve more effectively as convenient locations to collect Iraqi prisoners of war.

Kuwait War Slang

Every war has its slang, a mix of terms of peacetime duty and some new stuff invented on the spot. Herewith is a selection of what was heard in the Arabian Desert during the Kuwait War.

- Abdul—Generic term for any Arab
- Airedales—Navy aircraft (usually bombers in support of ground troops)
- Air-to-mud—Air-force term for ground attack missions
- Assets—Shorthand for troops, weapons, and equipment. Can refer to either enemy or friend by "assets."
- BAM—Big-Assed Marine (female marine)
- Bedouin Bob—Generic term for any Bedouin met in the desert (often a resourceful fellow with something useful to sell or trade)
- BMO—Black Moving Object (Arab woman wearing traditional veil and black dress that covers everything)
- Boloed—Destroyed, as in a Hummer crash or from an enemy bullet in the head
- Dossbag—Sleeping bag (British)
- Echelons Beyond Reality—Superior officers
- EPW—Enemy Prisoner of War. Because of all the angst and notoriety over Vietnam prisoners of war, the term POW has become touchy. So the U.S. Department of Defense decided to have one term for our troops held prisoner (POWs) and another for enemy troops held prisoner by us (EPWs). Got that? Good.

- Going up (or down) town—Flying bombing missions to Baghdad. The term also used for other targets as in "going up to Big Al," referring to places with names beginning with "Al" (as in Al Fallujah)
- Gopping—Dirty and grungy from being in the desert too long (British)
- HEMTT—Smaller version of HET, not a tractor-trailer, but able to move up to twenty tons or more of supplies over almost any kind of terrain.
- HET—Heavy Equipment Transporter. Very large tractor trailer capable of carrying sixty-ton M1 tanks (to save wear and tear on the tank, and use less fuel getting there) and up to seventy tons of other useful stuff (fuel, ammunition, and water)
- High-Speed, Low-Drag—State-of-the-art, or highly respected
- HMFIC—Head Military Fucker in Charge, senior officer
- Hogs—Popular term for U.S. Air Force A-10 Thunderbolt II ground attack aircraft. Also known as "Warthog." Flown by "hog drivers"
- Homer—Generic term for Iraqi soldier (after the hapless father in *The Simpsons* TV show)
- Hummer—Ubiquitous wheeled vehicle that replaced the jeep during the 1980s.
- Jib Rat—See *REMF*
- Johnny Weissmuller Shower—A cold shower that makes you bellow like Tarzan
- Liberty Chits—What the marines called the U.S. psyops surrender leaflets dropped by the millions on the Iraqi troops
- Minging—See *Gopping*
- MOPP 4—Wearing all your chemical-warfare protective equipment (mask, suit). From MOPP, Military Oriented Protective Posture, or to be mopped. MOPP 4 is the highest level of preparedness.
- MRE—Meals, Ready to Eat (or "Meals Refused by Everyone"). Dehydrated field rations. Not too bad, but not so hot if it's all you have three times a day for weeks on end
- Nuclear Coffee—A cup of what passes for water (in Saudi

Arabia) with instant coffee, chocolate, creamer, and sugar. Kills most of the bad taste of the water.
- Ponts—Persons of no tactical significance. Anyone who has no impact on getting your job done (reporters, senior officers, civilians, etc.)
- REMF—Rear Echelon Motherfucker. Anyone not suffering with you out in the desert
- Rotor Heads—Helicopter pilots and the people that work with them
- Sammy—Saddam Hussein
- Scud—As in "Go Scud yourself"
- Scud-a-vision—CNN and other news programs that show the world what you are doing
- Shamal—A local word meaning sandstorm. The heavy shamal winds blow across the desert in the spring, which was another reason for getting the war over with before March. Also, the movement of thousands of armored vehicles through the desert broke the hardened crust of so much ground that extremely heavy amounts of dust and sand were blown around during the April 1991 shamal storms. In Saudi Arabia, this proved to be a bigger health problem than the burning oil wells up north in Kuwait.
- Sludding—Effects of chemical attack
- Spud—Slang for Scud
- Tread Heads—People who operate tanks and other armored vehicles
- Tree Eaters—Special Forces troops
- Unhappy Teddy—A depressed soldier (British)
- Varks—F-111 aircraft, also known unofficially as Aardvarks
- Zoomie—Anyone in the air force

The Crucial Role of Noncombat Airpower

While the combat aircraft received a lot of well-deserved credit for defeating the Iraqi armed forces, little notice was given to the essential role played by transport aircraft. Aside from the obvious job of delivering most of the troops and initial equipment and supplies, transport aircraft were flying into Saudi Arabia intensively throughout the war. Particularly for the combat aircraft during the air war, there was an urgent need to get spare parts and new equipment from the United States (or Europe) to Saudi Arabia. Generating over 2,000 combat sorties a day over a period of weeks uses up hundreds of pounds of spare parts per aircraft per sortie, and if new spares are not delivered in a timely fashion, the bombers cannot fly. In addition troops and essential ground-combat equipment were still being rushed in through late January.

To provide all these transport services, the active duty and reserve transport pilots flew many more hours than they are normally allowed. Major air bases at Riyadh and Dhahran saw round-the-clock transport operations, and the intensity of these operations could be seen from the number of hours pilots were flying. In peacetime, U.S. Air Force rules limit pilots to 125 hours in any thirty-day period and no more than 330 hours in the air during any ninety-day period. Peacetime flying rarely gets pilots up to 100 hours in thirty days, even during large military exercises. With the coming of Desert Storm, these rules generally went out the window. Military transport pilots were flying up to 260 hours in a thirty-day period and up to 550 hours in ninety days. Many pilots were right up against that limit, and some were forced to lay over in Saudi Arabia or stateside until they were enough hours under the limit to take another long trip between North America and the Middle East (or Germany, where a lot of military equipment and supplies were taken out of the large stockpiles in the area).

Noncombat Losses

It was only in this century that wars were fought in which more troops were killed and injured by combat than by disease and sickness. This was a direct result of improved medical and sanitation practices. The United States has been one of the leading practitioners of these methods and its army has had proportionately fewer noncombat losses than any other army. The Persian Gulf War was no exception and, despite the abundance of diseases in the Gulf area, coalition losses of this kind were minimal. Not so the Iraqi Army. Of the 350,000 Iraqi troops in the Kuwaiti Theater of Operations (KTO), 85,000 were taken prisoner, up to 50,000 were able to retreat into Iraq as organized units or as individuals, over 100,000 deserted before or during the ground war, and the remainder died from either combat or noncombat causes. Prisoner interviews and an examination of the dead indicated that over half of those killed died from sickness and disease, while many of the deserters and prisoners were themselves not in the best of health. Had the air war gone on much longer, the losses from sickness and disease would have been much higher, and the bane of soldiers from the beginning of organized warfare would have again claimed more victims than combat itself.

Who Made the Iraqi Armed Forces Possible

Initially, it was the Turks, then the British, and, finally, the Russians and the Gulf Arabs who created the Iraqi Army. One reason Iraq's past was always so dominated by military coups and violence was because so many of Iraq's founders had served as officers in the Turkish Army. Service in the Turkish Army had been a common means of making a living in the relatively impoverished portions of the Turkish Empire that eventually became Iraq. There were over a thousand Iraqis serving as Turkish officers who rebelled in 1916–18 (during the general Arab Rebellion) and formed a large portion of the leadership in the new nation of Iraq. These officers were largely from the wealthiest families and, to a lesser extent, the sons of the Muslim clergy. After 1918, Britain was the big influence in the military, and young Iraqi officers were sent to British military schools while British officers and NCOs went to Iraq to train the Iraqi armed forces. When the monarchy was overthrown in 1958, more middle-class (and fewer royalist) officers became more numerous. When the Baath party took control in the 1960s, membership in the Baath party became a more important factor in officer selection and promotion than military skill. Russia also became the major arms supplier after 1958, although Iraq still looked to Britain for tactical doctrine and training. However, as the quantity of Russian arms increased to a flood during the Iran-Iraq War, with all this equipment came more Russian military advisers. Thus, by 1990 much of the Iraqi Army was trained in Russian methods of fighting.

The Iraqi Army went from a 330,000-man force in late 1980 to over a million in 1988. It went down to about 700,000 by early 1990, but was built up to over a million again in late 1990 after the Kuwait invasion. The equipment for this army came largely from Russia and other Communist nations (China, North Korea, East Europe). These sales amounted to over half the $40 billion Iraq had spent on arms. France was the next-largest supplier, providing about $10 billion worth, including a lot of the high-tech aircraft, missiles, and electronics. Other Western nations provided billions of dollars' worth of ammunition. Much additional "semimilitary" equipment was received from Russia and the West, including trucks, communications gear, and building material (for fortifications). And as we have seen, the Gulf Arabs (largely Kuwait and Saudi Arabia) provided most of the cash for the weapons that were paid for, even though Iraq still owes its arms suppliers (mainly Russia) over $10 billion for equipment received and not yet paid for. As one Saudi diplomat put it to a Russian who apologized for arming Iraq, "You may have supplied the weapons, but we *paid* for them."

The Mail-Order War

During the Persian Gulf War, troops in the field often had access to long-distance phones and fax machines. They were also able to receive airmail. Many took advantage of these capabilities to purchase mail-order items from American firms. Special tents, food (to break the monotony of MREs), clothing, and electronic gadgets were all ordered and received within weeks. One of the more interesting items some troops obtained in this way were $4,000 GPS (Global Positioning Satellite) receivers. Additional shelter and familiar brand-name foods were one thing, but not getting lost in the desert made a GPS unit an expensive but much appreciated mail-order advantage.

Necessity Is the Mother of Expediency

Many items that the armed forces needed in the Gulf, but did not exist when the troops were deployed, suddenly appeared in the hands of the troops when they were sorely needed. Some of this equipment, like J-STARS, was already in development, but was several years away from troop use. Electronic gear was taken out of the laboratory, or created from scratch and put into action successfully. Less exotic equipment, like add-on armor, heat shields, and sundry electronic gear was also acquired. One of these items was literally a "Twenty-four Day Wonder." A concerned engineering technician, looking for a way to avoid friendly-fire losses, sketched out a design for an infrared beacon that could be mounted on armored vehicles and give off a light signal that could only be seen by aircraft. This happened on February 2, 1991; twenty-four days later the first devices were delivered to combat units in southern Iraq. The small battery-powered devices cost $320 each. Although the fighting was over before many more could be delivered, the full 10,000 units ordered were taken so that there would not be as much of a problem with friendly fire the next time around.

The Aircraft Factory

One of the major items needed before the air war could begin in the Gulf was an aircraft maintenance facility. By the end of January 1991, such an operation was set up in central Saudi Arabia. Starting with only an emergency landing strip, within six weeks the air force had deployed 5,000 maintenance personnel and all their equipment and spare parts. The AMU (Aircraft Maintenance Unit) could do anything needed to get an aircraft flying again, including practically rebuilding it. In peacetime, combat aircraft normally fly only 300–400 hours a year. During the war, most aircraft did that much flying in a few weeks. Without the AMU—and its ability to turn damaged aircraft around in days, if not hours—the air war would have been less intensive and more expensive.

Bad Luck and Bad News

British Tornado fighter-bombers primarily flew low-level missions against Iraqi airfields during the first week of the air war, and four Tornadoes were lost. At first, it was assumed that because these aircraft had to come in so low and slow, they were more vulnerable to ground fire. This proved not to be the case, as only one of the Tornadoes lost was attacking airfields. The other Tornadoes were lost performing the same types of attack missions common to U.S. aircraft. The heavy Tornado losses were largely a result of chance, or, as the pilots would put it, "rotten luck." Rotten treatment in the news, also. In any event, the RAF, primarily the Tornadoes, flew 6,500 sorties (4,000 combat), with 6,000 (1,000 guided) bombs dropped. The Canadians, with 26 U.S. F-18 aircraft flew 994 sorties (770 CAP, 168 sweep, 56 CAS, averaging 5.7 hours each, 38 sorties and 220 hours per aircraft).

The Nine Nuclear Labors of Saddam

One of the great fears during the Gulf War was that Iraq would produce a nuclear weapon, and use it. Such an event was unlikely during the war, as can be seen from the list of nine areas of technology that Iraq must master. The future is another matter.

1. Nuclear Material   This is what explodes with thousands of times more force than an equal weight of conventional explosive. Not all nuclear material will react in this way; the stuff that fuels most nuclear-power plants won't work. Potent "weapons-grade" material is required, and Iraq has no easy way of producing it. Its only facility capable of producing it quickly was bombed by Israel in 1981. The only other way to produce nuclear-grade material is with an elaborate system of mechanical and chemical procedures (isotope separation via gas centrifuge), or even older (and less efficient) World War II methods. Iraq has been assembling the many components for both systems but apparently never got much nuclear fuel out of either system. Much of what it did have was bombed in January 1991.

2. Reflector   The nuclear material is formed into a ball, which is surrounded by a special tungsten alloy. The alloy speeds up the nuclear reaction and, for a crude weapon, may make the difference between an explosion and just some radioactive contamination. There is nothing particularly difficult with this component, and the Iraqis can probably handle it, if they can get the alloy.

3. High-Explosive Trigger   What sets off the nuclear reaction is nothing more than surrounding the nuclear material with high explosive that is shaped and positioned to direct most of its force onto the nuclear material. If the weapons-grade nuclear material is rich (radioactive) enough, such a squeeze sets off the nuclear explosion. Designing these explosives requires a high degree of chemical and mechanical engineering, and the Iraqis would probably have a problem with this item. There is no civilian equivalent they can buy on the open market.

4. Fuse   The conventional explosives must be set off with split-second precision. This requires special capacitors (to store the electric charge) and high-speed electrical switches (krytrons). The capacitors can be relatively easily obtained (or even made in Iraq). The krytrons are also rather common for use in commercial equipment. Iraqi agents were caught trying to smuggle krytrons in 1989. Additional smuggling attempts were complicated by the war and its aftermath.

5. Neutron Starter   The conventional explosion alone does not start the chain reaction, and there must be an additional source of neutrons directed into the nuclear material to ensure that the chain reaction gets going. The neutron source can be either a special metal alloy or an electromechanical device. Iraq can probably put together the alloy version.

6. Fabrication   The nuclear material (a rather heavy metal, something like lead) must be precisely shaped into a ball and fitted into the reflector. It is a nasty job, given the highly radioactive nature of the material, but technically not all that difficult.

7. Design Calculations   Lots of math and physics go into figuring out exactly what shape the crucial bomb components must take. You don't need a supercomputer to do this (although it helps), but you do need competent scientists. Iraq has them, although it probably lost a few when Iraqi weapons labs were bombed in 1991, and when other scientists fled in the aftermath of the war.

8. Implosion Testing   Before you risk your scarce nuclear material to a live bomb, you have to test the entire system several times and correct any problems you find. This requires several copies of the bomb to be detonated without the nuclear material but in the presence of a lot of expensive test equipment to record the results. Getting some of the test equipment may prove difficult, although the Iraqis could build a bomb without this stage and risk a dud (a high risk, given all their other problems).

9. *Warhead Design and Construction*   A nuclear device is not the same as a nuclear weapon. Getting the device into a shape (and robustness) that would work in a missile is very likely beyond the capabilities of most Third World engineering resources. The Iraqis can get it into a package that would likely survive (and explode after) being dropped from an aircraft. They could also deliver their bomb (weighing half a ton or more) by truck or ship.

Infrared

A term often heard during the Gulf War was infrared, which refers to a form of light that the human eye cannot see but electronic sensors can. Infrared light is present at night, as it is a by-product of heat. For this reason, there has always been a military interest in infrared detection as a means of seeing at night. Because military equipment, and troops, give off heat, they can be seen with the proper infrared detector. To make them more efficient, some infrared detectors only look for certain intensities of infrared light. This is the principal behind heat-seeking missiles and many modern "fire-and-forget" missiles.

Which Weapons and Doctrine Didn't Work

Most U.S. and NATO Allied weapons worked. The ones that didn't perform as expected were:

Cluster Bombs   Clusters didn't cause as much damage as precision-guided big bombs.

Low-Level Bombing   Though thought to be a natural protection from enemy air defenses, it was found that enemy ground fire was still a fatal factor. Low-level attacks on runways by Tornado aircraft were a particular example. The British RAF pilots were brave, but flying headlong down runways to drop the JP-233 runway attack bombs allowed Iraqi antiaircraft gunners to hit the attacking aircraft. While these airfield attacks later proved to be less dangerous to the Tornadoes than originally thought, it was quickly noted that most bombs could be accurately dropped at higher altitudes (12,000–20,000 feet) beyond the reach of the thousands of smaller antiaircraft weapons Iraq kept operational until the end of the war. One reason Baghdad was such a dangerous target was because a third of the Iraqi light antiaircraft guns and missiles were in and around Baghdad.

Helicopter-Based Naval-Mine Clearing   Minesweeping ships are still needed, particularly as naval mines become more versatile. This is one reason why Allied minesweepers and mine-warfare ships were significant contributions.

TOWs   When they worked, they worked well. However, firing a TOW over certain types of sand obstacles (such as a berm) was a recipe for a miss. The sand particles apparently affected the TOW's trailing guidance wires.

One Big Bomb Is Better Than a Lot of Little Ones

Over the last thirty years, much effort and many tax dollars have gone into developing cluster bombs. These air-delivered weapons substitute dozens or hundreds of smaller bomblets (submunitions) for the usual bomb filling of straight high explosive (HE). The theory behind cluster bombs was that the bomblets would fall over a wider area and do a lot more damage than just one large explosion, and this has proven generally true against infantry. In the Persian Gulf War, however, the antitank cluster bombs (containing fewer bomblets than the antipersonnel version, where a larger bomblet is required to destroy òr disable a tank) were not found to be as effective as expected. The problem was that you could see the antitank bomblets on the ground and avoid, clear, or destroy them. As the Iraqis avoided moving at night, when these bomblets were most effective (because they were less likely to be spotted), they were able to further limit the effectiveness of the cluster bombs.

In comparison, the GBU's (Glide Bomb Units) did work well. A GBU takes a basic "iron bomb" (a steel casing filled with explosive, costing about a dollar a pound) and adds a guidance-and-sensor kit (costing a few thousand dollars). An aircraft (not necessarily the one carrying the bomb) uses a laser that is aimed at a target on the ground. The sensor on the bomb homes in on the laser light reflected off the target. The air force found that one aircraft with a laser could cruise back and forth in front of an enemy unit (out of range of enemy ground fire) and move the laser from one target to another as other aircraft fly in and release their bombs. Dozens of enemy tanks were destroyed in a short time using this technique, and it proved to be one of the more useful new tactics developed during the campaign.

Special Operations Forces (SOF)

SOF played a significant, but little publicized, role in the Gulf War. SOF consists of special operations by small groups of highly trained troops. "High value, high risk" missions are often intertwined with intelligence work or areas that are best kept out of the spotlight. The United States only got into SOF during World War II, with its army Ranger and marine Raider battalions; and the OSS (Office of Strategic Services, a precursor of the CIA) also did a lot of what the Special Forces does today. In the early 1960s, the SOF was established in its current form, and the U.S. Special Forces made its reputation during the Vietnam War. Over 5,000 SOF troops were used in Kuwait and Iraq. In addition to the Special Forces (SF for short, also known as Green Berets or "beanies"), there were the navy SEALs (three teams of "Sea, Air, and Land" troops) and the air-force 1st Special Operations Wing (SOW). The SF antiterrorist "Delta Force" was also involved, as were members of Britain's SAS (Special Air Service), and one company of U.S. Army Rangers. The army provided most of the manpower on the ground, the SEALs worked along the coast and the air-force SOW's all-weather helicopters, transports, and gunships took people and equipment where they were needed.

The SEALs are classic commandos, trained to come from ships to land areas to scout or destroy enemy installations. The Ranger battalions are highly trained light infantry that can also be used as paratroopers. Each division has its own small units of SOF troops: LRS-Ds (long-range surveillance detachments) and LRRPs (long-range reconnaissance patrols). These recon troops are basically well-trained infantry volunteers who are flown up to 100 (or more) kilometers from their divisions to provide information on enemy activity that might affect their division during the war.

The SF troops (in teams of five or six men) were dropped deep in Iraqi territory, up to 500 kilometers into Iraq, at least several weeks before the ground war began. Many SF teams went deep into Iraq overland, using specially configured HMMVs (with silenced engines) to get around. These SF scouts were also used to locate Scud launchers and then target them with lasers. U.S. bombers then came in and used the laser reflections to guide smart bombs to the target. If targets were found in daylight, A-10s usually did the attacking.

The SF scouts also used other electronic equipment to get around and stay in touch. Teams were equipped with GPS navigation sets that enabled them always to know their exact location. Compact radio transmitters (equipped with antijamming and detection capabilities) enabled them to transmit information on Iraqi troop movements, military bases, and key civilian targets. The SF teams also helped rescue eight American pilots shot down over Iraq, including one as far north as Baghdad.

The LRS-Ds (long-range surveillance detachments) and LRRPs (long-range reconnaissance patrols) operated closer to the divisions they belonged to and usually went out for only three to seven days (compared to a week or more for the Special Forces teams). These troops were not Special Forces troops, but specially selected and trained reconnaissance troops belonging to the combat divisions. The LRRPs moved around on a preplanned route looking for such things as enemy activity or routes over which the division would later advance into Iraq. Out in western Iraq, there weren't many Iraqi troops, and the LRRPs just had to make sure that they saw the enemy first. With air superiority, Allied aircraft could work with the LRRPs to warn of any approaching enemy units. The LRS-Ds had a quite different job. They would select a site, dig themselves in, camouflage the position, and then wait for several days and observe any enemy activity. This was a mission uniquely suited to the sparsely populated desert of southern Iraq. In more densely populated areas, the LRS-D would more likely be accidentally discovered by civilians wandering by. In the desert, even passing civilians would usually not detect the concealed LRS-D. In Iraq, the LRS-D troops had silenced pistols to deal with any Iraqi troops that came too close. If a substantial Iraqi unit discovered them, they could call on U.S. bombers and helicopters to help them shoot their way out.

The LRRPs and LRS-D units allowed American troops to get and keep the intelligence advantage. Air and satellite reconnaissance had disadvantages, the chief ones being they are not there constantly and they cannot experience exactly what the conditions are on the ground. The greater accuracy and speed of ground reconnaissance provided a crucial edge. Because of such aggressive reconnaissance, U.S. forces knew a lot more about Iraqi forces than the other way around.

The British SAS, despite having only 200 of their number in the area, distinguished themselves in several daring missions inside Iraq. Many of those involved taking something back with them, either an Iraqi or a piece of equipment.

The air force was the latest of the U.S. services to get into Special Operations. They were represented in the Gulf by the 1st Special Operations Wing (1st SOW). Most of the air-force personnel were flying and maintaining helicopters and transports that assisted special-operations troops from other services. The 1st SOW had five squadrons, one each for MH-60 helicopters (specially equipped UH-60 "Blackhawks"), MH-53J heavy helicopters (four led the army Apaches on the opening attack deep in Iraq), AC-130 gunships (one was lost at Khafji), MC-130 long-range, all-weather transports (dropped 14 million surrender leaflets on Iraqi troops positions, as well as eleven 7.5-ton bombs and several SOF ground operations), and HC-130 tankers (for refueling all aircraft in the 1st SOW, and any other SOF aircraft that needed it). The helicopter squadrons contained ground teams that were placed within Iraq to collect information (often as individuals). Over sixty missions of this type were conducted, including a series of scouting missions in late February that discovered a concentration of twenty-nine Scud missiles aimed at Israel. The A-10s were called in to destroy the Scuds, and, as U.S. leaders put, "keep Israel out of the war."

Casualties You'll Never Hear About

One of the less discussed aspects of the SOF's missions is the reluctance to announce casualties. The names of some SOF troops killed in Vietnam do not appear on the Vietnam "wall" memorial in Washington, D.C., because of the sensitive nature of the missions they were on when they were killed. In addition, over a dozen Special Operations Forces troops killed in Latin America during the 1980s were never officially recognized as "killed in action"; their the next of kin were told the men died

in a training accident. Indeed, during the Gulf War several of
the helicopters that were reported as crashed in noncombat actions were actually SOF choppers downed deep inside Iraq. It
remains to be seen if all SOF casualties in the Gulf War will be
revealed for what they were.

The Prudent, Devious, or Deceived Intelligence Analysts

From early in the campaign, Allied intelligence analysts estimated that there were nearly half a million Iraqi troops in Kuwait and southern Iraq. This number was arrived at from
information obtained from satellite photos and intercepted radio
messages. From that data came the estimate that there were at
least forty divisions in the area. This number of divisions, with
the usual support troops, and even if somewhat under strength,
came to at least half a million troops. The number of tanks in
the area came from adding up the number of tanks (MBTs, or
Main Battle Tanks) normally assigned to the different types of
divisions, plus some confirmation from satellite photos and the
radio intercepts. The seven Republican Guard divisions had
1,300 to 1,400 MBTs. The nine army tank and mechanized divisions in the Kuwait Theater of Operations (KTO) had another
2,000–2,200 MBTs, and the twenty-five infantry divisions had
about 1,000 MBTs. From this calculation came the estimate of
4,000 to 4,400 Iraqi tanks in the KTO. But the crews on these
tanks amount only to about 15,000 troops. It's the 260 to 270
infantry battalions that contained most of the manpower
(156,000 men, if at nearly full strength). The estimated 3,000
artillery weapons in the KTO required another 35,000 troops.
Thus, the principal combat weapons occupied about 200,000
Iraqi soldiers, with the other 200,000 to 300,000 being occupied
with support roles within the divisions or at corps level.

After the ground war, the Allies found themselves with 85,000
prisoners and what appeared to be up to 100,000 dead Iraqis
(mostly from the air campaign and disease). There weren't that
many bodies in evidence, but there were a lot of caved-in bunkers and graves of Iraqis buried by their fellow soldiers. Iraqi
officers were not sure how many troops were in the area, nor
how many were killed. It was unlikely there were 100,000 dead,
or even half that number. It was estimated that nearly a third
of the Iraqi troops (up to 150,000) deserted before the end

of the ground campaign and that 20,000–30,000 Iraqis (in combat units) escaped to Iraqi-controlled territory. This left over 100,000 Iraqi troops unaccounted for. Or were they really unaccounted for?

The Allied intelligence effort began even before August, as U.S. satellites were constantly monitoring the Iraqi Army and were the first to note the size and composition of the buildup of Iraqi forces on the Kuwaiti border during July 1990. With only periodic (several times a day) satellite overflights, it was possible to get "snapshots" of what the Iraqis had on the ground and draw up a list of the major formations (combat divisions) being moved to the area. Stockpiled supplies ("supply dumps") could also be detected and this was the tip-off that the Iraqis could actually invade if they wanted to. Once the invasion took place, satellite (and reconnaissance aircraft) surveillance increased. But despite all this effort, one item in particular could not be counted with precision: people. This was not considered crucial, as it was known how many troops there were in a combat division. Or at least it was known how many troops there were supposed to be in a division, and that's apparently where the problems arose in getting an accurate head count.

The Kuwait invasion was not very popular within Iraq. Even less popular among the troops was the prospect of being sent off to sit in the Kuwait desert in the middle of summer. Desertion (or simply not showing up for duty) was thus common in the Iraqi Army. This was known from what went on during the 1980–88 Iran-Iraq War. At any given time, there were at least 100,000 Iraqi deserters during that war. Despite strenuous efforts at controlling the population, Iraq was never able to get a grip on the desertion problems. When reservists were called up in 1990 to man the divisions being sent to Kuwait, many troops simply did not show up. Some bribed local military officials, or let it be known that local political peace could be had if the Baath party officials in the area did not make a big deal about the absent soldiers.

Initial reports had indicated that up to 100,000 Iraqis had been killed in the KTO. When the survey of the area was completed, the evidence indicated that no more than 30,000 Iraqis had been killed by Allied attack, and probably considerably fewer. Allied forces buried the Iraqi dead who had not already been buried (by other Iraqis or left inside collapsed bunkers) during the bombing campaign. There were about fifty different burial sites, most of them containing fewer than a hundred bodies. It was too dangerous to go digging up collapsed bunkers. There were not enough Iraqi wounded to indicate a death toll of more than 20,000–30,000. Information from prisoners also confirmed this.

Therein lies the problem. Allied planning was heavily dependent on strategic reconnaissance systems, particularly satellites. While these systems are good for the long haul, they were insufficient to support combat operations. Battlefield commanders need detailed information and they need it quickly. A major reason for the Iraqi ground forces undercount was that the satellites did not pass overhead frequently enough to catch all the thousands of small unit movements. There was no way of knowing if a truck convoy in one satellite photo was the same one seen in another ten hours later. It's hard to tell if the trucks carried troops, food, ammunition, or whatever. Further complicating the satellite situation was the worst winter weather in Kuwait in several decades, the end result being that the area was covered by clouds half the time, and only a few of the U.S. satellites could penetrate the cloud cover, and then not in very much detail.

Satellites had yet another flaw: Their information was customarily sent directly back to Washington. Despite the needs in the Gulf, this satellite data did not always make it to the Gulf in a timely fashion, if at all. Initially, it was thought that the thousands of analysts in Washington could sort out the data and send it on to the Gulf quickly enough to be of use. However, not only did the stateside analysis slow things down, but it often conflicted with reports obtained on the ground (or close to it, from pilots and troops on the ground). This became particularly onerous because local resources (aircraft and helicopters) were able to cover the same ground in most of Kuwait as the satellites. Allied analysts in the Gulf could clearly see that the Washington-based analysts, working only with satellite sensor material, were making incorrect assessments. This was further confirmed after the ground war, when people were able to further check out the target status and damage situation at ground level. This was particularly the case with weapons that do their damage in such a way that massive destruction does not result. The best example was the laser-guided bombs, which many times were dropped down airshafts, causing massive internal damage while leaving what appeared to be an undamaged structure in a subsequent satellite photo. The same thing happened with tanks and aircraft. If an A-10 aircraft attacked a tank with its 30-mm cannon, the only external evidence of the massive internal damage to the tank would be a few one- to two-inch holes in the tank's armor. Satellite photos would often show these destroyed tanks still sitting there, seemingly intact. Tanks that were hidden in individual bunkers were equally difficult to assess as having been destroyed by precision munitions. The satellite analysts often disputed whether there was a tank in the bunker at all.

There were several hundred aircraft and helicopters in the Gulf equipped with reconnaissance cameras, but there were never enough of them. These recon aircraft were also needed to locate new targets, and the heavy cloud cover made it difficult even for low-flying aircraft to keep everything under observation. The satellites were supposed to be the solution, but there are obviously a few bugs still to work out.

Intelligence Breakdowns and Assessments

Why were U.S. and Allied intelligence forces caught so far off-guard by the Iraqi attack on Kuwait? Part of the reason is almost total reliance on electronic intelligence systems and their "operational indicators," especially in the case of the U.S. Apparently, the Iraqi units on the border of Kuwait were not informed until less than half a day before the attack began that they were to proceed with the invasion of Kuwait. Lack of "tactical" and "operational" traffic (and no intercepted orders) was perceived as an indicator that the Iraqis were not about to move. With few "Humint" assets (human intelligence assets—i.e., covert agents) in Iraq and with satellite photos confirming little activity among the Iraqi front-line units, the assessment remained that the Iraqis were not about to move.

Admittedly this is highly speculative, but there are indications that the Iraqi troops themselves were surprised by the order to go ahead with the invasion. Was Saddam being clever or had he decided, suddenly, to go ahead and gamble? He had perceived a strategic opportunity and had the instrument (the army), but the decision to go ahead on August 2 may have been spurof-the-moment, surprising his own troops as well as the enemy. If this was the case, then there is little wonder that the Iraqi forces stayed in Kuwait. Because of Saddam's sudden decision to go into Kuwait, they did not have the supplies and logistics capabilities to continue the attack into Saudi Arabia.

Friendly-Fire Losses (U.S. Only)

There were 107 killed and wounded by friendly fire. Nearly all confirmed friendly-fire incidents involved U.S. forces.

CONFIRMED FRIENDLY-FIRE INCIDENTS

Type of Incident	Number	KIA (killed)	WIA (wounded)
Air to ground	7	11	5
Ground to Ground	15	24	57
Air to Ship	2	0	0
Ship to Air	1	0	0
Ground to Air	1	0	0
Total	26	35	72

Friendly-fire losses received a lot of media attention. Casualties caused by one's own troops' weapons ("friendly fire") have been a problem for as long as there have been battles. In this century, the heavy use of firearms, artillery, and aircraft has increased the incidence of friendly fire. No one in the military likes to talk about it, although combat training stresses the many things the troops can do to avoid it. One official study done by the U.S. Army concluded that at least 2 percent of American casualties are from friendly fire. Other estimates go from 5 to 20 percent. The experience in the Persian Gulf was toward the high end. The U.S. Army's official 2 percent friendly-fire rate is suspect, as these were only the losses officially reported as such. Nearly every combat veteran can tell you of one or more unreported case of friendly fire. The combat officers who do the reporting have no incentive to report such incidents if they can avoid doing so. It does not do much for one's career to admit that you are shooting your own troops. This points out another aspect of friendly fire: The side with the most firepower in play can expect to take more losses from its own fire. The U.S. Army has generally had the most firepower to throw around in twentieth-century wars. This was the case in the Gulf. Note that planners during a previous high-firepower war (World War I) habitually planned on 10 to 15 percent losses from friendly fire, particularly if chemical weapons were being used.

The use of "smart" munitions increases the incidence of friendly-fire losses as, once launched, these somewhat more intelligent missiles have no way of distinguishing friend from foe. With more troops traveling in vehicles rather than moving by foot, the chance increases for a tragic loss resulting from a single missile. Nine of the twenty-six incidents involved missiles, another eight were from long-range M1A1 cannon fire.

One aspect of modern warfare that increases losses is the large proportion of combat troops traveling around packed into lightly armored vehicles. Most (73 percent) of the friendly-fire casualties in the Gulf were troops traveling in these armored vehicles (Bradley M2s/M3s, or similar marine or British vehicles). The long range and high accuracy of U.S. tank guns in the desert also made it easy to mistake vehicles two miles away for enemy targets. Seven of the nineteen friendly-fire incidents that caused casualties involved M1A1 tanks firing on other ground troops and causing seventeen dead and forty-eight wounded. Overall, the M1A1 tank accounted for over 60 percent of the friendly-fire casualties, most caused by the M1A1's 120-mm gun. There were about nine thousand 120-mm shells fired during the ground war. Including "friendly fire" that missed and didn't cause casualties, about one in five hundred 120-mm shells fired was aimed at friendly troops. So remember it was friendly tanks, not friendly aircraft, that were the most common cause of friendly-fire losses.

Friendly aircraft got most of the attention in friendly-fire incidents because the majority of the air-to-ground errors occurred before the ground war began, when not much news was available and friendly fire quickly became a hot item. All (seven) of the air-to-ground incidents occurred before the ground fighting began in earnest on February 24, resulting in eleven dead and fifteen wounded. There was one non-U.S. incident that occurred after February 24, when British armored vehicles were fired on by American aircraft, causing nine dead and eleven wounded. This was the handful of non-U.S. friendly-fire incidents of the entire war. Most of the other Allies did not even keep careful track of friendly-fire losses, as such incidents are traditionally regarded as the unfortunate "fortunes of war."

Seven of the twenty-six friendly-fire incidents resulted in no casualties at all; three of these involved missiles being fired at friendly aircraft or ships. In another incident, an A-10 fired at a marine observation post, where at least the troops could jump into a foxhole. Another involved M1A1 tanks firing at other M1A1 tanks.

The U.S. armed forces are apparently going to try and do something about friendly fire on the ground and adopt a solution the air forces have been using for over thirty years: IFF (Identify, Friend or Foe) devices. These are small radio mechanisms which, when they receive the right signal from a friendly aircraft, respond with confirmation that they are indeed a friendly. The IFF device may not work as well on the more cluttered ground battlefield, and it will increase costs by perhaps 1 percent, but it will reduce (but not eliminate) friendly-fire losses. A small, cheap device for identifying friendly armored vehicles from aircraft was delivered just as the ground war ended. But as air-to-ground errors are not as great a problem as ground-to-ground incidents, most of the future effort will go toward keeping the ground troops from shooting each other. One device, PLRS (Position Location Reporting System), is already being tested. It is a radio transmitter that links with headquarters to show on a computer screen where all the friendly units are. The radio signals are coded to avoid the enemy from using the information. This solution may turn out to be the most practical means of reducing friendly fire on the modern battlefield. Just knowing where all your own people are eliminates a lot of fatal errors.

Defending the Fort

The military buildup in the Gulf removed most of America's ground combat forces from the United States. Of the combat divisions in the U.S. Army, the movement to the Persian Gulf left the army's active divisions as shown on page 381.

Of the army's three active-duty armored cavalry regiments, two were in the Gulf (2nd and 3rd ACR), while one (11th ACR) remained in Europe.

1st Mechanized Infantry	Gulf
2nd Infantry	Korea
3rd Mechanized Infantry	Gulf, 1 brigade; Europe 2
4th Mechanized Infantry	U.S., 2 brigades
5th Mechanized Infantry	U.S., 2 brigades
6th Light Infantry	U.S. (Alaska), 2 brigades
7th Light Infantry	U.S.
8th Mechanized Infantry	Germany, 1 tank battalion to Gulf, 1 artillery battalion to Gulf
9th Motorized Infantry	U.S., being disbanded (1 brigade now)
10th Light Infantry	U.S., 2 brigades
24th Mechanized Infantry	Gulf
25th Light Infantry	U.S. (Hawaii)
82nd Airborne Infantry	Gulf
101st Air Assault Infantry	Gulf
1st Armored	Gulf
2nd Armored	Gulf 1 brigade from U.S. 1 brigade from Europe (remainder of division disbanded)
3rd Armored	Gulf
1st Cavalry (Armored)	Gulf

Good News/Bad News Summary

Within a month of the end of the "100 hour" ground war, it was clear that while an impressive victory had been won, there was a growing list of items needing improvement:

1. Friendly Troop Identification, in Order to Eliminate All Those Friendly-Fire Losses It was known that there could be problems, and while there were only about thirty incidents, the losses were considered avoidable. Most of the friendly vehicles fired on were those that looked like enemy vehicles (the USMC and British armored cars looked like the Russian armored cars the Iraqis used). The many measures that were taken did reduce

the number of friendly-fire incidents that could have been expected given the number of ground-support missions being
flown. GPS was a big help in keeping friendly-fire losses low.
Units reporting incorrect positions have, in past wars, often resulted in said units getting clobbered by friendly artillery and air
strikes, not to mention an occasional friendly ground unit.

*2. Better Integration of Navy Air Operations with Everyone
Else*   The U.S. Navy has always seen itself as a self-contained
armed force. It has ships, naturally, but it also has an army (the
marines) and an air force. However, the navy tends to operate
without much reference to the other services, and this became a
major problem in the Gulf. Naval aviation had serious problems
operating efficiently with air force, army, and Allied aviation.
Navy and air-force staffs knew little about how each other operated and had to get acquainted very quickly. Some problems
couldn't be overcome. For example, carriers were not equipped
to handle some of the specialized air-force bombs, forcing air-
force aircraft to perform missions against targets requiring those
weapons. Don't look for the admirals to be terribly contrite or
willing to implement efficient solutions.

3. Heavy Equipment Transport by Sea   Getting heavy equipment to the battlefield was a difficult job. Nearly all the armored
vehicles and trucks had to come by ship, and there were not
enough fast freighters to get over 6,000 armored vehicles (tanks
and APCs) and 30,000 trucks to the Gulf quickly enough. Earlier, the U.S. Navy was forced, by Congress, to buy eight fast
transport ships, and a few more may be purchased in the future
with somewhat less arm twisting.

4. Pilot Night Vision   Night-vision goggles have been used by
pilots for several years. Their principal limitation, the pilots'
difficulty in orientating themselves in featureless terrain, became painfully apparent after months of operations in the flat
desert. While U.S. helicopter pilots frequently train in desert
environments, they have never operated so intensively over
such areas as those found in northern Arabia. This has been
a problem for a long time, and a solution will not be found
quickly. More work will be done on navigation equipment for
helicopters in all types of terrain. Advances in this area will

also improve the effectiveness of night and thermal imaging fire-control systems.

5. Helicopter Communications During Low-Level Flight Aircraft radios are built with the understanding that they will usually be operating at some higher altitude. Helicopter operations in the flat expanses of the Arabian desert often had helicopters very close to the ground for extended periods of time. This limited the range and effectiveness of helicopter communications. As it has been known for some time that helicopters in combat are safer close to the ground, improvements in helicopter radio communications will now be made.

6. More Realistic Threat Modeling That's a ten-dollar phrase for more realistic representation of likely opponents in peacetime wargames. The air-force bombers, in particular, were caught short. They thought they could quickly reprogram their fire-control systems to hit Iraqi targets from higher altitudes. In practice, a combination of unpreparedness and complacency caused this reprogramming to be a problem. There were similar problems with the bombs themselves (not enough "bunker busters" of the right type).

7. Don't Cut the Tail Too Short The army, in its haste to provide more troops for combat units during the 1980s, came up with the "Army of Excellence" (AOE) program. The program was a bad joke to most of the troops who had to live with it, as the AOE meant you had to provide the same levels of support with fewer troops and equipment. You can kid yourself about this in peacetime, but in the Gulf, there weren't enough trucks or mechanics, and it was pretty obvious. The reserve troops solved some of the personnel problems, but equipment that no longer existed was another matter. Artillery units often had to use half their ammunition trucks to carry water and fuel.

8. Don't Play Games with the Reserves The army "Total Force" had some success, and some glaring failures. Put simply, vital units needed for a large combat force (as was needed in the Gulf) existed only as reserve or National Guard units. This worked out well with the combat-support units; combat units are another matter. The army had planned to send many combat divisions to war with a third of their combat troops coming from National Guard brigades. That didn't happen. We'll all be hearing more about this disaster, and can only hope that it won't be repeated.

9. Put Some Intelligence in Intelligence U.S. intelligence resources are formidable, and centralized in a number of Washington, D.C.–based bureaucracies. These information czars were reluctant to share their resources in a timely manner with mere field commanders. The folks in the field were not happy with this arrangement, and one of them, General Norman Schwarzkopf, was not shy about voicing his displeasure. Improvements in this area will not come easily, as the secretive intelligence magnates won't let go of anything without a fight.

10. Antijamming for Tactical Satellite Communications The army currently makes extensive use of satellite-based communications (setting up one of these stations has been used in a recruiting commercial). It was discovered during the Gulf operations that these communications could be jammed. So, a means has to be found to limit the effects of jamming.

11. More Firepower for Light Troops Throughout August 1990, American commanders were keenly aware of how vulnerable U.S. forces on the scene were to a move out of Kuwait by Iraqi armored forces. The only ground forces the United States could get to Saudi Arabia immediately were paratroopers and other light infantry. The firepower of these light forces was limited to what could be carried in the available air transport. This meant very little artillery, and what there was of it was in the form of light howitzers and mortars with not much ammunition. The solution will no doubt be a more rapid development of the robotic mines and other "smart weapons" that can do for the ground troops what laser-guided bombs have done for the air force.

Not Another Vietnam

There were some striking similarities between the Gulf War and Vietnam, as well as the obvious differences. Both wars involved the same number of troops in action at one time. In its peak year, the U.S. deployed 536,000 troops in Vietnam, organized

VIETNAM: TROOPS AND CASUALTIES

Year	Troops	Dead
1964	23,000	453
1965	184,000	2,532
1966	385,000	6,053
1967	486,000	11,058
1968	536,000	16,522
1969	484,000	11,527
1970	335,000	6,065
1971	158,000	2,348
1972	24,000	561

PERSIAN GULF

1991	540,000	331

into nine combat divisions and five separate brigades. The big differences between the two wars were in how long it took to get in to the area, how costly the fighting was, and how long it took to get everyone out. In 1968, the daily loss rate was higher in Vietnam than in the Gulf. Vietnam in 1968 was a 366-day war; the Gulf War was a forty-two-day air campaign, with a four-day ground battle at the end. The Gulf War killed less than 1 percent as many Americans as died in Vietnam. The buildup of forces was also quite different. It took four years to get half a million troops into Vietnam, versus six months in the Gulf. Because of the one-year tour of duty limitation in Vietnam, and the length of the war, there are over 2 million Vietnam vets; there will be fewer than 100,000 Gulf War vets. In Vietnam there were forty-five combat fatalities for every ten noncombat deaths. In the Gulf there were more noncombat deaths than combat fatalities.

The Better Part of Valor

Once the word got around among Iraqi troops about the accuracy and lethality of American firepower, many Iraqi crews simply got out of their tanks and other armored vehicles and walked away. U.S. helicopter and aircraft pilots often observed this happening, and several times an entire unit's worth of Iraqi armored vehicles (companies or battalions, ten to forty vehicles) were found lined up in formation and abandoned.

My, Aren't We Well Behaved?

For the first time in American history, U.S. combat units went into action with a lot of women officially in the ranks. While women cannot serve in combat jobs, there are many "noncombat" positions filled by women that bring them very close to the fighting. Headquarters and combat-support jobs are filled by women; so they are there, with the men, in the combat areas. Living conditions are quite crude in the field. Basically, men and women share living accommodations, just like in all-male units. If the troops are sleeping in large tents, the men and women use the same ones. The one difference is, usually, in how latrines and showers (when available) are used: Men and women take turns. Otherwise, it's strictly unisex at the front.

With 35,000 American women troops in Saudi Arabia, and over 500,000 male soldiers, sailors, airmen, and marines, you would think there might have been some problems with what the military calls "fraternization." Actually, the uniformed U.S. men and women got on very nicely, thank you. Perhaps it was the absence of alcohol (not to mention the lack of any local women to entertain the male troops). There were only two dozen reported instances of rape, attempted rape, "indecent assault," or the like. The way the military operates, there were far more cases that didn't make it into the military police reports. But even 100 attempted or actual rapes among 35,000 women and 505,000 men over a period of six months is a pretty low figure. There was, as the military puts it, "fraternization." Such relationships are illegal only between those of different rank, particularly between officers and the enlisted troops. Amatory relationships between troops of roughly the same rank are officially discouraged, but in practice they are tolerated as long as they don't cause any commotion. There were quite a few pregnancies. According to one source, over 1,200 female troops went home early because they were pregnant. On some navy ships with crews comprising one quarter or one third female sailors, the pregnancy rate was as high as 10 percent. It was lower among the ground-based troops, but, as the military pointed out, these pregnancy rates weren't much higher than normal. In the Gulf, there was plenty to do, and the most popular nonwork activity was sleep, just sleep. This contributed to above-average performance among the troops, a point noted by officers and NCOs, who observed that troop performance tended to be higher when alcohol was not readily available (as at remote bases in unpopulated or otherwise "dry" areas).

Not So Well Behaved

When U.S. troops began going home, special efforts had to be made to prevent large quantities of Iraqi Army weapons and equipment going with them. According to regulations, all captured enemy gear belongs to the U.S. government. The troops are generally allowed to keep things like clothing and small non-combat items. But some of the more popular souvenirs were AK-47s, along with ammunition, grenades, and even land mines. Sometimes units tried to send home large items, like antiaircraft guns, to decorate their barracks. At least one unit tried to send home a towed 23-mm antiaircraft cannon in pieces. The baggage of troops returning from the KTO had to be checked carefully for Iraqi weapons and explosives. Quite a lot was found. And quite a lot got through.

Premonitions

In the late 1980s, three years before Iraq invaded Kuwait, the U.S. Army greatly increased the number of troops it was training to act as Arabic language interpreters. No one has come forward to take credit for this bit of foresight.

Heroic Forecasts

Before the air and ground war began, the Pentagon ordered some 16,000 medals from manufacturers, so they would be available when needed. Most of these were Purple Hearts, medals for troops wounded in combat. This indicated the expectation of a relatively high casualty list or, more optimistically, as an estimation of the high end of the expected number of dead and wounded. Not all the medals ordered were Purple Hearts. Hundreds were reserved for the two most common awards for battlefield valor: the Bronze Star and the more rarely awarded Silver Star.

In fact, right after the cease-fire, the Pentagon put out a call to all commanders, asking for names to be recommended for medals (Purple Hearts were automatic, if you were wounded by enemy fire). There was practically no response, which may have partially been due to the shortness of the war, and the fact that so much of it was fought with longer-distance weaponry.

Nevertheless, there were many unusual instances of deeds that went "above and beyond the call of duty." These fell into several distinct categories, the strangest of which were those performed in rescuing Iraqi prisoners of war. Many of these Iraqis surrendered while trying to pass through their own minefields or while dodging fire from other Iraqis who wished to fight on. Some injured Iraqis in damaged and burning vehicles were rescued by Americans. It remains to be seen how much this particular brand of (quite humanitarian) heroism will be rewarded.

More common were those acts of heroism expected to occur during the penetration of the Iraqi fortified zones. Getting through unanticipated minefields and other obstacles often calls for extraordinary efforts. Traditionally, many medals are awarded for heroic acts performed during these operations.

Lethal Leftovers of War

One of the enduring legacies of the Gulf War will be the up to 100,000 undetonated mines and unexploded bombs and artillery shells scattered throughout Kuwait and Iraq. Even a war as short as six weeks leaves a lot of unexploded munitions around. Most of these are the land mines and naval mines emplaced by the Iraqis and not cleared by either side after the war.

The Iraqis are estimated to have laid down over half a million land mines and over 1,000 naval mines. As is commonly the case in wartime, not all the records of where the mines were placed survives the fighting. Allied intelligence reports (mostly aerial reconnaissance photos) and prisoner debriefings indicated where most of the minefields were located. But so many Iraqis were killed, or deserted, that a complete list of minefields could never be compiled. And just as the exact number of mines planted will never be known, nor will those planted ever completely be cleared. So for the next several generations, the Saudi-Kuwait border and many Kuwaiti beaches will be off-limits. Naturally, some people will ignore the warnings, particularly in the border areas where the Bedouin have been moving about with their herds of camels and sheep for centuries. A lot of livestock will be lost, and several hundred more people will be killed and injured before these mines finally become impotent. This will not happen until well into the next century.

Unexploded shells and bombs are a different matter. A few percent of artillery shells and bombs do not explode when they are supposed to. Fortunately, most Allied ammunition was pretty high-quality stuff, and so only a few percent were duds. But the Allies fired off several hundred thousand shells and rockets. This leaves up to 10,000 "duds" buried on the battlefield. This means more dead sheep, camels, and Bedouin for the next century. The Iraqis did not fire off as much ammunition, but much of what they were using was Russian-made, which has a much higher dud rate (often over 20 percent) than Western munitions.

The unexploded bombs pose another problem, particularly those dropped in built-up areas that don't explode. When the wrecked buildings are later cleared away, these bombs are often uncovered and sometimes jarred sufficiently to explode. Every year, Europeans are killed or injured in just this way from unexploded World War II ordnance. Newly developed and redeveloped areas in Iraq and Kuwait can expect to have the same problems.

Women at War

Women have served in all American wars. The Kuwait War was no exception, with 6 percent, or 35,000, of the U.S. troops in the Gulf being female, making it the largest percentage of female troops ever deployed to a combat area. Although women are still excluded from combat jobs, this does not keep them out of the line of fire; two were captured and several killed and injured by enemy action. While only 15 percent of the Army's jobs are directly related to combat, another 20 percent of the jobs (jobs that were often held by women) brought them right to the scene of recent, or imminent, combat. In effect, the exclusion of women from combat is not absolute but only a matter of degree. Women are trained in the use of infantry weapons, just as are all other troops, and carry rifles on the battlefield.

Not the Quickest

The Persian Gulf War is sometimes referred to as the 100-Hour War. That's stretching it a bit, as the air force pummeled the Iraqis for about 900 hours first. Actual ground operations took 400 hours. An 1,100-Hour War is still impressive, but doesn't have quite the same ring. The Israelis won their 1967 war in about 150 hours, and the all-time record is the thirty-eight-minute war (Britain versus Zanzibar, August 27, 1897). It was also achieved by high-tech bombardment, courtesy of the Royal Navy.

Delayed Casualties

Twenty years after Vietnam, thousands of veterans are killed or disabled each year by diseases they contracted in the jungle. The Arabian Desert may prove to be even more lethal to the veterans of the Gulf War. Many of the diseases in Arabia are difficult to detect immediately and take months or years to do their damage. While the immediate death toll of the war was under 500, there may be hundreds more added in the next two decades as the deadly bugs and microbes of the desert slowly and inexorably do their work.

Er, I Believe That's One of Ours

Kuwait managed to get most of its air force out of the country ahead of the invading Iraqi troops. The Kuwaiti Air Force consisted of twenty U.S.-built A-4 light bombers and twenty French-built Mirage F-1 fighters. As the Iraqis also used Mirage F-1s, the Kuwaiti Mirages were not allowed to fly in the early stages of the war lest they be mistaken for Iraqi Mirages and shot down. The Kuwaiti Mirage pilots were quite upset about this, as their fellow pilots took off each day in their A-4s to bomb Iraq. Finally, on February 7, the Kuwaiti Mirages were allowed to fly again (albeit in formation with Kuwaiti A-4s). Allied pilots were warned of this new arrangement, and it worked. The Kuwaiti Mirages kept flying for the rest of the war, and none were hit by friendly fire.

Accuracy in Weather Reporting

As an aftereffect of the Iraqis igniting several hundred Kuwaiti oil wells, the air in the area was covered with black, oily clouds. The weather reports on the U.S. Armed Forces Network radio station issued reports such as, "Air is partly oily, with winds from the southwest."

The Real Desert Storm

Saudi Arabia is an area of climate extremes. For most of the year, it is hot, with weeks on end of 100-plus daytime temperatures. At night it gets much cooler and in the winter months often falls below freezing in the predawn hours. Temperature was a problem for the troops, and often baked equipment left out in the open. A greater problem was caused by the various storm conditions common in the desert. There are two long storm seasons, summer (May–November) and winter (December–February).

There are two kinds of storms in the summer, the worst of which are the sandstorms. But these are not sandstorms like in any other desert. Arabia is noted for its lightweight sand, more like talcum powder than the stuff you find on the beach. The storms roll across the desert several times a month, pushed by gale-force winds and presenting aircraft with a 6,000–8,000-foot wall of sand, dust, and anything that is not tied down. When the gale-force winds die down to a breeze, the powdery sand stays suspended in the air, making visibility difficult. This became especially hard on reconnaissance, although some of the more modern and powerful sensors could handle it. There are still clear days, but it is more common to have a mist of desert dust suspended to an altitude of several hundred or several thousand feet. Because the sand just hangs there, it gets into everything, people as well as equipment.

The other type of "storm" is very local and often lethal to aircraft. These are the minitornadoes commonly known in North America as dust devils. The ones in Arabia are larger and more numerous and add a little more excitement for helicopters or small aircraft during takeoff and landing.

Winter brings with it rain—not a lot of rain, but when it comes, it tends to come all at once. Perhaps two or three storms that turn everything to mud, and if you are caught in one of the riverbedlike depressions called wadis, you can get caught in flash floods when they suddenly fill up with water.

Fortunately, the desert storms were just as hard on the Iraqis, and overall, the Iraqis came out worse with them. The Allied equipment was better maintained and more able to keep going when the weather got rough. The Allied units also had a navigation advantage with their GPS receivers, which allowed them to find their exact location no matter how thick the rain clouds or dust. So while many (but not all) Allied aircraft would be grounded during storms, this did not prevent Allied ground forces from using GPS receivers to find their way around the desert and into Iraq.

The Other "Iraqi Armies"

The decisiveness of the Allied victory over the Iraqi Army caused a stir among the leaders of many other of the world's large armies. The cause of this consternation was the similarity of the Iraqi Army to so many of these others. China, Syria, Egypt, North Korea, Cuba, and even Russia have armed forces that concentrate more on quantity than quality. Only America has such largely high-tech armed forces. The effectiveness of high-tech weapons has now moved from the realm of speculation to that of fact. All those nations with large, relatively low-tech armies can now be turned into wreckage. Just as the Iraqi Army was. The point many of these nations will miss is that the high level of training of the U.S. forces was ultimately more important than the gadgets. This was the lesson the Israelis have been demonstrating for the last thirty years. Another factor was that it was a desert war, which lends itself to decisive, lopsided victories. It will be interesting to see how these other armies adapt to what they thought they saw in the Persian Gulf.

The Russian Influence

It was not just Russian weapons and equipment that gave the Iraqi Army something of a Russian flavor. It had, ever since the 1980–88 war with Iran, operated very much in the Russian style. On the plus side, this instituted a lot of professionalism in an Iraqi Army long noted for its lackadaisical performance. Saddam Hussein was also well disposed toward the Russian way of operating as it strongly encouraged centralized control of the armed forces through the use of secret police and informers. While this gave Saddam a tight rein on the armed forces, this centralized system turned out to be vulnerable to the Allied air attacks that destroyed the extensive Russian communications system and left the troops paralyzed from lack of orders.

Highway Traffic

Why do cruise missiles like highways? U.S. cruise missiles find their way to their target by using an electronic map (in their guidance system) of the terrain they will be flying over. The guidance system periodically scans the terrain below and compares it with its electronic map. When the missile detects a deviation from where it's supposed to be, it changes its course accordingly. For this to work, the electronic map must be prepared beforehand and loaded into the cruise missile's electronic memory. When the Gulf War began, and the heretofore remote possibility of using cruise missiles over Iraq became a real opportunity to use them in combat for the first time, it was discovered that there were no electronic maps of Iraq available. To make matters worse, Iraq was a relatively featureless place. This made creating those electronic maps even more difficult. A solution was found in the wide highway the Iraqis had built that led from the Persian Gulf to Baghdad (where many of the cruise-missile targets were). After a while, the Iraqis began to notice that many of the incoming cruise missiles could regularly be seen zipping along at 500 miles an hour a few hundred feet above the highway. There was not a lot the Iraqis could do about it, as most of the attacks came at night.

The Sixty-Year Chemical-Warfare Truce

Never, since 1918, have two nations possessing chemical weapons used them against each other. Many feared that Iraq would break this legal (the Geneva Convention) and customary (everyone's afraid of them) tradition. But as it turned out, Iraq did not break this long, voluntary prohibition against using chemical weapons against someone who could use them right back at you. With Allied air superiority and most Iraqi artillery destroyed,

Iraq would have had a hard time using much in the way of chemical weapons anyway, and in return could have got back a substantially more lethal dose of them. Another problem was the crude nature of Iraqi chemical weapons, particularly their nerve gas. If there are too many impurities in a nerve gas, the lethality of the gas degrades. Iraqi nerve gas has a short, thirty-to-sixty-day shelf life; after that it loses most of its punch. In any case, the Iraqi nerve-gas factories were destroyed in the first week of the war. The ground offensive took place over a month after that. Mustard gas is more stable, but it requires tons of volume to seriously injure just a battalion-size unit. The Allies had several hundred combat battalions in action, and the Iraqis had little chance of delivering several tons of anything in one battalion's operating area.

The Arab-Israeli Wars

Before the Gulf War, the 1967 and 1973 Arab-Israeli wars were looked upon as brilliant examples of how to win a desert war quickly and with minimal casualties to the victor. The six-day 1967 war saw Israel deploy 200,000 troops against 800,000 Arabs. The Israelis lost about 1,000 dead, while the Arabs suffered nearly 20,000 fatalities. The 1973 war was not nearly so lopsided, with nearly 4,000 Israeli dead to some 20,000 Arab dead. In the 1973 war, the Israelis sent about a quarter-million troops against nearly 1 million Arab soldiers. This war took eighteen days. The Gulf War saw nearly a million Allied troops (including the Turks up north) arrayed against a little more than a million Iraqis. But this war went on for forty-two days, and this made all the difference in the casualty rate, with fewer than 500 Allied dead versus over 30,000 Iraqi dead. What made the difference was the five weeks of pounding the Iraqis took from the Allied air forces. In the Arab-Israeli wars, air power had also been decisive, but Israeli ground forces went into action simultaneously with Israeli aircraft. Any student of modern military history knows that air warfare, even against well dug-in and heavily armed ground forces, loses you far fewer people than when the ground forces engage. The Allied strategy in the Gulf was thus to minimize the ground fighting by demolishing most of the Iraqi ground-combat capability before sending in a massive ground assault. Israel never had the opportunity to fully exploit its air superiority, and suffered greater combat losses as a result.

Lessons of Grenada

The 1983 American invasion of Grenada was a relatively small operation, but it did involve units from all four services. One of the most embarrassing aspects of the campaign was the inability of the troops of each service to communicate with each other on their radios. This shortcoming was noted and a fix implemented. However, such changes make their way slowly through the military procurement channels, and the new radios were just reaching the combat units in 1990. Shipments had to be rerouted quickly to the Gulf so that the ground troops could, unlike the 1983 campaign, talk to the air force and navy.

Reinventing Doctrine and the Operational Art

Two of the less well known aftereffects of the Vietnam War were the U.S. Army's discovery of doctrine and the operational art. Doctrine is a well-thought-out and widely distributed set of techniques for actually fighting a battle. Prior to the late 1970s, what passed for doctrine in the army was, to put it kindly, somewhat deficient. Officers spent more time learning how to be managers, technicians, and diplomats than they did in studying how to actually deploy their troops on a battlefield.

Another curious lapse in U.S. Army military thought was the Operational Art. This is the study of combat between the tactical level (moving individual troops and vehicles, or small groups, around the battlefield) and strategy (moving armies and fleets around the world). The Operational Art is basically knowing what exactly you must do to fight and win a battle. After Korea, the army tended to just improvise as it went along, which tended to have less than favorable results. During the late 1970s, the army discovered what many European armies had known about, and been using, for over a century: doctrine and the Operational Art. Through the 1980s, the World War II blitzkrieg was reinvented as AirLand Battle, and everyone was taught the same set of combat procedures (doctrine) and drilled (and tested) relentlessly in the Operational Art. This drilling and testing involved a lot of realistic war games (which were also rediscovered by the army in the late 1970s). Effective doctrine and familiarity with the techniques of combat paid off in the liberation of Kuwait.

The Biology of Biological Warfare

One little-mentioned aspect of biological warfare is the fragile nature of the microbes and other little critters that are to inflict disease upon the troops. One reason biological warfare has been more a threat than a reality is the uncertainty about how much of the biological agent will survive being delivered on to the enemy troops. As with chemical weapons, you need a lot of the biological agent reaching the troops in order to inflict any damage. For this reason, anthrax spores (which are quite durable) are consistently mentioned as the most likely biological agent to be used. Even so, you must deliver a lot of the spores on the troops to have any effect and, even then, the afflicted soldiers can be put right with prompt medical attention. Because Allied troops had access to a lot more medical support than Iraqi forces, the Iraqis had to consider which side would suffer most if anthrax spores were used.

The Perilous Playing Field

One aspect of the low casualty rate in the Gulf War was a higher incidence of sports injuries. The general lack of other entertainments caused the troops to spend a lot of their limited time playing sports. As a result, sports injuries that required hospitalization were double the number of battlefield injuries. At one point, marine commanders noted the high number of football injuries and ordered the marines to play only touch (noncontact) football. The marines considered this beneath their dignity as combat troops, and so full contact football, and the injuries, continued.

Would You Settle for Fifteen?

A major navy hospital in Saudi Arabia, with its 900-member staff, was primed to deal with up to 500 marine and army casualties a day, yet never received more than 15 on any given day. No reports exist on how dangerous it may have been for injured troops who possibly got too much attention from bored doctors. The extra nursing care, however, was probably appreciated.

The Intelligence Troops

CENTCOM, the Central Command headquarters commanded by General Norman Schwarzkopf, had over 700 intelligence troops assigned to it by January 1991. There were another 300 intelligence troops in a Joint Intelligence Center and an additional 300 in an Imagery (photo interpretation and reproduction) unit. These troops found 200,000 targets worth hitting and then kept track of the progress in "servicing" each of these targets. Back in the Washington, D.C., area, over 3,000 analysts from several different agencies (Defense Department, CIA, etc.) were also analyzing their butts off.

But while the U.S. intelligence specialists in the Gulf were counting destroyed tanks, their counterparts back in Washington were giving contrary analysis of the same photographic evidence. This produced one of the major snafus of the war, as the Gulf commanders were caught between the assessments of their own intelligence specialists and the more numerous intel crowd eight thousand miles away. Unlike Vietnam, in the Gulf War, commanders in the field were left alone and proceeded using their own interpretation of intelligence. Their dissenting counterparts in Washington leaked the dissenting analysis to the media.

The Real Biological Warfare

Without any assistance from the Iraqis, the local bugs and microbes waged a fierce campaign against Allied troops. While most of Saudi Arabia is desert, the people have always lived where there was any water, and this is where a host of diseases and insects to carry them also live. Two generations ago, the average life span in the area was about forty years because of the multitude of diseases. The oil wealth has put the microbes on the defensive, but has not eliminated them. Most of these diseases can be (and were) taken care of by strenuous preventive medicine. Dysentery, an intestinal malady spread by flies and contaminated human (or animal) waste was controlled by going after the flies and keeping the crap underground. When American troops first arrived, many units had over half their troops hit with dysentery. After a month or so, the rate was reduced to a fraction of one percent. Malaria is another world-class killer that the Saudis have been trying to eradicate for several decades. Allied troops were shielded from malarial infection by destroying the mosquitoes that spread it. But a more worrisome intestinal disease is visceral leishmaniasis, which takes as long as two years to become active (and often fatal) after the victim gets a bite from a sand fly. Black flies can spread onchocerciasis ("river blindness"—in a country without rivers). This nasty item makes you blind, but can take months to show itself. A related disease, schistosomiasis, ravages the lymph and circulatory system. Strenuous medical efforts kept Allied losses very low (hundreds ill, a few dead). Iraq did little in this area and suffered thousands of dead.

Tomahawk Effectiveness

United States Navy surface ships and submarines fired 288 Tomahawk cruise missiles during the Gulf War. This action was the Tomahawk's first combat experience. At least 97 percent of the missiles made a successful launch, and settled down into the "cruise" speed the Tomahawks are named after and proceed on to their targets. Bomb damage assessment indicated that over 80 percent of the missiles fired hit their assigned targets. The exact percentage of hits (and their effectiveness) will never be known until—and this is unlikely—Allied technical teams are allowed into Iraq to examine the targets.

The Babylonian Captivity of Kuwait

The first thing Kuwaitis will remember about the invasion of their country is the looting. What arrived right behind the looting was the terror that the Iraqi soldiers and secret police brought with them. Iraqi documents captured during the liberation of Kuwait revealed that the looting was an official policy. Just about everything that could be moved was to be taken back to Iraq. Much of everything else was to be destroyed and the native population driven out. The Iraqi objective was apparently to destroy the nation of Kuwait by sending its people into exile and stealing or destroying all that the Kuwaitis had. During the five-month Iraqi occupation, over half the native Kuwaitis fled the country, and many were replaced by Iraqi civilians. The Palestinian workers in Kuwait were encouraged to think of

Iraqi-occupied Kuwait (now Iraq's "19th province") as the Palestinians' new homeland. In a strange historical irony, these policies were virtually identical to those practiced by the ancient Babylonians, who ruled what is now Iraq and visited such treatment on distant nations such as ancient Israel. And just as ancient Israel was destabilized from experiencing defeat by the forces of Babylon, so was Kuwait. After the Iraqis were driven out, in addition to the civilian damage and social disorder, Kuwait also found itself without any armed forces. Much of the Kuwaiti "Liberation Army" demobilized soon after arriving home. By the summer of 1991, the Kuwaiti armed forces amounted to about 6,000 troops (versus 24,000 in July 1990). The four army brigades contained only about 1,000 troops each, and had very little heavy equipment. Only about 20 of the prewar 250 tanks were still working. The rest had been destroyed by the Iraqis or by Allied air power during the war. Equal devastation was visited on the army's other equipment. The navy was essentially destroyed, and since 60 percent of the sailors were not Kuwaiti citizens, they were gone, too. Only the air force retained a lot of its prewar power, with about half its combat aircraft surviving. Kuwait has a squadron of U.S. F-18 aircraft on order, but it will be at least a year before there is an air base in Kuwait that can accommodate them. The army bought a hundred Yugoslav versions of the Russian T-72 (the M-84) for their Liberation Army. Another hundred were ordered, although the Kuwaiti troops were not happy with the M-84. Kuwait would like to get U.S. M1A1s. Other heavy equipment, including artillery and trucks, is also on order. It will be difficult for Kuwait to rebuild its army, as it is determined to have only Kuwaiti citizens in it. Since there are only about 600,000 officially recognized citizens of Kuwait, and only 1.5 million people living in Kuwait (down from 2 million in July 1990), and since Kuwaitis have never been particularly keen about military service, even building the force back to its prewar level of 24,000 will be a chore.

The Bedouin View of the War

Most Saudis saw very little of the war. Most of the action was of the noncombat variety, and most of that was confined to:

Ports—Most of the Allied equipment and some of the troops

came in by ship. Persian Gulf and Red Sea ports were used to bring this material in, and most of it was quickly moved inland. Several hundred thousand of the Allied troops were stationed in and around these ports to keep the supplies moving and provide maintenance and administrative support.

Roads—Most Saudis saw the war as endless convoys of trucks and armored vehicles heading north and west. Many enterprising Saudi merchants expanded their operations accordingly. Food (to alleviate the monotony of MREs), amenities (razor blades, suntan oil, nonalcoholic beverages, batteries, etc.) and other items were put out for sale to Allied troops and truck drivers at roadside shops and stopping points along the way.

Air Bases—Allied combat and transport aircraft crowded every major air base in Saudi Arabia. The pilots and their support personnel were quartered on or adjacent to these bases.

Desert Camps—Nearly half of the 700,000 Allied forces in Saudi Arabia lived and operated out of desert camps. The camps were not in unpopulated areas; some were in or close to Bedouin settlements and some of the still-nomadic Bedouin passed through the camps with their herds of camels and goats. The Bedouin and soldiers provided each other with some break from the otherwise bleak visage of the desert, and not much else.

Patriots and Expatriates

The half a million U.S. troops sent into Saudi Arabia in late 1990 joined an already substantial American community of 12,000 expatriates working for the Saudi government. Most of these offshore Americans are college-trained professional and managerial types, and they provided invaluable official, and unofficial, assistance to the military buildup. Aside from explaining to their military compatriots the sometimes inscrutable ways of Arabia, the local Americans also provided respite from the desert living the combat troops endured for the five months prior to the beginning of hostilities. Over 40,000 troops were guests in the homes of these expatriates, where the soldiers could take a shower in an American-type suburban home and then enjoy a backyard barbecue.

The NATO Coalition

While American forces predominated, they were joined by troops from most other NATO nations. This was the first time NATO troops have served together in combat, and outside the territory of a NATO nation at that. NATO nations serving in the Gulf were:

> *United States*—540,000 troops, 160 ships, 5,000 aircraft, 5,000 armored vehicles
> *Turkey*—150,000 troops (most on the Iraqi border), 60 aircraft on the border, 2 warships in the Gulf
> *Britain*—42,000 troops, 26 ships, 120 aircraft, 1,000 armored vehicles
> *France* (an "associate" member of NATO)—14,000 troops, 12 ships, 160 aircraft, 150 armored vehicles
> *Canada*—2,200 troops, 3 ships, 36 aircraft
> *Belgium*—4 ships, 18 aircraft in Turkey
> *Denmark*—1 ship
> *Germany*—5 minesweepers, 18 aircraft in Turkey
> *Greece*—1 ship
> *Italy*—3 ships, 18 aircraft
> *Netherlands*—2 ships
> *Norway*—1 ship
> *Portugal*—1 ship
> *Spain*—3 ships

Blood for Iron (and Silicon)

Throughout history, observers of military affairs have noted that the most successful generals were those who managed to win their victories with a minimum of fighting and loss of life (or at least loss of friendly troops). Most wars don't work out that way, but the Gulf War did. It was no accident. America's armed forces were designed to put machines rather than people in harm's way. The entire war was fought with that principle in mind, and it worked. The troops are taught "to generate maximum violence," and they did. The lesson of history is that if you can terrorize your opponent, he will surrender rapidly. The

Allies did, and the Iraqi surrenders rapidly followed. Saddam Hussein tried to put half a million of his troops in harm's way. A third of them got out of the way, half of them surrendered or fled, and the rest were killed. It could have been worse for the Iraqis, and for the Allies.

CHAPTER 11

Predicting the Past: The Military Game

Machiavelli writes of a Greek lord who never saw a hill as a hill or a road as a road. Hills were always potential positions for soldiers, his own or his enemies. Roads were always routes for advance or retreat or maneuver. He would incessantly question his lieutenants and courtiers with propositions like, "If you and a detachment were on that hill, and you saw me and five hundred soldiers in this defile, what would you do?" The lord expected reasoned answers. He expected his officers to think creatively. He wanted them to have already considered many basic issues of strategy and tactics so in the pressure of combat they would have an advantage over their opponents. The Greek lord was war-gaming.

For at least 3,000 years, war games and combat simulations have proved their usefulness as "thinking devices" for military planners and strategists. Several U.S. defense agencies, CENTCOM among them, had produced intricate logistical, strategic, and tactical analyses of combat scenarios based on a "theoretical" Iraqi attack on Kuwait and Saudi Arabia. Indeed, CENTCOM had made use of "gaming" techniques as late as July 1990, when General Norman Schwarzkopf had asked his staff to conduct an extensive review of the command's war plans. Immediately after the Iraqi invasion, several of the planning departments of the Office of the Secretary of Defense (OSD) ran an extensive war game analyzing both Iraqi and U.S.–Saudi strategic options.

Modern war games, both classified ones used by the military

and the ones you can buy in specialized game stores, are a cross between chess (which was originally a more complex game, and a war game as well) and modern statistical science (or operations research for those who have heard of that). Most computer war games have one of these chesslike "manual" war games within them (you push cardboard markers around a map); and most of the people creating computer war games started out with manual, off-the-store-shelf war games. These commercial war games became quite popular in the 1970s, and that's when the military picked them up in a big way.

There is no question that war games can also be utterly abused, especially if they are used as "predictors." The future cannot be predicted. War games, however, are useful "projections" of potential events. The difference between a prediction and a projection isn't wordplay. Projections clearly come from assumptions; the quality of a projection is drawn from the quality of the assumptions made and the analysis and thought that follows from the assumptions. On the other hand, predictions suggest certainty. In warfare there are no certainties.

But the insights gained from good war-gaming analysis are immense. At the minimum, they give the general public an idea of what can happen. Games also give the experts a means of testing opinions.

In late August 1990, one of us (Jim Dunnigan), then editor of the military history magazine *Strategy & Tactics,* decided to publish a war game on the Persian Gulf situation. Dunnigan had himself designed over a hundred war games, including several covering military events in the Middle East and the Gulf. He selected as the designer of the game Austin Bay (the other author of this book). The game, "Arabian Nightmare: The Kuwait War" (published in December 1990, with an update published in March 1991), gave the authors a means for identifying in detail the critical components of operations in Saudi Arabia, Kuwait, and Iraq, examining different strategic options, and portraying the results of different decisions.

Gaming provided CENTCOM with the same array of insights and would have done the same for the Iraqi Baathists running their side of the war. The problem for the Iraqi command, however, is that good gaming requires open minds willing to consider alternatives. It appears that the Iraqi high command, Saddam in particular, was not open to alternative suggestions.

We are devoting a short chapter in this book to war-game design because the Iraqi invasion of Kuwait and the subsequent operations, Desert Shield and Desert Storm, provide near-textbook examples of "gamed" (and gameable) military events. As we shall see, Arabian Nightmare serves as a "track record" for that assertion.

Building a Persian Gulf War Game

There are eight components of the war game:

Terrain

War games begin with a map. A map is (to quote a favorite old army sergeant) "a piece of paper which shows ya what the dirt might be like." The "theater of operations" (from Turkey's southern border to Riyadh) has a lot of different terrain, though in Kuwait and Saudi Arabia sand dominates. Still, the war could have been fought in the north, through mountains and rough, rocky terrain (similar to the terrain Iran and Iraq fought over in the Kurdish areas). The upper Tigris River Valley in Iraq has some clear areas, but between Samarra and Baghdad canalization develops. The further down the Tigris and Euphrates, the more swamps and lakes are found. Then there are the road networks, the types of which will require identification (superhighways, asphalt-topped, unimproved, etc.). Why is this important? Tanks and trucks move on the ground. The type of terrain effects speed.

Cities are also "key terrain" that have political value and military value as defensive positions and objectives. Strategic targets are also important; in Arabian Nightmare oil facilities, permanent Iraqi surface-to-surface missile sites, chemical-weapons facilities, and nuclear facilities were pinpointed.

Finally, air bases and seaports are critical items, both for logistics purposes (shipping in units and supplies) and in the case of air bases for basing aircraft.

Weather

Weather is also key to military operations. Many war games necessarily include extensive variable-weather rules. Arabian Nightmare did not play weather as an extensive problem except in

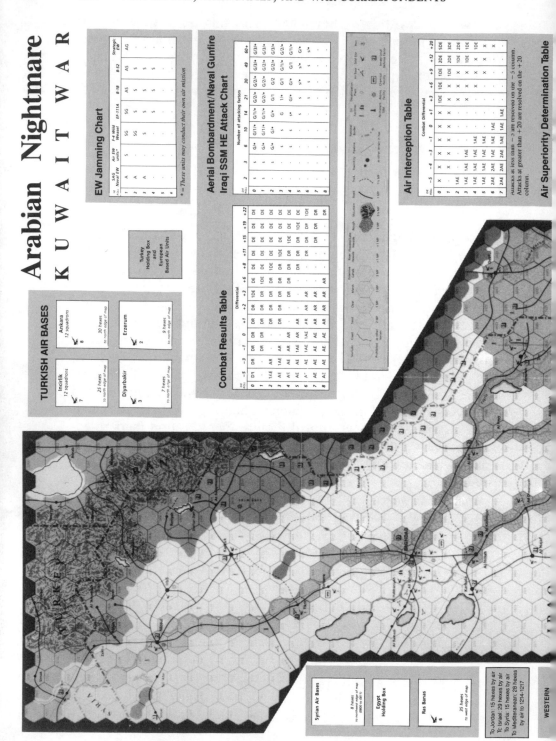

War-gaming map with hexagon grid
from the Arabian Nightmare war game

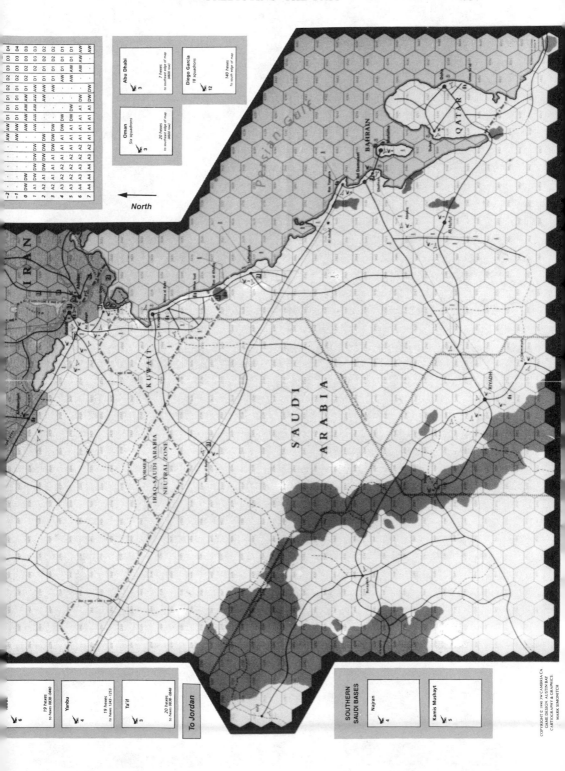

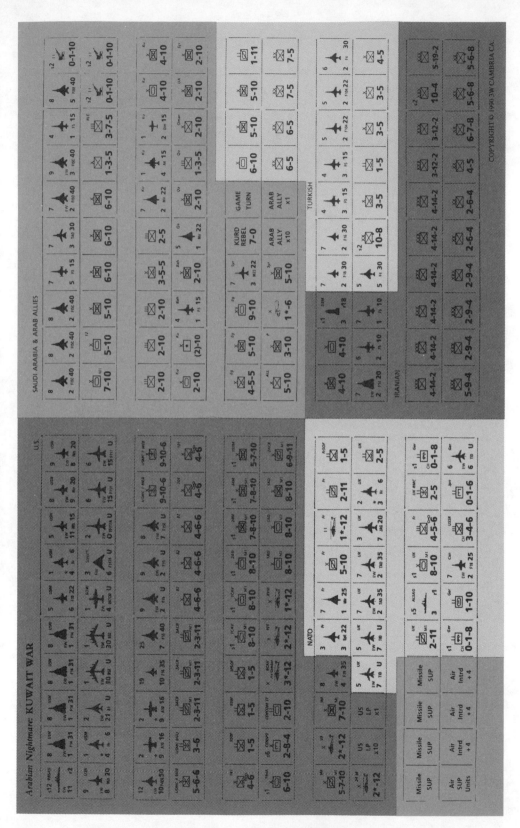

Playing pieces portraying U.S., Coalition and Iraqi forces

one scenario that began in late February (February 20, to be precise). In this scenario, "shamal" dust and rainstorms began to arrive, inhibiting Allied helicopter and air units and slowing down ground movement. Air-to-ground attack capabilities were limited. The weather change was based on a die roll. Note that in the course of the ground war, nearly twenty-four hours of such weather did occur.

Troops

The Institute for Strategic Studies' *Military Balance* handbook provided the basic information for Arabian Nightmare's initial Orders of Battle. These were continually refined (thanks to the press) through September and October of 1990. Talking to a couple of retired military officers experienced in the Middle East helped us get a better picture of local forces, the Republican Guard in particular.

Ground Forces: Ground forces were "modeled" based on unit size (battalion, brigade, division), equipment, and troop training. Mechanized and motorized forces move faster than infantry units that depend primarily on walking to supplement minimal motor transport.

Air Forces: Air forces were modeled based on unit size (squadron or wing), type aircraft in the unit, and pilot quality. What is pilot quality? Admittedly, it is based on military reputation, combat experience, training techniques, training time, and "gut estimate." Few people, however, would argue that Israeli, American, and RAF pilots have more experience and better training than most other air forces. Arabian Nightmare rated the Saudi Air Force quite highly. Events in the air war proved the rating was justified. Why? The Saudi Air Force attracts the elite of Saudi society. Also, USAF rumor had it that the Saudi F-15 pilots were very good. The Iraqi Air Force, however, performed abysmally in the Iran-Iraq War. The Iraqis received poor training and experience ratings even in formations flying excellent aircraft like the Mirage F-1.

Certain air units, such as the A-10, could be assigned "On Call Air Support" missions where they essentially served as part of the ground combat units. This reflected AirLand Battle Doctrine. When A-10 wings were added to a U.S. armored division and an attack helicopter brigade, the firepower virtually assured the elimination of an Iraqi division. This was criticized by several gamers, although events would show that this was, if anything, an understatement of the combined arms capabilities. Another underestimate (by the public, not by the game) was the lethality of current air weapons. What the air force was able to do to Iraq and the Iraqi Army came as no surprise to people in the business. The high-tech air weapons used have been around for a while and are regularly tested under realistic conditions. Those smiles you saw on the faces of aircraft and helicopter gunship pilots were not ones of relief that the weapons actually worked, but satisfaction that they actually got to use the weapons (and all that training) on a battlefield. In training exercises at night and in bad weather against tiny targets, all of those pilots had spent hundreds (and sometimes thousands) of hours delivering those weapons, and doing it successfully. Now, the world knows it, and that makes a pilot feel good. Even some of the people playing Arabian Nightmare were incredulous, but the authors had seen reports of the tests and training exercises and knew from past experience that the current weapons were a lot more lethal than anything in the past. The game was accurate, as good combat simulations usually are.

Special Forces: Special Operations Forces had special capabilities for conducting raids on enemy missile sites and strategic targets. They could also free hostages. Allied attacks received "combat bonuses" if Special Ops troops participated (reflecting their ability to improve air and artillery targeting).

Naval Forces: Arabian Nightmare was not a "naval game" although naval air units operated from carriers in the Red Sea and Gulf of Oman and Naval Surface Action Groups (centered around battleships). The battleships' firepower against Iraqi units along the coast was devastating. Rules also provided for marine Harrier air units to remain with marine ground units, providing continuous close air support. (The Harriers are "jump jets" that can operate without airfields.)

Smart Weapons

Naval Surface Action Groups with battleships could fire cruise missiles. These weapons were, in the game, particularly effective at suppressing enemy airfields and were most valuable in the first game turn when the Allies were trying to assure control of the air. F-117A Stealth fighters were essentially improved cruise missiles when it came to attacking and suppressing air bases and hitting strategic targets. The game portrayed them as being more effective than "regular" air units at taking out specific targets. F-111 and Tornado air units received combat bonus benefits for their accurate targeting capabilities.

Chemicals and Nukes

Only the Iraqi player could use chemical weapons. At the players' option, Scuds had the ability to carry chemical warheads (which was a pessimistic assessment based on the known technical difficulties of manufacturing workable chemical warheads). Iraqi Republican Guards and Special Forces units could also conduct "tactical chemical war"—chemical agents delivered by artillery. The game rules, which could be changed by the players, suggested that the efficiency of Iraqi chemical attacks would drop sharply after "first use": Allied forces would overcome their fear of chemical attack, and Allied artillery and air units would suppress the hell out of the Iraqi artillery firing the chemical munitions. (There was a penalty: The attack value of B-52 units, which was huge to begin with, doubled, reflecting the potential for "unrestrained aerial bombardment" based on anger at the Iraqis' use of chemicals.)

Logistics

Iraqi and Allied forces were both limited by logistics capabilities. Players were given a rate of supply (which could be adjusted by the players who wanted to experiment with variable rates of supply). The game did a fair job of portraying Iraqi logistical limitations but grossly underestimated Allied logistical capabilities after the end of November 1990. In reality, once the Allies had the logistical base in place in Saudi Arabia, they were able to supply virtually any military operation. Still, the first three months (August until the end of October) were logistically "tense." Allied forces, up until the end of November 1990, were indeed limited in what they could do offensively.

How far off was the game, however, in total Allied logistics points (the measure, in game terms, of logistic capability)? The game estimated that the Allied player would have around

135 logistics points on January 15. In reality, it seems that 450 would have been more accurate. What was missed? Basically, CENTCOM, the U.S. Air Force Military Airlift Command, U.S. Army, and U.S. Navy logisticians produced the greatest logistics effort in history. There is also the experienced war-gamer's tendency to pay close attention to the "worst case" side of a situation.

Strategy Options

Iraq:
Continued August Offensive—The war game suggested that Iraq's best strategy was to continue the attack straight through Kuwait and south to Dhahran and Riyadh. Don't stop. And early use of chemical weapons on Saudi troops concentrations would speed up the attack. The Iraqis had to keep moving, paying particular attention to taking airfields in Saudi Arabia. The trouble here was the lack of Iraqi logistics points. If the Iraqis didn't have to worry about supplying their units (and if Saudi generalship was poor), the Republican Guards blitzed right to Dhahran (the nerve center of Saudi oil operations).

Dispersed Defense—The second-best strategy was to dig in a "crust" of infantry units along the Saudi-Kuwaiti border and defend deep and dispersed across the entire Saudi-Kuwaiti border with mobile units. The problem here was that Iraq had to cover the Turkish, Syrian, and Iranian borders and began to run out of troops. Also, Iraq had insufficient surface-to-air missiles to protect the ground units.

Hedgehog Defense—The third-best strategy was essentially the one the Iraqis adopted: digging in all the way around Kuwait and fortifying mobile units. This strategy, however, "bunched" the Iraqi Army in a huge basket and sacrificed all mobility, although the units were better protected against air attack.

Coalition Options:
Initially, the coalition was put at an extreme disadvantage. The Allies had to rapidly build up forces in the theater of operations, and there were not enough logistics points. The question became: How could the Allies stop an immediate Iraqi invasion of Saudi Arabia? The key would be how fast B-52s and other

air units could get into the theater and start bombing Iraqi mobile units. Another key was how fast the 82nd Airborne Division could get to Saudi Arabia and hold on to the airfields. A U.S. Marine Amphibious Unit (reinforced battalion) backed up by air support from two carriers, with a Saudi mech brigade, might have held on to Dhahran. Could that have been history? Fortunately, we'll never know.

The two-front war (an attack on Kuwait and an attack from Turkey into Iraq) was another strategic option, but required a lot of political assumptions to engineer. A two-front war did not occur, though Turkey kept troops right at the border and allowed Allied air units to fly bombing missions from Turkey.

Amphibious operations against Iraqi units dug-in along the Kuwaiti coast or on the Al Faw Peninsula afforded another strategic option, though mines could have interfered with the assault. The presence of two battleships and air superiority assured the Allies of winning a beachhead. The question would always be, however, how many casualties would be sustained? As in the real war, though, the optimal Allied strategy was to keep USMC units afloat to threaten such an attack, thereby tying down Iraqi units.

What did continual war-gaming suggest was the optimal Allied strategy? Even against the "dispersed" Iraqi defense, and especially against the "hedgehog" (the historical Iraqi defense), the wide left hook, the third option, worked the best. The speed of Allied ground units, the use of airmobile forces and attack helicopters, and Allied close air support made for a certain breakthrough to the west of Kuwait. With just a little luck, the entire Iraqi Army was surrounded and cut off. To the author's knowledge, the quickest any player succeeded in accomplishing this feat did so within in six days (one complete game turn).

General Schwarzkopf and his forces bested that. Hats off.

Political Game

The Arabian Nightmare war game had an extensive political-events game that when integrated with the military game often skewed the best-laid combat plans. The war game used scripted political "endeavors" (representing both policy choices and specific tactical political decisions) and random events (portraying such events as changes in governments around the world, Iranian and Japanese waffling, and so forth). Success or failure of endeavors depended on the opponents' chosen political reaction and the results of a dice role. The comparative political strength (measured in political points for the Allies and military victory points for the Iraqis) also affected results. (The following chapter, The Political Game, discusses the political strategy and tactics in detail, using a "card game" as a model for understanding the opposing governments' political options.)

War is an extension of politics by other means. War does indeed take place inside the political sphere. The Vietnam experience weighed heavily on the American high command, as it did on the American people as a whole. Disdain, fear, envy, and suspicion of "the West" pervades many Arab states (Bahrain being one exception, Oman a possible exception). This political fact was also a political burden for the coalition. The Israeli-Palestinian conflict could have split the Allies into a hopeless mosaic. If the coalition had fallen apart, Saddam would have "won" Kuwait, and the Iraqi Army would be dominating the Arabian Peninsula. War games simulating the Persian Gulf War must recognize that the most potent weapons in Saddam's strategic bag were political, designed to attack U.S. "fatigue" (or Vietnam war-weariness) and Arab divisions.

Let the Games Begin

Many readers may have seen the ABC News *Nightline* show of October 3, 1990, where the authors of this book discussed two scenarios of Arabian Nightmare, and the "gamed results" were given to the audience and a panel of military strategists. (The panel included Colonel Harry Summers, who would later work with Jim Dunnigan as an analyst for NBC during the war itself.) The key military scenario portrayed a "wide left hook" into southern Iraq and around into Kuwait City and northern Kuwait (what became known as "the optimal move"). *Nightline*'s producers insisted on a U.S. Marine-led amphibious landing on the coast because, "Ted [Koppel] likes marines." (One might argue that anyone who really likes marines, however, wouldn't want them conducting opposed amphibious assaults.) Austin Bay argued with the *Nightline* producers, maintaining that "gaming" showed that the marines were most valuable as a "threat" so that the Iraqis had to cover the coastline. An actual amphibious attack risked too many lives, and that could put the United States and the coalition into a political bind. No dice—General Koppel ordered the invasion.

Nightline's producers and the authors agreed to run the game with the following assumptions: The Allies had at least five to six "armored division equivalents" in the theater (which they did not have in late September when the games were conducted), and the conflict would begin with an extensive air war followed by (within a week to ten days) a ground attack. It was assumed that Turkey would start a "second front" on Iraq's northern border and push south as far as Mosul. It was assumed that the Iraqis had chemical weapons and would use them on the Allies and Saudi civilians. Also, dug-in Iraqi ground forces were given a "high morale factor," military jargon for a strong will to resist the Allied attack.

The *Nightline* air and ground campaign was run six times. On average it took the Allies thirty to thirty-five days of combined air and ground war (five to six complete game turns) to destroy the Iraqi Army and retake Kuwait. The Turks never failed to take Mosul, and the Allies never failed to take Kuwait City. The air war alone was never prosecuted for more than twelve days (two game turns with four combat phases). The ground war never took less than nine days or more than twenty-eight (though in one game the ground war was arguably over in six days). Remember, the scenario called for a two-front war and a marine amphibious assault. Air units also continued to attack strategic targets (chemical, nuclear facilities, etc.) during the ground campaign.

The Iraqis also got off several Scud attacks with chemical warheads fired at Saudi cities. There was no real way of estimating how many civilians were hurt by ten to twenty Scuds carrying nerve-agent warheads, but looking at the population concentrations in Riyadh and Dhahran (a total of 2.5 million people in the target areas) and taking the standard unclassified casualty figure of 5 percent casualties for warned and protected troops, that worked out to between 100,000 and 125,000 casualties. That would have flooded hospitals and given the Iraqis a terrible political victory. (Patriot PAC-2s were given a 50 percent intercept rate in the October version of the game.) This portion of the war game drew considerable fire from critics who questioned

Iraqi chemical capabilities. (The authors also questioned Iraqi chemical capabilities. We didn't think the Iraqis could get off successful chemical-missile attacks, but for purposes of the game it was assumed they could.)

Rough estimates were made of casualties (which were based on historically derived estimation means). Allied killed were between 4,000 and 7,000, and wounded estimates were 15,000 to 20,000. Many of the killed and wounded occurred in battles on the northern front. The marine amphibious assaults were also bloody. Estimates for Iraqi killed and wounded were even higher, but 60,000 dead was the figure ABC used. Was anything of use gained? The fighting indicated the coalition needed more troops, especially if Iraqi morale was high.

In late October, several weeks after *Nightline* aired, Arabian Nightmare was "play-tested" in Washington by an odd collection of war-gamers. An analyst from the CIA played the Allied coalition. Mark Herman, designer of two other successful war games focusing on the Persian Gulf, commanded the Turkish front. Game-designer Austin Bay took the Iraqis. The game now posited an Allied attack in mid-January rather than mid-November. In response to the games conducted for *Nightline*, Allied units were heavily reinforced: The players had decided, based on political assessments, to go for overwhelming power. (These additional forces included the 1st Mechanized Infantry Division, an additional attack helicopter brigade, and the 1st and 3rd Armored Divisions from the U.S. 7th Corps were added to the Order of Battle. The 2nd Armored Cavalry Regiment was also deployed, but to southern Turkey rather than Iraq; and an Italian mechanized infantry regiment was also deployed with the Turkish Army. A second B-52 wing was added to the available air units.) The assumption was made that Egyptian and Syrian units would fight inside Iraq (which was contrary to what the Egyptian and Syrian governments were saying, but games give the players the opportunity to experiment freely).

Iraqi infantry forces were dug-in inside Kuwait, and Iraqi mobile units were in fortifications in southern Iraq and northern Kuwait. Only five of the eight Republican Guards divisions were deployed in southern Iraq, however. The Adnan and Al Faw divisions were in fortifications near Karbala, and the Baghdad Division remained in Baghdad. Otherwise, the Iraqi units were deployed in what was very close to their actual defensive positions. Last of all, it was assumed that Iraqi infantry morale was *very* low (which affected the units' ability to stand and fight in their positions).

On the southern front, the Allied forces opened up with what in real time would have been a twelve-day-long air campaign. Allied air forces attacked the fortified mobile units and eliminated two Republican Guards divisions and one motorized infantry division fortified in southern Iraq north of what was the old Saudi-Iraqi Neutral Zone. The Allies gained total air superiority (Iraqi planes remained in Iraq in their shelters, however. They did not fly to Iran, once again proving reality is far stranger than fiction.) No Allied air units were eliminated. About five Iraqi squadrons were eliminated as effective units (roughly fifty to eighty aircraft were destroyed in air combat). Navy cruise missiles suppressed Iraqi air bases and air defenses.

On the northern front, the Turks launched a ground attack on the first day of the campaign. By day three, the 2nd Armored Cavalry Regiment (ACR) had taken Mosul. The Iraqis counterattacked between days four and six and destroyed the 2nd ACR. (This would be the only Allied loss of a unit.) By day nine, however, virtually all Iraqi resistance north of Tikrit had ceased. The Turks ran out of supplies and dug in.

Back down south, the Allies launched a ground offensive on day twelve. The main attack was a huge left hook directed at An Nasiriyah on the Euphrates. Iraqi mobile units left their fortifications, and Allied air units destroyed them. A U.S. armored corps, consisting of the 1st Cavalry Division, the 3rd Armored Division, the British 1st Armored Division, and the 3rd ACR closed on An Nasiriyah and turned toward Basra, destroying the Republican Guards. The 24th Mechanized Infantry Division and the 101st Air Assault Division, supported by a French airmobile infantry regiment, destroyed a dug-in Iraqi motorized infantry division and pressed on to As-Samawah on the Euphrates.

Three Marine Corps expeditionary brigades attacked up the coast road from Khafji to Kuwait City. They were supported by one battleship. (When the Saudis actually attacked up the road, they also received battleship support.) Saudi, Egyptian, and other U.S. Army units conducted holding attacks against the dug-in Iraqi infantry divisions deployed along the Kuwait-Saudi border.

Way, way out west the French and Syrians, operating as a separate corps, attacked north to An Najaf. At the end of the nine days of ground war, they had destroyed two Iraqi divisions (including a Republican Guards division) and were outside of Karbala, linking up with the 82nd Airborne Division, which conducted a parachute airdrop just southeast of Karbala.

All coalition attacks received massive air support. The Allies succeeded in every attack conducted. The Iraqi line shattered in the first attack.

The entire ground war took what in real time would have been nine days. Estimates on Allied casualties were 2,000 killed and 4,000 to 5,000 wounded, half of the dead sustained in the loss of the 2nd ACR and a Turkish mountain unit's initial attack on an Iraqi division dug-in in the northern Iraqi town of Amadiyah. (Remember, these rough estimates were made using casualty rates drawn from analysis of past battles.) Still, Allied casualties on the southern front were around 1,000 killed and 3,000 wounded in what was a twenty-four-day air and ground war.

No one, of course, was prepared to believe that the battle would be "that easy."

So what, then, did gaming suggest? Given time, air power could greatly weaken the Iraqi Army, and if the Allied forces went deep into the desert then hooked back toward the sea, the Iraqi Army would be quickly smashed. Combined Allied air and ground attacks were devastating.

What was missed? The Iraqi Scud brigades got off only two "missile salvos" (both launched at Hafir al Batin) before all missile units were destroyed. (There were no Iraqi missile attacks launched at Israel.) Patriot Pac-2 units, however, were also underrated in the game. Patriots had a 50 percent hit chance against Iraqi Scuds instead of the 95 percent rate they showed in combat. Correcting that consisted of changing a result on a chart, but then no one, not even the strongest Patriot and SDI advocate, was prepared for Patriot's success.

War-gaming has been used in all the major wars of this century. CENTCOM had several dozen people in Saudi Arabia war-gaming the situation from mid-August to the end of the fighting. Their results were almost identical to those derived from the commercially available Arabian Nightmare game described in this book. For the first time in history, war games of professional quality were available to civilians while the war was going on. This availability will grow in the future and will change the way civilians, and the media, look at the unfolding operations with an unprecedented insight and accuracy. You saw it here first.

CHAPTER 12

The Political Game

As mentioned in the preceding chapter, the Arabian Nightmare war game contained a "political game," which could be played separately or along with the military game. The political game anticipated many of the actual political events that occurred during the war. In retrospect, the game's structure provides a simple and useful way of explaining to a broad audience Iraq's and the coalition's actual political options and strategies.

The Iraqi Game

Saddam Hussein waged the political war with far more skill, daring, and shrewdness than he managed on the battlefield. This was to be expected: Saddam is a politician, not a soldier. Though he likes to strut in uniform and preen with a black beret, the political sphere is his area of expertise.

Saddam's overall aim in the political war was to create strategic delay and disruption. Time, he concluded, was on his side. If he were given time, Kuwait would be dismantled, the Kuwaiti population exiled or decimated. If he were given time, his attack would become old news. Strategic delay and disruption would also be his aim if opposition to Iraq's invasion coalesced and hardened. And if a "worst case" evolved (rapid American intervention), he had plans for breaking U.S. and Arab cooperation. His range of political endeavor was broad: the spectacular gambit, the subtle pressure, and the exercise of continual pressure on the political edges and seams of his adversaries.

The Arabian Nightmare: Kuwait War political and military simulation provided a useful tool for projecting Saddam's political initiatives and gauging U.S., Saudi, and Allied action as well. The simulation used a system of competitive "endeavors" (political actions) the Iraqi player and the Allied player would conceivably use against one another in an attempt to affect national and international opinion and politics as well as strengthen military positions. The game used a die roll to determine results. In the game, playing an "endeavor" is very much like playing a card whose true strength and value will only be determined by events.

Saddam's pack of political playing cards is a strange and violent Tarot. The arcana includes: the Fear card, the War card, the Israeli card, the Palestinian card, the Great Leader card, the Pan-Arab card, the Arab Revival card, the Arab Weakness card, the Arab Street card, the 19th Province card, the Islamic card, the anti-Emirate card, the Hostage card, the Economic card, the Oil card, the Soviet card, the anti-American card, the Vietnam-Syndrome card, the Casualties card, the Peace card, the European (French?) card, the Third World card, the Rich-Poor card, the North-South card, the Iranian card, the Jordanian card, the Terror card, the Scud card, the Assassination card, the Chemical and Biological Weapons card, the Nuclear Weapons card, the Republican Guards card, the Ecological Destruction card, the Western Press card, the Cable News Network card, the Iraqi Suffering card, the Nihilist Destruction card, the Victory in Defeat card, and the Saddam Survival card.

This strange pack has Machiavellian and Manichean origins. Saddam had tested it during his bloody trip through the channels of Baath into the halls of power in Baghdad. During the course of the crisis, he would play all of his cards; many would be played several times as he worked the features of each political option. One of them, perhaps, would be his final trump.

A Quick Trip Through the Arcana

The Fear Card: A card with tentacles in the Terror card, the War card, and the Great Leader card. Iraq had built what some analysts had come to believe was the world's fourth-largest army, with land and air forces superior in size to those of acknowledged heavyweights like India, Germany, Turkey, and Egypt. Saddam had gassed Kurdish rebels. Saddam had promoted worldwide terror. Saddam told *The Wall Street Journal* that he would "burn half of Israel." Unlike the oil sheikhs who dealt in appeasement, he was a man who would act with force. The card's political objective: to say, Give me what I demand or I will kill you.

The War Card: This card works in several ways. It is the Big Fear card. Saddam rattled the sabers to threaten Kuwait. Then he actually invaded. He displayed bravado and daring. His power, regionally, was unmatched. Playing the War card made the statement that Saddam was ready to act and act violently. Who would challenge him? Playing the War card showed he was not restrained by fear of Israel or the West. The political objective: to take Kuwait by force. If successful, to play the card again and go for Saudi Arabia.

The Israeli Card: A most complex card, a ploy of immense potential power. The Arab-Israeli rift runs deep. The Palestinian issue is its wound, and a legacy of five major wars and continual conflict increases the agony. Many Arabs see Israel as a Jewish Crusader state planted in Arab lands by the West. Israeli military capabilities and economic facility increase envy and hostility. Nothing, Saddam's conventional wisdom went, drives Arabs together more quickly than the conflict with Israel. Mask any political endeavor with the Israeli card and you assure yourself of a strong cadre of Arab support. Saddam's political objective: to blame Israel for all regional evils and convince the Middle East that Kuwait was but a way station on the road to the liberation of Jerusalem and defeat of Israel. If a Western-Arabic coalition formed to oppose him, he would attack Israel and provoke the Israelis into entering the war. The coalition, Saddam reasoned, would collapse because Arab populations would not allow their governments to "side with Israel" against another Arab state.

The Palestinian Card: A card rooted to the problem of Israel. Ignore the fact that Palestinians and the Palestine issue have been the playthings of Arab governments. Remember that all Arabs support their Palestinian brothers against the Jews. The West is run by hypocrites who claim they wish to resolve the problem of the Palestinian diaspora. The West doesn't. The

Russians are no longer interested in confronting the West. The Palestinians need a champion, and Iraq will be that champion. The Palestinians can be a source of political support, and their guaranteed public reactions will play well in the Western media. The political objective: to mask the invasion of Kuwait behind the question of Israeli occupation of the West Bank and the question of Palestine.

The Pan-Arab Card: A tough card to play but one with emotional impact and appeal throughout Arab lands. The Pan-Arab card is actually the centerpiece of Baath ideology. Arabs once were great. Baghdad was the center of world learning. But Arabs were brought down by (Western, i.e., Crusader) subterfuge and imperialism. Ignore the fact that the Mongols and Turks from the East are the peoples who destroyed the Arab world after the Crusaders left. Or that it was the West that drove out the Turks and made many of the Arabs independent once more. Rather, declare that the Baath (Renaissance or Revival) party will restore Arab greatness. There will be one Arab state that will be the equal (or superior) of the Superpowers. The current borders between Arab lands, prescribed by Britain and France, are false. Arab blood and language erase those borders. The political objective: to take the focus off the fact that Kuwait was an Arab nation and make the case that the invasion was the first "erasure" of illegal borders.

The Great Leader Card: An outgrowth of Saddam's megalomania and the cult of the personality established in Iraq. Saddam has forged a mighty armed force. His voice is heard around the world. He acts while others hide. He is the heir of Hammurabi, Nebuchadnezzar, and Saladin, the other great warlords of Mesopotamia. Arabs need a great leader to confront the West. Saddam is that man. The political objective: to destabilize rival regimes by establishing himself as *the* Arab leader.

The Arab Revival Card: A jack to the Pan-Arab card's king, but a reaffirmation of the same appeal. Iraq has gained industrial, military, and political capability. Unlike Egypt, which capitulated to Israel, or the oil sheikhs, who have capitulated to money, Iraq, under Saddam's leadership, has reenergized the Arab world. The political objective: to enhance Saddam's personal prestige and portray Iraq as an "Arab alternative" to development models found in the capitalist West or the lapsing socialist East.

The Arab Weakness Card: A trey or so, but one that can ignite lingering Arab resentments of the West (particularly in Tunisia, Algeria, and Morocco) and plays well with the European and American left. Arabs have been intentionally weakened by the West. Arabs suffered for 400 years under the Ottoman Turks. Arabs have been persecuted by the Iranians. Arabs are persecuted in France. The political objective: to set up the Great Leader, Arab Revival, and Pan-Arab cards. Give the European and American leftists rhetoric that allows them to portray Iraq as another Third World underdog chased by the hounds of American imperialism.

The Arab Street Card: Another dangerous yet amorphous card because no one is quite sure where the Arab Street is and where it goes. Lots of folks in the West and the Middle East, however, think this political avenue is volatile and an alley to be feared. During the conflict, Amman, and to some extent Morocco and Tunisia, were the Arab Street (that's where television cameras could focus). The Arab Street is supposed to be filled with a host of the angry and the dispossessed (i.e., Palestinians) who will riot against local regimes and readily turn to terror. This street is looking for a gang leader who will set up shop on the block. Saddam said he was that gang leader. The political objective: to destabilize rival Arab regimes, convince the West, through the press, that the entire Arab and Islamic world supports Saddam. (Caveat: Make sure that no roads lead to Kuwait City. That town has no Arab Streets.)

The 19th Province Card: A domestic ace and an international joker, but in a pinch you play what you can play. As noted in an earlier chapter, Iraq's historical claim to Kuwait is very weak. The United States has a better legal claim to Wrangel Island (north of Russian Siberia) than Iraq does to Kuwait. But when drumming up support for an aggressive war, old historical claims help ignite martial fervor. Make no mention that the Turks merely tossed Kuwait into the millet (province) of Basra as a convenience. Make no mention that Iraq could be the victim of other, much more historically validated land claims (Kurd and Turk). The political objective: to enthuse the Iraqi populace and army for taking and holding on to Kuwait. Confuse the geographically and historically ignorant (i.e., the masses in the United States).

The Islamic Card: An ace with a club, if it had worked. Ignore the fact that Saddam was, at best, an agnostic, and that the Baath is a secular movement. Ignore the fact that the Baghdad government had spent years suppressing Shiite Muslims in southern Iraq and Kurdish Muslims in northern Iraq. Ignore the fact that more Muslims live in Indonesia and Malaysia than in the Arab world; and that Islam, like all great religions, has extreme sects and divisions. In the West, Islam tends to wear a monolithic face—the face of "jihad." An aspect of the Islamic card is Mecca, which may have very well been an ultimate objective for Saddam. The political objective: to create an image in the West that if the West aided Saudi Arabia and opposed Saddam, 400 million Muslims worldwide would side with him. In Islamic nations, the appeal would be to religious resentments of Western culture and influence. ("American Jewish soldiers are in Mecca," Baghdad radio said.) Here, once again, Saddam was Saladin, driving the immoral West out of Islamic lands.

The Anti-Emirate Card: A card entangled with economic and historical resentments around the Arabian Peninsula. The al-Sabah family and the Saudi royal family are portrayed in this endeavor as the tools of Western oil companies and the pawns of Washington. The political objective: to mask the Iraqi invasion of Kuwait as a strike against archaic autocratic regimes, and to destabilize the Saudi government and other Gulf emirates by alienating them from their people. Saddam would be portrayed as a liberator saving these populations from feudal domination. The card also played in the West. It raised the question of what a democracy like the United States was doing supporting feudal autocracy. Ignore the fact that the aristocracies of the Gulf have ruled their populations with far less bloodshed and terror than any of the more "progressive" Arab states.

The Hostage Card: A brutal play, reasserting aspects of the Fear and Terror cards. Saddam took people from Western,

Arab, and Third World nations hostage. He even used Western hostages as "human shields" to protect strategic targets from air attack. This card was finessed by diplomats who convinced the Baghdad regime that if Iraq wanted any hope of a settlement the hostages would have to be released. The Iraqis interpreted the diplomatic language as telling them that if they let the hostages go they would not be attacked. Apparently, there was some misunderstanding. Saddam seemed to forget that the rest of the world sees the taking of hostages as criminal behavior. The political objective: to obtain bargaining chips with the West and other Arab states, airtime on American television, to play on Western concerns for hostages held in Lebanon and the U.S. experience with hostages taken at the Tehran embassy during the early days of the Iranian revolution.

The Economic Card: A card primarily directed at Jordan and Turkey, but affecting many other Third World countries with workers in the Middle East (the Philippines, South Korea, and India in particular). Almost half of the Jordanian economy is directly tied to the Iraqi economy. Turkey made money off trade with Iraq and through oil-pipeline fees. Foreign workers earned money in Iraq. The political objective: to politically leverage these nations by promising economic pain if they failed to accept Iraq's invasion of Kuwait.

The Oil Card: The ace of spades, a source of power that is also the death card. Oil drives the economies of the industrialized world and the underindustrialized as well. Gaining direct control of 60 percent of the world's proven oil reserves, or at least the ability to dominate them, would have vaulted Iraq to near-Superpower status. The economies of the United States, Western Europe, and Japan were jolted. Possibly they could have been controlled. On the subtle side, Third World nations, who are even more vulnerable to oil-price fluctuations, would be leveraged. The political objective: to achieve genuine worldwide influence and effective control of oil pricing.

The Soviet Card: A ghost card, but a ghost with an arsenal. Yes, Soviet influence is lapsing, but for forty years the Kremlin had been a counterbalance to American power. Saddam had respect for Soviet capabilities and Moscow's demonstrated willingness to use force, overtly and covertly. Iraq and the USSR developed many ties. Moscow had been Iraq's largest arms supplier. As late as mid-August 1990, over 7,000 Soviet technicians were still inside Iraq, involved with both economic development and military projects. Saddam also saw that a "Stalinist backlash" was (and is) developing inside the USSR, a backlash against "accommodationist liberals." Saddam knew that Gorbachev relied on his foreign policy successes to reinforce his position in Moscow. Iraq and Syria were Moscow's best links in the Middle East. The political objective: to attempt to engage the USSR in any manner and get the Soviets to veto any UN action against Iraq. That failing, to allow Moscow to operate as a rogue intermediary.

(NOTE: Of course Moscow cooperated in the play of this card, but not as Saddam thought it would. The Cold War is over. The Soviets want influence in the Middle East, but they read Saddam's move as a huge mistake. There is also a "Chinese aspect" to this political move. China has a permanent Security Council seat and has also sold a lot of weapons to Iraq [through its Norinco weapons company]. The Iraqi ties to China are weaker than to the USSR, but Saddam tried to pull on them just as hard.)

The Anti-American Card: An oft-tried and sometimes useful trick, but one that has waned in value since the United States became the big pillar of the multipolar world emerging from the end of the Cold War. The card is a variant of the "North-South" and "Rich-Poor" suit. The political objective: to use simmering anti-Americanism (resentments of American success, American power, and/or resentment of American political depredations, real and imagined) to weaken and break the U.S.-led political coalition.

The Vietnam-Syndrome Card: Now we enter the U.S. domestic arena, as strange and inscrutable to the rest of the world as Saudi royal-family politics, Baath party feuds, and Tokyo land prices are to Americans. Saddam, in his February 1990 speech in Amman, said America was "fatigued." Vietnam had sapped American will. The rapid American withdrawal from Lebanon after the bombing of the marine barracks in Beirut had showed that the it had no staying power. All Saddam had to do was flip on CNN and watch American doves rattle on about the limits of

American power or the foolishness of American military action. Winston Churchill had once remarked that "the hope of the world lies in the strength and will of the United States." Vietnam, Saddam concluded, had weakened that will, perhaps fatally. He concluded that he could re-create a Vietnam situation. Antiwar protests would sow doubt and discord in America. Left-wing doves in the Democratic party, which controlled the U.S. Congress, would block or thwart U.S. military action. The political objective was clear: to convince the United States that engaging Iraq would produce another scarring Vietnam. To divide the American people, and in doing so, gobble Kuwait.

The Casualties Card: The scythe in the hand of the Vietnam syndrome. The rapid U.S. pullout from Lebanon convinced Saddam that the American military could not, at least politically, sustain large casualties. Iraq, on the other hand, could lose 10,000 men in one battle, and it would not matter. The Iraqi Army, Saddam said, was "battle-hardened." The U.S. military could not count on political support if it got bogged down. The political objective: to arm American antiwar protesters with visions of body bags and block the deployment of American troops. If they are deployed, to frighten the electorate into keeping them in a defensive posture. To sow discord in the United States.

The Peace Card: This card had appeal in Western Europe and Japan as well as the United States. It is tied closely to the 19th Province card. All Saddam wanted was justice, Kuwait returned to Iraq. Now there would be peace. The causes of violence in the Middle East were Israel and the United States. Iraq was misunderstood. Peace was what Saddam wanted. If the United States didn't want peace, he would give it another Vietnam. As for Europe, the European left was already convinced that the United States was (somehow) the aggressor in virtually every confrontation on the planet. The political objective: to gain time to solidify control of Kuwait and play upon isolationist and antiwar sympathies in the United States; to divide coalitions opposing the invasion by confusing the issue of aggression.

(NOTE: This card plays off of forty years of Kremlin Cold War rhetoric and twenty-five years of American trauma over Vietnam.)

The European Card: A minor card but one Saddam played. Europe, at least in the eyes of leftist intellectuals, had been dominated by United States imperialism. Europe should not be the puppet of America, which is a notion that has had particular appeal in France (across the French electorate) and with the German and Dutch left. The political objective: to divide Western Allies and exploit the political endeavors of European radicals.

(NOTE: Saddam, of course, misread the French, but then everyone does. France played both sides of the street, as it always does. The French recall, with disgust, American intervention in the 1956 Sinai War that forced them to withdraw from Egypt. But despite that snafu, since then the French supported the United States whenever it came to a military crunch in the Middle East. Paris wants to know that Washington means business. Lebanon, Chad, and now Kuwait illustrate this political and military truth.)

The Third World Card: This ploy is a magnification of the European card, but seeks to pit the so-called "Third World" (as if it were a monolith) against the "developed world." The tactical political objective: to gain control in the General Assembly of the UN. The strategic political objective: to unravel the coalition by portraying the Arab states opposing Iraq as dupes of the West; to sow sympathy among Western leftists who are wedded to "Third World causes" and perceive small, impoverished nations as the victims of the wealthy.

The Rich-Poor Card: In its international context, this card is an aspect of the Third World card, played with different rhetorical twists. There is also a regional echo in the Middle East that resonates with the "anti-Emirate" card. Some Arabs are fabulously wealthy while some are tragically poor. Kuwaitis and Saudis are the wealthy, Jordanians, Palestinians and Egyptians are the poor. Kuwait and Saudi Arabia, according to Saddam, should share the wealth. Ignore the fact that Iraqis could be among the wealthy if Saddam didn't squander Iraq's oil revenues on warfare. The political objective: to stoke the resentments of the Arab poor and the poverty-stricken nations around the globe; to divide political support for nations opposing Iraq, particularly in the UN.

The North-South Card: Again, found in the Third World and Rich-Poor suits. This has become a favorite phrase for describing the divide between wealthy industrialized nations and the impoverished underindustrialized.

The Iranian Card: A high-low card that may be an ace or a worthless deuce. Iran and Iraq were engaged in a bloody, eight-year war. But the Islamic revolutionary government in Tehran is anti-Western, both politically and culturally. The war had reduced the Iranian Army to a shell. When Saddam saw the coalition solidify against his invasion of Kuwait (in late August 1990) he withdrew Iraqi troops from the "wedge" they occupied inside Iran. He gave Tehran everything it had demanded politically, with the major exceptions of $150 billion in war reparations and his own head. Perhaps it was impossible that Iran would side with Iraq militarily, but there were avenues of mutual interest to explore: shares of future oil wealth, protection of Shiite shrines in Karbala and An Najaf, political cooperation against the West, and even Iraqi "payments" to Iran after the absorption of Kuwait. The downside of this argument, though, has more credibility: Why would Iran want to turn Iraq into a Superpower? Why should the radical ayatollahs cooperate with a secular leader hostile to their own political and religious objectives? How could the Iranians forget eight years of war? Likewise, the Iranians had a more valid land claim to the Basra region than Saddam did to Kuwait. The political objective: to use Iran as an economic embargo–breaker; to gain Iranian cooperation in an Islamic front against the West. At the minimum, to assure that Iran would not open a second front against Iraq.

The Jordanian Card: A card to be played in conjunction with the Economic and Arab Street ploys. Jordan proved to be the weak link in the UN-imposed economic sanctions. Indeed, the port of Aqaba, which had served as Iraq's seaport during the Iran-Iraq War, continued to do so now. The political objective: to break economic sanctions and use Jordan as a political front for Iraqi operations. (NOTE: In fact, the Iraqi embassy in Amman was the chief center of Iraqi espionage and political intrigue during the conflict.)

The Terror Card: A play from the shadows, with aspects of the

Fear card. Terrorism has been a plague in the Middle East and a thorn in the life of Western Europe. The Pan Am 103 (Lockerbie) bombing struck a chord of fear in the United States. Saddam had been a major supporter of several well-known terrorists and terror organizations. The Venezuelan Marxist terrorist "Carlos" had supposedly holed up in Baghdad sometime in late 1989 (and done a lot of drinking, according to several sources). Several Palestinian terror groups were on the Iraqi payroll. Saddam made no secret of his means. During the conflict, Baghdad radio broadcast mysterious "instructions" that many around the world interpreted as code telling terror networks where, when, and whom to strike. The political objective: to sow fear; to show the American and European publics that they have no sanctuary from the bloodshed.

The Scud Card: A spectacular card, tied to the Israeli card and the Chemical, Biological, and Nuclear card suit (trumped, however, by the U.S. Patriot Pac-2 ATBM). Iraq's surface-to-surface missile capability, demonstrated during the Iran-Iraq War, gave Saddam the ability to threaten population centers throughout the region. Turkey, Saudi Arabia, Syria, Iran, and Israel were all within range. If the Iraqis had possessed chemical or nuclear warheads, the Scud could have proved to be decisive (again, if the United States had not had Patriot Pac-2). As it was, the Scud served as a terror weapon. The political objective: to frighten populations in the region; to strike at Israel and antagonize the Israelis into joining the war, thereby splitting the coalition opposing Iraq. Scuds would also show the Arab world that Iraq possessed technological power.

The Assassination Card: An aspect of the Terror card. The Iraqis were involved in the assassination of an Egyptian government official in the fall of 1990. Some evidence exists that Iraqi agents were involved in another attempt in Saudi Arabia. The political objective: to eliminate opposition leadership.

The Chemical and Biological Weapons Card: This card was played right up until the coalition began the ground war. It was tied to the Casualties card. Saddam had used chemical weapons against the Iranians and the Kurds. Likewise, the fear of biological weapons had been repeatedly reinforced by the Iraqis. The political objective: to intimidate. These weapons terrorized opponents. If delivered by Scuds, they could result in massive civilian casualties. Tactical use of these weapons would increase the power of the Iraqi Army. This card actually worked, to a limited extent. The Allies expended a lot of effort and expense on preparing for chemical warfare. During the ground war, many Allied troops went into battle all suited up for chemical attacks that never came. This made the troops uncomfortable and slowed them down a bit. It may have even caused a few casualties. But in the end it didn't lessen the magnitude of the Iraqi defeat.

The Nuclear Weapons Card: Unquestionably, gaining nuclear technology and nuclear weapons was an active Iraqi aim and would have been a real ace. Indeed, nuclear-tipped ICBMs in Iraqi hands would have made Washington think twice about intervening. The political objective: to join the elite "nuclear club," which politically denotes superior power.

The Republican Guards Card: This card is tied to the Casualties card and the Fear card. Republican Guards units were ruthless and fearless and personally loyal to Saddam and the Baath. The Republican Guards emerged from the Iran-Iraq War with a fearsome combat reputation (which was more smoke than fire), and so led the invasion of Kuwait. The political objective: to convince peace groups in the West that tangling with Iraqi elite units was militarily futile; to convince opinion leaders in the West that huge casualties would result where the Republican Guards were engaged in ground combat.

The Ecological Destruction Card: Linked to the Nihilist Destruction card but designed to influence the Sierra Club, the German Greens, and ecological movements around the world. Iraqi propagandists and numerous ecological and peace groups around the world emphasized the potential for great environmental devastation resulting from war. Oil spills would destroy the Persian Gulf. In a redux of "nuclear winter," fires from burning oil wells would alter weather patterns worldwide. The political objective: to exploit a popular cause in the West and divide Western public opinion.

The Western Press Card: Saddam concluded that the Western press corps could be used to propagandize the world. Accurately or not, he believed that the United States in particular could not fight a war that was covered by the press. He had seen the videotape of Vietnam. In August the Western press came to him (Ted Koppel of ABC and Dan Rather of CBS did go to Baghdad). The Western press would be the conduit for his bluster, feints, and political gambits. The press's desire for "objectivity" would be warped so that Iraqi political claims would be portrayed as being on an equal footing with Washington's. Likewise, lingering press suspicions of the Pentagon would be exploited.

The Cable News Network Card: A technological aspect of the Western Press card. In a world of instant communications and spontaneous news (flashed around the globe with no context) there is opportunity for graphic propaganda. Western viewers might see through most of Saddam's theatrics, but the CNN feed to other Arab populations played a different way, and in Saddam's favor.

The Iraqi Suffering Card: A post–January 16, 1991, version of the Arab Weakness card that is closely tied to the CNN Card and Third World cards. In this play, Iraq is cast as a victim of Western technology and indiscriminate bombing. It appeals to the humanitarian instincts of human beings everywhere, i.e., stop the bombing because children are suffering. Ignore the fact of Iraqi terror and depredations against the Kuwaiti populace. Cameras can't get into Kuwait City. The political objective: to appeal to human compassion. In particular, stoke the Western peace movements and generate pacifist sympathy, so that the bombs stop falling on Baghdad.

The Nihilist Destruction Card: A dark blot of a card. Destroy Kuwait and the Kuwaiti oil fields. Loot and pillage. Destroy everything. Political objective: to show the world that Iraq and Saddam will not be toyed with. (NOTE: Of course this produced worldwide revulsion and backfired.) Why try it at all? Play it and show the world that it is dealing with a man who will stop at nothing. ("Better to appease me before I destroy us all.")

The Victory-in-Defeat Card: This might also be called the "Martyr" card. A tricky card to play. Observing Egypt's Gamal Abdel Nasser rise from defeat after the 1967 Arab-Israeli War, Saddam noted that no Arab leader in the last forty years has been thrown out of office by losing a war. Basically, this endeavor says that it doesn't matter what happens on the battlefield, the fact that Saddam took on the world will live on in myth. He will be remembered by Arab history as a giant. Smiting him will not destroy his power. The political objective: to discourage attacks on Iraq and Saddam. It's futile. If the coalition wins, Saddam will still appear as a victor in "the Arab Street."

The Saddam/Baath Survival Card: The "I'll always keep turning up" card. No matter what happens, the propaganda went, Saddam will remain in power in Baghdad. The political objective: to create doubt in the opposition. If Saddam would remain anyway, if the Baath stayed in power, why bother fighting the war?

Saddam tried them all. What kind of political card shark was Saddam? Go back and review the pack. He played them all. Of the lot, only the Baath Survival card remains in play. Literally, none of Saddam's cards worked. And it wasn't a game. Instead of a pile of chips, Iraq was left with a pile of rubble.

The Coalition

The Allied political game is much more complicated than that of Iraq. Coalition formation and coordination was the key strategy.

Internationalization was a corollary aim as was *personalization* of the conflict, that is, making Saddam the political and propaganda heavy. Directing barbs and blame at Saddam deflected the Iraqi attempt to portray the conflict as a struggle between Arabs and the West. Saddam was very accommodating on this point, but it may never be clear just how deeply the Revolutionary Command Council and other elements of Baath and Iraqi political power were involved in the escapade. Likewise, internationalization, primarily through the United Nations, reinforced the Allied political intent that the conflict be one of Civilization (the world) versus Barbarism (Saddam). Internationalization also brought extraordinary political legitimacy to the coalition's effort, and helped stifle leftist "antiwar" protests throughout the coalition countries.

As the conflict unfolded, other strands of Allied political strategy became evident. The political (and supposedly military) objective would be limited to the reestablishment of the situation antebellum and no more. Kuwait would be liberated, the Kuwaiti government reestablished; the Iraqi Army would return to Iraq. Elimination of Saddam and his Baath government would not (at least publicly) be a political and military aim.

Keeping Israel out of the conflict would also be an essential goal. Overt Israeli participation would split the coalition.

But the coalition was the key. Of course, United States and to a lesser extent British and French forces would be the military core of both the blockade and embargo phase of the conflict and the military. But the Bush administration had to remember never to get too far out in front of King Fahd and the Saudis or the Egyptian government of President Hosni Mubarak, whose support was absolutely central to success. Many commentators referred to the coalition as an "impossible" political construction. Admittedly, the integration of Syria into the coalition appeared illogical and grotesque, given the fact that Syria's president al-Assad has almost as bloody a record as Saddam. But Syria's participation illustrates once again just how deep runs the personal, political, and historical competition between the Syrian wing of the Baath and the Iraqi wing of the Baath. Saudi and Egyptian participation, however, is not so odd. Both the Saudi Arabia and Egyptian governments had been telling Washington (and Britain and France) for years that if and when a genuine military crisis developed in the Middle East, either perpetrated by Soviet, Iranian, Iraqi, or Syrian action, they would count on the West and the West could count on them. Mutual economic and political interests between Saudi Arabia, Egypt, and the United States supplanted mutual suspicions. At least that was the "sub rosa" message since the mid-1970s. And when the Kuwaiti crunch came, the coalition formed.

The Coalition Suit

The Kuwaiti Card: The first card played in response to the Iraqi invasion. On August 2 (Kuwait time), and the day of the attack, Kuwaiti crown prince Saad al-Abdullah al-Sabah called the American embassy in Kuwait and asked for immediate U.S. military help. Still, he was worried about other Arab reaction, so he asked that it "not be made public or treated as official." Four hours later, Kuwait's prime minister asked that the request be made open and official. Kuwait no longer cared about "Arab reaction." The political objective: to save the Kuwaiti state from Iraq's invasion.

The Saudi Arabian Card: At first the Saudis were flustered and caught off guard. By August 3, 1990, the day after the invasion, they had made their decision: to oppose Saddam, and rely on United States backing if that's what it took. The only caveat, at the time, was that the United States had to agree in writing to pull its troops out of Saudi Arabia and Kuwait after the conflict ended. Saudi Arabia's decision was pivotal. The Saudi objective was to insure the Saudis' own survival if Saddam continued the attack through Kuwait toward Riyadh or Dhahran. But Saudi economic and political influence in the world, and Saudi geography, were essential to coalition success.

The United States Card: Played both by Washington and Riyadh. With the end of the Cold War, the "multipolar world" emerged—with one big "pole" called the United States. No other nation on the globe could mobilize military assets as large as the United States, and no one could move them as rapidly. The Iraqi military machine was simply too large for an "Arab solution" or Arab force to confront alone. Likewise, no other nation had America's degree of influence, economic power, and esteem. The United States, of course, had its own interests and political objectives at stake: The U.S. economy is directly affected by the price of oil, and that of its European and Asian allies even more so. American leaders also saw Saddam in the 1930s context: He looked like a would-be Mussolini or Hitler, bent on expansion, bent on acquiring modern conventional weapons and nuclear power. Saddam was also a threat to Israel and America's Arab allies.

The Egyptian Card: With the largest population in the Arab world, Egypt was central to coalition success. Egypt was still in the process of "reintegrating" into the Arab world after years of being shunned because of its peace settlement with Israel.

Longtime historical and political hostility toward Iraq was also an issue. The Egyptian government also sensed a critical opportunity: A "U.S.-Egyptian-Arab Coalition" would be the first step to marginalizing both social and religious radicals. Such a coalition would be a risk, from the Egyptian perspective, a risk well worth taking. Besides, Saudi Arabia would be footing the bill. Although the prime political objective remained stopping Saddam, Egypt might also emerge from the conflict as the key Arab power. And "deradicalization" of the Middle East would allow Egypt to address domestic economic concerns.

The Syrian Card: Baghdad and Damascus have been at odds for centuries. The Syrian and Iraqi wings of the Arab Baath have been violently hostile since the mid-1960s. Syria, in fact, had supported Persian Iran during the Iran-Iraq War. Iraq's emergence as the regional superpower threatened Syria. If the coalition was to wage a successful sanctions policy against Iraq, Syria was essential. The invitation was made. From Syria's perspective, accepting the invitation reopened economic and political channels to Egypt, Saudi Arabia, and even the United States. With Soviet support fading, Syria was on a tenuous limb: Damascus needed a new relationship with the United States and Middle Eastern moderate regimes. The crisis, on the cynical side, also gave Syria an opportunity to attack the (Iraqi-supported) Maronite Christians in Lebanon and to try to break that lingering stalemate. If Syria cooperated with the alliance, France and the United States would have to look the other way as Syria "dealt with" General Michel Aoun, the renegade Lebanese commander of Maronite Christian forces. The central coalition objective: to surround Iraq.

The French and British Card: Despite France's tendency to play both sides of the fence, Paris began to cooperate. The French had been major arms suppliers to Saddam, as had Britain. But once Iraq moved, both Britain and France committed to the coalition. Common historical, political, and economic interests demanded the decision.

The Turkey Card: Turkey is the lurking powerhouse in the Middle East. For seventy years, Turkey had (more than less) followed Kemal Atatürk's dictum that Ankara must avoid

"Arab entanglements." Turkish prime minister Turgut Ozal overcame domestic dissent and placed Turkey squarely in the coalition camp—once he was sure the United States would truly lead (as opposed to the fiasco of America's retreat after the terrorist attack on the marine barracks in Beirut). This time, the Bush administration assured him that the United States would stay until the job was done. Turkey closed the northern door on Iraq. It also opened a potential "second front." The highway from Cizre to Baghdad (down the Tigris Valley) is an ancient invasion corridor. The Turks also knew they had a madman on their border. Participation in the coalition would gain Turkey political chits in its bid to join the European Economic Community. It would also strengthen Turkish ties with the United States. Likewise, Turkey stood to benefit economically if it helped Saudi Arabia. Many Arabs and Asians already consider Turkey "Europe," and the Turks would like to make it even more so.

The Russian Card: The coalition's version of Iraq's Soviet card. From the Allies' perspective, opposing the invasion as an effective coalition was only possible as long as Moscow cooperated. And Moscow had many reasons to cooperate. Despite Stalinist recidivism and trouble in the Baltics, the Kremlin had committed to a "West-politik" of common economic and often political cause with Western Europe and the United States. The USSR had interests in keeping Saddam in power, but it had no interest in allowing land grabs. The USSR and Eastern Europe are themselves a hodgepodge of border claims and counterclaims. Russian cooperation illustrated the changed nature of global politics and stressed Iraq's isolation. It also made UN action possible. Little could have happened without the end of the Cold War and the changes in Soviet domestic and international policy. The end of the Cold War gave the United States an enhanced freedom of action.

The China Card: Perhaps worth a point less than the Russian card, but still vital in gaining global cooperation. China, still semi-isolated by its government's massacre of dissidents in Tiananmen Square, saw an opportunity to regain some leverage with the United States. All Beijing had to do was abstain in the Security Council. It did.

The Security Council Card: Key to seeding the internationalization of the conflict and gaining legal authority to oppose Saddam. Security Council resolutions (by the end of the conflict
there would be thirteen of them) provided the political glue for
defeating Iraq.

The United Nations Card: In some ways subsidiary to its own
subsidiary (the Security Council), but a vital link in the coalition
process nonetheless. While the League of Nations could do
nothing about Mussolini's invasion of Ethiopia (1935) the UN,
with U.S. leadership, could confront Iraq when it attacked Kuwait. The political objective: to internationalize the conflict and
isolate Iraq.

The Political Operations Suit
(These cards were played in Washington, Riyadh, and the
UN.)

The Assets Freeze Card: Ordered early on by the Bush administration, the freeze of Kuwaiti and Iraqi bank accounts and a
hold on other assets in the United States, Japan, and Western
Europe would evolve into worldwide sanctions. The Assets
Freeze was the first card dealt in a straight flush of economic
warfare against Iraq.

The Political Isolation Card: An aspect of internationalization
but an important one. Iraq would be portrayed as a nation alone
led by a criminal leader rejected by all but a few crank supporters around the planet.

The Sanctions Card: Card two in the "economic straight
flush"—it let the Iraqi people know they would pay a deep economic price for Saddam's invasion.

The Embargo Card: Card three in the economic deal. A complicated card to play but one of strength, though it is very doubt-
ful that embargo and economic sanctions would have removed
Saddam from Kuwait before the coalition's political will fal-
tered. Still, the embargo hurt Iraq and reinforced the Iraqis'
sense of world isolation.

The Saudi Money Card: The Saudis and Kuwaitis had money stashed away for this contingency. Money bought supplies and fuel for American and coalition forces. It also helped ensure the participation of Turkey, Egypt, et al.

The Saddam Card: Portraying Saddam as the rascal, and not the suffering population of Iraq, served several political purposes: It began to drive a wedge between Saddam and the Iraqi people; and it gave television producers a bad guy straight from Central Casting.

The Palestinian Conference Card: Played by Paris overtly, but by Washington covertly. Almost everyone was interested in getting the Israelis and the Palestinians to the bargaining table, just as long as Saddam didn't get credit. France sought to blunt Saddam's appeal to the Palestinians. This card didn't work well during the conflict.

The Military Buildup Card: While the arms buildup had a military intent (i.e., to protect Saudi Arabia), it also had a political intent: to force Saddam to back down by convincing him that unless he pulled his troops out of Kuwait voluntarily he would face attack. It did not work as a threat, but provided the ability to implement a military solution.

The Kuwaiti Resistance Card: An important political card that ultimately proved to have military utility. The Kuwaiti armed resistance remained active inside Kuwait throughout the war, blunting Iraqi claims of the 19th Province.

The Counterterror Card: The United States and Saudi Arabia applied pressure on Syria to cooperate in counterterror action. Damascus agreed. Throughout the conflict, Iraqi attempts to launch terror strikes around the world were blocked. Several nations expelled Iraqi diplomats known to be contacts for terrorists. Britain even interned, as prisoners of war, several dozen Iraqis living in Britain who might assist terrorist acts.

The Information War Card: This is really a complex political play with many sides, a deck unto itself but a point worth specifically noting. The entire coalition made wise and effective use of the global communications network. Audiences around the world were swamped with information, largely from American and Western sources, but information that was "shaped" by coalition press controls.

The Television Briefing Process Card: A significant subset of the information war. Admittedly, live briefings are a risk, but they are also an opportunity, if you use the right briefer. Questions asked at the briefings in Riyadh would be analyzed and answers prepared for the briefings in Washington. But that was a tangential benefit. What the briefing process did, over time, was expose the foibles of the working press. U.S. and Allied military briefers became sympathetic and credible figures. The sharp-tongued and cynical press became the bad guys.

The Israeli Reassurance Card: Call this money and military assistance, but it was also politically important that Israel know it had not been abandoned by the United States. Interestingly, Egypt, Saudi Arabia, and later Syria reassured Israel that "all nations have the right to self-defense"—implicit recognition of Israel's national existence. The United States and Egypt intend to use this card as a basis for reaching new agreements on the Israeli-Palestinian problem.

The Arab Action Card: Whenever the coalition could do it, which was often, Arab members of the coalition did the talking, asserting that this effort was a united effort with willing Arab participation. The political objective: to blunt Saddam's appeals to pan-Arabism.

The International "Ante-Up" Card: If Japan and Germany won't show up with troops, they can pay for the protection. The Germans, of course, argued that they were still holding down the Central Front, and that it was the Bundeswehr's presence that allowed the U.S. 7th Corps to depart for the Middle East. But that perception didn't play well in the United States or Britain or France—or for that matter, Turkey. The Japanese argued that their post–World War II constitution forbade them from participating militarily. It even got to the point where the Japanese argued that they were still feared throughout Asia and they didn't want to return to bad old habits. Be that as it may, American taxpayers feared another Japanese and European free ride. The Japanese and Europeans responded with billions of dollars to support the Allied war effort.

The "Eco-Terrorist" Branding Card: Used successfully to counter Nihilist Destruction and Ecological Destruction cards. Really a propaganda card since Saddam's Ecological Destruction card had both a political and economic purpose that removed it from the realm of terrorism. Environmental destruction is a primeval tool in war. The Romans salted the fields of their vanquished enemies (e.g., Carthage, 146 B.C.), inhibiting their ability to recover from defeat.

The United States Domestic Front Suit
New World Order Card: Possibly as much an international as a domestic card and certainly one with possibilities. The political objective: to show that the Cold War is over and that old post–Vietnam era assumptions about the world no longer apply; to focus public opinion on the potential benefits for peace; to give the American people a New Crusade—and mean it.

The Command Group Card: Saddam really underestimated the depth, breadth, and strength of the U.S. "command group." George Bush, James Baker, and Richard Cheney provided cool and consistent political leadership. Colin Powell was the perfect swingman between the political and military sphere. Norman Schwarzkopf was the right general at the right time. Was the United States lucky? Probably. Some pundits have tried to imagine how a Michael Dukakis presidency would have handled or mishandled the Iraqi invasion. The operative issue is Dukakis's (and the liberal wing of the Democratic party's) suspicion of the use of American military power. But that is one of those questions of history that will never be answered.

The Domestic Coalition Card: The Bush administration got the support of key congressional Democrats. Their support was critical for the declaration of war, but also emphasized that this was not a Vietnam redux.

The Declared War Card: President Lyndon Johnson missed on Vietnam—American military forces need the commitment and political support of the American people to wage successful war. Congress, miserable as it may be, is the forum of that debate. The political objective: first, to show the Iraqis that the United States would go to war; second, that if the United States went to war, the war would be one waged with unquestioned domestic support.

The Respond to Other Crisis Card: A small but important move by the Bush administration in the early days of the conflict. Unlike President Jimmy Carter, who some came to believe was held "hostage in the Rose Garden" by the Iranian hostage crisis, President Bush spent the last months of 1990 making sure that that did not happen. Bush focused attention on events in Liberia, the Baltics, and Europe, and even (some would say minimal) to domestic concerns at home. The political objective: to ensure that Saddam would not be the only political agenda in town, at least until the other political and military elements of the coalition were ready to deal with him.

The Anti-Fascist Card: Saddam was a fascist. The left in Europe and America styles itself as "antifascist" (though it's hard to understand why when one considers Castro). Portraying the anti-Saddam action as an antifascist action blunted some left-wing protest.

The Military Suit
The Logistics Card: The United States and Allied military forces' logistical efforts were the most thorough and sophisticated in military history. What was needed to win could be brought into the theater and was brought into the theater. The political objective: to have the means at hand to continue politics by other means (i.e., war).

The Unity of Command Card: Even though the coalition was a multinational effort, the air and ground wars were run under the principle of unity of command. All air units were placed under a coalition "planning umbrella." The ground war was fought under unified command. Ultimately, success or failure of the military effort was placed on one man, General Norman Schwarzkopf. Take the responsibility and heat and take the glory—or the defeat. Schwarzkopf took the responsibility and did the job. The political objective: to avoid having a military machine organized to fight at cross-purposes and with murky chains of command.

The Intelligence Card: United States and coalition intelligence capabilities were near total. Apparently, the Allies could get electronic intelligence on all but Iraqi telephone communications over buried landlines (and sometimes they got that by tapping cables). Problems did develop in the speed of processing and interpreting intelligence, but coalition intelligence problems were nothing compared to the Iraqis', who barely had any intelligence on Allied plans, military moves, or political efforts.

The Patriot/SDI Card: The Patriot surface-to-air missile system was a potent antiaircraft weapon; the software and guidance improvements of Patriot Pac-2 would make the Patriot system effective against tactical ballistic missiles, like the Scud. But would they work? Actually, the Patriot Pac-2 almost didn't make it into the war. The first Pac-2s came into the army inventory in late July 1990. One of the first Pac-2 units to go to Saudi Arabia arrived in Dhahran with only three Pac-2 missiles. But the Patriot Pac-2 worked even better than anticipated. The Scud threat was stopped. Scuds, at least militarily, were a nuisance. Politically, they were a terror weapon and the weapon Saddam intended to use to drag Israel into the conflict. The Patriot stopped the Scud (more politically than physically), proving the necessity of Strategic Defense Initiative–type programs.

The High-Tech Weapons Card: With casualties a concern, pinpoint targeting, smart weapons, and advanced conventional weapons gave the coalition's political leaders confidence that Iraqi forces could be taken out with few casualties.

The Air War Card: Allied air power and air tactics developed by NATO gave the coalition a huge battlefield edge and one with a sharp political point: Allied air forces could attack the enemy army and cause it casualties with minimal killed and wounded among coalition forces. One political objective of the air war that did not come about, however, was Iraqi capitulation based on air attack alone.

The AirLand Battle Card: United States military doctrine had evolved since the mid-1970s. Future American wars would be fought with deep strikes at the enemy's rear. Air-force air support, helicopters, Special Forces operations, armor, infantry, and artillery would all be equipped, organized, and trained to fight together. Operations would stress speed and maneuver. Advanced equipment (to allow pinpoint targeting) would improve the military's ability to fight at night. The U.S. Army expected to fight outnumbered and win. The political argument: Training and tactics would, in all likelihood, make for a quick ground war, especially if the air war was successful. Note that this is basically an update of the successful 1940s blitzkrieg tactics, which the Israelis adopted for their wars with Arab armies.

The National Training Center Card: The U.S. Army that fought in the Persian Gulf War was trained at Fort Irwin, California. The training at the "NTC" is thorough and realistic, and produced a desert army schooled in AirLand Battle Doctrine and tactics. Perhaps even more than the Israelis, the United States possessed the best-trained desert army in the world.

A deck of cards, a host of options. International diplomacy has often been compared to a game of poker. Diplomats use a larger deck, and a more complex one. The cards keep changing, although many remain constant (terror, threats, subsidies, and so on). But a card game it remains, as in the phrase, "playing the China card." The stakes are often quite high, for when a war breaks out, everyone loses. Those who declare themselves winners are those who have lost the least.

CHAPTER 13

AirPrint Battle:
The Adventures of the Press Brigade

Nearly 2,000 journalists of various types went to the Middle East to cover the war. Most of them were in Saudi Arabia, where they largely languished under military press restrictions. On the home front, the major networks scrambled to assemble teams of experts to analyze and give perspective to the unfolding situation, and explain it to their millions of viewers.

This was a TV war, expedited by the presence of instant satellite transmission. However, one important link in this chain of reporting was missing. The reporters at the front were not free to go after the story. Realizing that the enemy could see the television news reports as quickly as the folks back home, the military tightly controlled where the press could go and, to a lesser extent, what it could report. This state of affairs did not satisfy the press.

The American media is never satisfied with much of anything, but then, satisfaction isn't the job of a free press. Informing the public, touting points of view, and exposing malfeasance among the powerful (while securing sufficient advertising revenues) are more or less the basic duties of a free press in a free society.

The U.S. military's job is to deter wars and, that failing, win wars. Both deterrence and victory require "operational security," that is, the maintenance of some degree of secrecy. For the military, secrets, facts, and analysis are the essence of "military intelligence." Tactical, operational, and strategic secrets—information about friendly and enemy troops, terrain, missions, communications, enemy intentions, etc.—are vital to success. Military "opinions" are the initial ingredients of operational plans and the basis for analysis of both friendly and enemy intentions.

Yet "secrets," (or at least the "stuff" some folks don't want others to know), and "opinions" (the "stuff" others *do* want others to know) are the fodder of journalism. For the reporter and editor, secrets and opinion are headlines, news stories, and op-ed columns.

Thus, between U.S. media and U.S. military, to paraphrase that prince of indecisiveness, Hamlet, lies the *perpetual* rub.

Certainly, the press is bound to clash with all of the other institutions of society. Out of this clash is born two things: enough truth to help insure a more just society on the one hand, and on the other, the sense of "arrogance of power" on the part of reporters, newscasters, and editors so often despised by press critics.

The clash between military and press, however, may be more fundamental, especially in a free society. Debating budgets, cost overruns, and base closings is one thing; however, friction between the free press and the military of a free society during a war, given the life-and-death stakes, twists the clash into something else. Reporters, always nosy and investigative, may play the unwitting spy. The rub between inquisitive press and wartime military may produce real wounds and devastating military defeat.

The Persian Gulf War demonstrated the velocity and ferocity of the U.S. Army's AirLand Battle Doctrine. But the war was also an "AirPrint Battle," a battle of broadcast, televised, and newsprint commentary and opinion, where members of the press fought among themselves for "scoops" but also fought with the military leadership. The AirPrint Battle was also quick and volatile, and in its own way, bitter.

The Ghosts of Vietnam and Waging War in the "Strategic Information Environment"

Like Hamlet, American military operations and military-press relations have been stalked by a ghost: the ghost of Vietnam. The old "Vietnam suspicions" lurk around the edge of every briefing and every interview. On the part of the military, the ghost takes the line that the press "lost" the war and treated soldiers unfairly. The press counters that the military and the government (the Kennedy, Johnson, and Nixon administrations at least), lied.

For the military, press leaks are not a new problem. The combination of mass circulation newspapers and telegraph in the 1860s gave the American Civil War generals (particularly those on the Union side) severe problems. Several times, Confederate commanders did obtain militarily useful information from northern newspapers. A reporter could telegraph news to his paper, have it appear in the next day's edition, and have a copy of that edition find its way to a Confederate general in a few days' time. The Spanish-American War, thirty-three years later, was too short and too spread out to offer the enemy a lot of useful information via the American press. World War I, twenty years further on, was the first time when reporter/editor patriotism, plus military censorship of dispatches, withheld useful information from the enemy. World War II and Korea carried on that tradition, with the press benefiting from briefings by commanders on key operations before the operations occurred. The press was trusted, the military didn't lie, and the system worked. Then came television, and Vietnam. Television made a big difference. It was relatively immediate. The military didn't know what hit them, and were not able to impose the degree of press control they had in Korea and World War II. Vietnam was unique in the respect that it was relatively wide open to the press. Pictures of dead and wounded American troops were common early on. Yet, while there was grousing among the Gulf camera crews about not being able to film dead Americans, few were probably aware that no pictures of dead Americans were allowed to be shown during World War II until 1943.

But in order to understand the dimensions and appreciate the crucial aspects of the Gulf War's "AirPrint Battle," one must understand the new "strategic information environment," which is newly coined military jargon for the instantaneous global information communications network. Instantaneous communications and the rapid dissemination of information are critical features of today's world.

The communications technologies have a political impact. In fact, to an increasing extent, political borders have been erased by fast, cheap, and *reliable* (at least in terms of hardware) communications and information technology. The profound political effects are worth taking a moment to consider, and the end of the Cold War provides an interesting example. At the very least, 1989's Eastern European revolutions were encouraged (if not directly promoted) by the penetration of the Iron Curtain by Western radio and television, and by the increasing availability of individualizing, choice-producing technologies, such as the microcomputer, videocassette tape player, home-satellite dish antenna, and the "backpack" video camera.

Given these technologies and their "creep" eastward (through smuggling, gifts, etc.), the Communist regimes of Eastern Europe were no longer able to seal their populations to alternative opinions. The truth of Western political and economic success could not be denied—the totalitarian regimes could not compete with the information barrage from the West nor could they close all of the multiple information "invasion" routes.

Certainly, a great deal of the information that reached Eastern Europe might be viewed as "incidental." Western advertising for blue jeans and Coca Cola isn't government-produced propaganda. But Western information success was not incidental in the sense that it reflected the benefits of economic, political, and social freedom. Freedom, blue jeans, rock-and-roll, and Coca Cola (i.e., Western political, economic, and social success) behind the military shield of NATO won the Cold War.

Thus, the "strategic information battle" was vital to Western success. Indeed, the Cold War was fought in a "strategic information environment" characterized by massive amounts of free and open information flowing through multiple human and technological channels. The world, and not simply Eastern Europe, was the audience for this information. The amplification effect of Western media reinforced the fact that "government channels" (such as Voice of America, BBC, Radio Free Europe, Deutsche Welle, etc.) were generally telling the truth. The Communist dictators were caught in a bind: Development and economic competitiveness required communications technology and a population familiar with its operation. Western success could not be hidden without Eastern Europe falling even further behind economically.

The military and press experience in operations Desert Shield and Desert Storm reinforce the fact that all contemporary military operations are waged in the context of this "strategic information environment" where anyone with a video camera (or a ham radio, extension telephone, and so forth) can tap into the world's information network (via satellite, broadcast, or for that matter, fax) and a secret military operation can become the lead story on CNN's *Headline News* within ten minutes.

Sun-tzu's strategic commentaries, Machiavelli's *The Prince,* and Carl von Clausewitz's *On War* all focus on the fact that war is conducted in a political context and that the "moral aspect" of war, if only reflected in a society's will to fight the war, is always critical to success or failure. Clausewitz in particular reminds his readers that military action is always part of the political sphere.

In free societies, and, as communications technology proliferates, in all but the most restrictive societies around the globe, the press and "advertising" are critical political connections. Multiple information sources and multiple access are positive resources for the world public. Free information tends to reinforce democratic values and institutions. Yet the ability of new media technologies to disseminate (quite rapidly) unchecked, biased, and decontextualized information is a threat to freedom because it is a threat to the truth. It is certainly a threat to a military operation, for military operations, by their very nature, rely on an element (be it at the strategic, operational, or tactical level) of surprise in order to achieve success. To paraphrase one U.S. tank officer, it's very difficult to surprise an enemy if he is watching you prepare your troops for battle, live and in color on CNN.

Most of the information the media presented during, and even after, the war could charitably be called disinformation. A combination of ill-educated (in military affairs) reporters and fragmentary release of data by the military resulted in a guessing game wherein the truth—or at least some semblance of reality—tended to come last. For example, press estimates of aircraft in the KTO varied from 2,000 to 2,800 (combat aircraft from 1,200 to 2,000). Similarly, the number of combat sorties reported varied from 108,000 to 114,000. There was a great deal of misinformation about the effectiveness of the bombing, largely derived from the disparate bits of information released by the USAF in support of F-117 effectiveness. There was a general misunderstanding about how bombers and attack helicopters operate and how to evaluate their work. It's no wonder that spectacular bits of film footage, no matter how out of context, were eagerly snapped up and shown by perplexed reporters for their equally perplexed viewers.

AirPrint Battle: Press Focus by the Week

How did the press look at the war? Some critics thought they detected coverage "themes": General emotional content of the time period's press coverage. The months leading up to the beginning of the air offensive were another story. After five months of waiting, speculation ruled the airwaves and editorial pages. While some commentators gave an accurate rendering of what would happen when the shooting started, much of this was lost amid a wail of fear and speculation about the competence of America's forces and the number of casualties that might be anticipated. Careful observers could see that the buildup was moving toward a "hit-them-hard-and-fast-with-a-lot" strategy intended to minimize casualties. But fear played better, and attracted more people to such stories. Newspaper and magazine circulation soared. CNN quadrupled its ratings (and raised its rates accordingly). Then the air war began.

January 11–17: Themes: Apprehension, Doubt, and Gloom. *Major Stories:* The United States Congressional debate on the war resolution, the vote on the war resolution, dire predictions of U.S. casualties, the looming January 15 deadline, the initial Allied air attacks.

January 18–24: Themes: Optimism, bordering on euphoria, Glee, Gee-Whiz. *Major Stories:* The success of the initial Allied air attacks; the success of "smart munitions"; the first Iraqi Scud attacks; the apparent success of Patriot missiles; Iraqi Scud attacks on Israel.

January 25–31: Themes: Return to Sobriety, the Gloom of Ecological Disaster. *Major Stories:* The reemergence of "worst case" scenarios for the ground war as pessimism replaced the previous week's optimism; more Scud attacks on Saudi Arabia and Israel and Patriot interceptions; the deliberate release of oil into the Persian Gulf by the Iraqis; displays on Iraqi television of Allied POWs; the Iraqi attack on Khafji.

February 1–7: Theme: Impatience (with bomb damage assessment and "what Khafji means"). *Major Stories:* Bomb Damage Assessment and the air war (reporters demanded precise quantification of effects); the Battle of Khafji; casualties from friendly fire (provoked by casualties sustained at Khafji); ecological damage, military-media relations and how pools were denying reporters access to the troops; the battlefield, and "the real story."

February 8–15: Themes: Impatience and Angry Clamor. Major Stories: The Cheney-Powell trip to Saudi Arabia to assess the progress of the air war; what can be done about friendly fire; why are Scuds still being launched; the bombing of the Baghdad command bunker; civilian casualties; the Iraqi government's extremely conditional statement over Baghdad Radio that it was ready "to withdraw from Kuwait."

February 16–23 (early afternoon): Theme: Return to Apprehension. *Major Stories:* Deadline for withdrawal of Iraqi ground troops from Kuwait; women-in-the-military; concern about excessive "casualties among troops from minority groups"; The Endgame (how the war will end).

February 23 (late afternoon) through March 1: Theme: Excitement and Optimism. *Major Stories:* Allied ground offensive; surrender of Iraqi troops (even to journalists); the success of the air war against Iraqi ground units; the Iraqi "withdrawal/retreat" from Kuwait City and the air attacks on the Iraqi units; Iraqi atrocities against Kuwaiti civilians; military-media relations and how pools were being denied access to the battlefield; the liberation of Kuwait City, the Allied armies' destruction of the Iraqi Republican Guard; the cease-fire; the escape of remnants of the Republican Guard, Kuwaiti resistance fighters' first "reprisals" against "Palestinian collaborators"

The Center for Media and Public Affairs kept track of the TV network coverage of the Gulf War and came up with some interesting statistics. From August 2, 1990, to February 27, 1991, the networks' evening news shows ran 4,283 stories, or about seven stories per network each night, each story taking about 104 seconds. But the forty-two days of the actual fighting got 1,733 of those stories (averaging 112 seconds each). Thus 20 percent of the 210 "newsdays" got 40 percent of the stories. Which makes sense, as combat is a lot more newsworthy than a bunch of diplomats yelling at Saddam to get out of Kuwait or else. The "or else" does attract attention, however. Following the ancient (and highly practical) policy that bad news gets more attention than good, the network news tended to emphasize items that were critical of United States efforts in the Gulf. The sources for stories tended to be against the war (55 percent of them, although 64 percent of ABC's sources were hostile to U.S. policies). President Bush, when mentioned, was criticized 44 percent of the time. The Battle of Khafji, for example, merited forty-two stories, while the bombing of an Iraqi command bunker full of civilians got forty-four. The war definitely was big news. It got over twice as many stories in seven months than the 1988 presidential campaign in 22 months. That angle probably deserves a little more media coverage.

The Baghdad Bunker Bombing

The "Baghdad Bunker Bombing" is perhaps one of the best (or worst) examples of limited context of a "battlefield report" creating a terrible media controversy that affected military and political operations. During the week of February 8–15, the topic of Iraqi civilian casualties caused by Allied bombing received a tremendous amount of news coverage. The central event was the bombing on the night of February 12–13 of a command-and-control bunker by U.S. Stealth fighters using precision-guided 2,000-pound bombs. The bunker also sheltered Iraqi civilians, some of whom were relatives of elite Baath party members.

CNN broadcast footage showing the smoking, destroyed bunker and civilian casualties, complete with comments by Peter Arnett, the CNN correspondent in Baghdad. Clearly, the attack was a valid news story, especially since Allied policy was to limit civilian casualties as much as possible. Arnett reported what the Iraqi government claimed had happened and, in responding to live questions from the CNN anchor, Arnett said that *he* could find no evidence of military activity in the bunker. Arnett was caught between "Iraq and a hard truth." Other reporters, however, among them a reporter for a British news service, claimed that the devastated reinforced-concrete facility had no military function. The pictures and comments shot around the world instantly, pictures of *Arab* civilians killed by *American* bombers. No doubt, this was instant fodder for the angry Arab Street—Saddam Hussein's propaganda case was made, wasn't it?

But within an hour, one of CNN's military consultants, USAF Major General (retired) Perry Smith, was on CNN live, going over the tape. Smith pointed out that the top of the bunker was camouflaged, that the concrete was thicker and more expensive than what usually went over an air-raid shelter, that a cyclone-wire fence ringed the bunker (suggesting limited access, associated with command posts, not shelters), and that communications cables filmed inside the bunker were protected in hardened ducts (a visual signal that the facility wasn't a shelter but a hardened command-and-communications bunker). Smith suggested that reporters who were unschooled in intelligence analysis shouldn't make judgments one way or the other about a facility's capabilities and how they were used, especially when the judgments reinforced the propaganda line of a dictator like Saddam. He also said that the bombing could have been indicative of an Allied intelligence failure—in all probability the Allies did not know civilians were also using the bunker. A number of other commentators would also examine the evidence. Still others would ask CNN why they did not wait and show the videotape until the network could document Iraqi depredations in Kuwait City.

Everything cleared up, right?

Wrong. The *initial* broadcast, especially the images of destruction and civilian deaths, continued to ignite a firestorm of rage and outrage. Review of the videotape supported Arnett's contention that he tried to contextualize the report as best he could, given his circumstances. But contextualizing images is exceedingly difficult. This is one of the key problems of television journalism. Television treats journalism as another "show." The criticism that CNN was not reporting on Iraqi attacks on civilians in Kuwait also hit home. Reports after the war would verify the USAF's contention that at least during the day the facility had been used as a military bunker and that Perry Smith's analysis was quite accurate.

What can be done? In truth, not much, except to ask that reporters and anchors do a better job of defining the background and circumstances of a report, especially a live report. Few real journalists doubt the validity of showing the public just what a 2,000-pound guided bomb does when it strikes its target very precisely. Anyone who thought the air war really was a video game got a hard dose of necessary reality.

One suggestion that later made the rounds does have some merit: War footage where one side is clearly making an emotion-laden propaganda appeal should be telecast inside a red "videobox" that reads on the top and bottom of the screen, UNDOCUMENTED BY OTHER SOURCES.

The classic example of press controversies in the Persian Gulf War, and a controversy that still lingers, centered on Peter Arnett, CNN's correspondent who stayed in Baghdad.

Arnett, an outstanding combat reporter with a long record for guts, determination, and fearlessness, personally bore much of the brunt of the public anger and disgust that pummeled "the press" during and immediately after the Persian Gulf War.

Among most reporters, however, Arnett is a hero. He decided to stick out the war in Baghdad. He is a brave man; thugs like Saddam may threaten him but he doesn't get intimidated. His live morning reports from the Iraqi capital were one of the more fascinating and risky press events of the war.

Clearly, CNN benefited from Arnett's presence and Iraq's decision to let him stay. The Iraqis thought they would benefit as well, by restricting what Arnett could see and what he could say. From the beginning, the Iraqis planned on using CNN as a window on civilian casualties and other exploitable events.

Yet Arnett was consistently clever. When asked what he saw on the highways moving to and from sites the Iraqis wanted CNN's crew to film, Arnett would reply that he had not seen "much in the way of civilian traffic." Uh-huh. Then Arnett looks carefully into the camera. If one and one make two, is it fair to conclude that the highways were packed with military traffic? Slip one past the Iraqi censors and give Arnett another point toward his next journalistic prize. People, that is heroism.

Still, Arnett's reporting illustrates the compromises news organizations make when covering an event from inside a dictatorship. The ground rules in a free society and those in a closed society are very different. This fact is hard to communicate when the reporter faces either expulsion or arrest or death for an unpleasing comment. This is the kind of compromise reporters would rarely allow a business or a government agency to make, and another reason why many people in the United States think the press is hypocritical and unfair.

Up Front with the PAOs (Public Affairs Officers): Pool Sharks, Briefing Bummers

"You are broadcasting our war plans," was the U.S. military's basic case. The reporters at the front countered with, "We're not free to go after the story."

Here, in short, is the problem: Could live, real-time television reports provide live, real-time reconnaissance for an enemy? The CNN cameras at the Al Rashid Hotel in Baghdad provided an excellent example on the first night of the air war (January 16). The live reports by the Peter Arnett-Bernard Shaw-John Holliman CNN crew did more than confirm that Allied air strikes were arriving on schedule. The pictures taken by CNN camera crews could have provided (and perhaps did provide) Allied intelligence officers with a detailed positioning of Iraqi antiaircraft guns on the perimeter of Baghdad. The intelligence analysis process would have been simple: Take the known position of the Al Rashid, identify the camera direction from terrain features, and work the angle of fire back from the antiaircraft artillery tracer fire. At the origin point of the tracer fire is an antiaircraft gun, the weapon caliber of which could be identified by a trained analyst using the tracer. Admittedly, this information may not have been so critical to the Allied air campaign, since the vast majority of Allied air raids on Baghdad were carried out by F-117A Stealth aircraft that had already struck and left the scene by the time the antiaircraft guns began to light the sky. Yet this does provide a stunning example of what could be gleaned from a seemingly "innocuous" shot. There are many more. American "Stealth" fighter pilots, returning from bombing sorties over Baghdad, used CNN footage to identify individual bombing missions.

Of course, live television can be used as a means of tactical and operational disinformation. Road signs can be changed, unit equipment switched; unit patches from units 300 kilometers away can be sewn on the uniforms of local troops. This kind of deception is as old as warfare itself, and the backpack television camera becomes another means of spreading false rumors. Such fakery, however, when passed through free-press channels, sullies everyone's reputation and sacrifices the credibility of the press.

Actually, using the free press in direct, calculated deception has grave strategic risks, even if the reporter and his editor give their okay. This applies in particular to the United States, where one of the "strategic restraints" on U.S. disinformation operations is risking the credibility of the free press, precisely because the free press is the key link to the American citizenry (the source of political power). The American public will accept deception of the enemy, but it will not accept lies. Americans enjoy criticizing the press, but they also want to trust the press, as they want to trust their political and military leadership. The backlash of the American people, when they believe trust is violated, is deep and bitter.

Vietnam is again the lesson. As a result of Vietnam, the United States military became much more aware of the importance of the public's perception of events on the battlefield. The North Vietnamese 1968 Tet offensive is the crucial example. While the Tet attack was, in military terms, an extraordinary operational defeat for North Vietnam and the graveyard of the Viet Cong, the fact of the North Vietnamese attack produced a palpable political darkness where "light at the end of the tunnel" (victory in Vietnam) had been promised to the American people by their political and military leaders. The North Vietnamese struck at the *exposed* political will of the American people, a strategic weakness made vulnerable by the Johnson administration's poorly developed, usually inconsistent, and at times completely fraudulent information policy.

The decision during the Kuwait War to use as spokesmen the senior military officers who were actual operational leaders and planners was taken to establish credibility with the press and the American people. The officers could respond with drilled professionalism and insight.

That was the upside of the use of spokesmen. There was also a devious side. During the Gulf War, the technique of using so-called "subject matter experts" also became a means of attacking the news media's credibility as analysts and critics of military policy. How? Only a handful of reporters and correspondents have sufficient expertise in military affairs to challenge a senior colonel's or general's presentation or analysis of military information. Most reporters have little or no knowledge of military affairs. In truth, reporting is an often tedious and dirty business of probing and analyzing and asking the wrong questions until the right questions are struck. Few members of the public see anything but the final copy in the newspaper or the seamless news broadcast. Live briefings, on the other hand, portrayed informed military officers being asked apparently foolish questions by half-informed reporters. Unprepared reporters appeared to be incompetent, especially when the military officer was crafty and had personality and media pizzazz.

White-haired, joke-cracking, and crusty General Thomas Kelly is the classic case in point. By the close of the 100-Hour War, U.S. Army lieutenant general Thomas Kelly, Joint Chiefs of Staff operations officer and the primary Pentagon military briefer, was more or less commanding the briefings, as chastened reporters (some scalded by press satires on NBC's *Saturday Night Live* and in the comic strip *Doonesbury*) soft-pedaled questions. When it came to running press briefings in the AirPrint Battle, General Kelly and CENTCOM commander General Norman Schwarzkopf were past masters. Crew-cut and angular Marine brigadier general Richard Neal, complete with a Boston working-class accent straight from the television show *Cheers,* also played the snake-charmer. They were soldierly, intelligent, and much to the chagrin of their would-be adversaries in the press gallery, very real and warm human beings. They were not jargon-mumbling military martinets. The French (French Air Force general Claude Solanet and Frency Army brigadier general Daniel Gazeau) demonstrated constant media savoir faire; British (in particular RAF group captain Niall Irving, whose delivery was as precise as a smart bomb), and Saudi briefers from Riyadh also served important roles. Their continuing appearance on international television sent a political message: The war was an international effort, not a U.S. show. Oftentimes the briefings in Washington were directly affected by the questions in Riyadh. Riyadh became a "rehearsal" for Washington. As noted previously, briefers in Washington prepared answers to questions that were raised in Riyadh.

"Pooling" was another part of the Pentagon's strategy in the AirPrint Battle. Everyone who has had an association with the military is familiar with the term "motor pool." The military defines "pool" as "to maintain and control a supply of resources and personnel on which other agencies may draw. A pool promotes maximum efficiency of the use of resources. It is a combination of resources that serve the common purpose." In other words, what's good for trucks and Hummers is good for handling reporters, too.

More to the point, a "media pool" ("pooling" of reporters) is organized when there are more journalists interested in a particular military operation than the commanders of the operation feel they can reasonably accommodate. Media pools take selected print, electronic, and photojournalists into the field with the unit. The journalists then write or produce stories that are shared with all the reporters who didn't get to make the trip. One Pentagon media-relations officer defines "media pool" as any group of discontented journalists attempting to cover a military event.

That's the military's point of view. The press, of course, sees it differently. From the media's perspective, pools are tools of intimidation and denial, fundamental attacks on the First Amendment and on the people's right to know. Pools limit the number of reporters, thereby limiting the number of eyes and ears. The pooled reporters aren't free to roam; they are paired off with military escorts, usually trained public-affairs officers who know the reporters' tricks (that's because a lot of them have worked as reporters). The escorts keep tabs on what the press sees and writes. The escorts "eavesdrop" to inhibit interviews. A baby-sitting act is tough to hide; a "tight escort" also amounts to a form of censorship. A clever escort officer, by delaying the pool in the field, could "pigeonhole" what might have been an unfavorable story even if there were no reasonable concerns for military security. And the delay could continue until the story was no longer timely.

This of course angered the press immensely.

The military responds that to accommodate every reporter would create a "logistical overload," and that reporters have to respect operational security. At the same time, the military points out that the pool reporters are free to report what they see, and that, according to the Pentagon, military censors only objected to five filed reports between January 17 and February 28. The military says the press's grousing about pools is really self-serving, not public-serving—since news agencies spend money to send their own reporters to an event they want their guy to report, not to submit or rewrite the copy of another news agency's reporter. Finally, the magnification of every petty inconvenience into an issue of constitutional prerogative can become absurd.

The press responds that the pool system broke down in the latter stages of the war as Allied forces pushed into Kuwait City and to the Euphrates River. The military shrugs and says, Yeah, once we've won, there's no need for operational security.

Would the media be willing to go to a system where twenty-five or so selected news agencies provided all of the coverage? Essentially, under such an arrangement, an informed "elite" of combat and military journalists would do all of the reporting. They would be subject to cursory censorship before filing a story but be given free reign on "getting the story." This "solution" of course plays into the hands of *The Washington Post, Time* magazine, *The New York Times.* The major regional dailies, like *The Dallas Morning News* or *The Denver Post,* if they were excluded, might label such a "solution" nothing more than a "superpool." Press critics of the far right and far left would call such an arrangement "too cozy."

Still, it is easier to be frustrated with the U.S. military than it is with the Iraqi military or those political and military establishments in less open societies. When it comes to wars, free and democratic Britain puts the clamp on journalists. But America has its Bill of Rights—and the Bill of Rights guarantees (thank God) that there will continue to be an "AirPrint Battle."

Quick Study 9:
Talking Heads and Truculent Prattle

Everyone has seen them: "the talking heads," the usually erudite-looking characters who are hauled onto the TV news set to give an "expert opinion." During the Persian Gulf War, a number of "expert consultants" appeared on the tube and in print, many of them retired military brass or scholarly denizens of Washington's infamous Beltway.

Indeed, at times the networks seemed to be desperate for information and analysis of the sudden yet obscure events. There were several reasons to call out the experts. Television in particular was caught in a monster of its own making: Many events in the Gulf could be seen almost as soon as they occurred. Cameras could cut from live pictures of Iraqi tanks rolling south to an interview with Saddam, then back to live debate on the U.S. Senate floor. The pictures were there, but what did they all mean? Many editors and programmers argued that the (alleged) *lack* of information given by the military to the press necessitated they turn to extensive use of expert analysis to "fill in the gaps in information." Coverage critics replied that the experts appeared to fill in the yawns between commercials. Inside the Pentagon, military officials winced at the inaccurate comments and winced even more painfully at the accurate speculations.

When it came to television in particular, there was yet another edge to this irony: Military affairs and military analysis, as opposed to procurement scandals, normally get little attention in the mass media. Yet when war breaks out, the bum's rush for instant expertise begins. Who can explain what's happening, and do it in two comprehensible sentences? *Does* Kuwait belong to Iraq? Where is Kuwait, anyway? Can you explain cruise-missile technology in a soundbite?

In many cases, the on-camera expert-and-anchor experience turns into a round of the blinded leading the blind; the TV and radio interviewers don't know what questions to ask, and the experts they round up often don't know how to deal adequately with the rapidly developing situation or to explain it to the beer-and-pretzels crowd.

The usual result is the safe route of "follow the trend" in current reporting. A smaller version of the "follow the trend" reporting that created the weekly "press themes" previously mentioned in this chapter. Here's how the "trend analysis" bit works: One news show picks up (or invents) a juicy item, and everyone else feels compelled to follow it up. Often the item picked up and followed by everyone is not the most accurate or informative one at the moment, but it is the one most likely to get attention. As one newspaper publisher put it long ago, "Dog bites man isn't news, man bites dog is." This "follow the trend" line of commentary led to many of the "news stories" about how formidable the Iraqi armed forces were and what severe problems U.S. troops were having with their equipment. The American public was prepared for battlefield and political catastrophes whose likelihood of occurrence was actually minimal. Readers and critics, please allow the authors this bit of truculent prattle: Commentators who insisted on pointing out that the recent Iraqi track record in warfare was poor and that Baghdad's situation was decidedly grim did not play well on the TV circuit, at least between August 2, 1990, and January 17, 1991.

The uneven quality of the experts recruited by the news media further muddied efforts at clarity and reason. In *most* cases *perceived* stature (i.e., former military rank, number of doctorates, clout in the Carter or Reagan State Department, friendship with political cartoonist Garry Trudeau) counted for more than knowledgeability. Perceived stature gave many talking heads more credibility than they deserved. Worse yet, many of the talking heads used the electronic and print soapboxes they were given to sound off with their favorite ideas on how things *should* be. In the early days of the crisis, a man from Mars might have got the impression that the United States had invaded Iraq as partisan "Middle East experts" repeated the cant about an inevitable conflict between "Islam and the West" and the mythic "power of the Arab Street" which would "act against U.S. aggression." This selective focus ignored years of Arab and Western economic, political, and even military cooperation. Many of us found it hard to ignore ARAMCO, the Camp David accords, "Bright Star" US-Egyptian defense exercises, and thousands of other less dramatic but politically and culturally cooperative events and organizations. Optimistic pragmatism, however, just doesn't raise the blood pressure and the ratings like the stench of catastrophe. Reality took a hike as pet ideas and sensationalism elbowed aside the historical record.

Television news programs are the major source of news for most people, so there must have been more than a little confusion in many people's minds as they were bombarded with an often contradictory picture of what was allegedly going on in the war. From August through December, the prophets of doom got a lot of airtime. The population was anxious, and those commentators who would play up all the things that could go wrong were deemed the most newsworthy. During this period, anyone describing the most realistic outcome was treated with some incredulity by the TV-news crowd, although this attitude changed as January 15 came closer and many of the more sober-minded predictions began to jibe with reality.

The bright side of the general expert wrongheadedness was that when the shooting started and reality finally took over, the war's actual events appeared even more startling. However, in one of those choice ironies, it cost the electronic media, particularly TV, a bundle. Major advertisers refused to allow their products to be promoted during regular TV news broadcasts or the many special shows covering the war. So while the print and radio news were taking advantage of the vastly increased audiences for war news, the television news operations took a bath (for over $100 million). Worse yet, without the ads to run, the TV news shows now had a lot more "air" to fill, thus providing far more opportunities for talking heads to pontificate as the war continued.

To be fair, genuine attempts were made to get reliable and accurate consultants. Many former military officers were brought on board, especially if they had some reputation as writers on military affairs. The civilian talking heads were a more mixed bag. Most were defense consultants and scholars ("beltway bandits" is the Washington terminology). A few (the most helpful) won their spurs writing on military affairs for the general public. The retired officers suffered from knowing too much of the detail of military operations and a tendency to revert to that distinct (and baffling) military dialect (professional jargon). To make matters worse, the retired generals and colonels tended to use a variation of the military dialect favored by active duty generals and colonels. Most people watching the news who had military experience were familiar only with the coarser enlisted dialect (which consisted primarily of words that make even less sense and are generally so rude they can't be used on TV, or even in this book. Deep kimchee, yobo). Trying to say too much in a language few viewers understood simply gave the TV pros more work, as they struggled to get their talking heads' commentary to make some kind of sense. The beltway bandits weren't much easier to understand, as they tended to use a political-science dialect familiar only to academics, a few government officials, and reporters for *The New York Times* and *The Washington Post.*

A few of the consultants, however, were overly knowledgeable. Some members of the military got antsy, especially when the "deep left hook" option was discussed. Sometimes, however, the obvious is difficult to hide even from consultants.

After the war was over, the print media in particular raked many of the talking heads over the coals for their earlier off-base commentary. This, once more, played down the work of those talking heads who did get it right. To say, back in the fall of 1990, that the Allied air forces would pound the Iraqis to pieces, that the coalition would hold together, and that Allied ground forces would sweep deep around the Iraqi western flank, was still not very newsworthy—even if it did proved to be correct.

Quick Appendix: AirPrint Battle
War-gaming as a Tool in Explanatory Journalism

Newspaper journalism is a daily act of risk. Thus, an editorial written by author Austin Bay, which appeared in the August 3, 1990, edition of *The Houston Chronicle,* is reprinted below. The *Chronicle* op-ed piece illustrates what war-gaming can do for explanatory journalism, especially when a crisis first breaks and the public is fired with a need for accurate information and an accurate direction as to how and why the crisis began and how it could unfold.

War-gaming, journalism, and military analysis are not discrete disciplines. In fact, when it comes to anticipating, analyzing, and explaining an event, they are mutually reinforcing. When Iraq invaded Kuwait on August 2, Saddam brought "the threads of a crisis" together into a knotty historical fact. War-gamers, analysts, and journalists make careers of following the indicators that precede a crisis.

Still, "daily journalism" is ripe with pitfalls; the mistakes stay in print. The historian, going through an old newspaper clipping file, may chuckle at an error of misperception. The journalist knows, however, that the unforgiving finality of a deadline entails risk and compromises. Sure, there are mistakes, but the journalist leads and the historian follows.

With that in mind, these caveats: (1) Iraq fielded forty to forty-five divisons in early July, prior to remobilization; (2) "The Persian Gulf War" the essay mentions is now referred to as "The Iran-Iraq War"; (3) as of August 2, 1990, Iraq had not officially annexed Kuwait (though it would do so within a week; (4) in the fourth paragraph, "west of Kuwait" should read "northwest of Kuwait" (that is, the Rumailia oil field).

The Houston Chronicle, FRIDAY, August 3, 1990

Iraq's invasion of Kuwait is more than just another Middle Eastern border war. Oil prices are the most obvious indicator Baghdad's attack and annexation of the sheikhdom is an attack on the economic stability of the world.

With 5,500 main battle tanks, 43 ground combat divisions, and an air force with 700 French- and Russian-supplied planes, Iraq has a horde of sophisticated weapons. Bombs and artillery filled with chemical nerve agents and mustard gas, and possibly the makings of a small nuke or two, are also in the arsenal.

The Iraqis—and their leader, Saddam Hussein—are no strangers to aggression. Iraq invaded Iran in 1980 and precipitated the Persian Gulf War. While Baghdad came out of the conflict the "victor," the Iraqis were very lucky. The war became a grinding battle of attrition, with the Iranians and their superior population holding the upper hand. Iraqi perseverence—and Arab money to buy weapons and ammuniton—eventually prevailed. (The Islamic Revolution also wreaked economic chaos in Iran, which benefitted Iraq.)

Iraq invaded Iran to "retake" the mouth of the Shatt-al-Arab waterway (the mouth of the Euphrates River), Iraq's chief outlet to the sea. Iraq also has a second exit to the Persian Gulf, the Khawr Abd-Allah, situated between Iraq and a Kuwaiti sandbank called Bubiyan Island.

On several occasions Iraq has pressured Kuwait for a lease on Bubi-yan. Kuwait has refused. Iraq and Kuwait have also had several dis-agreements over their so-called "neutral zone"—an oil-soaked stretch of sand west of Kuwait.

Saddam Hussein doesn't believe in negotiations—especially when his army is 50 or so times stronger than his opponents, as was the case with tiny Kuwait.

Saddam has become the Mussolini of the 1990s. Like the Italian Fas-cist, he has huge romantic dreams. Saddam speaks of his intention to "lead the Arab world." His dreams of "Greater Iraq" dominating the whole of the Arabian peninsula and "Mesopotamia" are no secret. With over 100 billion barrels of proven reserves, Saddam sees Iraq as the new chief of OPEC. Crack the whip and Saudi Arabia gets in line, right?

But with this invasion, Iraq has now condemned itself to the political fringe. It is also a nation surrounded. The Iranians to the east hate the Iraqis. The Persian Gulf War is still not officially over.

Syria and Iraq are bitter enemies. The Syrian wing of the Baath (Arab Renaissance Party) and the Iraqi wing are long-time rivals. In 1975, Iraq and Syria mobilized their armies along the frontier. The immediate cause of the dispute: Syrian construction of a dam complex on the Euphrates River. Water resources, a touchy subject in the Mid-dle East long before oil became the economically dominant liquid, was the question. Saudi Arabian intervention defused the crisis.

To the north lies Turkey. Saddam Hussein threatened Turkey over the latter's construction of the Ataturk Dam on the Euphrates. Turkey and Iraq are both fighting their Kurdish minorities, but Iraqi mistreat-ment of Turks in northeastern Iraq has already disturbed Ankara.

West lies Jordan and Israel. Jordan has been Iraq's best ally, but Saudi Arabia holds Iraq's first allegiance. The Jordanians will play their invasion politics close to the vest. Iraqi and Israeli political and military relations are best described as terrible.

To the south, Kuwait may be sacked, but the Saudis aren't so vulner-able, not with their allies, Egypt and the United States. Though a fur-ther push into Saudi Arabia would certainly overrun the big Abqaiq pumping station and huge Gawahr oil fields, the Saudi coast and the interior toward Riyadh is real estate where U.S. air strikes (Air Force F-111s from Europe, other tactical air from ground bases in the region, and Navy air off carriers in the area) can shut down an armored ad-vance.

The Iraqis may be able to produce 6.5 million barrels of oil a day, but if they are surrounded, how will they sell it? And where is Washington in all of this? The United States wants to ensure stable Persian Gulf governments so that the oil flow isn't interrupted. The United States knows this could mean that a military commitment must be made. The United States has a bilateral defense agreement (and several UNDERSTANDINGS) with the Saudis. The U.S. Navy has spent the last week exercising with several of the Persian Gulf states' small coastal forces. The U.S. Central Command—the global cavalry of Army light divisions, the 24th Mech Division, and associated Marine units—has trained in Egypt and planned for critical logistical support in the Middle East by improving airstrips in Saudi Arabia and storing supplies on the Indian Ocean island base of Diego Garcia.

Saddam Hussein gambles that Saudis and the rest of the world will tremble, and that oil prices will skyrocket. He gambles that the world will ignore Kuwait just as the world ignored Mussolini's invasion of Ethiopia. Unfortunately, Saddam has missed a critical bit of information: Ethiopia wasn't in the oil business.

PART IV

After the Storm

Where does it lead? George Bush called the war a "defining moment." History has a bad tendency to bring optimists to heel; on the other hand, the pessimists also do poorly. The chapter in this section peers into several alternative futures.

CHAPTER 14

Scenarios of Hell, Scenarios of Hope: The Aftereffects

In 1989 Eastern Europe experienced rapid political upheaval and change. The Berlin Wall cracked. Communism in Poland, Czechoslovakia, Hungary, and East Germany died within weeks, and even the curious Stalinist autocracies in Bulgaria and Romania toppled. Effectively, World War II *finally* came to an end. Soviet armies remained in place, but the Stalinist system no longer had the political will to continue to rule. The seemingly "intractable problem" of the Cold War was resolved—allowing a whole host of new problems to appear.

It is conceivable, though highly unlikely, that the Persian Gulf War sparked by Iraq's invasion of Kuwait will also take four decades to settle and subside. The "fog of peace" is as impenetrable as the "fog of war." What passes for peace in the Middle East is only slightly less contentious than combat.

Yet that could change. Wars can be defining experiences, for the "good" of future peace as well as the "bad" of further conflict. In the aftermath of the Persian Gulf War may arise the opportunity for establishing a new set of political ground rules for resolving conflict without lapsing into ethnic feuds, religious hatred, economic strangulation, and bloodshed.

Much has been made in this book and elsewhere about the rapid formation of an international coalition to confront Iraq's aggression. The continuity of coalition cooperation—or the increasing lack of cooperation—is one of three central features to the many potential "futures" resulting from the war. The second center is the "question of Palestine," the search for a new and less conflicted accommodation between Israelis and Palestinians in the Middle Eastern political scape. The third center is economic development in the "have-not" Middle Eastern countries. Wealth *tends* to breed stability and minimize ethnic and historical friction.

Yet, as Eastern Europe in 1989 illustrated, rapid and profound change can occur. What seemed to be an intractable set of problems may no longer be. Even as Europe experienced rapid upheaval and change, as parts of Asia flirted with democracy or challenged autocratic rule, the problems of the Middle East seemed fixed and relatively stable. Saddam's attack, because of its audacity and the clarity of its violation, destroyed the "stability" of Middle Eastern conflict. The "clarity" of Saddam's attack on Saudi and Israeli civilians, the "clarity" of Iraq's rape and pillage of Kuwait (once the world's cameras returned to Kuwait City), and the world's increasing awareness of Saddam's and the Baath party's savagery toward the Kurds and Shia minorities demonstrated across the Middle East the immense danger of the fascist in pan-ethnic garb.

Two "rules" of regional existence were smashed by Saddam. The attack on Kuwait directly challenged the "inviolability" of political frontiers. Almost all of the "lines in the sand" demarcating the boundaries between states in the region have been drawn in this century, with most of the artwork supplied by Britain and France. The border between Iran and "Arab lands" was drawn by Turkey and Iran in 1914, with Russian and British backing. Likewise, Saddam's attack destroyed any remaining substance to the "rule" prohibiting inter-Arab warfare. Much less a rule than an aspiration, the bias against Arabs taking arms against other Arabs had had a dampening effect on warfare.

Human beings are condemned to being human. Europeans fight among themselves; Americans slay one another in street violence. And Arabs have *always* fought other Arabs: Arab Bedouin used to raid Arab cities. Arab slavers and pirates used to tangle with merchants and fishermen in Aden, Oman, and the Trucial Coast. Hashemites fought the Sa'ūds over the Hejaz and lost. In more recent times, Oman and South Yemen waged a quiet "camel war" for a decade in the Dhofar Province. South Yemen and North Yemen, in the twenty years prior to their rapprochement, fought a continual series of border wars. Algeria and Morocco have been essentially at war for fifteen years in the Western Sahara (Algeria sponsoring the Polisario guerrilla movement and Morocco trying to absorb the old Spanish colony). Libya has fought Muslim tribesmen in Chad and Egypt, and Libya fought a brief border war. Libya has also squared off against Tunisia. Syria and Jordan have had several near clashes, and Iraq and Syria have faced off across their mutual border a half-dozen times since 1970. Jordanians have fought Palestinians. Christian and Muslim Arabs have bloodied themselves in continual warfare in Lebanon.

The list could go on. Yet, to a great extent, these conflicts have indeed been restrained. Then Iraqis invaded Kuwait. Saddam's invasion of Kuwait and slaughter of Arab civilians snapped, perhaps forever, any notion of inter-Arab restraint.

On the other hand, the passionate embrace of Saddam as "Arab champion" by disenfranchised Palestinians and the semi-Westernized Arabs of the Mahgreb (Tunisia, Algeria, and Morocco) impressed the rest of the world with the depth of disillusionment affecting significant segments of the Arab body politic. Arguably, Saddam's destruction of Kuwait hurt the economy of the West Bank Palestinians almost as much as it hurt the pocketbooks of wealthy Kuwaitis. Certainly, the Iraqi invasion beggared the Jordanian economy. Several estimates placed Palestinian losses (in remittances, wages, investments) in the $8–$10 billion range—a figure that will take the meager Palestinian economy a decade to recoup.

Yet for the displaced and culturally alienated, for the Palestinians facing an increasingly powerful Israel (an Israel reinforced by the influx of Russian Jews), Saddam's pro-Palestinian rhetoric and missile shots at Tel Aviv were enough to gain him political support despite his theft.

The fact of Iraq's immense defeat, however, cannot be erased, even by gifted Arab rhetoric. The UN coalition's devastating destruction of the Iraqi Army established a new military and political balance of power in the Middle East. Egypt will now assume the role of regional Arab military powerhouse. Israel has no contenders for dominant regional military power. Saudi Arabia, with its crack air force and Patriot missile batteries in place, is much less subject to military intimidation. The demonstration of America's high-tech military capabilities intro-

duced the world to twenty-first century warfare. Would-be saber
rattlers around the globe must rethink the utility of saber rat-
tling without sophisticated offensive and defensive weapon
systems.

The gray-and-bloody world of the international terrorist appears to have been hemmed by the collapse of Eastern European Communist regimes, the international coalition's military
victory, and the withdrawal of Gulf Arab subsidies to the PLO.
But the hem can tear—it is easy to stall peace plans by tossing
a grenade or blowing up an airliner. Still, if the KGB chooses
to cooperate with other intelligence and police agencies, global
terrorist operations will become more difficult to execute.

The reshaped political landscape, to a degree, mimes the military power balance. Radical Arab states are weakened; the
wealthy, more conservative Arab states are, in some dimensions, politically strengthened. Egypt rises in esteem and influence.

Yet the "traditionalist" Arab states, Saudi Arabia, Qatar, and
the UAE, also face a slew of troubles brought on by victory:
Open alliance with "the West" exposes their nations to change,
a change perhaps more rapid than desired by the conservative
autocracies. Kuwait and Bahrain are already facing this fact;
soon Saudi Arabia will as well. The "high-tech feudal" societies
of wealthy Arabs will evolve, and the evolution will not be
smooth.

What will a future Middle East look like in the wake of war?
A political-military "scenario" is a lace of fantasy and reality
created for the purposes of planning for events. They are not
predictions, though in the context of a particular moment certain scenarios are "more plausible" (more likely to happen) than
others. This chapter offers six different scenarios featuring an
interplay of problems, opportunities, and "historical issues" that
will only be addressed by time, leadership, and luck. Each is
drawn from a set of assumptions, more or less a "fictive plot"
of future events, many of which we hope do not occur. A sev-
enth scenario is also included ("Saddam's Scenario") for comparative purposes. It, too, could have been history—a terrifying
history.

Earlier, we identified three central issues: Coalition cooperation (or lack thereof), the "question of Palestine," resolved or
not resolved, and new economic accommodations between Mid-

dle Eastern "haves" and "have-nots." In creating the following scenarios, these central issues are broken down more finely and bedded with a host of other issues. All of the issues have aspects that may be looked at as "problems," "opportunities," and "specific historical considerations" that affect the future.

Problems

The scenarios address either directly or indirectly the following problems confronting the Middle East and the parties involved in the Persian Gulf War:

1. Cooperation, or lack thereof, among the UN and "coalition" partners. Old suspicions of the West, on the part of Arabs, could resurface now that the enemy is gone. Western doubts of Arab intents may also be renewed. Or, given a different assumption, the UN can continue to grow in power and respect.
2. The Middle East must navigate the Palestinian issue. An accommodation between Israelis and Palestinians is the explicit centerpiece for all "peaceful" scenarios.
3. Protection of the human rights of minority populations is another major issue, one often lost in the images of oil sheikhs and Israeli-Palestinian conflicts. The populations of all Middle Eastern nations, Iraq in particular, feature diverse ethnic, religious, and social backgrounds, where the ruling tend to abuse, on a daily basis, the ruled. The Iraqi murder of the Kurds after the end of the war demonstrated this issue all too well.
4. Economic-development issues and economic-development rights are another major problem. The sharp divide between "Arab rich and Arab poor" (e.g., rich Kuwaitis versus poor Jordanians) was exploited by Saddam—crudely since Iraq clearly was among the Arab rich squandering its cash on armaments and Saddam's megalomaniacal dreams. But the problem and its intense political repercussions remain.
5. Leadership in the region is another issue. New leadership, and not merely new leaders but greater participation by the citizenry, is a demand being felt worldwide. It is being felt in the Middle East as well. Call it "democ-

ratization" of sorts, but in autocratic societies democratization usually produces, at least in the short term,
political instability. An aspect of this problem is addressing governmental corruption, which is rampant
throughout the Middle East.

6. Peacemakers in the Middle East must also bridge the appeal of so-called "fundamentalist Islam" with economic
development and integration into a world characterized
by instant communications and integrated economies.
There is a tragedy of perception. Islam is not antidevel-
opment. The lie is tied to the appeal of a "lost Islamic
(read Arab) golden age."

7. Weapons are another regional problem; that is, the number, density, and cost of weapons. Economies have stagnated and died beneath the "weight" of tanks, bombers,
and military establishments. Iraq and Iran beggared
themselves in their eight-year-long war. Israel suffers
from the burden of its defense requirements. Europe has
used the end of the Cold War as a chance to disarm.
Will the end of the Persian Gulf War give nations of the
region a chance to balance military establishments?

8. Relations with "the West": Will the West be a trading
partner, a region of technological inspiration, a place of
social and religious threat, or a mix of all three? The
West, at least for Kuwait and Saudi Arabia, was a saving
ally. Will Western forces remain in the region, and if
they do, to what extent? (This is a further refinement of
the mutual suspicions discussed in Problem 1.)

9. Add to the mix an unstable USSR and a USSR that may
need to import oil by the end of the 1990s. What of the
potential trouble of Russian recidivism, not quite a new
Cold War, but of a provocateur seeking to spread its
own instability around the globe, so that no one "gets
too far ahead" of Russia?

Opportunities

The scenarios consider these political opportunities:

1. Coalition politics as a model of Arab and "Western" cooperation. Emphasis on partnership, not domination.

Allied (particularly U.S.) acknowledgment of the Middle East's importance to "Western" stabilization.

2. Emphasis on "nonradical" models of development. The Turkish model of development, touted as not *an* example but the *only* example of integrating into the modern world. Secularist Kemalism (the "ideology" developed for Turkey by Kemal Atatürk) with acknowledgment of Islamic traditions. New funds provided by oil-rich nations for economic development may be forthcoming. They may prove to be necessary, to resolve (or inoculate) the region against further rich-poor conflict.

3. "Media" success. The war emphasized the immediacy of communications around the globe, illustrating the fact that someone else's problems may indeed be your own. This could translate into cooperation on ecological as well as economic issues.

4. Finally ending World War I. The Persian Gulf War may offer the opportunity to address the political and geographical imbalances that were "hardened" after World War I. It may be done by drawing new borders, though the general political attitude is that borders are inviolate. It could be done with new political accommodations.

5. Changes in Arab domestic political situations. To some degree the Western "bogeyman" (and the Israeli bogeyman), the outsider responsible for Arab problems, has been exposed as a strawman. Likewise, Arab human-rights activists in the United States and elsewhere have been heard from and will not be as easily silenced or ignored as in the past. Kuwaiti calls for democracy in Kuwait have already had a profound impact on the coalition. Could Kuwait become an example for regional democratization?

6. Calculated disarmament. Requires establishing political procedures for conflict resolution. Frees economies to develop and not stagnate amid their tanks, fighter-bombers, and long-sought nuclear weapons.

7. Recognition of Israel. Last but not least, increasing opportunity for official Arab governmental recognition of Israel and a chance to begin to resolve the Israeli-Palestinian conflict.

Making historical predictions is a futile exercise. Analyzing the potential effects of possibilities is a necessity. The following historical issues, how they come to pass (if they occur), and how they are perceived regionally and globally directly affect regional problems and opportunities.

Specific Historical Considerations

1. The leadership in Iraq will be crucial. What will the Iraqi government look like? This becomes even more specific: Does the Iraqi Baath party survive as a coherent leadership force? Does Saddam himself survive in power a year, a decade? Will a "Kurdish autonomous zone" develop in Iraq?
2. Will Iraq's political isolation remain? What are the effects of economic isolation? Part of this question will be: How economically significant was the destruction of Kuwait's infrastructure by Iraq and the destruction of Iraq's infrastructure by Allied bombing?
3. What is the perception of Saddam, either as a living leader or as a legacy? Will his elimination and humiliation be the pertinent political fact? Will Iraq's crushing one-sided military defeat be blamed on Saddam?
4. Will the clarity of the coalition victory be obfuscated by "media myths"? That Saddam stood up to the United States, that he punished the wealthy Kuwaitis, or that he promoted an international conference on Palestine. This also introduces a curious but important and prickly "sub-issue"—what will be the effect of Western leftists and neutralists who believe the United States is the central source of conflict and evil in the world, on those who, if not directly propping up Saddam, like the Palestinians in the streets of Amman, need a "figure" standing defiant against their tarred image of "Amerika." (The fact that Saddam and the Baath are classic fascists has yet to sink in on many of these groups.) These groups may be small in number, but they have what is ruefully known as "media access." Many European leftists are intensely respected in the impoverished corners of the globe. Their personal influence is direct. Will they mythologize Saddam? Will the mythology stick?

5. Will the end of the Cold War eliminate the chance of "Nasserite survival" for Saddam's supporters? Nasser succeeded in turning military defeat into political victory by playing the USSR off against the West. The current USSR is only an outline of its former self, though still a potent political force. The overwhelming coalition air and ground victory makes such an outcome unlikely, but it must be considered.

6 What Palestinian leadership will develop out of the chaos of intifada and Iraqi failure? Yasir Arafat chose to support Saddam, but then he was reflecting the appeal of Saddam among Palestinians, wasn't he? What kind of Israeli leadership will direct Israeli policy? Has the Likud become increasingly intransigent, and will it decide to opt for absorption of the West Bank into a Greater Israel as the radical Molodet party advocates?

The following scenarios are drawn form the interplay of problems, opportunities, and historical issues. They are by no means definitive, but are rather suggestive of trends that could emerge from the aftermath of the war.

Scenario 1:
New World Chaos

As a territorial entity, Iraq is less a nation-state than a political-geographic creature of post–World War I political maneuvering. Essentially drawn, with some minor adjustments, from three Ottoman provinces (Basra, Baghdad/Mesopotamia, and Mosul), Iraq could just as easily disintegrate into an enlarged Lebanon despite coalition insistence on maintaining current (preinvasion of Kuwait) boundaries.

The local battle lines would be a replay of 1,200 years of tribal and ethnic squabbling. Sunni Arabs in the Baghdad region would battle Kurds to the northeast and Shiites to the south, as they did at the end of the ground-war phase of the Persian Gulf War. Other "traditional" disputes would enter the fray: city dweller versus desert dweller; Euphrates River farmer versus

Bedouin; people living in the oil-field areas versus those living elsewhere; development advocates versus religious fundamentalists; and an entire hidden range of personal conflicts among would-be leaders.

Iraq, in this potential outcome, would become a "center that does not hold"—a land of a thousand tiny whirlwinds that becomes a central storm, sucking its neighbors into the trouble.

Turkey would be involved. As previously noted, Turkey already has its own Kurdish problem. Would Turkey allow a de facto Kurdistan to evolve from the chaos in Iraq? Would the Turks allow the Kirkuk and Mosul oil fields to be abandoned, with the loss of millions in pipeline fees that would result? What happens if the fields are attacked by the Kurds, or Syria makes a move into northern Iraq in the direction of the oil fields? Turkey has more historical claim to Mosul than Iraq ever had on Kuwait. Would the opportunity to gain 50 billion barrels in potential oil reserves cause Turkey to turn its back on seventy years of anti-irredentist policy?

Syria also becomes a candidate for Lebanization. Syria, too, is a mosaic of religious, social, and ethnic competitions, held in check by the Alawite-led police state of the Syrian wing of the Baath party.

Jordan is already afflicted by severe instability as the Palestinian majority continues to clash with the ruling Hashemite Bedouin minority. With an economy harmed by the war, could Jordan withstand an Iraq in total chaos? Jordan itself is ripe for political change. If King Hussein falls in a coup or is replaced by a "weaker ruler," the trouble in Jordan could increase Iraq's instability.

Iran would be drawn into the conflict because of its historical relations with Arab Shiites and, perhaps, a desire to "protect" Shia holy sites in An Najaf and Karbala. Iraqi troops damaged those sites in the postwar internecine battles. Next time a militarily reinvigorated Iran could choose to defend them.

On the far side of Jordan, chaos also continues. There is no move toward a resolution of the "Palestinian problem," so in Israel and the West Bank the intifada continues, with Jewish settlers from the Soviet Union taking Arab jobs in Israel and more Jewish settlements rising on the West Bank. "Moderate" Palestinian leaders are jailed by the Israelis and murdered by Arab radicals. The PLO may be poorer, but it remains deadly.

To the south Kuwait rebuilds itself as an oil enclave, Saudi and Gulf Arab states in the Gulf Cooperation Council arm themselves to the teeth. Egypt benefits economically from serving as a mercenary force in the Persian Gulf, but Egyptian relations with Israel deteriorate. But embittered oil sheikhs see no profit in establishing an "Arab Development Bank" in order to promote economic opportunity in poorer Arab nations. The impoverished pay attention only to their rage, paving the way for religious radicals and terrorists of all philosophic stripes and faiths.

Poverty and low-grade yet bloody warfare continues. New World Chaos differs little from the prewar past.

What brings this scenario about? (1) Arab dissension in the wake of victory; (2) United States focus on another region or other issues; (3) continued "Saddamist" leadership in Baghdad.

Scenario 2:
Jihad, and Other Old Middle Eastern Woes Enhanced

Call this future a variant of New World Chaos: Allied victory is perceived as less than complete, and lingering Western military forces exacerbate anti-Western feelings. The arrogance—and alienation—of the oil sheikhs increases. The old oligarchs stifle protests. Then radical Islamic fundamentalists and Arab nationalists topple the fragile autocracies and nascent Arab democracies. Those with petrodollars flee to luxurious exile in Cannes. Anti-Americanism and anti-Western sentiments are the breaking edge of an "Eastern tidal wave" to drive the West back into Europe. Turkey is caught in the throes of Islamic radicals fighting Kemalist Euro-Turks. The oil fields, in the hands of the religious radicals, become economic weapons against the West and Japan.

What brings this scenario about? (1) Failure to address the political and economic expectations created by the UN victory; (2) the rise of a *more* radical Shiite regime in Tehran; (3) the creation of a Shiite Arab state, effectively run by Tehran, in what was southern Iraq.

Scenario 3:
The Egyptian-Saudi Axis

This scenario assumes cooperation between wartime-coalition allies continues, at least the primary allies. Saudi Arabia and Kuwait fund an Egyptian Army presence (two or three divisions) based out of northern Saudi Arabia and Kuwait. Essentially, Saudi money and Egyptian arms (and population size) provide the Arab counterweight to Iran, which Riyadh and Cairo conclude is sufficient. Saudi largess is focused upon Egypt.

The Palestinian issue becomes a side issue for Saudi Arabia and Egypt, both deciding the question is unanswerable. The Saudis conclude that it is better to let Israel and the Palestinians suffer. Both can become convenient scapegoats for regional troubles (as they've been since 1947). Syria is consulted but "loosely"; in the main Syria is left to stew in its own internal problems and in Lebanon. (Besides, the Saudi logic goes, Assad and his Alawite clique are heretics anyway.) If Assad or his successors turn to terror *against* Egypt or Saudi Arabia, then the petrodollar flow to Damascus is reduced.

Iran becomes the oil salesman to Russia. Iraq develops the "northern" market as well. The Iraqi Baathist government, steeped in blood, continues to conduct a low-level war against the Kurds. Saudi Arabia judges that Baghdad remains "just stable enough" not to make trouble for anyone except the Kurds.

What brings this scenario into being? (1) Internal Egyptian economic and political problems that Saudi Arabia and the Egyptian government judge come first and foremost. Egyptian guns and general Egyptian reliability are judged so precious that the rest of the region is ignored; (2) Lack of U.S. and European (and UN) pressure to force a new and more permanent accommodation on the Palestinian homeland issue; (3) Simmering Saudi and Kuwaiti anger at Jordanian, Yemeni, and Palestinian support for Saddam that is translated into a policy of angry neglect; (4) Syrian domestic political concerns, which lead the Syrian government to be "less cooperative" with its "new allies." (5) Likud intransigence at working toward Palestinian autonomy; (6) Maintenance of power in the PLO by the old "Arafat leadership."

Scenario 4:
Permanent Intifada—Revived Arab-Israeli Conflict and Increased U.S.-Israeli Strain

This scenario takes Scenario 3 and gives it an Israeli twist. Assume that right-wing Israeli political parties gain control of the Knesset and as part of their domestic agenda vehemently refuse to deal with the Palestinian issue. The pressures of Soviet Jewish immigration are cites as the primary reason: Judaea and Samaria must be integrated into Greater Israel.

The United States is portrayed not as a protector of Israel but as an "unreliable imperial state." This tack leads to a more permanent U.S.-Israeli stress—a fracture in the old strategic relationship. United States leverage over Israel weakens.

Violence on the West Bank, however, does not diminish. Vigorous Egyptian and Saudi leadership, while promoting moderate Palestinians, is boxed by resistance from Israeli radicals.

Meanwhile, back in Tehran, with the intifada once again distracting the world, the Iranians decide it's time to renew support for Shiite separatists in southern Iraq.

In Baghdad a post-Saddam Baath government offers Saudi Arabia and Egypt a new alliance, one that would combat Shia trouble in southern Iran and add ground divisions for the looming war with the expansionist Israelis.

Simultaneously, in Damascus the Alawite dictatorship, pressed for change by the Sunni majority, turns to the "foreign enemy option." Syria (or was it Israel?) provokes a brief border clash in the Golan, or ersatz Syrian and Israeli forces battle in South Lebanon.

The right-wing Israeli government decides to up the ante by quietly informing Damascus that if the Syrians don't cease and desist, Israel will launch a nuclear strike on Syrian air and army installations.

The border clash stops. The Saudis and Egyptians accept the Iraqis' alliance offer. The New World Order goes tilt.

This scenario assumes (1) An aggressive, expansionist, xenophobic government in Israel that is *not* Arab propaganda; (2) Ineffectual leadership in the United States; (3) A weakened

UN; (4) An increasingly desperate and isolated Syrian leadership; (5) A post-Saddam leadership in Iraq willing to accept Saudi leadership in intra-Arab affairs (in return for Saudi dollars).

Scenario 5:
Patchwork Development, Patchwork Peace

This scenario is a mosaic of hope and sorrow. If the authors were to bet, given the situation in the summer of 1991, this would be the most likely immediate future (1991 through 1995 or so):

Iraq's economy remains hostage to the UN. Turmoil continues in Kurdistan. The lingering Baath government (eventually minus Saddam Hussein) is kept just strong enough to keep Iraq together but too weak to be a threat to its neighbors. Kuwait begins a rapid rebuilding process. Still, internal frictions between "those who stayed" and "those who fled" during the war remain. Iran slowly reenters the world.

Turkey is beset with a familiar set of problems; a low-grade war with its Kurdish minority continues in southeastern Turkey, the discontent fired by the continuing troubles in Iraq. The Turkish economy stabilizes, though promised Japanese investment fails to materialize. Turkey, however, does get increasing support from its European allies, and the fundamentalist threat to Turkish Europeanization decreases (as the Iranian "model" of Islamic revolution fades).

The Egyptian economy also stabilizes, thanks to Saudi investment. Egypt and Saudi Arabia participate in regional negotiations with the Israelis regarding creation of an autonomous but demilitarized Palestinian political "zone." After fitful negotiations, a consensus emerges that such a state must be created. The timetable, however, does not suit Palestinian radicals. Israeli right-wingers object to the loss of "Samaria and Judaea." Tension increases, but progress continues.

Yemen and Jordan continue to suffer severe economic losses as the Saudis and Kuwaitis continue to punish the Yemeni and

Jordanian governments for cooperating with Saddam. The Jordanian monarchy is toppled, stalling Palestinian autonomy talks. Yemenis clamor to have their old jobs back in Saudi Arabia.

This scenario assumes: (1) Saudi recognition of Israel as a legitimate state; (2) steady and farsighted diplomacy in Israel, Saudi Arabia, the United States, and the United Nations.

Scenario 6:
New World Order

We might call this the George Bush Dream Scenario.

Oil prices stabilize between twenty-one and twenty-six dollars a barrel in 1991 U.S. dollars. The Saudis and other Gulf Arab states create and begin to fund a Middle Eastern Development Bank. The name "Middle Eastern" is important. Non-Arabs living in the Middle East (to include Turks, Israelis, Kurds, and Persians) are invited to participate.

A new Palestinian leadership acceptable to Israelis emerges from Arafat's "great mistake" of backing Saddam. Likud falls from power, supplanted by either a coalition government or a Labor "peace" government strong enough (and wise enough) to negotiate over the West Bank.

The Arab Middle East organizes politically along the lines of the Grand Coalition. Saudi Arabia is the economic arbiter and Egypt the political center, with a "deradicalized" Syria participating. Kuwait rebuilds. The emirate establishes a constitutional monarchy that is a model for democratic evolution in the Gulf region. This model is emulated in Bahrain and Qatar. Iraq evolves into a semiauthoritarian state run by the military. The Tikriti-Baath clique is toppled from power. In return, the UN eases its debt demands on the Iraqi economy.

Iran decides to opt for selling oil rather than promoting Islamic revolution. A vote in the parliament decides to ask Abolhassan Bani-Sadr (the only democratically elected head of state in Persian history) to return to Tehran for "political consultations." The wounds of the revolution begin to heal.

Turkey makes large economic strides and achieves an internal settlement with its Kurdish minority.

The United Nations begins to function as the world decision maker and enforcer it always could have been. Why? The United States shows that the coalition lived up to the letter of the UN mandate for action against Iraq. The mandate stands as an example of what can be achieved through cooperation.

This scenario assumes that: (1) political change in Russia is evolutionary rather than revolutionary (i.e., Russia remains stable and continues to cooperate with the UN. Likewise, the KGB cooperates in reducing the threat of regional and worldwide terrorism); (2) China continues to cooperate with the United States and the UN (i.e., change in China from the "Old Guard" of Deng Xiaoping to a younger, economically progressive leadership is managed without a change in foreign policy); (3) United States leadership remains firm, consistent, and internationalist (rather than turning isolationist, which is the classic U.S. pattern after an international conflict); (4) Western Europe provides massive aid, credits, and markets to Turkey (Turkey is indeed established as a "bridge" between the West and the Middle East).

Scenario 7:
Saddam's Outcome

Saddam invades Kuwait. The response by Saudis is frightened, confused, and muddled. United States president Michael Dukakis suggests Saddam be respected and reasoned with. No U.S. forces show.

Iraq topples Saudi Arabia, either by invasion or assassination, and annexes the northeastern provinces (that is, the area where the oil is). The 12,000-strong foreign contingent of ARAMCO workers and their families captured in Dhahran are held hostage. "If the United States tries another Desert One," Saddam boasts, referring to the failed Iranian hostage rescue attempt, "we will turn the desert into a lake of burning ARAMCO blood."

The House of Sa'ūd flees west into the Hejaz. Saddam's forces pursue as Jordanian forces enter the fray against the Saudis. Jordan takes the Hejaz, an area the Hashemites clan now ruling Jordan traditionally controlled. Now tradition, with the help of Iraqi arms, is back. King Hussein has always wanted his people to call him Sharif Hussein, his grandfather's name— Hashemites had ruled Mecca and Medina until the 1920s, when the area was conquered by the Sa'ūd clan.

Saddam now controls or threatens 55–65 percent of the world's proven oil reserves. His puppet Jordan (at least temporarily) controls Mecca. King Hussein has, for the moment, become Sharif Hussein, and the Hashemites rule the Hejaz—as long as Saddam lets them. What has Saddam gained? Saddam has "ideological leverage" over the world's 450 million Moslems. The world's worst Arabian Nightmare has just begun.

NEW POLITICAL ACCOMMODATIONS IN PALESTINE

A common theme in populist Arab politics since early in this century has been the arrogance and interference of the Western nations (particularly Britain, to a lesser extent France, and increasingly the United States) in the internal affairs of Arab nations. It was the Western powers that liberated most Arab nations from the centuries of rule by the Ottoman Turk Empire and designated the boundaries of most (new, and often quite artificial) Arab nations during the 1920s and 1930s. It was also Western governments and corporations that discovered Arab oil and provided a market for it in the 1930s and 1940s. But none of these actions were done with just Arab well-being in mind, and the Arabs remember that more than non-Arabs. There is also a clash of cultures involved. There is a general yearning for a return to the (largely mythical) glory days of an Arab Empire of united Arab peoples. The first, and last, Arab Empire collapsed in a bloodbath of civil and religious wars over a thousand years ago. But the empire angle still plays well among Arabs, and the Western nations are seen as being an obstacle to reestablishing that long-lost unity. A large part of this Western "plot" to thwart Arab unity (and prosperity, power, dignity, etc.) is perceived as connected with Western efforts to establish the state of Israel in 1948.

While Israel is often considered the primary cause of unrest in the Middle East, more ancient, or practical, causes of war have prevailed. Since 1948 Arab has fought Arab more than Arab has fought Israeli; and more Arabs have killed Arabs than the Israelis have. The causes have been purely political (Egypt and Libya, Jordanians and Palestinians, etc.), civil war (Lebanon, Syria, Iraq, Yemen, Oman, Sudan, etc.) or territorial (Morocco and Algeria, Iraq and Kuwait). The web of mutually antagonistic ethnic rivalries in the Middle East has largely Arab threads. The Israeli strand stands out largely because it is the most recent one and because it is different. Israel is different for several reasons, each an illuminating insight on why Arabs are angry, embarrassed, ashamed, and ultimately a little encouraged at having Israel in their midst:

1. Israel is the only functioning democracy in the Middle East. A few Arab countries come close (Egypt), but most do not even attempt broad-based democracy. (Interestingly, Kuwait has had a more democratic tradition than the other Gulf Arab states.) Increasingly, the democratic form of government is seen as the most effective one, and it is one form of government that the Arabs have never been able to make work. Israel is coming to be seen as a model for a "Middle Eastern" democracy, or at least a working example. Egyptian and Israeli politicians have long met to compare notes, and Egypt is the most democratic of the Arab states.

2. Israel's population is largely composed of European Jews, or their descendants. Unlike the neighboring Arab populations, who can often trace their local roots back for centuries, most Israelis are newcomers. The new people in the neighborhood are always held in somewhat lower esteem, particularly if they are as powerful as Israel. But now, after five wars and one act of self-control (not retaliating against the Scud attacks), there is an increasing acceptance. In the wake of Israel's performance during the Gulf war, Kuwait, Saudi Arabia, and even Syria expressed an interest in improving their relations with Israel.

3. Israel has a modern (although shaky) economy. One could say that this demonstrates what other Arab nations could do under similar circumstances.

4. Israel has a modern and effective armed forces. This is largely a result of its high level of education, modern economy, and its host of (external) enemies.

5. Israel is the biggest recipient of foreign aid in the region. Don't underestimate this one, as no other Arab nation is likely to get anything near as much as Israel (especially on a per capita basis). Each year Israel receives several thousand dollars per family. It makes a big difference.

6. Israel has no oil. No oil means dependence on foreign aid, but one less thing for a greedy neighbor to go to war for.

7. Israel is a largely non-Moslem country in a Moslem region. Jews, Christians, and breakaway Islamic sects comprise most of Israel's population. This is not unique; look, for example, at Lebanon. But then, look at Lebanon again, and you wonder what could happen in Israel.

8. Israel has a highly literate, well-educated population. This is the key to much of what does work in Israel and an object lesson for its Arab neighbors.

Israel does have a number of things in common with its Arab neighbors (Semitic language, religious fundamentalists, etc.). But it is the differences that define the Arab-Israeli relationship. This has not always been a barrier to working relationships between nations in the area. After World War I, when the Arabs were freed from the Turkish Empire and more Jews were emigrating into Palestine, Arab leaders were not opposed to a Jewish presence in the region. For example, Emir Faisal (son of the British backed leader of the Arabs, Sharif—later King—Hussein) expressed a common feeling among Arab leaders. Faisal felt the Jews in Palestine, and those continuing to move there, could live in peace with the Arabs. But when it came to sorting out which group would get what part of the Arab lands for their "homeland," there was then, as now, sharp disagreement over which real estate "belonged" to which ethnic or religious group. The number of inter-Arab and civil wars in the last forty years attests to that. Armed force, diplomacy, and possession of the land in question is the usual solution. The Gulf War went one more step toward establishing Israel's acceptance in the Middle East, if only by eliminating one of the more strident opponents (Saddam Hussein) to its existence.

Saddam was not able to make the Israeli situation a decisive element of his war plan because other local Arab governments were finally forced to confront the reality that Israel's situation vis-à-vis the Palestinians is not much different than that of many other Arab nations and the minorities they have subjugated within their own borders. Iraq's Kurds are a prime example of this, but every other nation in the region has similar situations. While Israel did seize parts of Syria, Jordan, and Egypt, it was not without provocation. Iraq seized all of Kuwait with practically no provocation. Iraq went too far, and Iraq's neighbors were willing to take joint action against that degree of aggression.

The Persian Gulf War could be a turning point for Arab-Israeli relations for three reasons:

1. Most Palestinians supported Iraq's aggressions, while most other Arabs did not. This cost the Palestinians diplomatic support they could ill afford to lose, as well as generous subsidies and wages from Gulf states. What makes the Palestinians, and the PLO, weaker makes Israel stronger.
2. Israel refused to be drawn into the war even as Iraqi Scud missiles killed and injured Israeli citizens. Israeli military action would have caused political problems in most pro-Kuwait Arab nations as this would have turned the war into an Arab-Israeli affair.
3. Iraq made it quite clear that Arab nations had more serious problems than Israel.

The truth of the matter is that the reality of Israel's persistent existence, the growing danger of other Middle Eastern problems (as in Iraq invading Kuwait), and the increasing attractiveness of some kind of solution to the mess has brought a solution to the "Israel problem" closer than at any other time in the last fifty years. To implement this solution requires that four problems be taken care of:

1. Recognition of Israel's right to exist and survive. Arab nations have been weakening on this one from the moment Israel was created. Egypt took a lot of diplomatic

heat for recognizing Israel during the 1970s. But now Egypt is the leading power of the Arab world (as much as one can be a leader in such a situation). Israel has also established numerous economic and diplomatic relationships with Arab nations. That most of these had to be done in secret did not make them any less real.

2. Neutralization of radicals on both side of the issue. The PLO had always been the primary source of radicalism on the Arab-Israel issue. The radicals attacked government officials in states that supported Kuwait. This makes it easier to crack down on the Arab and Israeli radicals. If any radicals are allowed to run loose after an Arab-Israeli agreement, the agreement won't last long.

3. Guarantees of economic opportunities for both Jews and Arabs. Although the Israelis have gone out of their way to favor Israelis over Palestinians, the Arab population has still managed to do better economically than any other (non–oil rich) Arabs. Evening up the playing field would make the Palestinians even more well off and go a long way to keeping the peace.

4. Effective policing of threats. All the terror doesn't come from terrorists. Lebanon stands as a constant reminder of how words between different ethnic groups can quickly escalate to an artillery barrage. Making peace is not as important as doing whatever has to be done to keep it.

Afterword

To speak of a major war as lasting eight months (August 1990 to March 1991) is at best to express a hope—a very unlikely hope. The "100 Hour War" was pure Madison Avenue, catchy and slick but not very accurate. Despite the immediate impact of the international coalition's war against Iraq, the basic political and geostrategic problems and relationships modify slowly. In the Middle East, the post–Gulf War political landscape has changed and yet it hasn't. The region's prewar political, historical, and economic strains remain. Few Middle Eastern potentates relinquish power without dying by either assassination or (rarely) of old age. Imbalances of wealth affect disgruntled and jealous populations. The Israel-Palestine problem, slouching toward a conference table, leaves a deep legacy of human bitterness. The anti-Gorbachev Moscow coup tosses one more troubling element into the stew.

Yet both politically and militarily, the Persian Gulf War has had and will have profound effects. For once, the United Nations did serve as a major force for combined, international, and consensus *armed* peacekeeping. Can it do so again remains for history to see. Next time, will Russia and China go along? Next time, will the United Nations, Western, and regional leadership find the means and will to cooperate?

Militarily, the Persian Gulf War gave the world a peek at the twenty-first century, at the power of precision-guided weapons, at the speed of combat. We hope that a peek is enough to convince everyone that in the next millennium, turning to war to resolve disputes is a terrible choice; however, as historians we know better.

The Persian Gulf War will be historically notable for several unprecedented things that happened in the American armed forces. It was the first war in which the U.S. forces fighting the first battle were well-trained and well-equipped professionals. The results were unlike the embarrassing performances common in America's previous "first battles." This was also the first war in which all three services actually cooperated, or at least cooperated without a tremendous amount of arm twisting. These two factors were largely responsible for the outstanding performance of the U.S. and coalition forces.

Two other factors were equally responsible for the dramatic Allied victory, and should not be ignored. First, the war was fought in the desert. This has always been ideal terrain for the side with air superiority. The Allies had air superiority, and massive air forces to make the most of it. Second, this was the war American air and ground forces have been preparing to fight since World War II. The Gulf War was the massive armor and air campaign that was to be fought in Central Europe against the Russians. Instead, it was fought in a desert against Russian equipment, but with less capable Iraqi troops operating that equipment.

There was also one more element that made a major contribution: the shadow of Vietnam. The U.S. military has been trying to live down the Vietnam experience since the 1970s. While not the decisive factor, the nightmare played its role, affecting both leadership and doctrine.

These five factors resulted in an unprecedented military victory. Never has such a large campaign resulted in so few casualties for the winning side. The war was noticeable for one other uncharacteristic event: the U.S. Navy did not get a share of the credit commensurate with its size. The navy is the largest (when one eliminates all the strategic weapons) of the conventional services. America is a maritime nation: Its navy is the first, and primary, line of defense. The navy guards America's crucial access to maritime trade, and it provides the first line of defense any invader would have to get by. The navy has capitalized on its position to make itself a very self-contained service. It has a large air force and its own army (190,000 marines). In the Gulf, the navy provided crucial service as the blockading force, but its marines were turned over to the U.S. Army to act as just one more ground force. Naval aircraft were dependent on air-force tankers to get to their targets and on air-force headquarters and air-control units to show them what to hit and when. Compounding this was a lapse in the public-relations department. Even considering its military situation, the navy did not get its share of the ink.

This bodes ill for postwar wrangling over which service should shrink how much in the post–Cold war, post–Gulf War world. This assumes that the Cold War and the Persian Gulf War are "post." Indeed, the euphoria that swept Eastern Europe in November 1989 and the euphoria in March 1991 at the liberation of Kuwait may prove to be have been the most fleeting of exultations.

James F. Dunnigan and Austin Bay

Sources and Further Reading

Our best source happened to be a book we were just completing writing as the war broke out: *A Quick and Dirty Guide to War* (1990s edition). Several chapters were devoted to the Gulf, and a lot of material could be recycled.

For the uniquely military aspects of this book, we had to go beyond secondary sources and get the information from the scene. Our friends and acquaintances in the military were invaluable for this: There were a lot of long-distance conversations and numerous documents from the front. But if you don't want to get into the subject as deeply as we did, the widely available news media (particularly print) are an excellent source of raw material and even more analysis. In addition to major newspapers and news magazines, specialist publications like *Jane's Defense Weekly, Aviation Week, International Defense Review, International Security,* and *Foreign Affairs* are also excellent sources. If you have access to periodicals published within the military (*Infantry, Armor,* etc.), or foreign general and specialist publications, you will uncover even more gems.

Unfortunately, for a subject like this, most of the books with a broad perspective haven't been written yet. Except for this one.

Index